After years of writing unpublished children's books, short stories and a few unfinished YA novels Jen Atkinson started a little chick-lit book she called *Am I 30 Yet?*. After six months she finished the first draft of the work now known as *Roses Don't Have to be Red*. She and Samantha Blake were so different and yet like a good friend she loved and understood her well.

Jen adores a good clean love story as well as a fun, unpredictable, young adult, dystopian. She enjoys blogging and speaking about the wonderful world of writing, her books and the joys and hardships of being a wife and mother. Her family is her life. She falls in love over and over again with her husband Jeff. She adores her three boys, Tim, Landon and Seth. And couldn't live without her cherry-on-top, Sydney Belle. Jen lives next to one of Wyoming's many mountains where she enjoys getting blown away by the Wyoming wind on a regular basis.

Read more about Jen at:
jenatkinsonauthor.wixsite.com/jenatkinson

CPSIA information can be obtained
at www.ICGtesting.com
Printed in the USA
FFOW02n1613231017
41466FF

CARING FOR THE DEAD IN ANCIENT ISRAEL

ARCHAEOLOGY AND BIBLICAL STUDIES

Brian B. Schmidt, General Editor

Number 27

CARING FOR THE DEAD
IN ANCIENT ISRAEL

Kerry M. Sonia

SBL PRESS

 **PRESS**

Atlanta

Copyright © 2020 by Kerry M. Sonia

Library of Congress Cataloging-in-Publication Data

Names: Sonia, Kerry M., author.
Title: Caring for the dead in ancient Israel / Kerry M. Sonia.
Description: Atlanta : SBL Press, [2020] | Series: Archaeology and biblical studies ; 27 | Includes bibliographical references and index.
Identifiers: LCCN 2020012839 (print) | LCCN 2020012840 (ebook) | ISBN 9781628372854 (paperback) | ISBN 9780884144618 (hardback) | ISBN 9780884144625 (ebook)
Subjects: LCSH: Death—Palestine. | Dead—Religious aspects—Judaism. | Ancestor worship—Palestine. | Ancestor worship—Middle East. | Funeral rites and ceremonies, Ancient—Palestine—History. | Funeral rites and ceremonies, Ancient—Middle East—History. | Jewish funeral rites and ceremonies—Palestine.
Classification: LCC GT3274.5.P19 S6 2020 (print) | LCC GT3274.5.P19 (ebook) | DDC 393/.930933—dc23
LC record available at https://lccn.loc.gov/2020012839
LC ebook record available at https://lccn.loc.gov/2020012840

In loving memory of my grandfather
John Ambrose Ford
who encouraged me to write clearly,
read widely, and learn ancient languages

CONTENTS

Acknowledgments

Over the course of this project, I have been fortunate to have the help and support of a broad community of mentors, colleagues, friends, and family. First and foremost, I must thank my doctoral advisor, Saul M. Olyan, whose teaching and research initially sparked my interest in the study of Israelite religion and the Hebrew Bible. I continue to be inspired by the rigor and creativity of his work, and I deeply appreciate his mentorship over the years. Many readers have provided invaluable feedback on this project, particularly members of my dissertation committee—Matthew T. Rutz, Michael L. Satlow, and Susan Ackerman. I have greatly benefited from their close and insightful reading.

I feel extremely fortunate to have engaged with so many brilliant and supportive scholars while writing this book. I have found our conversations not only personally enriching but also vital contributions to the project. Among them, I would especially like to thank Ross Shepard Kraemer, Brian Schmidt, Seth Sanders, Matthew Suriano, and the anonymous reviewers of this manuscript, all of whom raised important questions and offered incisive feedback. I must also thank my graduate student colleagues, who have witnessed and encouraged the development of this project from its infancy. It gives me great joy to thank Dana Logan, Sonia Hazard, Elizabeth Angowski, Andrew Tobolowsky, Daniel Picus, M. Willis Monroe, and Zack Wainer for their collegiality and friendship.

Over the course of writing this book, I have been part of several academic institutions, all of which have been instrumental in the process. I would like to thank the Department of Religious Studies at Brown University, the Department of Religion at Bowdoin College and the Andrew W. Mellon Foundation, the Department of Religion at Washington and Lee University, the Women's Studies in Religion Program at Harvard Divinity School, and the Religious Studies Department at Colby College.

Finally, to my friends and family, I am so grateful for your ongoing support. And thank you to my parents, John and Gail Sonia, for your incredible love.

ABBREVIATIONS

ABD	Freedman, David Noel, ed. *Anchor Bible Dictionary*. 6 vols. New York: Doubleday, 1992.
AfO	*Archiv für Orientforschung*
ANET	Pritchard, James B., ed. *Ancient Near Eastern Texts Relating to the Old Testament*. 3rd ed. Princeton: Princeton University Press, 1969.
AnSt	*Anatolian Studies*
AOAT	Alter Orient und Alten Testament
ARRIM	*Annual Review of the Royal Inscriptions of Mesopotamia Project*
AS	Assyriological Studies
BA	*Biblical Archaeologist*
BABELAO	*Bulletin de l'Académie Belge pour l'Étude des Langues Anciennes et Orientales*
BaghM	*Baghdader Mitteilungen*
BAM	Köcher, Franz. *Die babylonisch-assyrische Medizin in Texten und Untersuchungen*. Berlin: de Gruyter, 1963–.
BASOR	*Bulletin of the American Schools of Oriental Research*
BARIS	BAR (British Archaeological Reports) International Series
BDB	Brown, Francis, S. R. Driver, and Charles A. Briggs. *A Hebrew and English Lexicon of the Old Testament*. Oxford: Clarendon, 1907.
Bib	*Biblica*
BibSem	The Biblical Seminar
BM	Tablets in the Collections of the British Museum
BMS	King, L. W. *Babylonian Magic and Sorcery*. London: Luzac, 1896.
BRA	Beiträge zur Religionsgeschichte des Altertums
BWANT	Beiträge zur Wissenschaft vom Alten und Neuen Testament

BWL	Lambert, Wilfred G. *Babylonian Wisdom Literature*. Oxford: Clarendon, 1960.
BT	*The Bible Translator*
CAD	*The Assyrian Dictionary of the Oriental Institute of the University of Chicago*. Chicago: The Oriental Institute of the University of Chicago, 1956–2006.
CBQ	*Catholic Biblical Quarterly*
COS	Hallo, William W. *The Context of Scripture*. 3 vols. Leiden: Brill, 1997–2002.
DAS	Documents d'Archéologie Syrienne
DDD	van der Toorn, Karel, Bob Becking, and Pieter W. van der Horst, eds. *Dictionary of Deities and Demons in the Bible*. Leiden: Brill, 1995.
EncRel	Eliade, Mircea, ed. *The Encyclopedia of Religion*. New York: Macmillan, 1987.
EPRO	Etudes préliminaires aux religions orientales dans l'empire romain
HALOT	Koehler, Ludwig, Walter Baumgartner, and Johann J. Stamm. *The Hebrew and Aramaic Lexicon of the Old Testament*. Translated and edited under the supervision of Mervyn E. J. Richardson. 4 vols. Leiden: Brill, 1994–1999.
HAR	*Hebrew Annual Review*
HBAI	*Hebrew Bible and Ancient Israel*
HSS	Harvard Semitic Studies
HTR	*Harvard Theological Review*
HUCA	*Hebrew Union College Annual*
IBHS	Waltke, Bruce K., and Michael O'Connor. *An Introduction to Biblical Hebrew Syntax*. Winona Lake, IN: Eisenbrauns, 1990.
IEJ	*Israel Exploration Journal*
JAEI	*Journal of Ancient Egyptian Interconnections*
JANER	*Journal of Ancient Near Eastern Religions*
JANESCU	*Journal of the Ancient Near Eastern Society of Columbia University*
JAOS	*Journal of the American Oriental Society*
JBL	*Journal of Biblical Literature*
JC	*The Jewish Chronicle*
JCS	*Journal of Cuneiform Studies*
JHS	*Journal of Hellenic Studies*
JJS	*Journal of Jewish Studies*

JMA	*Journal of Mediterranean Archaeology*
JNES	*Journal of Near Eastern Studies*
JQR	*Jewish Quarterly Review*
JSOTSup	Journal for the Study of the Old Testament Supplement Series
K	Kuyunjik collection of the British Museum
KAI	Donner, Herbert, and Wolfgang Röllig. *Kanaanäische und aramäische Inschriften.* 2nd ed. Wiesbaden: Harrassowitz, 1966–1969.
KTU	Dietrich, Manfred, ed. *Die keilalphabetischen Texte aus Ugarit.* 3rd enl. ed. of *KTU: The Cuneiform Alphabetic Texts from Ugarit, Ras Ibn Hani, and Other Places.* Edited by Manfred Dietrich, Oswald Loretz, and Joaquín Sanmartín. Münster: Ugarit-Verlag, 1995.
LAS	Parpola, Simo. Letters from Assyrian Scholars to the Kings Esarhaddon and Assurbanipal. 2 vols. Kevelaer: Butzon & Bercker; Neukirchen-Vluyn: Neukirchener Verlag, 1970–1983.
LKA	Ebeling, Erich. *Literarische Keilschrifttexte aus Assur.* Berlin: Akademie, 1953.
LXX	Septuagint
MS(S)	manuscript(s)
MT	Masoretic Text
NEA	*Near Eastern Archaeology*
Or	*Orientalia* (NS)
PWCJS	*Proceedings of the World Congress of Jewish Studies*
QSS	Qatna Studien Supplementa
RA	*Revue d'assyriologie et d'archéologie orientale*
RGG	Betz, Hans Dieter, ed. *Religion in Geschichte und Gegenwart.* 4th ed. Tübingen: Mohr Siebeck, 1998–2007.
RGRW	Religions in the Graeco-Roman World
RS	Ras Shamra
SAOC	Studies in Ancient Oriental Civilizations
SAQPC	Studi Archeologici su Qatna è Pubblicata in Coedizione
SpTU	Weiher, Egbert von, and Hermann Hunger. *Spätbabylonische Texte aus Uruk.* 5 vols. Berlin: Mann, 1976–1998.
StPohl	Studia Pohl
STR	Studies in Theology and Religion
TCL	Textes cuneiforms. Musée du Louvre

TDOT	Botterweck, G. Johannes, and Helmer Ringgren, eds. *Theological Dictionary of the Old Testament*. Translated by John T. Willis et al. 8 vols. Grand Rapids: Eerdmans, 1974–2006.
UF	*Ugarit-Forschungen*
VC	*Vigiliae Christianae*
VT	*Vetus Testamentum*
VTSup	Supplements to Vetus Testamentum
WA	*World Archaeology*
WAW	Writings from the Ancient World
ZA	*Zeitschrift für Assyrologie*
ZAW	*Zeitschrift für die alttestamentliche Wissenschaft*
ZDPV	*Zeitschrift des deutschen Palästina-Vereins*

Introduction

"All culture is a struggle with oblivion."[1] Reflecting on the role of writing in the construction of memory, Egyptologist Jan Assmann cites this assertion by sociologist Thomas Macho. A provocative and, perhaps, overgeneralizing statement, it nevertheless invites us to think about the pull of memory in different cultural spheres—the individual, family, community, and nation—and what is at stake in its production. People often speak of making memories, but how is memory, especially collective memory, actually made? And to what extent does memory construction take for granted the threat of forgetfulness and annihilation, as indicated by the quotation above? After all, cultural landscapes are never static but continuously contested and reconstructed by individuals and social groups through their practices, ideologies, and narratives. Buildings, monuments, and the spaces they create give a sense of fixity, of relative permanence, which makes their destruction all the more traumatic and disorienting for those who move in and around them and invest meaning in them. Burial sites are particularly notable for their fixity—or, rather, the ideal of fixity. Tomb inscriptions from ancient West Asia, for instance, often refer to the permanence of the tomb, its inviolability, and the curses against those who would disturb it. Indeed, ideal burial for these ancient societies requires that the tomb be not only undisturbed but also marked and actively remembered in perpetuity. This idealized permanence of the tomb, its function as a memorial for the dead, and its nature as a locus for ritual activity make it a particularly effective site for the construction of memory.

It should come as no surprise, then, that tombs are among the features of the landscape most often targeted for destruction by those who wish to eradicate a people and its claims to territory and the past. Nor should it surprise us that curses against tomb violation abound in ancient West

---

1. Jan Assmann, *Religion and Cultural Memory: Ten Studies*, trans. Rodney Livingstone (Stanford, CA: Stanford University Press, 2006), 81.

Asia, a clear expression of anxiety about the materiality of memory and its vulnerability. The more descriptive curses vividly depict what terrible fate befalls those who would disturb the dead. In effect, these curses afflict on tomb violators a fate similar to one violators impose on the dead—annihilation of their memory. The significance of dead bodies and the spaces they occupy is intertwined with concerns about family religion and the performance of filial piety, part of the bedrock of ancient West Asian societies. Indeed, the treatment of dead bodies in the Hebrew Bible and other texts from ancient West Asia highlights the importance of ritual and space in the preservation of personhood and group identity. It is, after all, no accident that the quest for immortality in the Epic of Gilgamesh begins and ends with a description of the king's construction projects in the city of Uruk. In this ancient text and others, buildings are construed as monuments to the king's memory, physical reminders of his great deeds in life. These buildings, the spaces they create, and the commemorative rituals they house comprise in effect a kind of structured remembering and, thus, a kind of immortality.

This study is an examination of commemoration and care for the dead in ancient Israel, against the broader cultural backdrop of ancient West Asia. It takes as its starting point what I refer to throughout as the "cult of dead kin" and analyzes the constitutive practices and principles of this cult. It goes on to evaluate the relationship between the cult of dead kin and other forms of cult in Israelite religion, including the cult of the Jerusalem temple. Reconstructions of an Israelite cult of dead kin have circulated within biblical studies for several decades.[2] Despite a wealth of schol-

---

2. Scholarly treatments in the last few decades of the textual and material evidence of Israelite cult of dead kin include Klaas Spronk, *Beatific Afterlife in Ancient Israel and the Ancient Near East*, AOAT 219 (Neukirchen-Vluyn: Neukirchener Verlag, 1986); Theodore J. Lewis, *Cults of the Dead in Ancient Israel and Ugarit* (Atlanta: Scholars Press, 1989); William W. Hallo, "Royal Ancestor Worship in the Biblical World," in *Shar'arei Talmon: Studies in the Bible, Qumran, and the Ancient Near East Presented to Shemaryahu Talmon*, ed. Michael Fishbane and Emanuel Tov (Winona Lake, IN: Eisenbrauns, 1992), 381–401; Elizabeth Bloch-Smith, *Judahite Burial Practices and Beliefs about the Dead*, JSOTSup 123 (Sheffield: Sheffield Academic, 1992); Brian Schmidt, *Israel's Beneficent Dead: Ancestor Cult and Necromancy in Ancient Israelite Religion and Tradition* (Winona Lake, IN: Eisenbrauns, 1994); Joseph Blenkinsopp, "Deuteronomy and the Politics of Post-mortem Existence," *VT* 45 (1995): 1–16; Karel van der Toorn, *Family Religion in Babylonia, Ugarit, and Israel: Continuity and Changes in the Forms of Religious Life* (Leiden: Brill, 1996); Thomas Podella, "Ahnenverehrung

arship on death and the dead in the Hebrew Bible, treatments of the cult of dead kin often rely on methodologies and theoretical assumptions that require significant revision. This study focuses on two pervasive problems in reconstructions of the cult. The first is a problem of definition and categorization. Previous studies differ in how they refer to a cluster of cultic practices pertaining to the dead, sometimes conflating them into overgeneralizing categories, such as "death cult practices" and "cult of the dead." Others distinguish some death-related rituals, such as necromancy, from care for the dead.[3] Scholarship refers to the latter variedly as "ancestor cult," "cult of the dead," "care of the dead," or, in the case of this study, "cult of dead kin." The varied terminology used for this cultic activity indicates the uncertain categories used by scholars to understand these practices and their unsuccessful attempts to theorize the underlying principles of these cultic phenomena. Thus, it is essential in a discussion of the Israelite cult of dead kin to consider what this term entails and what theoretical assumptions undergird it.

Second, many reconstructions of Israelite religion argue that biblical writers attack cultic practices pertaining to the dead, particularly during the postexilic period. These reconstructions differ concerning what social, political, or cultic forces may have influenced this shift; yet, they often depend on Max Weber's paradigm of centralized authority to argue that centralization of Yahwistic cult in Jerusalem necessitates an attack on

---

III," *RGG* 1:227–28; Rachel Hallote, *Death, Burial, and Afterlife in the Biblical World: How the Israelites and Their Neighbors Treated the Dead* (Chicago: Dee, 2001); Philip S. Johnston, *Shades of Sheol: Death and Afterlife in the Old Testament* (Leicester: Apollos, 2002); various essays in Angelika Berlejung and Bernd Janowski, eds., *Tod und Jenseits im alten Israel und in seiner Umwelt* (Tübingen: Mohr Siebeck, 2009), including Rüdiger Schmitt, "Totenversorgung, Totengedenken und Nekromantie. Biblische und archäologische Perspektiven ritueller Kommunikation mit den Toten," 501–24; and Jens Kamlah, "Grab und Begräbnis in Israel/Juda: Materielle Befunde, Jenseitsvorstellungen und die Frage des Totenkultes," 257–97; Francesca Stavrakopoulou, *Land of Our Fathers: The Roles of Ancestor Veneration in Biblical Land Claims* (New York: T&T Clark, 2010); Christopher B. Hays, *Death in the Iron Age II and in First Isaiah* (Tübingen: Mohr Siebeck, 2011); Rainer Albertz and Rüdiger Schmitt, *Household and Family Religion in Ancient Israel and the Levant* (Winona Lake, IN: Eisenbrauns, 2012).

3. See, e.g., Mark S. Smith and Elizabeth M. Bloch-Smith, "Death and Afterlife in Ugarit and Israel," *JAOS* 108 (1988): 281; Schmidt, *Israel's Beneficent Dead*, 11–12; Rainer Albertz, "Family Religion in Ancient Israel and Its Surroundings," in *Household and Family Religion in Antiquity*, ed. John Bodel and Saul M. Olyan (Oxford: Blackwell, 2008), 99.

local, kin-based religious authority, epitomized by the cult of dead kin.[4] Thus, many treatments focus on the supposedly adversarial relationship between the cult of dead kin and the so-called official Yahwistic cult centered in Jerusalem.

In this study, I hope to offer three correctives to the study of the cult of dead kin in the Hebrew Bible and ancient Israel. First, the failure of previous studies to separate necromancy from the cult of dead kin has led to a misreading of biblical polemic against necromancy as polemic against the cult of dead kin and its constitutive practices. Second, this conflation has contributed to the pervasive notion that the cult of dead kin is antithetical to Yahwistic cult. Third, reconstructions of an adversarial relationship between centralized cult and care for the dead depend on problematic readings of key biblical texts and on a Weberian paradigm that does not adequately account for the dynamics of Israelite religion, particularly the overlapping interests of family and temple cult.

I use the term *cult of dead kin* to refer to a complex of practices in which the living offer ritual care to the dead.[5] As an essential part of family religion, the cult of dead kin extends participation in the family unit and its religious practices beyond its living members to include kin who have died. This care negotiates the ongoing relationship between the living and the dead and, in doing so, helps structure current social, political, and topographical landscapes in terms of the past.[6] For instance, the recitation

---

4. Susan Ackerman provides a helpful examination of the influence of Weber's *Ancient Judaism* on reconstructions of the Israelite cult of dead kin. See Ackerman, "Cult Centralization, the Erosion of Kin-Based Communities, and the Implications for Women's Religious Practices," in *Social Theory and the Study of Israelite Religion: Essays in Retrospect and Prospect*, ed. Saul M. Olyan (Boston: Brill, 2012), 19–40.

5. See below for a discussion of the term *care* and its range of meaning.

6. Modern anthropological and ethnographic studies support this assessment. See, e.g., Richard Huntington and Peter Metcalf, eds., *Celebrations of Death: The Anthropology of Mortuary Ritual* (Cambridge: Cambridge University Press, 1979); Maurice Bloch and Jonathan Parry, eds., *Death and the Regeneration of Life* (Cambridge: Cambridge University Press, 1982); Paul Connerton, *How Societies Remember* (New York: Cambridge University Press, 1989); Gerdien Jonker, *The Topography of Remembrance: The Dead, Tradition, and Collective Memory in Mesopotamia* (New York: Brill, 1995); Michael Parker Pearson, *The Archaeology of Death and Burial* (College Station: Texas A&M University Press, 1999); Gordon F. M. Rakita and Jane E. Buikstra, eds., *Interacting with the Dead: Perspectives on Mortuary Archaeology for the New Millennium* (Gainesville: University Press of Florida, 2005).

of lineages and their claims to certain territories, whether real or fictive, provides a basis for such land rights among those who claim descent from those lineages.

Recent scholarship on family religion in ancient Israel helps us further contextualize the cult of dead kin. In fact, scholarship on the cult of dead kin from the last few decades coincides with a broader paradigm shift within the field of biblical studies toward greater consideration of internal religious plurality in the Hebrew Bible and ancient Israel and, more specifically, varied manifestations of local and family religion. Articulations of what constitutes family religion vary; in general, however, family religion includes veneration of family or household gods and rituals surrounding important life events such as birth, illness, marriage, and death.[7] From a social perspective, participation in these rituals may affirm or challenge membership in the family unit, the relative status of individual members in that unit, and the relationship between the family and perceived outsiders.

Defining *family* or *kinship*, however, is notoriously difficult.[8] The sociological and anthropological literature on the topic is extensive, and a full account of it is beyond the scope of this study.[9] In the field of biblical studies, scholars have similarly considered the family, its defining characteristics, and the range of its membership.[10] Some recurring themes emerge in these

---

7. For a discussion regarding the contours of family religion, see Van der Toorn, *Family Religion*, 4; John Bodel and Saul M. Olyan, "Introduction," in Bodel and Olyan, *Household and Family Religion*, 1.

8. In this study I use the terms *family* and *kinship* interchangeably. I emphasize that both terms signify flexible, socially constructed concepts that depend on ideologies of shared identity, often mediated through ritual.

9. A survey of kinship as a concept in anthropological discourse can be found in Janet Carsten's "Introduction: Cultures of Relatedness," in *Cultures of Relatedness: New Approaches to the Study of Kinship*, ed. Janet Carsten (Cambridge: Cambridge University Press, 2000), 1–36. Another helpful survey examining the development of kinship in this discourse since the mid-twentieth century is Bernard Chapais, "From Biological to Cultural Kinship," in *Primeval Kinship: How Pair-Bonding Gave Birth to Human Society* (Cambridge: Harvard University Press, 2008), 48–59. A more extensive examination of this development is the focus of Marshall Sahlins, *What Kinship Is—And Is Not* (Chicago: University of Chicago Press, 2013).

10. For an overview of the family in biblical scholarship over the past few decades, see Patricia Dutcher-Walls, "The Clarity of Double Vision: Seeing the Family in Sociological and Archaeological Perspective," in *The Family in Life and in Death: The Family in Ancient Israel; Sociological and Archaeological Perspectives*, ed. Patricia Dutcher-

treatments. Most important, the conception of family is not universal but highly dependent on the particular cultural context in which it appears. In a ritual context, however, the family includes those persons who recognize affiliation through rituals accompanying childbirth, marriage, adoption, and death. Analyses of the family also emphasize the role of materiality in defining this social unit.[11] Those who inhabit the same built environment, such as the domicile, often comprise the family. Servants and slaves residing within that domicile, for instance, may sometimes claim membership in the family unit (e.g., Gen 17:10–14; Exod 12:43–45). In some treatments, the same can be said for those who share hardware, such as tools and agricultural implements, essential for their survival. In short, a variety of factors may determine who is and is not a member of any culturally constructed family. Ultimately, the cohesion of the family unit relies primarily on the mutual recognition of social relations on the basis of any of these factors.[12] This mutual recognition becomes particularly relevant in a discussion of family religion, including the cult of dead kin, since ritual in general creates a richly symbolic space where this kind of recognition can take place and where the reciprocal duties among family members may be affirmed, challenged, and terminated.

But why is the term cult of dead kin preferable to other terms for this phenomenon? As I note above, previous studies have used different terminology, and this inconsistency highlights some of the broader interpretative issues that divide scholarly opinion on the subject. Indeed, defini-

---

Walls (New York: T&T Clark, 2009), 1–15. Albertz and Schmitt offer a helpful overview of the terms *family* and *household* and their use in sociological and biblical scholarship (*Household and Family Religion*, 21–46). See also various essays in Leo G. Perdue et al., eds., *Families in Ancient Israel* (Louisville: Westminster John Knox, 1997).

11. Recent work in biblical scholarship also considers this aspect of the family. See, e.g., Carol Meyers, "The Family in Early Israel," in Perdue et al., *Families in Ancient Israel*, esp. 13–17; Meyers, *Households and Holiness: The Religious Culture of Israelite Women* (Minneapolis: Fortress, 2005), 24; Susan Ackerman, "Household Religion, Family Religion, and Women's Religion in Ancient Israel," in Bodel and Olyan, *Household and Family Religion*, esp. 127–32.

12. "While biological relations are important in defining family membership, the real issue is the *recognition* of a familial relationship." See Bryan S. Turner, "The Sociology and Anthropology of the Family," in *Classical Sociology* (London: Sage, 1999), 232, emphasis original. Similarly, Sahlins refers to the "mutuality of being" inherent in kinship: "kinfolk are persons who participate intrinsically in each other's existence; they are members of one another" (*What Kinship Is*, ix).

tion and its correlate, taxonomy, often reveal the fundamental theoretical assumptions underlying such an analysis,[13] and scholarly terms for cult reflect both first- and second-order categories used to understand the relationships among various cultic practices. Thus, in order to examine the cult of dead kin, we must define the parameters of that cult, including its constitutive practices and its participants. In doing so, we must confront some of the perennial issues in reconstructions of Israelite cult of dead kin, such as the role of the family in ancient societies, the nature of care for the dead, and distinctions between this cult and other practices related to death.

In studies of Israelite religion, care offered to dead kin is often called "cult of the dead" or "ancestor cult," both of which are insufficient in describing the object of study. Cult of the dead is overly vague and conflates various death-related practices that may take place in different contexts, are performed by different kinds of actors, and pursue different ends. Mourning and necromancy, for example, both entail rituals oriented toward the dead, but those rituals differ significantly in form and function.[14] Placing them in the same cultic category, cult of the dead, obscures fundamental features that make them distinct, while being more precise with our terminology for these cultic phenomena helps draw attention to their various points of divergence and, sometimes, overlap. Ultimately, this terminological distinction contributes to a more nuanced understanding of the phenomena themselves. Some studies have recognized the need for such nuance, drawing a distinction between funerary and mortuary ritual.[15] However, the ongoing tendency to conflate care for the dead with other death-related ritual necessitates further analysis.

Despite its helpful focus on the familial context of the cult, ancestor cult also has significant limitations in its ability to adequately describe the

---

13. For a discussion of definition and classification in the study of religion, see Jonathan Z. Smith, "A Matter of Class: Taxonomies of Religion," in *Relating Religion: Essays in the Study of Religion* (Chicago: University of Chicago Press, 2004), 160–78. See also Bruce Lincoln, "The Tyranny of Taxonomy," in *Discourse and the Construction of Society: Comparative Studies of Myth, Ritual, and Classification* (New York: Oxford University Press, 1992), 131–41.

14. While some death-related practices demonstrate a degree of conceptual overlap, I argue that more specific terminology helps us identify the differences between these practices that previous studies have neglected. I will examine the nature of such a categorical distinction more fully in ch. 2's discussion of necromancy and its relationship to the cult of dead kin in ancient Israel.

15. Schmidt, *Israel's Beneficent Dead*, 5–7.

scope and nature of the available evidence. In fact, when scholars refer to Israelite ancestor cult, what they are usually referring to is a broader category of practice, more accurately conveyed by cult of dead kin.[16] *Ancestor*, after all, typically denotes an elder predecessor, and both biblical and cuneiform evidence cited as representative of ancestor cult often involves dead who are not one's elder kin. In the biblical text, for example, Jacob's construction of a commemorative monument for his wife Rachel (Gen 35:20) or Rişpah's protection of her sons' remains (2 Sam 21:10) are arguably manifestations of the cult of dead kin but kin who are not one's elders.[17] Evidence for the Mesopotamian *kispu* (the Akkadian term for the cult of dead kin) follows a similar pattern: while some texts depict the *kispu* offered to parents or grandparents, others depict the *kispu* offered to non-elder kin.[18] Biblical texts that describe care for dead elders, such as 2 Sam 18:18 and Neh 2:3, constitute one facet of this broader category, cult of dead kin, and perhaps its ideal configuration. After all, elders ideally precede younger persons in death. Moreover, the focus of the Hebrew Bible on male ancestors—particularly the patriarchs and former kings of Israel and Judah—has likely led scholars to focus on care for dead elders, while fail-

---

16. I speak of Israelite kin and family here referring to practices of both the royal and nonroyal spheres. While members of the royal family are prominent actors in multiple texts depicting cult of dead kin (2 Sam 18:18; 2 Kgs 9:34–37), it seems unlikely that the cult of dead kin is limited to the royal family since other texts suggest that care for the dead was practiced more broadly. Isaiah 56:6, for instance, refers to the care offered by YHWH to the eunuch, while the first-person speaker in Deut 26:14 (who must not offer any of the tithe to the dead) seems to be any Israelite offering the tithe. Moreover, Mesopotamian evidence for cult of dead kin suggests that its constitutive practices could be performed in both royal and nonroyal spheres.

17. A more detailed analysis of the biblical texts cited here will appear later in this chapter as well as other chapters that focus on specific issues in the reconstruction of the cult of dead kin in ancient Israel. For a comment on the rationale for my interpretation of 2 Sam 21:10 as an example of the cult of dead kin, see my discussion below.

18. For example, citing a letter from King Hammurabi of Babylon to Sin-iddinam, Dina Katz notes that a father offers the *kispu* to his missing son. Without the corpse or even assurance of his son's fate, the father makes offerings as if his son were dead. See Katz, "Sumerian Funerary Rituals in Context," in *Performing Death: Social Analyses of Funerary Traditions in the Ancient Near East and Mediterranean,* ed. Nicola Lanieri (Chicago: Oriental Institute of the University of Chicago, 2007), 168–70. Katz also notes that a Sumerian text, called The Messenger and the Maiden, may similarly depict the performance of the *kispu* for one who died abroad and did not receive proper burial.

ing to acknowledge its broader ritual genus, care for dead kin. This revised taxonomy of cult has the advantage of recognizing the cult of dead kin as a more pervasive phenomenon in the Hebrew Bible and ancient Israel, thus introducing new and relevant evidence to an examination of it. Furthermore, by reframing the discourse surrounding care for the dead in this way, we may better understand the internal ritual and social logic of this cult and its embeddedness in the life of the Israelite family.[19]

In addition to this group of texts involving kin, there is another that depicts the use of the cult of dead kin to create social bonds among ostensibly nonkin actors. I argue that these texts draw on the imagery and individual practices of the cult of dead kin and apply them to nonkin in order to form new social and political relationships, especially in times of crisis when the dead lack living kin to care for them. Such biblical texts include the depiction of the relationship between the men of Jabesh-Gilead, Saul, and Jonathan in 1 Sam 31:11–13; David, Saul, and Jonathan in 2 Sam 21:12–14; Jehu and Jezebel in 2 Kgs 9:34; YHWH and the eunuch in Isa 56:5; and YHWH and Israel in Ezek 37:1–14. Isaiah 56:3–5 is particularly interesting in this regard because it not only assumes the ideal configuration of care for the dead—a dead parent cared for by living offspring—but also the recognition of nonideal death of the eunuch, who dies without descendants, and the substitution of a nonkin caregiver (YHWH) for those descendants. Similarly, 2 Sam 18:18 both assumes the ideal parent-offspring configuration and renegotiates it in light of Absalom's lack of a son. Cuneiform evidence also demonstrates this usage of care for the dead by nonkin actors. For instance, the *kispu* appears in a text called the Genealogy of the Hammurapi Dynasty, in which the new king Ammiṣaduqa makes offerings to different groups of the dead who, for various reasons, lack someone to care for them.[20] The offering of the *kispu* to these groups helps establish the nascent reign of the king, who is responsible for the cultic maintenance of his whole kingdom. Therefore, all of these texts constitute evidence for the cult of dead kin because they either involve cult offered to kin or use its constitutive rituals to create social and political bonds between nonkin actors.

---

19. For instance, previously overlooked biblical texts reflecting the cult of dead kin may change the way we think about the role of women in the cult, as I argue in ch. 3.

20. Jacob J. Finkelstein, "The Geneaology of the Hammurapi Dynasty," *JCS* 20 (1966): 95–118.

Indeed, the use of familial terminology and imagery to depict social relationships between nonkin actors is prevalent throughout ancient West Asia, including the treaty language used for suzerain ("father"), vassal ("son"), and ally ("brother"). The relationship between god and worshiper also uses such terms. For instance, in 2 Sam 7:14, YHWH uses the language of adoption to describe his relationship with David's offspring: "As for me, I will become his father. As for him, he will become my son." The use of familial terminology also appears in Exod 4:22–23 and Hos 11:1, in which Israel is described as YHWH's son, and Mal 1:6, in which YHWH refers to himself as a father deserving of honor. In these texts, family members serve as paradigmatic intimates for biblical ideologies about YHWH. Such use of the family as a model for various nonkin social relationships is well attested in the biblical text and further supports the use of the term cult of dead kin, since this model of kin providing cult to their dead family members informs not only familial but also nonkin configurations of this ritual care.

In short, I argue that nonkin actors utilize the practices of the cult of dead kin in order to create social bonds with the dead. By performing the cult, these nonkin actors tacitly (and sometimes explicitly) assert their status as friends, allies, and sometimes kin of the dead. Thus, nonkin actors may strategically use the cult to assert continuity through kinship and, thus, mitigate perceived social and political ruptures. Indeed, several biblical and nonbiblical texts from ancient West Asia depict nonkin actors using the imagery and individual practices of the cult in times of crisis, especially when the dead lack kin to care for them. This real or fictive lack of care for the dead creates an opportunity for nonkin to claim that affiliation with the dead and the social and political authority it may entail. As I argue in chapter 4, this strategic use of the cult of dead kin becomes particularly useful for biblical writers working in the postexilic period as they rationalize the social, political, and religious trauma of the exile.

The inclusion of the Jehu and Jezebel narrative in a discussion of the cult of dead kin also requires comment and raises the issue of discerning which texts are indicative of the cult of dead kin, rather than funerary or mourning practices. The language with which Jehu orders his men to care for the remains of Jezebel (*piqdû*) in 2 Kgs 9:34 is similar to that of the cult of dead kin in Mesopotamia (*pāqidu*).[21] It is important to note,

---

21. Lewis, *Cults of the Dead*, 120–22.

however, that the care offered by Jehu's men occurs prior to the burial of Jezebel, and one of the hallmarks of the cult of dead kin emphasized in previous studies is its performance after the burial of the dead.[22] Thus, the act of burial is often used as a dividing line between funerary and mourning rituals on one hand and cult of dead kin on the other. Indeed, such a distinction may hold in cases where the dead are given proper burial in a timely fashion, but this delineation between funerary/mourning ritual and cult of dead kin seems less clear in cases of corpse exposure or other forms of nonideal burial, as in the case of Jezebel in 2 Kgs 9:34 and the Saulides in 2 Sam 21:10. In these cases of corpse exposure, it is possible that the protection and care offered to the physical remains of the dead belong more to the realm of cult of dead kin than to funerary or mourning ritual. Evidence for the Mesopotamian *kispu* supports this categorization. In two cases of nonburial, the Genealogy of the Hammurapi Dynasty and the letter from King Hammurabi of Babylon to Sin-iddinam, the *kispu* is offered to those who have not received proper burial and who probably never will. In the former case, the dead are explicitly referred to as those lying exposed in foreign lands, while the latter text refers to a missing son, the whereabouts of whose corpse are entirely unknown. Despite their lack of burial, the dead in these texts nevertheless receive the *kispu*. Therefore, nonburial seems to complicate the distinction between funerary/mourning ritual and cult of dead kin because the customary line of demarcation, proper burial, is absent. In such cases, it seems plausible and, perhaps, more accurate to classify acts characteristic of the cult of dead kin—even prior to burial of the dead—as manifestations of that cult rather than funerary or mourning acts. In addition, these acts are not typical of funerary or mourning rites as far as we know.

My use of the terms *cult* and *care* also requires some unpacking. Referring to certain death-related practices as cult has the advantage of viewing them as a coherent cluster of practices. These practices comprise a cult

---

22. See, e.g., the thorough discussion of the cult of dead kin in terms of time-sensitive rites—specifically when they occur in relation to the moment of death—in Schmidt, *Israel's Beneficent Dead*, 4–12. Dennis Pardee draws a similar distinction between funerary and mortuary rites in the Ugaritic corpus. See Pardee, "*Marzihu, Kispu*, and the Ugaritic Funerary Cult: A Minimalist View," in *Ugarit, Religion, and Culture: Proceedings of the International Colloquium on Ugarit, Religion and Culture, Edinburgh, July 1994*, ed. John C. L. Gibson, Nick Wyatt, Wilfred G. E. Watson, and Jeffrey B. Lloyd (Münster: Ugarit-Verlag, 1996), 273–87.

of dead kin in the sense that they resemble both the care for living elders and the maintenance of a deity.[23] While the former entails the provision of sustenance and protection, the latter additionally concerns practices of invocation. After all, the Akkadian term *pāqidu*, the cultic custodian of the *kispu*, and its related verb, *paqādu*, are used in contexts depicting the care for animals, living people, houses, and temples.[24] Indeed, a neglected aspect of the cult of dead kin is its similarity to the care of deities, a point I will return to later in this chapter. Therefore, the use of *cult* in reference to both the temple cult of a deity and the cult of dead kin highlights the similarities between these two phenomena, including their reciprocal logic and embeddedness in ancient societies.

Regarding the term *care*, I do not use *care* as it appears in other studies to suggest the dependent, nondivine status of the dead.[25] For instance, in their recent, coauthored study *Family and Household Religion in Ancient Israel and the Levant* (2012), Rainer Albertz and Rüdiger Schmitt reject the terms ancestor cult and cult of the dead and instead opt for "care for the dead" because this latter term avoids issues regarding the supernatural powers of the dead and their status as divine cultic recipients. They use this term (analogous to the German *Totenpflege*) because, they argue, it more adequately reflects the social function of rituals involving dead kin, rather than veneration or worship of the dead as divine beings.[26] They argue against the divine status of the dead, saying that the biblical text

---

23. The essays in Marten Stol and Sven P. Vleeming, eds., *The Care of the Elderly in the Ancient Near East* (Boston: Brill, 1998), examine the phenomenon of care for living elders more fully.

24. *CAD* 12:126–27.

25. For instance, Schmidt considers "care for" or "feeding of" the dead as indicative of their weak status and thus evidence against the interpretation that the dead were worshiped or venerated (*Israel's Beneficent Dead*, 10). Other scholars have already addressed the problems with this argument. See, e.g., Elizabeth Bloch-Smith, "Death in the Life of Israel," in *Sacred Time, Sacred Place*, ed. Barry M. Gittlen (Winona Lake, IN: Eisenbrauns, 2002), 140; Theodore J. Lewis, "How Far Can Texts Take Us? Evaluating Textual Sources for Reconstructing Ancient Israelite Beliefs about the Dead," in Gittlen, *Sacred Time, Sacred Place*, 189–202. The most persuasive critique is that care and commemoration are common aspects of the worship and veneration of deities in ancient West Asia; therefore, these acts do not necessarily indicate weak, nondivine status. If we were to accept Schmidt's argument, then we would have to interpret sacrifice to YHWH as indicative of YHWH's inability to care for himself, a clear misreading of the biblical evidence.

26. Albertz and Schmitt, *Family and Household Religion*, 430.

does not explicitly depict the dead as venerated or worshiped by the living. For instance, they argue that the term *'ĕlōhîm* and its application to the dead (1 Sam 28:13; Isa 8:19) "is best understood as ascribing special status to the dead as preternatural beings, who thereby possessed qualities not shared by the living, especially knowledge of things to come." Therefore, according to their reconstruction, "ancestors were to be honored but not worshiped."[27]

One fundamental problem with this interpretation is that it creates a new category of divine being that is not supported by the ancient evidence. On the contrary, the terminology used for biblical necromancy suggests that the dead are, in fact, divine. That biblical writers use the term *'ĕlōhîm* for the dead in some biblical texts describing necromancy suggests that (in these texts, at least) the dead belong to the same conceptual category as other divine beings. Instead of dismissing this use of the term as indicative of a linguistic deficiency,[28] we might instead take this usage at face value— in the context of necromancy, the dead are divine, they possess powers to influence the world of the living, and they may offer those powers in exchange for care just like major and minor deities in ancient West Asia. Based on this usage of the Hebrew term *'ĕlōhîm* as well as cognate terms in other ancient West Asian textual corpora, it seems that biblical studies might benefit from recent discussions in Assyriology regarding the category "god" and its broad range of usage.[29]

---

27. Albertz and Schmitt, *Family and Household Religion*, 433. According to this argument, the fact that the dead are not worshiped explains why there is no polemic against the cult of dead kin in the Deuteronomic or Deuteronomistic texts, Priestly law codes, or prophetic texts. In their view, the writers of these texts would never condone such cult for the divine dead.

28. For instance, Lewis attributes the application of this term to the dead as indicative of the "poverty of ancient Near Eastern vocabulary rather than an attempt to deify the dead fully (in the sense of making them equal to the high gods of the pantheon)" ("How Far Can Texts," 198). Similarly, John Day asserts, "This term ['ĕlōhîm] had become something of a linguistic 'fossil,' since they are no longer regarded as literally divine." See Day, "The Development of Belief in Life after Death in Ancient Israel," in *After the Exile: Essays in Honor of Rex Mason*, ed. John Barton and David James Reimer (Macon, GA: Mercer University Press, 1996), 233. Both of these interpretations presume that the text could not possibly mean what it states. Instead, they begin with the assumption that the dead cannot be divine and proceed with a theorization of the divine category and the term *'ĕlōhîm* based on that assumption.

29. See various essays in Barbara Nevling Porter, ed., *What Is a God? Anthropomorphic and Non-anthropomorphic Aspects of Deity in Ancient Mesopotamia* (Winona

But what of the cult of dead kin? Although biblical writers never explicitly refer to the dead as *ʾĕlōhîm* in the context of the cult of dead kin, references to care for the dead, especially food and drink offerings as well as the invocation of their names,[30] demonstrate parallels with the cult for ancient West Asian deities. For example, taking temple cult in ancient West Asia as our paradigmatic model, we might observe that this cult entails not only regular food and drink offerings for the deity but also rites of temple and icon maintenance, on an as-needed basis. All of these rites concern the maintenance of the deity and its abode. Similarly, we observe that the cult for dead kin entails care performed with varying degrees of frequency, dictated by custom or necessity—food and drink offerings, invocation of the name of the dead, and rites of repatriation, reburial, and tomb maintenance as needed. Therefore, the different modes of offering and maintenance that constitute the cult of deities are strikingly similar to those constitutive of the cult of dead kin.[31] It is unclear what worship would entail in Albertz and Schmitt's analysis if not the performance of these modes of care. Unfortunately, Albertz and Schmitt do not elucidate their usage of these terms (*veneration*, *worship*, and *honor*), what they entail in terms of practice, or how they differ from one another. Thus, it is difficult to determine the criteria by which they designate the dead as nondivine, despite the fact that they receive cult characteristic of the worship of ancient West Asian deities.[32]

Lake, IN: Eisenbrauns, 2009). These discussions focus on the various manifestations of the divine in ancient Mesopotamia, which expand conceptions of deity to include entities that were previously overlooked by scholars.

30. Invoking the name of the deity appears frequently in the biblical text. Such idioms include *qrʾ bšm* (Gen 4:26) and *hzkr šm* (Exod 20:24; Isa 26:13; 62:6).

31. In fact, Matthew Suriano notes similarities in syntax between Iron Age funerary inscriptions and biblical references to care for the dead, including Num 19:11: "Again –ל is used to signify any general care given for the dead. The preposition implies purposeful action on the part of the person who is in contact with the dead and hence is defiled by the defunct soul" (*A History of Death in the Hebrew Bible* [New York: Oxford University Press, 2018], 147). Suriano later argues that this use of the preposition marks a dialectical relationship between the living and the dead, one modeled after dedicatory inscriptions to deities. For instance, in his examination of the inscription on the Ahiram sarcophagus, Suriano argues: "The formulaic beginning of this inscription identifies the object—the sarcophagus—as well as the person for whom it is dedicated. Although this formula usually appears in inscriptions where an object is dedicated to a god, the tenth century BCE Ahirom sarcophagus (*KAI* 1) marks an early example of its use on behalf of the dead" (*History of Death*, 173).

32. We may observe a similar ambiguity regarding these cultic categories in

When we look more broadly at the practice of sacrifice in the ancient Mediterranean and West Asia, we might ask whether sacrifice presumes a reciprocal relationship between the one who offers sacrifice and the one who receives it. If so, offerings to the dead seem to assume that the dead have enough agency to respond in kind and to exert their will with respect to the living. Although we lack explicit biblical evidence of reciprocity between the living and the dead, many studies take this reciprocal dynamic for granted. Thus, Theodore Lewis defines cult of the dead as "those acts directed toward the deceased functioning either to placate the dead or to secure favors from them for the present life."[33] Indeed, the reciprocity inherent in *cult* in general finds support in recent work concerning the nature of ancient Judean sacrifice and Mediterranean religion. Aaron Glaim examines the practical logic of the sacrificial cult of YHWH at the Jerusalem temple in the late Second Temple or Herodian period, arguing that nearly all of the ancient evidence for the Jerusalem temple explicitly or implicitly demonstrates the reciprocal logic of sacrifice.[34] Examining Mediterranean cult more broadly, Stanley K. Stowers delineates the religion of everyday social exchange, of which family and household religion is part, and outlines four characteristics of gods in this everyday exchange:

> People interact with them as if they were persons; they are local in ways that are significant for humans; one maintains a relationship to them with practices of *generalized reciprocity*; and humans have a particular epistemological stance toward them.... The default position found very widely around the globe is types of religiosity with gods and similar beings who are conceived as interested parties with whom people carry on mundane social exchange.[35]

---

other treatments of the cult of dead kin as well. In her study *Land of Our Fathers*, Stavrakopoulou vacillates on which term she prefers—*commemoration*, *veneration*, or *worship*—but suggests that *worship* may be the most accurate term: "And food and drink rituals and the invocation of the dead signal a response from the living less like commemoration and rather more like veneration, if not—sometimes—worship" (*Land of Our Fathers*, 23). More often, however, she refers to the veneration of ancestors, and this is the term she uses in the title of her book.

33. Lewis, *Cults of the Dead*, 2.

34. Aaron Glaim, "Reciprocity, Sacrifice, and Salvation in Judean Religion at the Turn of the Era" (PhD diss., Brown University, 2014).

35. Stanley K. Stowers, "The Religion of Plant and Animal Offerings versus the Religion of Meanings, Essences and Textual Mysteries," in *Ancient Mediterranean*

Although Stowers speaks of gods in this passage, his observations may equally apply to characterizations of dead kin.

Thus, I understand the logic of *cult* and its constitutive practices, such as sacrificial offerings, to be reciprocal in nature, even where we lack explicit allusions to this reciprocity in the extant textual evidence. Since reciprocity is so central to ancient conceptions of cult, it is difficult to imagine a ritual logic underlying the cult dead of kin in which reciprocity is entirely absent. Though the biblical evidence does not explicitly refer to reciprocity between the living and the dead, we may plausibly infer from the principles underlying cult more generally throughout ancient West Asia—and the fundamentally reciprocal nature of sacrifice in particular— that such reciprocal relations also exist between the dead and the living who care for them.

We must ask to what extent some scholars' rejection of *worship* in favor of *honoring* the dead is special pleading in order to avoid what some may perceive as a threat to supposed Israelite monotheism. In fact, earlier proponents of Israelite monotheism, such as Yehezkel Kaufmann, also created separate categories for describing ritual activity associated with the dead, calling it "ethical behavior" instead of "religious acts,"[36] in order to distinguish it from the kind of cult offered to YHWH. It seems no coincidence that treatments asserting Israelite uniqueness—particularly with regard to monotheism—would reject the existence of an Israelite cult of dead kin, likely to avoid the theological problems posed by the divine status of the dead, the offering of sacrifice to the dead, and the relationship between

---

Sacrifice, ed. Jennifer Wright Knust and Zsuzsa Varhelyi (New York: Oxford University Press, 2011), 37, emphasis added.

36. Yehezkel Kaufmann, *The Religion of Israel: From Its Beginnings to the Babylonian Exile*, trans. and abridged by Moshe Greenberg (New York: Schocken Books, 1972), 315. See also G. Ernest Wright, *Deuteronomy*, IB (New York: Abingdon, 1953), 486–87; Roland de Vaux, *Ancient Israel: Its Life and Institutions* (London: Darton, Longman & Todd, 1961), passim. An illustrative argument from de Vaux states: "People have wanted to interpret these funerary rites as manifestations of a cult of the dead ... but the Old Testament does not furnish any solid foundation for these opinions" (*Ancient Israel*, 100). However, not all scholarship from this era denied the existence of cultic practices pertaining to the dead. For instance, Gerhard von Rad argues that the dead continue to exist after death, have a "positive sacral value" among the living, exert influence on the living, and know the future. See von Rad, *The Theology of Israel's Historical Traditions*, vol. 1 of *Old Testament Theology* (Louisville: Westminster John Knox, 2001), 276–77.

the divine dead and YHWH. Therefore, we must ask to what extent this categorization and its theological underpinnings continue to influence reconstructions of the cult of dead kin in the Hebrew Bible and ancient Israel. Indeed, more recent treatments of the Israelite dead also use terms that differ ever so slightly from more common terminology of cult, perhaps to avoid these theological problems. Thus, the dead are not divine but preternatural.[37] They are not worshiped but honored.[38] The ritual activity surrounding them is not cult but care.[39] In all these cases, the preferred terms are vaguely defined—if defined at all—and the distinctions between them and rejected terminology are rarely explained. In short, each of these terms in the scholarly discourse deserves thorough analysis, but their similarity to previous terminological discussions demonstrating theological influence suggests that they may also be semantic dodges in order to avoid modern theological problems.[40]

While Albertz and Schmitt rightly emphasize the social function of rituals concerning dead kin, it is unnecessary to eliminate the religious dimensions of these rituals and cult. After all, as noted above, care for the dead (e.g., provision of offerings, protection, commemoration) is strikingly similar to the care of a deity in a temple cult, and the underlying logic of such cult assumes reciprocity between the one who sacrifices and the divine recipient. Furthermore, the fact that this cult has a social function does not mean that it operates solely in that way for cultic actors; in fact, it is unlikely that participants would justify the ongoing performance of these rituals by referencing their social utility. Cult and its constitutive rituals generally operate on multiple levels of interpretation dependent on the symbolic and social world of a particular tradition; although they may be used strategically to influence social worlds, ritual

---

37. Lewis, *Cults of the Dead*, 173; Lewis, "How Far Can Texts," 198; Albertz and Schmitt, *Family and Household Religion*, 430.

38. Van der Toorn, *Family Religion*, 233; Albertz and Schmitt, *Family and Household Religion*, 430.

39. Albertz and Schmitt, *Family and Household Religion*, 430.

40. Indeed, after reviewing the history of debates concerning an Israelite cult of the dead, Bloch-Smith posits that current scholarly attempts to minimize the scope of the cult of the dead may derive from these theological interests: "Given the Biblical Theology movement's influence in the 1950s and 1960s, one may wonder if theological forces are at work in the current backlash against the cult of the dead" ("Death in the Life of Israel," 142).

practice is rarely couched in just these terms.[41] While it is important to analyze the social utility of these rituals, social utility alone is insufficient in understanding the underlying logic of this cult and its significance among practitioners. Thus, the elimination of *cult* from terminology referring to rituals involving dead kin runs the risk of ignoring parallels with other cultic practices in ancient West Asian traditions—thus tacitly asserting the uniqueness of Israelite cult—and making social function the sole focus of the scholarly discourse.

Finally, we must examine the terms *Israelite* and *biblical* and to what extent we may reconstruct either an Israelite or biblical cult of dead kin. Throughout this study, I focus primarily on the biblical evidence for the cult of dead kin. For Israelite religion, the Hebrew Bible is our most extensive, descriptive body of evidence for reconstructing religious practices and ideologies. Yet, I often use the term *Israelite cult of dead kin* to describe my object of study because many of the practices and ideologies depicted in the Hebrew Bible seem to reflect the material evidence from the archaeological record in Israel. Previous studies have cogently argued that material evidence from Iron Age burials indicates the practices of care and commemoration for the dead in this period.[42] In addition, much of this material evidence, most notably the types of grave goods buried alongside the dead, is consistent with even earlier periods in the Levant. Such continuities suggest that these religious practices and ideologies concerning the dead have deep cultural roots in this region. For instance, Middle Bronze grave goods, such as ceramics containing food and drink residues, suggest that these offerings were intended as sustenance for the dead.[43] Treatment of dead bodies, particularly the practice of secondary burial, is another

---

41. Catherine Bell describes this aspect of ritual thus: "Ritualization is embedded within the dynamics of the body defined within a symbolically structured environment. An important corollary to this is the fact that ritualization is a particularly 'mute' form of activity. It is designed to do what it does without bringing what it is doing across the threshold of discourse or systematic thinking." See Bell, *Ritual Theory, Ritual Practice* (New York: Oxford University Press, 1992), 93.

42. See, e.g., Bloch-Smith, *Judahite Burial Practices*; Hallote, *Death, Burial, and Afterlife*; James Osborne, "Secondary Mortuary Practice and the Bench Tomb: Structure and Practice in Iron Age Judah," *JNES* 70 (2011): 35–53.

43. Rachel S. Hallote, "Tombs, Cult, and Chronology: A Reexamination of the Middle Bronze Age Strata of Megiddo," in *Studies in the Archaeology of Israel and Neighboring Lands in Memory of Douglas L. Esse*, ed. Samuel R. Wolff, SAOC 59 (Chicago: Oriental Institute of the University of Chicago, 2001), 208; Jill L. Baker, "The

indication that care for the dead continued after mourning and funerary rituals.[44] Other features of the cult of dead kin as I define it in this study, however, are unlikely to leave a material residue. Invoking the name of the dead, for instance, is less likely to leave a trace in the archaeological record unless that invocation includes the inscription of the name of the dead on a stela or similarly durable medium.

Comparative evidence from contemporary ancient West Asian cultures also suggests continuity with the cult of dead kin depicted in the Hebrew Bible. Although we must allow for local variation in particular practices, many of the practices and ideologies of family religion, including the cult of dead kin, are pervasive throughout ancient West Asia. Thus, this comparative analysis—between the Hebrew Bible and epigraphic evidence from Judah on one hand and evidence from other ancient West Asian cultures on the other—supports use of the term Israelite cult of dead kin, not merely a biblical cult of dead kin. The latter implies that this cult only exists as a literary fiction, but the extent of the evidence for the cult both in and outside the Hebrew Bible suggests that it did, in fact, exist in ancient Israel. Indeed, reconstructions of the Israelite cult of dead kin greatly depend on analogies drawn between the biblical evidence (as well as material remains from Judah) and evidence from other ancient West Asian cultures.

One of the persistent problems in the reconstruction of the Israelite cult of dead kin is the relative scarcity of biblical evidence for this cultic phenomenon compared to other ancient West Asian corpora and what this scarcity suggests about the cult in Israel: Was it widespread? Was it marginal? Although the Hebrew Bible contains no explicit references to the cult of dead kin (the Hebrew Bible contains no analogous term to *kispu*), the appearance of one or more characteristic elements of the cult in a familial or funerary context has led some scholars to reconstruct the cultic activity taken for granted by passages such as Deut 26:14, 2 Sam 18:18, and Isa 56:3–5. However, a minimalist interpretation of the Israelite cult of dead kin would argue that the lack of explicit reference to the cult in the Hebrew Bible indicates the historical absence of such cult in ancient Israel. While it is true that the biblical text does not include detailed pre-

---

Funeral Kit: A Newly Defined Canaanite Mortuary Practice Based on the Middle and Late Bronze Age Tomb Complex at Ashkelon," *Levant* 38 (2006): 5.

44. Melissa S. Cradic, "Embodiments of Death: The Funerary Sequence and Commemoration in the Bronze Age Levant," *BASOR* 377 (2017): 220.

scriptions of such rituals or articulations of Israelite ideologies regarding the benevolent powers of the dead, my analysis takes an optimistic view of the material.[45] Like many other features of family religion in ancient West Asian cultures, the cult of dead kin is perhaps so deeply interwoven into the fabric of Israelite society that its presence goes largely unremarked on in the Hebrew Bible, which tends to be more interested in centralized or state-focused ideologies. Indeed, in his influential article examining kinship, cult, and property, Herbert Chanan Brichto notes, "The Hebrew Bible is the visible tip of the iceberg; the mass below the surface, respecting quantity, distribution and contours, lends itself not to precise knowledge but to informed guesses."[46] Borrowing Brichto's metaphor, it seems that the bulk of family religion and, thus, the vast majority of ancient Israelites' engagement with religious practice lies below the surface of the biblical text. Yet, we may discern some of those underlying practices and ideologies from the ways in which the text moves over and around it.

Take, for example, the opposite end of the human life cycle: pregnancy and childbirth. The importance of progeny is a recurring theme throughout the Hebrew Bible and other cognate literatures; therefore, it is likely that rituals concerning conception, pregnancy, and childbirth would have played a role in securing offspring in ancient Israel. However, the Hebrew Bible contains no detailed account of any such rituals in literary, ritual, or legal genres.[47] Are we to conclude that no such rituals existed in ancient Israel? I find such a scenario unlikely, especially when we consider the material evidence that suggests otherwise.[48] Instead, this

---

45. For a relatively recent example of a minimalist interpretation, see Schmidt, *Israel's Beneficent Dead*, 164–65, 201, 262–63, and passim; or Johnston, *Shades of Sheol*, 193–95 and passim.

46. Herbert Chanan Brichto, "Kin, Cult, Land and Afterlife—A Biblical Complex," *HUCA* 44 (1973): 2.

47. However, the biblical text does include some brief references to parents petitioning the deity regarding conception (Gen 25:21; Judg 13:8; 1 Sam 1:11) and implies that YHWH has the ability to facilitate or prevent conception (Exod 23:26; Deut 7:14; Gen 17:16).

48. For instance, images identified as the Egyptian god Bes, who is associated with mothers, infants, and childbirth, have been found on Iron Age amulets at Beth Shean, Beth Shemesh, Lachish, Megiddo, Tell Jemme, Ashkelon, Tell el-Hesi, and Khirbet el-Qôm. In his treatment of Bes images in ancient Israel, Ziony Zevit estimates that around 146 Bes amulets have been discovered. See Zevit, *The Religions of Ancient Israel: A Synthesis of Parallactic Approaches* (New York: Continuum, 2001), 381–89.

example suggests the relatively limited cultic interests of the biblical writers, whose discourses about Yahwistic cult and covenant largely ignore the central issues of family religion. Thus, I am skeptical of the interpretation of this biblical lacuna as an intentional omission meant to silence or condemn the practice of such cult.[49]

In sum, the cult of dead kin was a widespread phenomenon in ancient West Asia. Its ritual components—provision of offerings, the construction of commemorative monuments, invocation of the name of the dead, and the protection and, when necessary, repatriation of human remains—appear in varying configurations in several corpora, including those of

---

Another well-attested object that seems to pertain to lactation and childrearing is the Judean pillar figurine. Some studies have interpreted the Judean pillar figurine as representative of either the goddess Asherah or an unidentified fertility goddess. For such an interpretation, see John S. Holladay, "Religion in Israel and Judah under the Monarchy: An Explicitly Archaeological Approach," in *Ancient Israelite Religion: Essays in Honor of Frank Moore Cross*, ed. Patrick D. Miller Jr., Paul D. Hanson, and Samuel D. McBride (Philadelphia: Fortress, 1987), 278; William G. Dever, "The Silence of the Text: An Archaeological Commentary on 2 Kings 23," in *Scripture and Other Artifacts: Essays on the Bible and Archaeology in Honor of Philip J. King*, ed. Michael D. Coogan, J. Cheryl Exum, and Lawrence E. Stager (Louisville: Westminster John Knox, 1994), 150–51; Raz Kletter, *The Judean Pillar-Figurines and the Archaeology of Asherah*, BARIS 636 (Oxford: Tempvs Reparatvm, 1996); Othmar Keel and Christoph Uehlinger, *Gods, Goddesses, and Images of God in Ancient Israel*, trans. Thomas H. Trapp (Minneapolis: Fortress, 1998), 333–36. I am more convinced by interpretations of the Judean pillar figurine as a ritual object meant to encourage lactation and/or weaning. For this interpretation, see Meyers, *Households and Holiness*, 54; Bloch-Smith, *Judahite Burial Practices*, 94; Saul M. Olyan, "What Do We Really Know about Women's Rites in the Israelite Family Context?," *JANER* 10 (2010): 61. The lack of explicitly divine attributes and the emphasis on the breasts suggests that the Judean pillar figurines do not represent goddesses but instead human women. Their appearance in a variety of domestic contexts, including the tomb, suggests that the Judean pillar figurines may have taken on a broader significance as well. Since care for the dead in ancient West Asia entailed provision of food and drink, the emphasis of the Judean pillar figurines on sustenance and nurturing may have made them relevant to the cult of dead kin and its focus on providing sustenance and protection for the dead.

49. In this regard, I disagree with Wayne Pitard's assessment that the relative silence of the biblical text on the matter of death indicates a deliberate choice by postexilic religious leadership in Judah to undermine the cult of dead kin in this period. See Pitard, "Tombs and Offerings: Archaeological Data and Comparative Methodology in the Study of Death in Israel," in Gittlen, *Sacred Time, Sacred Place*, 146. Similar arguments appear in Van der Toorn, *Family Religion*, 206, and Hays, *Death in Iron Age II*, 174–75.

Mesopotamia, Ugarit, and the Iron Age Levant. Through comparison of these corpora, we may recognize features of a cult of dead kin depicted in the Hebrew Bible, which suggests continuity between Israelite practice and that of surrounding cultures with regard to family religion. Situating the Israelite cult of dead kin within this broader cultural landscape helps us understand the dynamics of this cult—its participants, constitutive practices, and its relationship to other forms of cult. Though culturally specific manifestations of these practices naturally appear, the consistency of this broad framework for the cult of dead kin among different ancient West Asian cultures is striking. This study focuses on the manifestation of the cult in the Hebrew Bible and ancient Israel and continues to interrogate the relationships between the Israelite cult of dead kin, the Jerusalem temple, and the various ideologies of the biblical writers.

Chapter 1 situates the Israelite cult of dead kin within its broader ancient West Asian cultural landscape. Using the extant evidence, it reconstructs the constitutive rites of this cult, including offerings to the dead (food, drink, or other items), the construction of commemorative monuments, invocation of the name of the dead, protection/repatriation of the corpse or bones, and maintenance of the burial site. The chapter examines similarities and differences between bodies of evidence relating to the cult of dead kin from Mesopotamia, Ugarit, the Iron Age Levant, and the Hebrew Bible as well as material culture from ancient Israel. Through comparative analysis of this evidence, the chapter argues that there was likely a cult of dead kin active in ancient Israel, reflected in the texts of the Hebrew Bible.

Chapter 2 focuses on the cultic categories "necromancy" and "cult of dead kin," arguing that necromancy must be considered separate from the cult of dead kin in ancient Israel and in ancient West Asia more broadly. Both cultic phenomena concern the dead, but their purposes, principles, and participants are different. Moreover, their conflation in previous studies of the Hebrew Bible has led to problematic interpretations of the polemic against practices pertaining to the dead in certain strands of the biblical text. However, if we excise biblical polemic against necromancy—deemed by some texts an illegitimate means of procuring privileged information—from our evidence for the cult of dead kin, then we are left with the sense that the biblical text is largely uninterested in practices meant to commemorate and care for the dead. Therefore, the supposed biblical polemic against the cult of dead kin in the Hebrew Bible is less clear than previous studies assert, which has important implications for how we reconstruct the cult and its relationship to the ideologies of the biblical writers, especially their views of normative Yahwism and the Jerusalem temple.

Chapter 3 examines the role of gender in depictions of the cult of dead kin in ancient West Asia, particularly the extent to which women may have had access to the cult. Using textual and iconographic evidence, it explores whether women were excluded from the cult, as some previous studies suggest. Contrary to these studies, it seems that women could act as either participants or recipients in the cult, and the chapter focuses on the social and political settings in which women are depicted acting in either capacity. In general, I argue that the role of women in the cult of dead kin is more pervasive than previous studies have posited. That role is particularly well attested in moments of crisis when social and political order was disrupted in various ways. Though the cult of dead kin was fundamentally patriarchal and concerned primarily with male actors, women did occupy an important position within this cult, one that has been overlooked in the biblical text and cognate literatures.

Chapter 4 evaluates the Israelite cult of dead kin in light of previous reconstructions, many of which argue that biblical ideologies of the Jerusalem temple directly oppose the cult of dead kin. Such arguments often posit that such ideologies developed during the exile and the postexilic period and view Yahwism and the temple cult as antithetical to care for the dead. According to these treatments, some biblical writers attempt to undermine care for the dead in order to ensure centralization of the cult, the erosion of lineage systems, and the flourishing of new ideologies of affiliation. The chapter challenges those reconstructions of the cult of dead kin through a close examination of biblical evidence often cited in such treatments. Ultimately, it argues that, rather than undermining the cult of dead kin, biblical depictions of the temple cult in the postexilic period draw on the imagery and individual practices of the cult of dead kin in order to articulate the relationship between YHWH, the temple, and the people in Persian Yehud. Far from overturning the cult of dead kin, such allusions seem to reassert its validity and significance to the writers and audience of these biblical texts.

This study concludes by suggesting some potential avenues for further research. It also outlines the relevance of this study to the field of biblical studies (1) as a reexamination of the underlying ritual logic of the Israelite cult of dead kin and (2) in terms of the usefulness of a paradigm shift away from a Weberian model of centralized authority in favor of a model that better accounts for the often overlapping, symbiotic relationships between cultic spheres. For instance, this study contributes to a better understanding of the relationship between Israelite family religion, epitomized by the cult of dead kin, and its relationship to the Jerusalem temple cult. This study is relevant to the study of religion more generally because it is a reaction against reconstructions of ancient religion that overemphasize the development of cult away from more so-called primitive practices, such as the cult of dead kin, and its eventual conformity with modern theological concepts, such as monotheism and transcendent conceptions of the divine. Although many scholars have previously pointed out this teleological tendency in the study of religion and its theological biases, the pervasiveness of this tendency requires close and ongoing examination.

1

THE ISRAELITE CULT OF DEAD KIN
IN ITS ANCIENT WEST ASIAN CONTEXT

This chapter aims to situate the Israelite cult of dead kin within the broader cultural landscape of ancient West Asia. I begin by examining the comparative evidence for ritual care for the dead from ancient West Asian cultures outside Israel in order to identify some recurring principles and practices of the cult. Based on these parallels, this chapter argues that biblical writers assume the existence of such a cult of dead kin in ancient Israel. A fundamental assumption in this analysis, which is nearly universal in the field of biblical studies today, is that ancient Israel must be understood in its ancient West Asian context and that comparative evidence from other ancient West Asian societies may illuminate features and principles of Israelite religion that would otherwise remain obscure or unintelligible to us. Through an examination of this biblical and comparative evidence, the chapter outlines the constitutive practices of the cult of dead kin, including offerings of food and drink (and sometimes other items, such as incense), the construction of commemorative monuments, and the invocation of the name of the dead. While previous studies have examined the prevalence of these aspects of the ancient West Asian cult of dead kin, I argue that protection and (when necessary) repatriation of human remains should also be included among these practices. This protection may take the form of maintaining the burial site or defending the bones or corpse from disturbance by animals or looters. The expansion of the cult to include these practices has important implications for reconstructing who may participate in this cult and the contexts in which the cult takes place. As I argue in chapter 3, closer examination of these practices shows that both women and nonkin were more involved in the cult of dead kin than previous studies have recognized.

Locating the Cult of Dead Kin in Non-Israelite Ancient West Asian Textual and Material Evidence

An examination of non-Israelite ancient West Asian textual and material evidence shows a widespread concern for the care of the dead among the living, an ongoing interest and intervention in the welfare of the dead that extends beyond rites of mourning and burial. This ancient West Asian evidence for the cult of dead kin often falls into three broad corpora: material and textual evidence from Mesopotamia,[1] Late Bronze Ugarit, and the Iron Age Levant. As I note above, an examination of these corpora illuminates five recurring components of the cult of dead kin: offerings of food and drink (and sometimes other items, such as incense), the construction of commemorative monuments, invocation of the name of the dead, the protection and (when necessary) repatriation of human remains, and maintenance of the burial site.[2] Though they rarely all appear together in the same text and may overlap (e.g., a commemorative monument inscribed with the name of the dead), these components individually and in combination comprise ritual care for the dead in ancient West Asia. Though not exhaustive, the following survey provides a frame of reference for different modes of care for the dead in ancient West Asia, including some aspects that have been overlooked by previous studies.

---

1. This corpus is admittedly very broad since the evidence cited here consists of texts from the Old Babylonian to the Late Babylonian period. My intention is not to minimize the differences between these periods and, in doing so, imply an utter lack of change in practice or ideology over time and geographical space. Gathering these sources under the heading "Mesopotamia" is merely a heuristic for introducing the extant evidence from this general region before examining it in more depth in the pages that follow.

2. However, scholars must resist relying too heavily on this evidence in order to synthesize sparse data into a more compelling reconstruction of Israelite cult, and often they have not. Pitard cogently critiques this scholarly tendency in his survey of the textual and material evidence cited in reconstructions of the cult of dead kin: "I believe that the study of Israelite concepts of death and afterlife has often suffered from a tendency to overinterpret one's evidence, overgeneralize from limited data, overrely on meagre and weak evidence in drawing up complex reconstructions of systems of practice and belief, and to overuse cultural parallels from neighboring or more distant societies for interpreting unattested or ambiguous aspects of Israel's thought" ("Tombs and Offerings," 147).

The largest body of textual evidence from which to reconstruct the cult of dead kin in Mesopotamia comes from Old Babylonian references to the *kispu* ritual, which most frequently involves food and drink offerings for the dead.[3] In fact, this term, *kispu*, derives from the Akkadian verb *kasāpu*, meaning "to break off a piece,"[4] which likely refers to the breaking of bread as a food offering in this ritual. Providing fresh water (*mê naqû*) and invoking the name of the deceased (*šuma zakāru*) are also important elements of the *kispu*. The significance of the latter is evident in the term *zākir šumi*, "the one who invokes the name," which refers to the person who is the central ritual actor in the *kispu*. Another term used to describe one who cares for the dead is *pāqidu*, "provider, overseer, caretaker."[5] In most cases, the eldest son is designated as the *pāqidu* and the one who has primary responsibility for performing the cult of dead kin; however, there is also evidence of women fulfilling these responsibilities, especially when male descendants were unavailable or failed to do so.[6]

In other cases, nonkin may effectively construct social bonds with the dead by offering them ritual care, a phenomenon I examine more closely in chapter 4. As I note in the introduction to this study, this use of the *kispu* is particularly prevalent in royal inscriptions and facilitates political transitions of power. This use of ritual care for the dead to forge social bonds between offerer(s) and recipient(s) is well attested in different historical periods in Mesopotamia. For instance, in the Genealogy of the Hammurapi Dynasty, the new king offers the *kispu* to all the untended dead, near and far.[7] In doing so, he establishes himself as the pious, benevolent ruler of his new kingdom and the recipients of the *kispu* as his subjects. In a

---

3. The contours of the *kispu* and its centrality in Mesopotamian family religion have become more widely recognized among scholars following the publication of Miranda Bayliss, "The Cult of Dead Kin in Assyria and Babylonia," *Iraq* (1973): 115–25; Akio Tsukimoto's *Untersuchungen zur Totenpflege (kispum) im alten Mesopotamien*, AOAT 216 (Neukirchen-Vluyn: Neukirchener Verlag, 1985); and Van der Toorn, *Family Religion*, esp. 48–52. A shorter, more recent overview of the *kispu* appears in Van der Toorn, "Family Religion in Second Millennium West Asia (Mesopotamia, Emar, Nuzi)," in Bodel and Olyan, *Household and Family Religion*, 25–28.

4. *CAD* 8:241–42. See also the entry for *kispu*, *CAD* 8:425–27.

5. *CAD* 12:137–38.

6. In ch. 3, I further examine the role of women as both participants and recipients in the cult of dead kin in ancient West Asia, including the Hebrew Bible.

7. Jacob J. Finkelstein, "The Genealogy of the Hammurapi Dynasty," *JCS* 20 (1966): 95–118.

later text from the Neo-Babylonian period, the mother of King Nabonidus, Adad-guppi, claims to offer the *kispu* to the dead kings Nebuchadnezzar and Neriglissar when their living kin fail to do so.[8] Thus, the *kispu* resonates in different cultic spheres, nonelite family religion as well as royal cult.

While the contours of the *kispu* have been thoroughly examined by previous studies, other forms of care for the dead have been largely overlooked. Cuneiform evidence from Mesopotamia suggests that the protection and repatriation of human remains constitutes another significant aspect of care for the dead. For example, several attestations of a Late Babylonian (ca. 1000–500 BCE) funerary inscription refer to both the importance of preserving the burial site and the resulting reciprocity between the living and the dead.[9] The text implores its reader to restore the tomb in which it is found instead of destroying or ignoring it:

> In the future,
> A long time from now,
> For all time,
> Should someone see this grave,
> May he not remove it
> From its place. May he return it.
> May he return it to its place.
> That man who sees this,
> He will not forget it.
> Thus, he will say:
> "As for this grave,
> I shall return it to its place."
> May he repay him for the favor he did.
> Above, may his name prosper.
> In the netherworld, may his spirit [*eṭemmu*] drink
> clean water.[10]

---

8. Paul-Alain Beaulieu, *The Reign of Nabonidus, King of Babylon 556–539 B.C.* (New Haven: Yale University Press, 1989), 78–79.

9. Benjamin R. Foster examines these variants and suggests that the inscription is an archaizing Late Babylonian composition. See Foster, "Late Babylonian Schooldays: An Archaizing Cylinder," in *Festschrift für Burkhart Kienast: Zu seinem 70. Geburtstage dargebracht von Freunden, Schülern und Kollegen* (Münster: Ugarit-Verlag, 2003), 79–87. See also Rients de Boer, "A Babylonian Funerary Cone," in *Annual Report*, ed. Jesper Eidem (Leiden: Netherlands Institute for the Near East, 2012), 42–47.

10. Unless noted otherwise, all translations of ancient texts are mine. For further commentary on this text, see Foster, "Late Babylonian Schooldays," 82–87.

Through restoration of the burial site, reciprocal benefits are established between the living and the dead. Also noteworthy is the fact that the inscription does not identify the relationship between the dead and the one who would restore this burial site. It seems that the most plausible audience for the inscription would be a nonkin individual who maintains the tomb in the absence of living kin of the dead. Indeed, it seems that the inscription is geared more toward one who encounters the tomb by chance ("that man who sees this," *awīlum šū ša annittam immaruma*, l. 8–9) and is not already aware of its existence. The implicit anxiety reflected in the inscription concerns the possible neglect of the burial site and corpse disturbance. Indeed, we know from other sources that corpse exposure and "malevolent tomb opening"[11] (either by political enemies or looters) are common topoi in cuneiform texts, as in the case of Assurbanipal exhuming the bones of the Elamite kings and transporting them to Assyria in order to deprive the dead of care: "I took their bones to the land of Assyria, imposing restlessness on their ghosts. I deprived them of ancestral offerings (and) libations of water."[12]

Saul Olyan has recently identified particular settings, however, in which exhumation and removal of bones from their burial settings can be construed positively.[13] In the case of the Nebi Yunus slab inscription, for instance, Merodach-Baladan flees from Babylon with the bones of his ancestors in order to prevent their violation by his advancing enemy Sennacherib. Olyan also cites Assur-etel-ilani's transport of the tomb of the Dakkurian Šamaš-ibni from Assyria to his homeland in Bit Dakkuri, another instance in which the removal and subsequent repatriation of bones may be construed as care rather than violation.[14] Building

---

11. Here I am borrowing the terminology for this practice introduced in Saul M. Olyan, "Unnoticed Resonances of Tomb Opening and Transportation of the Remains of the Dead in Ezekiel 37:12–14," *JBL* 128 (2009): passim. On corpse exposure, see, e.g., Seth Richardson, "Death and Dismemberment in Mesopotamia: Discorporation between the Body and the Body Politic," in *Performing Death: Social Analyses of Funerary Traditions in the Ancient Near East and Mediterranean*, ed. Nicola Lanieri (Chicago: Oriental Institute of the University of Chicago, 2007), 189–208.

12. Rykle Borger, *Beiträge zum Inschriftenwerk Assurbanipals: Die Prismenklassen A, B, C = K, D, E, F, G, H, J, und T sowie andere Inschriften* (Wiesbaden: Harrassowitz, 1996), 55 (Prism A vi 74–76 = F v 53–54), cited and translated in Olyan, "Unnoticed Resonances," 495–96.

13. Olyan, "Unnoticed Resonances," passim.

14. Olyan, "Unnoticed Resonances," 497.

on Olyan's analysis, I argue that this discourse about physically moving human remains, construed as benevolent or malevolent depending on the context, derives its force from the cult of dead kin. More specifically, the actions of both Merodach-Baladan and Assur-etel-ilani reflect the custodial interests of the cult of dead kin, while the ritual violence of Assurbanipal against the remains of the dead is construed as the opposite of that care.[15] Similarly, the aforementioned Late Babylonian funerary inscription presents neglect and violation of the burial site as the opposite of care for the dead, which establishes reciprocity between the living and the dead. Thus, our framework for understanding the cult of dead kin and its constitutive practices should include this facet of care for the dead—the protection of human remains and, if necessary, the exhumation and later repatriation of those remains. Another important aspect of the cult illuminated by this evidence is that the ritual caretaker of the dead may be a family member (e.g., Merodach-Baladan) or a nonrelative who seeks to provide benefits to the dead and, possibly, their descendants.

In many ways, attestations of a cult of dead kin in cuneiform texts from Mesopotamia provide us with important insights about commemoration and ritual care. The living offer food, drink, and other items to the dead. The dead are invoked by name, sometimes in conjunction with these offerings. Though overlooked by previous studies, there is also an emphasis on the preservation of the physical remains of the dead as well as the burial site in which they are housed. Disturbance of either is often construed as leading to the disruption of *kispu* offerings to the dead and restlessness in the afterlife. Conversely, preservation of both could result in reciprocal benefits for the living and the dead. Those who care for the dead may include kin as well as nonkin, especially in times of crisis when living kin have not provided proper care for the dead. Although the construction of commemorative monuments does not appear in textual attestations of the *kispu*, it is possible that the Late Babylonian funerary cone may be construed in this way, a grave marker that helps perpetuate the (unnamed)

---

15. For an analysis of ritual violence and its role in the Hebrew Bible, see the essays in Saul M. Olyan, ed., *Ritual Violence in the Hebrew Bible: New Perspectives* (New York: Oxford University Press, 2015). Several of the essays refer to violence and death, but Olyan's treatment of corpse abuse ("The Instrumental Dimensions of Ritual Violence against Corpses in Biblical Texts") is particularly relevant to the present study, because such violence against corpses is antithetical to the cult of dead kin.

dead. Some studies have also interpreted the *sikkānu*-stones of Emar and Nuzi along these lines.[16]

Another rich source of evidence for ritual care of the dead comes from the Late Bronze city-state of Ugarit, located on the northern coast of modern-day Syria. Its textual corpus includes several texts pertaining to the relationship between the living and the dead; however, it is not always certain to what extent they concern the cult of dead kin. Included among these texts are the so-called Duties of the Ideal Son in the Aqhat Epic (*KTU* 1.17 i.26b–33), the Ugaritic Funerary Ritual (*KTU* 1.161), the Ugaritic King List (*KTU* 1.113), multiple references to a group of divine dead kings called the *rapi'ūma*,[17] and an inscribed clay liver model (*KTU* 1.142). This evidence demonstrates significant parallels with depictions of the cult of dead kin from Mesopotamia, yet demonstrates some distinctive features as well, including the designation of royal ancestors as divine.

The Duties of the Ideal Son in the Aqhat Epic may be the most extensive description of a cult of dead kin at Ugarit; yet, the interpretation of the passage is highly contested among scholars. The epic begins with a childless man named Danel who successfully petitions his patron deity for a son and heir. During this petition, he describes formulaically the cultic activities that the ideal son would perform. These activities include erecting a stela (*sikkānu*) for the son's "divine ancestor" or patron deity (lit. "god of the father") in the sanctuary, burning incense,[18] maintaining his father's

---

16. For an overview of such arguments, see Karel van der Toorn, "Ilib and the 'God of the Father,'" *UF* 25 (1993): 384 n. 36.

17. There is debate concerning the proper vocalization of the *rp'um*. Throughout this analysis, I use *rapi'ūma*, a stative form meaning "healthy ones." This, of course, is speculative. Another possible vocalization, *rāpi'ūma*, interprets the term as a participle, meaning "healers." Because the extant evidence of the *rapi'ūma* does not include any depictions of healing but rather depicts the *rapi'ūma* as strong warriors, I have opted for the former interpretation and vocalization. For a discussion of these different renderings of *rp'um*, see Conrad E. L'Heureux, *Rank among the Canaanite Gods: El, Ba'al and the Rephaim* (Missoula, MT: Scholars Press, 1979), 215–21. I refer to "divine dead kings" because of their designation as kings who receive sacrifice in *KTU* 1.161 and as divine dead in *KTU* 1.22. I will address both texts more fully in the discussion that follows.

18. The nature of this activity is contested; yet, as I argue below, the offering of incense seems the most plausible interpretation in this context. References to the *sikkānu* in texts from both Emar and Mari suggest that the term refers to a stela. For instance, in the *zukru* festival texts from Emar, the *sikkānu* stones stand outside the city gate and are anointed with oil (Emar 373, 375). See also their more recent treat-

abode, and eating his father's portion in the temples of Baal and El. Previous interpreters have argued that these custodial duties performed by the son for his father are informed by the same cultic concerns as the *pāqidu* in the Mesopotamian *kispu*.[19] However, the relevance of this passage to the cult of dead kin primarily hinges on the interpretation of the term *'il'ibu*.

The term *'il'ibu* has been translated either as "divine ancestor" or patron deity ("god of the father") in different scholarly interpretations.[20]

---

ment in Daniel E. Fleming, *Time at Emar: The Cultic Calendar and the Rituals from the Diviner's House* (Winona Lake, IN: Eisenbrauns, 2000), 76–93. This comparative evidence casts doubt on the interpretation of *skn* in the Ugaritic context as a G infinitive meaning "to care for," as it is interpreted in Mark J. Boda, "Ideal Sonship in Ugarit," *UF* 25 (1993): 13. Previous studies have vocalized this term *siknu* on the basis of Akkadian *šiknu*, meaning "appearance, shape, structure" (*CAD* 17:436–39). See, e.g., Lewis, *Cults of the Dead*, 55; and William F. Albright, *Archaeology and the Religion of Israel*, 5th ed. (Garden City, NY: Doubleday, 1968), 201 n. 28. However, the commemorative aspects of the *zukru* festival at Emar and its *sikkānu* stones provide a compelling parallel to the kind of commemorative monument in the Aqhat Epic, so I have opted for that vocalization.

19. See, e.g., Robert R. Wilson, *Genealogy and History in the Biblical World* (New Haven: Yale University Press, 1977), 121 n. 182; Marvin H. Pope, "The Cult of the Dead at Ugarit," in *Ugarit in Retrospect*, ed. Gordon D. Young (Winona Lake, IN: Eisenbrauns, 1981), 159–62. Others, however, have challenged this interpretation of the text, noting that some of these custodial actions seem to take place while the father is still living. See, e.g., Dennis Pardee, *Ritual and Cult at Ugarit*, WAW 10 (Leiden: Brill, 2002), 279; Schmidt, *Israel's Beneficent Dead*, 62. Despite the fact that some actions are directed to a living father, Lewis argues that other duties listed in the text, especially the construction of a stela (*sikkānu*) for the *'il'ibu* (a divine ancestor in his analysis) do suggest a cult of dead kin (*Cults of the Dead*, 69–71, 96). Indeed, the construction of a commemorative stela in the Ugaritic context may roughly correspond to the Mesopotamian duty of invoking the name if, for instance, the inscription of a name on a monument is understood to be a way of invoking that name through a material medium. Furthermore, some biblical references to the commemorative monument, such as 2 Sam 18:18 and Isa 56:5, closely associate it with the name of the dead.

20. For those who translate this term as "divine ancestor/father," see William F. Albright, *Yahweh and the Gods of Canaan: A Historical Analysis of Two Contrasting Faiths* (London: Athlone, 1968), 141–42, 204–5; John Gray, "Social Aspects of Canaanite Religion," in *Volume de Congres Geneve*, VTSup 15 (Leiden: Brill, 1966), 174; Lewis, *Cults of the Dead*, 56–59; Van der Toorn, *Family Religion*, 154–68. For those who interpret it as referring to a major deity, see Jimmy J. M. Roberts, *The Earliest Semitic Pantheon: A Study of the Semitic Deities Attested in Mesopotamia before Ur III* (Baltimore: Johns Hopkins University Press, 1972), 35, 125; Wilfred G. Lambert, "Old Akkadian Ilaba = Ugaritic Ilib?," *UF* 13 (1981): 299–301; Pardee, "*Marzihu, Kispu*," 279–80. For a

In addition to the Aqhat Epic, the term ʾilʾibu appears in two Ugaritic pantheon lists (*KTU* 1.118 and 1.47). The debate over the interpretation of this term primarily concerns the element ʾil, which can either function as a determinative—an untranslated marker of a noun's category (a deity, in this case)—or as the noun "god." The translation "divine ancestor" relies on the interpretation of ʾil as a determinative, while "god of the father" assumes the latter.[21] There is consensus among scholars that the second element of the term, ʾibu, means "father." For instance, a bilingual god list (RS 20.24:1) equates the Ugaritic term ʾilʾibu with Akkadian DINGIR *a-bi*. This Akkadian rendering of the term suggests interpreting ʾibu as "father," despite its uncharacteristic i-vowel.[22]

Various pieces of evidence have been marshaled in support of either interpretation. Noting that pantheon lists containing ʾilʾibu list deities in descending order of eminence within the Ugaritic cult, Lewis, among others, interprets the term ʾilʾibu as referring to "the divine ancestor *par excellence* who seems to have functioned as the primary family god."[23]

---

discussion of the few attestations of ʾilʾibu outside Ugarit, see Van der Toorn, "Ilib and the 'God of the Father,'" 379 n. 1.

21. Schmidt proposes an alternative interpretation in which ʾilʾib is a summarizing heading ("gods of the fathers") that encompasses the many deities listed after it, a theory that has not found wide acceptance among scholars (*Israel's Beneficent Dead*, 56–59).

22. In fact, Lewis notes that another common familial term, "brother," shows similar variation at Ugarit (ʾiḫ, ʾaḫ). Van der Toorn argues that the i-vowel in ʾib is the result of vowel harmony with the genitive ending on the term (*Family Religion*, 157). See also the discussion of ʾuḫ, ʾiḫ in Josef Tropper, *Ugaritische Grammatik* (Münster: Ugarit-Verlag, 2012), 176, 305. Thus, the interpretation of ʾib as "father" seems quite compelling.

23. Lewis, *Cults of the Dead*, 58–59; see also Van der Toorn, *Family Religion*, 156–60. Baruch Margalit not only interprets ʾilʾibu as a reference to the dead father but also understands *skn* as a tomb: "To set up the tomb of his (father's) ghost, (to set up) in the sacred precinct the ZTR of his clan." See Margalit, *The Ugaritic Poem of Aqht* (New York: de Gruyter, 1989), 144. Margalit interprets the first two duties of the son, using the verbs *nṣb* and *yṣ'*, as referring to proper burial of the dead father and necromancy, respectively. He also argues for the relevance of these activities to the *marzaḥu* (*Ugaritic Poem of Aqht*, 267). For a discussion of the vocalization of *marzaḥu*, see my comments below. Margalit's interpretation assumes that *qṭr* in this passage is the "smoke" or disembodied spirit of the dead father raised in necromantic invocation. This association between necromancy, cult of dead kin, and the *marzaḥu* is particularly problematic, as I argue in ch. 2.

Karel van der Toorn also draws parallels between this god list and a Hurrian god list found at Ugarit: in place of 'il'ibu is the Hurrian en atn, which he argues is an equivalent term.[24] Because a version of this Hurrian list (*KTU* 1.125) includes the Hurrian term without the element *en*, "god," Van der Toorn argues that this element and its Ugaritic equivalent, 'il, are marking the divine status of the "father" in both lists. However, others argue that the term more likely refers to a clan deity.[25] Dennis Pardee, for instance, notes that the Akkadian translation (DINGIR *a-bi*) of the Ugaritic term 'il'ibu that appears in *KTU* 1.41 and 1.47 suggests that these texts understand the term to refer to the "god of the father"—a family deity, not one's dead, deified father.[26] In addition, Schmidt argues that 'il'ibu cannot be a divine ancestor because none of the other god names that appears in these lists is preceded by the divine determinative.[27]

However, other features of 'il'ibu challenge its interpretation as a patron deity. For instance, contrary to Schmidt's argument, 'il'ibu is different from other divine names of the pantheon lists because it does not seem to be the proper name of a deity but rather a category of deity, "divine father," which may explain why it receives a divine determinative while other deities do not. In addition, Van der Toorn convincingly argues that the use of DINGIR *a-bi* in the Akkadian ritual series, *Bīt mēseri*, seems to use this term to refer to the "ghost of the father" rather than a patron deity.[28] The term DINGIR *a-bi* appears in a gendered pair with [d]INNIN *um-mi* in this text (l. 37). Since patron deities are typically associated with the father and not the mother, Van der Toorn argues that [d]INNIN *um-mi* more likely refers to the "ghost of the mother" rather than the mother's patron deity. Although Van der Toorn does not include this point in his analysis, a compelling datum supporting the interpretation of DINGIR *a-bi* and [d]INNIN *um-mi* as the ghosts of the father and mother in this passage is that the

---

24. Van der Toorn, *Family Religion*, 157–58.

25. See, e.g., Schmidt, *Israel's Beneficent Dead*, 56–58; J. David Schloen, *House of the Father as Fact and Symbol: Patrimonialism in Ugarit and the Ancient Near East* (Winona Lake, IN: Eisenbrauns, 2001), 343–45. In Schmidt's case, he views the term as a collective, "gods of the/his/my fathers," as noted earlier.

26. Pardee, "*Marzihu, Kispu*," 279–80.

27. Schmidt, *Israel's Beneficent Dead*, 54.

28. Van der Toorn, "Ilib and the 'God of the Father,'" 382. In his translation of the text, Tzvi Abusch suggests a similar interpretation of these terms as "ghost of the father and ghost of the mother." See Abusch, *Babylonian Witchcraft Literature* (Atlanta: Scholars Press, 1987), 58–59 n. 79.

lines immediately preceding them list various beings associated with the dead. The text lists these dead beings—along with various demons—as those who may be responsible for the current plight of the sufferer in the text. Among these beings are demons of the grave (*utukkī*) and ghosts (*eṭemmī*) in line 34 as well as the "hand of the ghost" (ŠU.GIDIM) in line 36, immediately preceding DINGIR *a-bi* and ᵈINNIN *um-mi* in line 37.[29] The occurrence of these terms together suggests that the text considers them to be associated with the same category of being, the dead. Indeed, there is abundant Akkadian evidence for the malevolent interference of ghosts in the realm of the living.[30] Therefore, it seems likely that DINGIR *a-bi* in the *Bīt mēseri* passage refers to the "ghost of the father," which may illuminate the usage of the same term in the Akkadian god list from Ugarit and the analogous Ugaritic term *'il'ibu*.

Another potentially illuminating piece of evidence regarding the interpretation of *'il'ibu* in the Aqhat passage is the parallelism between *'il'ibihu* ("of his *'il'ibu*") in line 27 and ʿ*ammihu* ("of his kinsman/clan") in line 28:

The one who sets up the *sikkānu*-stela of his *'il'ibu*
In the sanctuary [*bi-qudši*][31] the *zittaru*-stela[32] of his ʿ*ammu*

---

29. For a treatment of this text, see Gerhard Meier, "Die zweite Tafel der Serie *bīt mēseri*," *AfO* 14 (1941–1944): 139–52. For the range of meanings for the term *utukkī*, including "ghost, demon of the grave," see *CAD* 20:339–42.

30. For several examples of the malevolent behavior of ghosts in Akkadian texts, see Bayliss, "Cult of Dead Kin," 118; JoAnn Scurlock, *Magico-Medical Means of Treating Ghost-Induced Illnesses in Ancient Mesopotamia* (Boston: Brill, 2006).

31. Margalit's rendering of *qudši* in this passage as "cemetery" and thus *sikkānu* as "tomb" is unconvincing. Nowhere else do we find *qudšu* referring to a cemetery, and the single incantation text from Ras Ibn Hani on which this interpretation is based does not provide cogent proof that we should include "cemetery" among the range of meanings for *qudšu*. It seems more plausible that the commemorative stela erected in the Aqhat passage is placed within a sanctuary or temple precinct, much like the *yād wā-šēm* in Isa 56:3–5, a text I will return to later in this study. Indeed, the coincidence of cult offered to major deities and the dead in Syro-Phoenician mortuary inscriptions, such as the Hadad inscription, which I will discuss below, suggests a significant overlap between the cult of major deities and the cult of dead kin. Therefore, we should not be surprised to find this overlap manifested in terms of physical space as well.

32. On the translation of *zittaru* as "solar disc," see Matitiahu Tsevat, "Traces of Hittite at the Beginning of the Ugaritic Epic of Aqhat," *UF* 3 (1971): 352. See also Johannes C. de Moor, "Standing Stones and Ancestor Worship," *UF* 27 (1995): 8. Margalit argues against Tsevat's interpretation of *zittaru* as a Hittite loanword (*šittari*) meaning "sun-

Such parallelism suggests that *ʾilʾibu* and *ʿammu* are being treated here as roughly equivalent or at least related terms, which might help us determine the nature of *ʾilʾibu*. The Ugaritic term *ʿammu* can be rendered either as "kinsman, father's brother" or "clan, father's relatives" (compare Hebrew *ʿam*).[33] If the term refers to one's kinsman, then the parallelism of the lines would suggest that *ʾilʾibu* also refers to a member of one's family, albeit one who has died and achieved divine status.[34] Indeed, a morphologically similar term, *ammati*, appears in three Akkadian texts from Ugarit (V 2.4; V 81.4; V 82.5–6)[35] and may lend further support to the interpretation of *ʿammu* in the Aqhat Epic as "kinsman" rather than "clan." In each of these

---

disc," instead interpreting it as metonymy for the stela on which the sun-disc appears. This interpretation has been accepted by other scholars, including Meindert Dijkstra and Johannes C. de Moor, "Problematic Passages in the Legend of Aqhatu," *UF* 7 (1975): 175, and Dennis Pardee, "West Semitic Canonical Compositions," *COS* 1:344 n. 7. Despite Margalit's claims that Ugaritic texts do not employ Hittite loanwords frequently, the iconographic evidence from nearby Zincirli in the first millennium does show that a winged sun-disc sometimes appears in the upper registers of mortuary stelae. See, e.g., Dominik Bonatz, "Katumuwa's Banquet Scene," in *In Remembrance of Me: Feasting with the Dead in the Ancient Middle East*, ed. Virginia Rimmer Herrmann and J. David Schloen (Chicago: Oriental Institute of the University of Chicago, 2014), 40, fig. 3.1. The use of such iconography on mortuary stelae should not be surprising in a Ugaritic context either, since the sun-goddess Šapšu is closely associated with the dead in textual depictions, much like the close association between the Mesopotamian sun-god Šamaš and the dead. This interpretation of *zittaru* as referring to a sun-disc— or, perhaps, the stela on which it appears—is more convincing than interpreting the term as referring to thyme or marjoram (see, e.g., Pope, "Cult of the Dead," 160 n. 4; Boda, "Ideal Sonship in Ugarit," 14). Thus, I have rendered the term *zittaru* as "*zittaru*-stela" in the translation above to signify its association with a cultic monument either similar or equivalent to the *sikkānu* in the preceding line.

33. For the translation of *ʿammihu* as "his clan," see Yitzhak Avishur, "The 'Duties of the Son' in the 'Story of Aqhat' and Ezekiel's Prophecy on Idolatry (Ch. 8)," *UF* 17 (1985): 51. Interestingly, Van der Toorn only notes the interpretation of the term as "kinsman," which he uses to support his interpretation of *ʾilʾibu* as a divine ancestor (*Family Religion*, 157). Lewis also interprets the term as "clansman" (*Cults of the Dead*, 54). Margalit, on the other hand, prefers interpreting the term as referring to the clan (*Ugaritic Poem of Aqht*, 271).

34. Indeed, this is the interpretation preferred by Simon Parker in his translation of the parallelism: "To set up his Ancestor's stela, the sign of his Sib in the sanctuary." See Parker, *Ugaritic Narrative Poetry* (Atlanta: Scholars Press, 1997), 53 n. 9.

35. See John Huehnergard, *Ugaritic Vocabulary in Syllabic Transcription* (Winona Lake, IN: Eisenbrauns, 2008), 189. Huehnergard also notes the recent argument of Ignacio Márquez-Rowe that the term may be related to Hurrian *ammade*, "grand-

texts, the term appears in the phrase DUMU *am-ma-ti* in the context of an adoption contract. Such a context suggests the close association between this term and one's immediate (adoptive) family, perhaps more than it does one's clan. Therefore, based on the similarity between these terms, it is perhaps preferable to interpret ʿ*ammu* as "kinsman" in the Aqhat passage rather than "clan," which supports the argument that ʾ*ilʾibu* is a dead, divine member of one's kin group. For these reasons, I prefer the interpretation of Ugaritic ʾ*ilʾibu* as referring to a divine ancestor rather than a patron deity.

Ultimately, if we interpret ʾ*ilʾibu* in the Aqhat Epic as referring to one's divine dead ancestor, then some of the duties of the ideal son listed in the text could be construed as constitutive of the cult of dead kin. For instance, erecting a commemorative stela for one's ʾ*ilʾibu* (ll. 27–28) and burning incense for him (l. 28) seem like ritual acts for the dead rather than the living, as comparative evidence suggests:[36]

One who sends up his incense [*quṭru*][37] from the earth

_____

father, ancestor," which would make the Ugaritic term something akin to "inherited sonship," (*Ugaritic Vocabulary*, 399).

36. For instance, the construction of a commemorative monument for the dead appears in biblical texts, such as 2 Sam 18:18 and Isa 56:3–5, as well as various inscriptions and extant stelae from ancient Samʾal, which I discuss below.

37. The offering of incense to the dead in l. 28, however, is disputed by some interpreters. Lewis argues that *quṭru* in this line refers to the dead man's life force rather than smoke or incense (*Cults of the Dead*, 61–62). His argument is based in large part on the parallelism of this line and the one following it, "one who guards his footsteps from the Dust." Nicolas Wyatt also interprets the term in this way, noting that the imagery of smoke coincides with other depictions of death in other Ugaritic texts (*KTU* 1.18 iv.24–26 and 1.169.2–3), which describe the moment of death as a man's life departing from him *kīma quṭri*, "like smoke" (*Religious Texts from Ugarit: The Words of Ilimilku and His Colleagues*, Biblical Seminar 53 [London: Sheffield Academic Press, 2002], 257). However, as John F. Healey points out, it is unclear that a reference to "smoke" alone denotes the departure of one's spirit. See Healey, "The *Pietas* of an Ideal Son at Ugarit," *UF* 11 (1979): 356. Other translators prefer to interpret this line as a reference to the burning of incense: "to send up from the earth his incense, from the dust the song of his place" (Schloen, *House of the Father*, 344). Schmidt also prefers understanding the term as a reference to burning incense but cautions that this practice may take place in a funerary, not mortuary, context (*Israel's Beneficent Dead*, 61). I find the interpretation of *qṭrh* as "his incense" more convincing, especially in light of the care offered by Adad-guppi to the dead Nebuchadnezzar and Neriglissar. In this inscription, she claims to offer both *kispu* offerings and incense to these dead

One who protects [*ḏāmiru*][38] his tomb [*'aṭru*][39] from the dust

Such acts of care are strikingly similar to the pouring of water, invocation of the name, and the giving of *kispu* offerings in texts from Mesopotamia. As we have noted previously, the protection of the burial site is an essential component of the cult of dead kin and appears in this passage. Protecting the father's tomb from the dust may refer to general maintenance of the burial site or may refer metaphorically to its protection from neglect and destruction. Either interpretation fits well with what we know about the cult of dead kin and how living caregivers should treat the burial sites of the dead. The relevance of line 28B to the cult of dead kin, however, has been overlooked or dismissed by previous studies.[40] Yet, read in this way, both 28A and B show a coherent concern for the performance of rites constitutive of the cult of dead kin—making offerings to the dead and protecting the integrity of the burial site and those housed within it.

Other duties listed in the text seem to take place while the father is still alive, such as supporting him when he is drunk (ll. 31–32), patching his roof on a rainy day (l. 34), and washing his muddy clothes (l. 34). The temporal context of other duties—whether they occur prior to or after the death of the father—is less clear. For instance, the ideal son may defend his father against slander both before and after his death (l. 30). The son may eat his father's portion in the temples of Baal and El (l. 32) while he is still

---

kings. Since the Aqhat passage focuses on care for the father, either living or dead, the offering of incense makes more sense in this context than releasing his life force or ghost from the underworld, as Lewis and Wyatt suggest. In fact, nothing about the passage suggests a necromantic dimension to the duties of the ideal son. Thus I have opted for the vocalization of the Akkadian form, *quṭru*.

38. For a review of the literature supporting the interpretation of this term as "to protect," see Lewis, *Cults of the Dead*, 62–63.

39. The interpretation of this term as "tomb" appears in John C. L. Gibson, *Canaanite Myths and Legends*, 2nd ed. (London: T&T Clark, 2004), 104; Pope, "Cult of the Dead," 161. Although Lewis opts for the interpretation of *'aṭrh* as "his steps," he concedes that its interpretation as "his tomb" is possible and notes several contexts in which similar language is used to denote the tomb. The term *māqôm*, he notes, refers to the abode of the dead in Qoh 3:20; Job 16:18; Ezek 39:11; KAI 14.3–4 (Lewis, *Cults of the Dead*, 64 n. 61). Although it appears in a different cultural setting, we may also note the close association between the grave and its "place" (*ašru*) in the Late Babylonian funerary inscription discussed above.

40. "Are we actually to believe that one of the son's duties was to keep dirt out of his father's tomb?" (Lewis, *Cults of the Dead*, 64).

living, though it is unclear why he would take his living father's cultic place except in the event of his recent or imminent death. Perhaps his father is too feeble at this point to do so, though (if that were the case) the text does not include this context. In any case, the *'il'ibu* is closely associated with the family in the Aqhat Epic, particularly the duties rendered by the ideal son to his father. Even if *'il'ibu* were a clan deity rather than a divine ancestor, the cult offered to this deity is still construed by the text as helping the son's father and, presumably, honoring him after his death. Thus, even in this context, it seems that preserving this cult is also a form of care for the dead father.

In light of the debate surrounding *'il'ibu* in the Aqhat Epic, it is important to note that other Ugaritic texts are more explicit with regard to the divine status of the dead and the offerings they receive. The depiction of the *rapi'ūma*, former kings of Ugarit,[41] suggests that the dead could become divine in some contexts. These fragmentary texts provide some useful information about the divine status of the *rapi'ūma* and their receipt of sacrificial offerings, particularly their lavish consumption at feasts. For instance, in *KTU* 1.22, the *rapi'ūma* are referred to both as divine dead (*'il mitūma*, l. 6) and divine helpers (*'il ġazirūma*, l. 7),[42] and after slaughtering

---

41. The identification of the *rapi'ūma* as former kings of Ugarit depends on their depiction in *KTU* 1.161, which I will examine below. For an in-depth examination of the Ugaritic texts in which the *rapi'ūma* appear, see Wayne T. Pitard, "The *Rpum* Texts," in *Handbook of Ugaritic Studies*, ed. Wilfred G. E. Watson and Nicolas Wyatt (Leiden: Brill, 1999), 259–69.

42. The vocalization of this term is unclear. It is possible that the root of the term, *ġzr*, is a cognate of Hebrew *ʿzr* and Akkadian *azāru*, "to help." Stanislav Segert also notes that this term appears in apposition to the Hebrew term *gibbôrîm* in 1 Chr 12:1, 22, which may suggest a close association between this term and military strength. See Segert, *A Basic Grammar of the Ugaritic Language* (Berkeley: University of California Press, 1984), 197. In the absence of a clear nominal form using this root in either language, I have chosen to vocalize the Ugaritic term as a G participle, *ġazirūma*, "helpers." Again, the crux of this interpretation depends on the nature of the term *'il*, either as a determinative or noun. The interpretation of *'il mitūma* and *'il ġazirūma* as divine beings in the passage is possible, though not accepted by other treatments such as Lewis, *Cults of the Dead*, 49–50, 96; Mark S. Smith and Simon B. Parker, *Ugaritic Narrative Poetry* (Atlanta: Scholars Press, 1997), 203; Gregorio del Olmo Lete, *Mitos y leyendas de Canaan: Según la tradición de Ugarit* (Monterrey: Institución San Jerónimo, 1981), 422–23. However, del Olmo Lete and Joaquin Sanmartín do recognize that *'il* may function as a determinative. See del Olmo Lete and Sanmartín, *Dictionary of the Ugaritic Language in the Alphabetic Tradition* (Leiden: Brill, 2015), 1:24. Marvin Pope

oxen, sheep, and rams, these *rapi'ūma* feast for days. In *KTU* 1.21, the *rapi'ūma*—referred to in this text as "gods" (*'ilānyūma*, l. 4)—are summoned by an unknown speaker to a *marzaḥu*,[43] well known from other texts (e.g., *KTU* 1.114) as a sumptuous feast. A third text (*KTU* 1.108) begins by inviting a god named Rapi'u, the "eternal king," to drink. The close association between the *rapi'ūma* and feasting in these texts suggests that the royal dead receive food and drink offerings from the living, in the context of either actual ritual performance or mythological narratives.

Other Ugaritic texts, such as the Ugaritic Funerary Text (*KTU* 1.161), provide further evidence of cult performed for the royal dead at Ugarit. This text describes a ritual that likely coincides with the burial of the recently deceased king Niqmaddu as well as the coronation of his son Ammurapi.[44] The ritual depicted in the text includes both the invocation of previously deceased kings (called *rapi'ūma* and *malkūma*) and the presentation of sacrificial offerings. Lewis argues that Ammurapi may have performed such cultic rites in order to ensure the blessings of the dead on his nascent reign, and Wayne Pitard highlights the similarities between the ritual depicted in the text and the *kispu*, particularly the invocation of Ammurapi's dead ancestors (ll. 2–12), food offerings (ll. 13–17), water libations (ll. 20–26), and, ultimately, the blessing bestowed on the new king (ll. 31–34).[45] These offerings are explicitly referred to as

---

also agrees with this interpretation of the term. See Pope, "Notes on the Rephaim Texts from Ugarit," in *Essays on the Ancient Near East in Memory of Jacob Joel Finkelstein*, ed. Maria deJong Ellis (Hamden, CT: Archon Books, 1977), 167. A comparable attestation of *'il* in support of its usage as a divine determinative is *'il ṣpn*, "divine Ṣapānu," in *KTU* 1.47 and 1.3 iii.29, and elsewhere. This usage of the term *'il* seems to refer to the divine nature of mountain Ṣapānu so closely associated with Baal.

43. For a discussion of the vocalization of this term, see Huehnergard, *Ugaritic Vocabulary*, 178. There is some variation in the spelling of this word (*mrzḥ/ʿ*) in the Ugaritic corpus. As Huehnergard notes, some syllabic writings of the term (*mar-za-i* and *mar-zi-i*) suggest the presence of ʿ instead of ḥ, as does the alphabetic spelling [*m*]*rzʿy*. For the sake of consistency, when referencing this cultic phenomenon, I use the *mrzḥ* spelling and follow Huehnergard's vocalization of the term (*marzaḥu*), which presents it as a *maqtal* form.

44. For an analysis of this text, see Baruch A. Levine and Jean-Michel Tarragon, "Dead Kings and Rephaim: The Patrons of the Ugaritic Dynasty," *JAOS* 104 (1984): 654.

45. Lewis, *Cults of the Dead*, 171; Theodore J. Lewis, "Feasts for the Dead and Ancestor Veneration in Levantine Traditions," in Rimmer Herrmann and Schloen, *In Remembrance of Me*, 69–70; Wayne T. Pitard, "The Ugaritic Funerary Text RS 34.126," *BASOR* 232 (1978): 65–75. See also Pierre Bordreuil and Dennis Pardee, "Le rituel

"sacrifices" (*dabḥūma*), and line 30 specifically refers to the offering of a bird (*ʿuṣṣūru*).[46] Thus, this text describes a ritual whose underlying logic depends on reciprocity between the living and the dead mediated by care for the dead in the form of sacrifice. In these ways, the text seems to draw on characteristic features associated elsewhere with the cult of dead kin. In this particular case, those dead kin are both the distant and more recently dead kings of Ugarit.[47] The invocation of the sun goddess Šapšu in this text (ll. 18–19) likely reflects her unique ability to traverse the underworld and, thus, to ensure that the dead in the underworld receive the offerings bestowed on them in the ritual. Here we may compare the role of Šapšu with that of the Mesopotamian sun god Šamaš in depictions of the *kispu*— both act as mediators between the living and the dead in the context of care for dead kin.[48]

Other interpreters, however, have argued that *KTU* 1.161 is funerary, not mortuary, in nature and thus does not count as evidence of a cult of dead kin:

> Though the departed ancestors participated in this Ugaritic funerary rite—and quite plausibly in all others—it is clear that the primary function of the cultic event was to ensure that the deceased king take up his proper place among the ancestors. The difference in function between this cultic act and those associated with the regular care and feeding of the dead is thus rather sharply defined.[49]

---

funéraire ougaritique RS. 34.126," *Syria* 59 (1982): 121–28; Levine and Tarragon, "Dead Kings and Rephaim," 649–59.

46. For the Akkadian cognate *iṣṣūru*, see *CAD* 7:210–14. However, the syllabic writing of the term appears to suggest *ʿuṣṣūru* (Huehnergard, *Ugaritic Vocabulary*, 143).

47. Although four of the names invoked in the text (Ulkn, Trmn, Sdn-w-rd[n], and Ṯr) are unattested in other extant Ugaritic texts, their appearance alongside the term *rapiʾī*, often understood to be a collective of dead kings, suggests that they are dead kings from a distant past. The appearance of two more recently dead kings, Ammiṯtamru and Niqmaddu, whose names also appear in the so-called Ugaritic King List (*KTU* 1.113), provide further evidence that the entities invoked in this text are dead kings.

48. See, e.g., Bendt Alster, "Incantation to Utu," *ASJ* 13 (1991): 27–96, esp. 75–76. In the Mesopotamian evidence, Šamaš also acts as a mediator between the living and the dead in the context of necromantic ritual, a facet of necromancy I will explore further in ch. 2.

49. Pardee, "*Marzihu, Kispu*," 275.

Pardee's analysis assumes a common scholarly distinction between rites of burial and rites of ongoing care for the dead. Despite the primacy of the burial act in this text, however, its depiction of the ancestors is relevant to a discussion of the cult of dead kin as well. The dead ancestors are invoked and fed during this ritual, and the cultic logic of reciprocity appears in the blessing bestowed on Ammurapi, which is entirely consistent with the cult of dead kin.[50] Furthermore, the cult of dead kin need not be the central concern of a text in order for that text to draw on it. In fact, one might argue that this text (and the supporting role the cult of dead kin plays within it) indicates the pervasive nature of the cult of dead kin and its influence on other forms of cult at Ugarit, including royal burial and succession, thus offering the modern reader a glimpse into the practice and broader application of the cult.

Another text relevant to the divine status of dead kings at Ugarit is the Ugaritic King List (*KTU* 1.113). Although the brokenness of the recto makes it difficult to read—much less interpret in relation to the verso—the verso includes a list of several personal names preceded by the divine determinative. Some of these names, such as Niqmaddu in line 25′, are known Ugaritic kings. Regarding the status signified by the divine determinative accompanying these names, Lewis states, "While the living king may have been deified to a degree at Ugarit, perhaps under Egyptian influence, it was certainly only a low-grade divination and did not include any notion of immortality.… It seems that the rulers were not 'deified' upon death at all in this sense; rather, they simply 'became an *ilu*.'" According to Lewis, this designation signifies the "transcendent" or "preternatural" nature of the dead.[51] However, it is difficult to reconcile Lewis's argument—that these dead kings were not divine or immortal—with the depiction of divine dead kings receiving offerings and bestowing blessings on the living in texts such as *KTU* 1.161. Unfortunately, the context in which the Ugaritic King List was used is difficult to establish. Lewis notes that the badly preserved recto refers repeatedly to musical instruments, which may suggest that the dead kings listed in the verso are being invoked with music. However, such a reconstruction is ultimately speculative, and the

---

50. For other instances of reciprocity in the cult of dead kin in cuneiform evidence, see my discussion of *LAS* 132.1–11 in ch. 2 and the Late Babylonian funerary inscription above.

51. Lewis, *Cults of the Dead*, 49–50. See the introduction to this study for a critique of this terminological distinction.

relationship between the two sections of the tablet remains unclear. It is perhaps for this reason that Pardee argues against interpreting this text as an offering list for dead kings used in a *kispu*-like ritual.[52]

Another text, an inscription on a clay liver model (*KTU* 1.142), does seem to refer to sacrifices for the dead. The text states: "Sacrifices of *byy*, son of *try*, for ʿ*ttr* who is in the grave."[53] While the inscription does not indicate whether the sacrifices were made in a funerary context or as a part of ongoing care for the dead, it does provide some evidence for sacrificial offerings to the dead.[54] It is also interesting to note that the one receiving these offerings, ʿ*ttr*, is not identified as the parent of the offerer, *byy* son of *try*. Thus, this inscription may be another example of nonkin offering care for the dead. It is also possible that the text depicts care for the dead beyond the typical father-son dyad. At the very least, both the offerer and the recipient are named in this inscription, which suggests that they may derive some benefit from being thus identified.[55]

---

52. Pardee, "*Marzihu, Kispu*," 276. He similarly points out the uncertain association between the *kispu* and *KTU* 1.108, in which the god Baal seems to act as an intermediary between the living king and the *rapiʾūma* (277).

53. For a survey of scholarship interpreting this text as a *kispu*-like ritual, see Schmidt, *Israel's Beneficent Dead*, 48 n. 5. The identification of this text as referring to the dead depends on reading the last word as *qbr*, "grave." Del Olmo Lete emends the text to *qbr* in del Olmo Lete and Sanmartín, *Dictionary of the Ugaritic Language*, 2:682. Elsewhere, however, he posits that the final word may be a place name, ʿAttartu. See del Olmo Lete, *Canaanite Religion according to the Liturgical Texts of Ugarit*, 2nd ed., trans. Wilfred G. E. Watson (Münster: Ugarit-Verlag, 2014), 292.

54. Schmidt himself does not dispute the translation of the text but rather argues that it refers to a funerary practice instead of a more regular practice constitutive of mortuary cult (*Israel's Beneficent Dead*, 49).

55. Some interpreters have also argued that two stelae from Ugarit, *KTU* 6.13 and 6.14, similarly attest to the reciprocal benefit of food offerings and commemorative monuments for the offerer and recipient. See, e.g., Herbert Niehr, "Two Stelae Mentioning Mortuary Offerings from Ugarit (*KTU* 6.13 and 6.14)," in *(Re-)Constructing Funerary Rituals in the Ancient Near East: Proceedings of the First International Symposium of the Tübingen Post-graduate School "Symbols of the Dead" in May 2009*, ed. Peter Pfälzner et al., QSS 1 (Wiesbaden: Harrassowitz, 2012) 149–60. Found outside the cella of the eastern temple of the Ugaritic acropolis, the inscriptions on these stelae refer to the *pagru*, which some interpreters view as a mortuary ritual, an interpretation based especially on texts from Mari and elsewhere at Ugarit. In addition, both *KTU* 6.13 and 6.14 refer to the god Dagan as the recipient of a *sikkānu* or *pagru*, respectively. Other interpreters, however, reject that the Ugaritic *pagru* refers to a mortuary rite on the basis of the Mari evidence (see, e.g., Van der Toorn, *Family Religion*, 162–63;

The evidence for a cult of dead kin from Ugarit offers some intriguing parallels to the Mesopotamian evidence, yet much of it remains problematic and highly contested among scholars. It is still debated, for instance, whether the term *'il'ibu* in the Aqhat Epic refers to a divine dead ancestor and thus reflects the performance of rites constitutive of the cult of dead kin. The reading of the clay liver model (*KTU* 1.142) as evidence of feeding the dead is also problematic because this interpretation hinges on the damaged final word of the inscription, read by some interpreters as *qbr*, "grave." The Ugaritic Funerary Text is perhaps our clearest evidence of the cult of dead kin at Ugarit, since it entails sacrifices to dead royal ancestors in exchange for blessings on the new king's reign, a reciprocity we have seen in other depictions of the cult.

Although the relationship between some of the Ugaritic evidence and the cult of dead kin remains uncertain, the textual and iconographic evidence from Iron Age Sam'al is quite striking. Located near the border of modern-day Syria and Turkey, the eighth-century kingdom produced commemorative monuments and inscriptions that illuminate modes of care for the dead. The most convincing piece of evidence supporting the connection between these inscriptions and the cult of dead kin is the recently discovered Katumuwa stela.[56] According to the inscription on this stela, which features a feasting scene characteristic of other mortuary monuments from this region, Katumuwa sets up the stela (*naṣīb*) for himself while he is still living. The inscription explicitly states that the soul (*nabš*) of Katumuwa resides within the stela itself, and it so closely associates sacrifice to the gods with sacrifice to the dead.[57] After stipulating

---

Schmidt, *Israel's Beneficent Dead*, 51–53). Niehr argues further that the stelae were set up in a public place and under the protection of the god's sanctuary, presumably to ensure the ongoing performance of these offerings and, perhaps, to allow the dead to continue paying homage to the deity ("Two Stelae," 156).

56. For a discussion of the inscription and its interpretation, see Dennis Pardee, "A New Aramaic Inscription from Zincirli," *BASOR* 356 (2009): 51–71; J. David Schloen and Amir S. Fink, "New Excavations at Zincirli Höyük in Turkey (Ancient Sam'al) and the Discovery of an Inscribed Mortuary Stele," *BASOR* 356 (2009): 1–13; Eudore J. Struble and Virginia Rimmer Herrmann, "An Eternal Feast at Sam'al: The New Iron Age Mortuary Stele from Zincirli in Context," *BASOR* 356 (2009): 15–49; K. Lawson Younger, "Two Epigraphic Notes on the New Katumuwa Inscription from Zincirli," *Maarav* 16 (2011): 159–79; and several essays in Herrmann and Schloen, *In Remembrance of Me*.

57. The term *nabš* and its Hebrew cognate, *nepeš*, are often translated "soul," but

sacrifices for multiple deities, including Hadad, Šamaš, and Kubaba, the speaker—Katumuwa himself—also requests "a ram for my *nabš* that is in this stela."[58] The findspot of this stela in relation to surrounding buildings at Sam'al may be another indicator that commemoration of the dead coincides with the cult offered to deities. Virginia Herrmann argues that A/III, the building immediately adjacent to the mortuary chapel of Katumuwa (A/II), was a temple, which may indicate that the mortuary chapel was intentionally positioned close to it.[59] This proximity may have helped ensure the longevity of Katumuwa's cult while bolstering the prestige of that cult through close association (through physical proximity) with the cult of a deity or deities.

Other inscriptions on commemorative monuments from Sam'al similarly attest to this close association between the ritual care of deities and the dead. For instance, an eighth-century inscription refers to the invocation of Panamuwa I, king of Yadi, by the son who succeeds him to the throne (*KAI* 214).[60] When his successor invokes Panamuwa, he entreats

---

this translation evokes anachronistic concepts that obscure the term's use in ancient West Asian texts. For instance, Suriano argues that the *nepeš* is unlike the Platonic concept of soul because the *nepeš* is not necessarily immortal, nor is it released from the body at the time of death (*History of Death*, 5). The term in Aramaic inscriptions, like that on the Katumuwa stela, often refers to a physical object that ritually embodies the dead, such as a stela where offerings to the dead can be made (*History of Death*, 150–54, 163–70).

58. The term *ybl* may be vocalized differently depending its relationship to either Hebrew *yôbēl*, "ram's horn," or Akkadian *iābilu*, "ram." For a discussion of *ybl* and its likely interpretation as "ram," see Pardee, "New Aramaic Inscription," 61.

59. Virginia Rimmer Herrmann, "The Architectural Context of the KTMW Stele from Zincirli and the Mediation of Syro-Hittite Mortuary Cult by the Gods," in *Contextualising Grave Inventories in the Ancient Near East: Proceedings of a Workshop at the London Seventh ICAANE in April 2010 and an International Symposium in Tubingen in November 2010, Both Organised by the Tubingen Post-graduate School "Symbols of the Dead,"* ed. Peter Pfälzner et al. (Wiesbaden: Harassowitz, 2014), 77–82; Herrmann, "The Katumuwa Stele in Archaeological Context," in Herrmann and Schloen, *In Remembrance of Me*, 52–53. Though at a significant remove chronologically and geographically, this proximity of the Katumuwa stela to a temple also calls to mind the commemorative monument of the eunuch in Isa 56:3–5, which is set up in the sanctuary of YHWH.

60. For a treatment of the inscription, see Josef Tropper, *Die Inschriften von Zincirli* (Münster: Ugarit-Verlag, 1993), 54–97; *COS* 2:156–58. For an argument against this inscription as evidence for the cult of dead kin, see Schmidt, *Israel's Beneficent Dead*, 132–35.

him to eat and drink with the god Hadad. This inscription, sometimes called the Hadad inscription, is even inscribed on a statue of the storm god himself. Via the inscription, Panamuwa instructs his descendants to say, "May the soul [nabš] of Panamuwa eat with Hadad, and may the soul of Panamuwa drink with Hadad" (KAI 214.21–22). That a statue of Hadad is the medium for this commemorative inscription of Panamuwa I is significant in the sense that it further demonstrates the role of deities in the cult of dead kin and, through their mediation, the greater likelihood that care for the dead would continue.

Indeed, the iconography accompanying the inscriptions cited above often evokes food or drink offerings to the dead as well as the presence of major deities, particularly a solar deity. Dominik Bonatz notes the similarities between the banquet scene on the Katumuwa stela and other depictions of a "mortuary repast" on commemorative monuments from Sam'al and nearby Marash.[61] One such commemorative stela from Sam'al depicts a woman sitting before a table of food, an attendant, and a winged sun-disc centered above the scene.[62] A winged sun-disc also appears on the Katumuwa stela and is reflected in the inscription that accompanies it, since one of the ritual instructions stipulates the offering of a ram for Šamš (l. 4). Unfortunately, the winged sun-disc at the top of the Katumuwa stela has been almost entirely effaced by repeated disturbance from plowing. The iconography of Katumuwa seated alone before a table of food, Bonatz argues, is also characteristic of other stone monuments from Luwian and Aramaean territories in the ninth to eighth centuries BCE. In fact, of the seventy-two stelae in Bonatz's study, only thirteen lack the depiction of this mortuary repast.[63] This iconographic association between mortuary feasting and a solar deity offers a striking parallel to the textual depictions of the relationship between solar deities and the dead in both Mesopotamia and Ugarit.

The first-millennium inscriptions of Sam'al offer evidence of other aspects of the cult of dead kin as well. For instance, an inscription com-

---

61. Bonatz, "Katumuwa's Banquet Scene," 39–44; Dominik Bonatz, "The Iconography of Religion in the Hittite, Luwian, and Aramaean Kingdoms," in *Iconography of Deities and Demons in the Ancient Near East*, 2nd ed., ed. Jürg Eggler and Christoph Uehlinger (Leiden: Brill, 2000).

62. See Bonatz, "Katumuwa's Banquet Scene," 40, fig. 3.1, or Dominik Bonatz, *Das syro-hethitische Grabdenkmal* (Mainz: von Zabern, 2000), C46.

63. Bonatz, "Katumuwa's Banquet Scene," 39, 43 n. 2.

missioned by Barrākib, the son of Panamuwa II, refers to the construction of a commemorative monument and the "benevolent transportation" of his father's remains.[64] According to the inscription, Barrākib erects a commemorative monument for his dead father and inscribes on that monument a description of his father's successes as king and his loyalty to the Assyrian king Tiglath-pileser III. The inscription also notes that after Panamuwa dies on campaign, Tiglath-pileser himself mourns him, erects a commemorative monument for him, and transports his body from Damascus to Assyria. This portrayal of the circumstances surrounding the death of Panamuwa shows not only different ritual components of the cult of dead kin but also the possibility that a suzerain could function as caregiver for the dead. In this case, the fact that Panamuwa dies on campaign—presumably along-side Tiglath-pileser—might suggest that his son Barrākib is absent and thus unable to provide timely care for his recently dead father. Another possible reading is that such care undertaken by one's suzerain is exceptionally honorable to the dead and demonstrates the degree of loyalty shown by the dead vassal. Such an interpretation might explain why Barrākib chooses to include the description of these events in the monument he himself erects for his father later. It is also interesting to note that the performance of care for the dead by the suzerain (Tiglath-pileser, in this case) does not forestall care for the dead by their living kin (Barrākib). Such observations concerning the performance of the cult of dead kin by different actors, including nonkin, will become especially relevant in the discussion of chapter 4.

Other evidence from the Iron Age Levant demonstrates both parallels with and divergences from the modes of commemoration and care in Mesopotamia, Ugarit, and Sam'al. For instance, the Phoenician inscription on King Ahiram's sarcophagus (*KAI* 1), composed circa 1000 BCE, states that Ahiram's son, Ittoba'l, makes a sarcophagus for his father, which the text refers to as his "eternal dwelling-place,"[65] thus emphasizing the inviolability

---

64. See Olyan, "Unnoticed Resonances," passim. For a discussion of this inscription, see *KAI* 215; Tropper, *Die Inschriften von Zincirli*, 98–131; K. Lawson Younger Jr., "The Panamuwa Inscription," *COS* 2.37:158–60.

65. For an examination of the inscriptions, see Reinhard G. Lehmann, *Die Inschrift(en) des Ahirom-Sarkophags und die Schachtinschrift des Grabes V in Jbeil (Byblos)* (Mainz: von Zabern, 2005), 38; Javier Teixidor, "L'inscription d'Aḥiram à nouveau," *Syria* 64 (1987): 137–40; Hayim Tawil, "A Note on the Ahiram Inscription," *JANESCU* 3 (1970–1971): 33–36; Menahem Haran, "The Bas-Reliefs on the Sarcophagus of Ahiram King of Byblos in Light of Archaeological and Literary Parallels from the Ancient Near East," *IEJ* 8 (1958): 15–25.

of the burial site. The inscription also curses those who would open (*wygl*) the sarcophagus, including kings, governors, and army commanders. While the lid of the sarcophagus depicts two human figures facing each other, commonly interpreted as Ahiram and Ittobaʿl,[66] the carvings on the sides of the sarcophagus depict a procession leading to a male figure seated on a throne of winged sphinxes set before a table laden with food. The figures in this procession carry various items and hold their hands up in a gesture of reverence, or, in the case of the women depicted on the short sides of the sarcophagus, tear their hair and garments in mourning. Such iconography is similar to the banquet scenes found on the stelae from Samʾal noted above. These scenes suggest the ongoing importance of not only providing food and drink to the dead but also honoring the dead through gifts and honorific gestures. The inscription also emphasizes that Ittobaʿl provides a proper burial for his father and that the burial site shall be inviolable in perpetuity.

However, most Iron Age burial inscriptions from the Levant show less interest in depicting care for the dead in the form of offerings and focus instead on preservation and protection of human remains and the burial site. Moreover, unlike the Ahiram sarcophagus, these commemorative inscriptions are not usually accompanied by the scenes typical of commemorative monuments at Samʾal. Instead, these inscriptions focus on dissuading potential tomb violators, claiming that no luxury objects are buried in the tomb and cursing anyone who would disturb it. In fact, Seth Sanders notes that this shift in focus is characteristic of Iron Age funerary inscriptions.[67] For instance, the Tomb of the Royal Steward inscription from Silwan (*KAI* 191), composed circa 700 BCE, states: "There is no silver or gold here, only [his bones] and the bones of his maid-servant with him. Cursed is the person who opens this (tomb)."[68] Similarly, the fifth-century BCE inscription found on the sarcophagus of Tabnit, the king of Sidon,

---

66. See, e.g., Edith Porada, "Notes on the Sarcophagus of Ahiram," *JANESCU* 5 (1973): 359.

67. Seth L. Sanders, "Words, Things, and Death: The Rise of Iron Age Literary Monuments," in *Language and Religion*, ed. Robert Yelle, Courtney Handman, and Christopher Lehrich (Berlin: de Gruyter, 2019), 327–31.

68. For further discussion of this inscription, see Nahman Avigad, "The Epitaph of a Royal Steward from Siloam Village," *IEJ* 3 (1953): 137–52. On the title "royal steward," see Hannah J. Katzenstein, "The Royal Steward (*Asher ʿal ha-Bayith*)," *IEJ* 10 (1960): 149–54; Scott C. Layton, "The Steward in Ancient Israel: A Study of Hebrew (ʾăšer) ʿal-habbayit in Its Near Eastern Setting," *JBL* 109 (1990): 633–49. On the shorter, more difficult inscription that accompanies it, see David Ussishkin, "On the

indicates a concern about thieves disturbing the grave.[69] Like the inscription of the royal steward, lines 3–4 explicitly state that one should not loot the tomb because there is no silver or gold buried in the grave with Tabnit, only the corpse of Tabnit himself. The term used for this grave disturbance is *rgz*, which the text explicitly states would be an abomination to the goddess Astarte. The curses against those who would violate the tomb include lack of both progeny and a resting place with the *rp'm*. The fifth-century BCE Eshmunazar inscription describing the burial of Eshmunazar II, son of Tabnit,[70] refers to the lack of grave goods buried with Eshmunazar and beseeches the reader not to open (*ptḥ*) the grave or to move the remains of Eshmunazar to a different burial place. The curses against those who would disturb the grave include lack of their own resting place, lack of proper burial, divine retribution, and lack of offspring.

Thus, these Iron Age inscriptions share some characteristics with the commemorative monuments and inscriptions from Mesopotamia, Sam'al, and perhaps Ugarit concerning the protection and preservation of the burial site, but it is less clear that the former are concerned with other aspects of the cult of dead kin. The Ahiram sarcophagus depicts the offering of food to the dead, much like the feast scenes of Sam'al. It also refers to the fact the Ittoba'l provides a burial site for his father, thus portraying the common dyad of the father-son relationship in the cult of dead kin. However, the overwhelming concern of other Iron Age inscriptions from outside Sam'al is the protection of the burial site from violation at the hands of political enemies or looters. Such violation results in curses on those who would disturb the tomb and its contents, and in some cases specific gods are invoked to enact such curses on violators. Such curses, though, do assume a principle of reciprocity between the living and the dead. In this case, violators suffer a similar fate to the one they inflict on the dead, a

Shorter Inscription from the 'Tomb of the Royal Steward,'" *BASOR* 196 (1969): 16–22; Suriano, *History of Death*, 103–5.

69. For a discussion of this inscription, see *KAI* 13; John C. L. Gibson, *Phoenician Inscriptions, Including Inscriptions in the Mixed Dialect of Arslan Tash*, vol. 3 of *Textbook of Syrian Semitic Inscriptions* (Oxford: Oxford University Press, 1982), 101–5; P. Kyle McCarter, "The Sarcophagus Inscription of Tabnit, King of Sidon," *COS* 2:56.

70. For a discussion of this inscription, see *KAI* 14; Gibson, *Phoenician Inscriptions*, 105–14; Jean-Claude Haelewyck, "The Phoenician Inscription of Eshmunazar: An Attempt at Vocalization," *BABELAO* 1 (2012): 77–98; James B. Prichard and Daniel E. Fleming, *The Ancient Near East: An Anthology of Texts and Pictures* (Princeton: Princeton University Press, 2010), 311.

kind of *lex talionis* for one's care and commemoration (or lack thereof) in death. Yet, aside from the Ahiram inscription and those from Sam'al, the epigraphic evidence from the Iron Age Levant is largely silent concerning the potentially positive role of the living in caring for the dead. Instead, the inscriptions emphasize the potentially negative role of the living—the possibility of tomb violation—and its deleterious effects on the both the living and the dead.

Overall, the evidence from ancient West Asia shows a shifting constellation of ritual care for the dead. These modes of care include offerings to the dead, commemoration through both invocation of the name and monuments, and protection and repatriation of human remains. The evidence from Mesopotamia, by far our largest body of evidence, demonstrates all of these features. The Ugaritic evidence shows an interest in providing sustenance and commemoration for the dead through sacrificial offerings and monuments. The evidence from Sam'al shows more concern with monuments, though this evidence is admittedly skewed more toward the concerns of royalty, who had the means of providing such an elite form of commemoration. The iconography of these stelae emphasizes the offering of food and drink to the dead. The inscriptions from the Iron Age Levant outside Sam'al show a concern for the integrity of the burial site and its contents, including the remains of the dead, but are largely silent regarding other aspects of care for the dead. What can we glean from this assemblage of data, especially when we consider that it comes from disparate time periods and geographic locales? Despite the incompleteness of the data, the recurring themes we find in these bodies of evidence provide a rough framework for ritual activity geared toward the dead in ancient West Asia. The nature of these ritual acts, particularly their emphasis on nurture and protection, indicates that their ultimate goal is to provide ongoing care for the dead. At the same time, the evidence suggests a reciprocal logic underlying the offering of this care. Thus, these modes of care are characteristic interactions between the living and the dead in ancient West Asia and comprise the cult of dead kin in this region. Since ancient Israel is also part of this region, we must evaluate its rituals and ideologies concerning the dead in light of this broad cultural framework.

Locating the Cult of Dead Kin in the Hebrew Bible and Ancient Israel

Using this brief survey of the cult of dead kin in Mesopotamia, Ugarit, and the Iron Age Levant as our frame of reference, we can see that the Hebrew

Bible also shows signs of a cult of dead kin. The most relevant biblical evidence for reconstructing such a cult includes (1) food offerings to the dead in Deut 26:14 and, perhaps, in 1 Sam 20:6;[71] (2) invocation of the name of the dead in 2 Sam 18:18 and, perhaps, in 2 Sam 14:7; Isa 56:3–5; and Ruth 4:10; (3) commemorative monuments in Gen 35:20; 2 Sam 18:18; and Isa 56:5; (4) protection and/or repatriation of human remains in Gen 49:29–32; 50:12–14; Josh 24:32; Judg 16:31; 2 Sam 2:31; 21:10, 12–14; and Ezek 37:11–14; and (5) maintenance of the burial site in Neh 2:3, 5.

Of the biblical texts that take for granted the ritual care of the dead, Deut 26:14 is perhaps the most debated among biblical scholars. The text states: "I have not eaten any of [the tithed offering] while in mourning; I have not consumed any of it while unclean; and I have not given any of it to the dead."[72] It is important to note that this passage contains no prohibition against offering food to the dead, despite studies that interpret it as a condemnation of the cult of dead kin.[73] Instead, this passage is concerned primarily with avoiding contamination of the tithe, a "holy thing" according to verse 13, including that which results from corpse contact (e.g., Lev 21:1–6, 10–12). In either interpretation, however, the text explicitly refers to the possibility of Israelites offering food to the

---

71. Food vessels and fragments from Judahite tombs may provide further material evidence of these practices. Later texts, such as Tob 4:17 and Sir 30:18, refer quite explicitly to food and drink offerings placed on graves. The former states, "Place your bread on the grave of the righteous, but give none to sinners," while the latter states, "Good things poured out upon a mouth that is closed are like offerings of food placed upon a grave." Van der Toorn also notes their similarity to Syriac Aḥiqar no. 10, which states: "My son, pour out your wine on the graves of the righteous" (*Family Religion*, 209 n. 9).

72. My rendering of *ləmēt* as "to the dead" deviates from Schmidt's interpretation, "on account of the dead" (*Israel's Beneficent Dead*, 199). According to Schmidt's interpretation, the underlying logic of Deut 26:14 is that the speaker in the text gives food to those who are mourning, not to the dead. This interpretation is ultimately unsatisfying because the syntax of the last phrase ("I have not given any of it on account of the dead") seems awkward due to its lack of an indirect object for *ntn*, "give."

73. On the basis of Deut 26:14, Lewis argues that "it seems safe to infer that any offerings to the dead would have been considered offensive to Deuteronomistic theology" (*Cults of the Dead*, 172 n. 2). See also Blenkinsopp, "Deuteronomy and the Politics," 15; Van der Toorn, *Family Religion*, 208; Herbert Niehr, "The Changed Status of the Dead in Yehud," in *Yahwism after the Exile: Perspectives on Israelite Religion in the Persian Era*, ed. Rainer Albertz and Bob Becking, STR 5 (Assen: Van Gorcum, 2003), 142.

dead and, perhaps, their assumption that these cultic spheres, the cult of dead kin and the cult of YHWH, are compatible. If the new moon festival of 1 Sam 20 is an occasion of commemoration for dead kin analogous to the Mesopotamian *bubbulum*, as Van der Toorn suggests,[74] then it constitutes another context for food offerings to the dead in the Hebrew Bible. In this case, the offering of food to the dead takes place at a feast where members of the same clan gather. A possible reference to feeding the dead also appears in Ps 106:28, "Then they joined themselves to Baal Peor and ate sacrifices of the dead."[75] However, the relationship of this passage to Num 25:2 complicates this interpretation. Numbers 25 contains the original Baal Peor account to which Ps 106:28 refers, and this passage lacks any reference to the dead. However, it does refer to sacrifices to Moabite women's gods (*ʾĕlōhîm*). Since the "dead" in Ps 106:28 may be a polemical reference to the powerlessness of these Moabite deities, rather than the dead, the relevance of Ps 106:28 to a discussion of the cult of dead kin is possible but not certain.

---

74. Van der Toorn, *Family Religion*, 211–18. However, for an argument against this interpretation of 1 Sam 20, see Jon D. Levenson, *Resurrection and the Restoration of Israel: The Ultimate Victory of the God of Life* (New Haven: Yale University Press, 2006), 57–58.

75. Schmitt interprets the reference to the dead in this passage as a pejorative epithet for illicit deities. Thus, he dismisses the passage as a reference to food offerings to the dead, since it seems to refer to the "dead" gods of Num 25:2. Therefore, he argues, the term *dead* is polemical in this context, used to denigrate the power of other gods, and does not refer to the care of the dead (Albertz and Schmitt, *Household and Family Religion*, 456). Lewis prefers reading Ps 106:28 as a reference to sacrifices for the dead and notes that the LXX rendering of the passage explicitly refers to these offerings as *thysias nekron*, "sacrifices of the dead" (*Cults of the Dead*, 167 n. 6). Lewis further argues that nowhere else does the biblical text refer to images of foreign deities as *mētîm* or "dead" (*Cults of the Dead*, 167, 176). However, recent work on icon polemics in the Hebrew Bible and ancient West Asia challenges this argument. See, e.g., Nathaniel B. Levtow, *Images of Others: Icon Politics in Ancient Israel* (Winona Lake, IN: Eisenbrauns, 2008). After all, in Jer 10:1–16, the reference to YHWH as a "living god" is contrasted with the images of other deities in which "there is no breath," which suggests that these images (and perhaps the deities they index) are dead. Furthermore, if we consider the recurring biblical depiction of the dead as ineffective and ignorant (e.g., Job 14:21; Qoh 9:5, 10), then referring to non-Yahwistic deities and their images as dead would be one more articulation of their many disabilities expressed in prophetic texts (e.g., Jer 10:5; Isa 44:18).

Other biblical passages suggest that the construction of a commemorative monument and invocation of the name of the dead were fundamental aspects of the Israelite cult of dead kin. For instance, in Gen 35:20, Jacob sets up a *maṣṣēbâ*, often translated "standing stone" or "cultic pillar," at the grave of his recently deceased wife Rachel. In other passages, erecting a monument and invoking the name seem inextricably linked. In 2 Sam 18:18, Absalom erects a *maṣṣebet* because he lacks a son to invoke his name. Lewis notes that the terminology used in the Absalom passage (*hazkîr šamî*) is similar to what we find in texts from Sam'al and Mesopotamia (*yzkr 'šm* and *šuma zakāru*, respectively) regarding the commemoration of the dead.[76] In Isa 56:3–5, YHWH claims that he will set up a *yād wā-šēm* greater than sons and daughters for the eunuch. The *yād wā-šēm*, literally "a hand and a name," is probably best understood as a hendiadys referring to a commemorative monument, and its presence in the sanctuary of YHWH also recalls the imagery of the *sikkānu* for the *'il'ibu* in the Ugaritic Aqhat Epic and the Katumuwa stela from Sam'al, both of which are placed in close proximity to a temple.[77]

Other possible references to the cult of dead kin, specifically the preservation of the name of the dead, appear in 2 Sam 14:7 and Ruth 4:10. In 2 Sam 14:7, a mother describes the death of her husband's heir as the removal of his name and "remnant" (*šə'ērît*) from the earth.[78] In light of the biblical evidence cited above, it is plausible to interpret the removal of the father's name as a lack of commemoration stemming from the absence of an heir to invoke his father's name. The imagery in Ruth 4:10 may also assume this threat to care for the dead.[79] When Boaz buys the former property of Mahlon, he takes Ruth, Mahlon's widow, as his wife, after which he states that he will set up Mahlon's name on his inalienable inheritance (*naḥălâ*) so that his name will not be cut off from his kin and

---

76. Lewis, *Cults of the Dead*, 173.

77. I will return to Isa 56:3–5 and the issue of YHWH as divine caregiver in ch. 4.

78. In his commentary on 2 Samuel, P. Kyle McCarter also draws a parallel between the "quenched ember" of 2 Sam 14:7 and the Old Babylonian expression describing a man with no heir as one "whose brazier has gone out." See McCarter, *II Samuel: A New Translation with Introduction, Notes, and Commentary* (Garden City, NY: Doubleday, 1984), 345.

79. See also Herbert Chanan Brichto's analysis, in which he argues that the "name" in Ruth 4:10 here stands for continuation of Mahlon's family line ("Kin, Cult, Land," 20–21). Part of the importance placed on continuation of the family line, he argues, is the performance of custodial acts by heirs for their dead kin.

from the gate of his "place."[80] Indeed, levirate marriage in Deut 25:6 is another way in which the name of the deceased is preserved through offspring. The text even specifies that the offspring produced through levirate marriage will assume the name of the deceased, thus preventing it from being "wiped out from Israel." It seems that the cult of dead kin provides a plausible rationale for this concern about the name of the dead in these instances. Someone—either one's own offspring or a child born through levirate marriage—must act as caregiver for the dead, invoking the name and thus preserving the memory of the dead.

Finally, several biblical texts attest to care for the dead in the form of protection and repatriation of human remains. This protection entails preserving the physical integrity of the corpse and/or burial site, while repatriation is the transportation of human remains to the territory associated with one's family or tribe. Biblical texts such as 2 Sam 21:10; 2 Kgs 9:34–37; and Neh 2:3 depict this protection of the remains of the dead, while texts such as Gen 49:29–32; 50:12–14; Judg 16:31; Josh 24:32; 2 Sam 2:32; and Ezek 37:11–14 depict the repatriation of human remains to their ancestral lands. In 2 Sam 21:10, Rişpah protects the remains of her dead sons and other executed Saulides from violation by wild beasts and birds.[81] Furthermore, when Jehu commands his men to care for Jezebel's corpse in 2 Kgs 9:34–37, the term used to describe this care (*piqdû*) may also indicate ritual care for the dead analogous to Mesopotamian practice. After all, the root *pqd* is the same as that of the Mesopotamian *pāqidu*, and the terminology and context of the passage suggest that burying Jezebel was construed as an act of care for the recently deceased.[82] In fact, Matthew Suriano notes that the phrase in 2 Kgs 9:37b, "This is Jezebel," is reminiscent of the syntax of Iron Age funerary inscriptions, including that of the Tomb of the Royal

---

80. The term *māqôm* has a range of meanings, including "sanctuary," which would be of great interest in the present analysis due to its possible parallels with the Aqhat Epic and Isa 56:3–5. However, the phrase "gate of his place" also appears in Deut 21:19, where it seems to refer to the gate of a town where elders would gather.

81. That Rişpah offers this care prior to burial should not disqualify it as an example of cult of dead kin. After all, in multiple instances of the *kispu*, the living may make offerings to the dead who lack proper burial. For further discussion of the inclusion of this and similar texts depicting nonideal burial, see the introduction to this work.

82. For similar interpretations of 2 Kgs 9:34–37, see Lewis, *Cults of the Dead*, 174; Bloch-Smith, *Judahite Burial Practices*, 146; Mark S. Smith, *The Early History of God: Yahweh and the Other Deities in Ancient Israel* (Grand Rapids: Eerdmans, 2002), 169.

Steward, which begins "This is the tomb of [PN]-yahu, the royal steward."[83] Such parallels suggest that this was a set phrase used to mark the space where bones were housed and protected and thus ritual spaces for the commemoration and care of the dead. In Neh 2:3–5, Nehemiah laments to Artaxerxes about the desolate state of Jerusalem, which he refers to as "the city of my fathers' tombs." He beseeches the king to allow him to return to the city so that he may rebuild it, couching his return in terms of tomb maintenance. This reference to preservation of the burial site and thus the protection of human remains is central to the cult of dead kin. Thus, the passage draws on the concerns of the cult of dead kin in order to justify Nehemiah's rebuilding project.

Biblical references to repatriation of human remains are more explicit, though their relationship to the cult of dead kin has been overlooked by previous studies. For instance, Gen 49:29–32 and 50:12–14 refer to Jacob's sons transporting their father's corpse in order to be buried in his ancestral tomb. In Judg 16:31, Samson's kinsmen transport his corpse from the Philistine city of Gaza to the tomb of his father Manoah, likely in the territory of the Danites. In Josh 24:32, Joseph's bones are brought from Egypt to Shechem.[84] In 2 Sam 2:32, Joab and the servants of David bring back the corpse of Joab's brother, Asahel, from battle in Gibeon to be buried in his father's tomb in Bethlehem. The narrative of 2 Sam 21:12–14 depicts David bringing the bones of Saul and Jonathan to their ancestral tomb in Benjamin. YHWH himself repatriates the bones of the figuratively dead Israel in Ezek 37:11–14, thus drawing on the imagery of the cult of dead kin to articulate Yahwistic ideology.[85]

This brief survey demonstrates how a comparative reading of the biblical material with evidence from other ancient West Asian cultures helps us recognize resonances of the cult of dead kin in the Hebrew Bible. In fact, we find nearly all of the recurring ritual components of the cult depicted in the

---

83. Suriano, *History of Death*, 196–97.

84. As Suriano points out, the term *pqd*, referring to care for someone's bones, appears in the description of Joseph in Sir 49:15, "Was a man like Joseph ever born? Even his body was cared for" (*History of Death*, 188). This later reference in Ben Sira seems to recall the earlier treatment and repatriation of Joseph's bones (Gen 50:24–26; Josh 24:32). The repetition of this term in the oath Joseph makes the Israelites swear in Gen 50:25—"God will surely care [*pāqod yipqod*] for you if you bring up my bones from here"—is intended to evoke the imagery of this care for his bones.

85. I will return to Ezek 37:11–14 and the issue of repatriation as an aspect of the cult of dead kin in ch. 4, which will address postexilic attitudes to the cult.

texts from Mesopotamia, Ugarit, and the Iron Age Levant in the Hebrew Bible as well. There are significant parallels concerning the participants of the cult and the social and political circumstances in which it was practiced. That we must read against the grain of the biblical text in order to notice the influence of the cult of dead kin suggests its pervasive nature, particularly as a fundamental aspect of family religion. The cult was likely a deeply embedded aspect of family life and thus may have been either taken for granted by biblical writers or simply outside the scope of their interests.

Material Evidence and the Cult of Dead Kin in Ancient Israel

While the evidence for burials in ancient Israel is rich, it is often difficult to determine its relevance to the cult of dead kin. Of particular interest in a discussion of the cult of dead kin is the Judahite bench tomb, which becomes well attested in the late eighth to early sixth century BCE in the southern highlands. This tomb type is notable for its similarities with the Israelite domicile. For instance, features such as imitation sunken wood panels, gabled ceilings, lamp niches, and headrests are similar to those found in domestic architecture. In her study of burial practices in Iron Age Judah, Elizabeth Bloch-Smith catalogues the different items in grave assemblages: vessels for food and liquid, lamps, tools, rattles, and an assortment of figurines. These figurines include birds, dogs, horses, the much-analyzed Judean pillar figurines, and imitation Mycenaean male and female figures as well as model thrones, beds, and shrines.[86] Similarities between the grave goods found within these tombs and those found in domestic contexts have led some scholars to argue that there was a conception of life after death or "functional immortality" for those who received such offerings.[87]

Another reason why bench tombs have been considered an important datum for cult of dead kin is the practice of secondary burial that took place within them. By the seventh century BCE, bone repositories are prevalent in Judahite bench tombs and may contain between fifteen and one hundred disarticulated skeletons. In this practice, a new corpse was laid on a stone bench, where it eventually decayed. Later (unfortunately, we do not have a textual account of this process including a time

---

86. Bloch-Smith, *Judahite Burial Practices*, 148.

87. See, e.g., Amihai Mazar, *The Archaeology of the Land of the Bible, 10,000–586 BCE* (New York: Doubleday, 1990), 521; Suriano, *History of Death*, 33.

frame), someone would gather the disarticulated bones and move them to a repository elsewhere in the tomb. Since bench tombs often contain the remains of multiple corpses, scholars have posited the relationship between this burial practice and a concern for maintaining the cohesion of a family lineage and the veneration of ancestors.[88] However, archaeologists have not always been able to adequately test the bones from these burials due to modern religious restrictions on osteological analysis.[89] Therefore, the genetic relationship of the individuals buried in some tombs remains unclear.

Some scholars of Israelite religion argue that the process of secondary burial in the bench tomb signifies the ritual transition of the dead into ancestors in ancient Israel.[90] This argument is similar to earlier work on secondary burial in the field of anthropology, such as that of Maurice Bloch, who observes the change in social status between decaying corpses, considered dangerous and marginal, and dry bones, which could be safely reintegrated into the community as ancestors.[91] In fact, the handling of bones during secondary burial seems like a crucial ritual aspect of caring for the dead, as Suriano notes: "The custom of secondary burial resonates with the concerns found in biblical and ancient Near Eastern sources for

---

88. On maintaining the cohesion of a family lineage, see, e.g., Avraham Faust and Shlomo Bunimovitz, "The Judahite Rock-Cut Tomb: Response at a Time of Change," *IEJ* 58 (2008): 150–70; Matthew Suriano, *The Politics of Dead Kings: Dynastic Ancestors in the Book of Kings and Ancient Israel* (Tübingen: Mohr Siebeck, 2010), 52–53. On the veneration of ancestors, see, e.g., Osborne, "Secondary Mortuary Practice," 35–53.

89. For a discussion of the limits of osteological analysis, see Elizabeth Bloch-Smith, "From Womb to Tomb: The Israelite Family in Life as in Death," in Dutcher-Walls, *Family in Life*, 125; Hallote, *Death, Burial, and Afterlife*, 194–207; Cradic, "Embodiments of Death," 221.

90. See, e.g., Suriano, *History of Death*, 39–40, 54; Osborne, "Secondary Mortuary Practice."

91. Maurice Bloch, "Death, Women, and Power," in *Death and the Regeneration of Life*, ed. Maurice Bloch and Jonathan Parry (Cambridge: Cambridge University Press, 1982), 211–30. Not only does Bloch describe the gendered nature of these ritual roles, but he also notes that the role played by the women in this secondary burial served as the antithesis of the social ideal the Merina hoped to effect through the ritual: "Women as agents of death and division therefore have the central role, not only the negative role but also the creative role, since the creation of symbolic order is dependent on negation. Death as disruption, rather than being a problem for the social order, as anthropologists have tended to think of it, is in fact an opportunity for dramatically creating it" ("Death, Women, and Power," 218–19).

protecting bones (e.g., 2 Sam 21:12–14)."[92] Thus, we may construe second-ary burial of bones as another form of caring for and protecting the dead. It is noteworthy, however, that while some or most Israelites may have taken this distinction between the social roles of corpses and bones for granted, the Priestly material in the Hebrew Bible finds them both equally polluting (Num 5:2; 19:11–21). Indeed, the prevalence of extramural buri-als in Iron Age Judah seems to reflect widespread anxieties about burying the dead within urban areas, despite some evidence of intramural royal burial in Jerusalem and Samaria.[93]

Although the bench tomb emerged as a quintessential Judahite burial type in the Iron Age, archaeological evidence from the second-millen-nium Levant suggests that some features of Iron Age care for the dead are continuations from earlier periods, including patterns of grave goods left in and around burial sites as well as the practice of secondary burial. Rachel Hallote emphasizes the rhetorical force of burial assemblages in Middle Bronze tombs in the construction of identity: "[Burial practices] reflect a wide range of emphases, omissions, and archaisms, and present an idealized view about individuals, families, and societies. All of this is based on shifting situational principles, which may fundamentally obscure or at least resist the contemporary world as much as situate the deceased within that world."[94] Indeed, almost every burial in the Middle Bronze period included food and drink vessels in those assemblages as well as nonedible offerings.[95] Melissa Cradic also points out indications of ongoing visita-tion to a Middle Bronze tomb at Tel Megiddo, including "stratified artifact and faunal remains outside the burial chamber and grave markers" as well as "high degree of corporeal fragmentation and commingling of disarticu-lated human skeletal remains."[96] There are also indications of mortuary as well as funerary ritual in the Late Bronze period. For instance, Aaron

---

92. Suriano, *History of Death*, 50.

93. For a treatment of royal death notices in the Hebrew Bible referring to intra-mural burial, see Suriano, *Politics of Dead Kings*. On the evidence for intramural burial at Samaria, see Norma Franklin, "The Tombs of the Kings of Israel: Two Recently Identified Ninth Century Tombs from Omride Samaria," *ZDPV* 119 (2003): 1–11.

94. Rachel S. Hallote, " 'Real' and Ideal Identities in Middle Bronze Age Tombs," *NEA* 65 (2002): 108.

95. Hallote, "Tombs, Cult, and Chronology," 208; Baker, "Funeral Kit," 5. Baker notes that there are very few cooking vessels found in the assemblages, which suggests that food was prepared in advance and brought to the tomb.

96. Cradic, "Embodiments of Death," 234.

Brody notes that objects discovered in the fill above a Late Bronze tomb in Grid 38 at Ashkelon, including part of a sheep skeleton, ceramics, thirteen jar stoppers, blade fragments, a scarab, and charred olive pits, suggest that mortuary rites continued after burial.[97]

The well-preserved royal hypogeum of Qatna, an important royal center in Bronze Age Syria, provides more elaborate comparative evidence of such mortuary practices. Peter Pfälzner, for instance, characterizes pottery deposits accompanying secondary burials at Qatna as evidence of *kispu*-like practices.[98] The ongoing use and care for the tomb seems to have lasted hundreds of years, well into the Late Bronze Age.[99] Pfälzner interprets the layout and faunal remains of the tomb as indicative of ongoing feasting for the living and dead.[100] Indeed, Sarah Lange distinguishes four types of offerings indicated by remains in the tomb: (1) offerings to dead individuals laid out in the southern chamber and afterward when the dead received primary and secondary burial, (2) offerings to royal ancestors in general, (3) offerings in the corridor and antechamber with unknown addressees, and (4) offerings consumed by the living in a funerary or commemorative "banquet."[101]

In addition to food offerings, the practice of secondary burial is also prevalent in the Bronze Age, and treatments of this archaeological material

---

97. Aaron J. Brody, "New Perspectives on Levantine Mortuary Ritual: A Cognitive Interpretative Approach to the Archaeology of Death," in *Historical Biblical Archaeology and the Future: The New Pragmatism*, ed. Thomas E. Levy (London: Equinox, 2010), 131–34. Brody notes similar depositions of offerings on top of and next to burials at Middle Bronze Tel Dan, Tell el-Dabʿa, and Tell el-Maskhuta. See Brody, "Late Bronze Age Intramural Tombs," in *Ashkelon I: Introduction and Overview (1985–2006), Final Reports of the Leon Levy Expedition to Ashkelon*, ed. Lawrence E. Stager, J. David Schloen, and Daniel M. Master (Winona Lake, IN: Eisenbrauns, 2008), 1:527.

98. Peter Pfälzner, "How Did They Bury the Kings of Qatna?," in Pfälzner et al., *(Re-)Constructing Funerary Rituals*, 213–16.

99. Peter Pfälzner, "Royal Funerary Practices and Inter-regional Contacts in the Middle Bronze Age Levant: New Evidence from Qatna," in Pfälzner et al., *Contextualising Grave Inventories*, 144; see also Sarah Lange, "Food Offerings in the Royal Tomb of Qatna," in Pfälzner et al., *Contextualising Grave Inventories*, 244.

100. Peter Pfälzner, "Archaeological Investigations in the Royal Palace of Qatna," in *Urban and Natural Landscapes of an Ancient Syrian Capital Settlement and Environment at Tell Mishrifeh/Qatna and in Central-Western Syria: Proceedings of an International Conference Held at Udine 9–11 December 2004*, ed. Daniele Morandi Bonacossi, SAQPC 1, DAS 12 (Udine: Forum, 2007), 58.

101. Lange, "Food Offerings," 255.

often associate this practice with the ritual transition of the dead into ancestors. For instance, Cradic argues that the "funerary sequence" at Middle Bronze Tel Megiddo consists of three phases: preinterment, interment, and postinterment.[102] The skeletal fragmentation of interred corpses was not merely functional, she argues, but also a part of the process by which the living and dead continued to interact and the dead became ancestors. Disarticulation of the skeleton facilitated the decomposition of the body and the individual so that it could become a "non-corporeal, nameless ancestor with a shared biography."[103] Pfälzner similarly argues that the process of distancing the dead from the world of the living involved the dissolution of the individual into the collective dead. He concludes: "The funerary rituals at Qatna, thus, resulted in the forming of collective ancestors as part of the collective remembering of the kingdom of Qatna."[104]

Such continuities in burial and mortuary practice between the Bronze and Iron Ages have led some scholars to argue that use of the bench tomb likely developed out of earlier tomb types, such as the loculus tomb, which "served similar mortuary needs."[105] In fact, Suriano further argues that this similarity in the ritual space of tomb types likely appealed to traditional tastes and contributed to the adoption of bench tombs in the Iron Age: "Even though the widespread adoption of repositories is a general innovation of the Iron II, it could still be seen as how 'things have always been done' (to use Bell's words) because this innovation was set within the multigenerational house of the bench tomb."[106] Other studies of the bench tomb focus on the political context of such burials, including the use of tombs and burial rites to convey and affirm a family's status within a community. For instance, Avraham Faust and Shlomo Bunimovitz argue that the emergence of the bench tomb type coincides with various threats to the Israelite family, including the rise of Neo-Assyrian hegemony, the population influx in Judah from the recently conquered Northern King-

---

102. Cradic, "Embodiments of Death," 220.

103. Cradic, ""Embodiments of Death," 225. While Cradic assigns ritual significance to the ways in which these bodies and their items were handled during secondary burial, Jill L. Baker and Rachel Hallote suggest that this was more haphazard. See Baker, "Form and Function of Mortuary Architecture: The Middle and Late Bronze Age Tomb Complex at Ashkelon," *Levant* 42 (2010): 11; Hallote, "Mortuary Archaeology and the Middle Bronze Age Southern Levant," *JMA* 8 (1995): 103–4.

104. Pfälzner, "How Did They Bury," 217–18.

105. Suriano, *History of Death*, 93.

106. Suriano, *History of Death*, 96.

dom, and resulting urbanization.[107] In their view, the similarities between the tomb and the typical Israelite house reflect an attempt to establish the permanence of the *bêt ʾāb* ("house of the father"), which they interpret as the extended family, through a material medium: "Since the house, in its social meaning (i.e., the family) was threatened, the adoption of the house (in its structural meaning, i.e., the four-room house) as a 'counter symbol' was to be expected."[108] The adoption of the bench tomb type was thus a reaction by extended families to such threats against their cohesion and came to represent the social status of the family, its generational continuity, and ongoing claims to land and property.

Like the design of the tomb itself, the burial assemblages within tombs offer both tantalizing details about burial practices and unsatisfying answers to questions about ideologies concerning the dead. Past studies, including Bloch-Smith's survey and the more recent study by Albertz and Schmitt,[109] have examined these assemblages in order to glean information about Israelite conceptions of the dead, including their powers, the afterlife, and their relationship to the living. For instance, the most common type of object in grave assemblages in ancient Judah is the ceramic dish or bowl. The prevalence of this grave good might suggest that there was a widespread concern for feeding the dead, a concern that fits well with what we know about the cult of dead kin in ancient West Asia. However, it is unclear whether these food vessels (and, in some cases, food fragments) were intended to feed the dead or were left over from a graveside meal meant solely for the living.[110] Another interpretative issue with such objects is that—if they were intended to feed the dead—we do not know

---

107. Faust and Bunimovitz, "Judahite Rock-Cut Tomb," 150–70. Their argument draws on Baruch Halpern's theory of changing kinship structure in the seventh century BCE, which argues that the rise of urbanization and centralized industry led to the growing dominance of the nuclear family as the primary social unit rather than large, extended families. See Halpern, "Jerusalem and the Lineages in the Seventh Century BCE: Kinship and the Rise of Individual Moral Liability," in *Law and Ideology in Monarchic Israel*, ed. Baruch Halpern and Deborah W. Hobson (Sheffield: JSOT Press, 1991), 91.

108. Faust and Bunimovitz, "Judahite Rock-Cut Tomb," 161.

109. Bloch-Smith, *Judahite Burial Practices*, 63–108; Albertz and Schmitt, *Family and Household Religion*, 438–55, 457, 462–69.

110. However, as Bloch-Smith notes, food left in simple, jar, and urn burials suggests that the food was intended for the dead, not the living (*Judahite Burial Practices*, 105).

whether this provisioning was temporary or was intended to feed the dead in perpetuity. The time of deposition of offerings in and outside tombs differs across burial sites. Some tombs in which the primary burial remains undisturbed contain grave goods, such as lamps, positioned around the corpse.[111] In Tomb 1 at Khirbet Beit Lei, the absence of grave goods alongside primary burials may suggest that such deposits would have been left sometime between primary and secondary burial. Suriano further suggests that inscriptions may have accompanied these grave goods placed before or during secondary burial. In other tombs, it appears that these grave goods were collected along with disarticulated skeletons into repositories during secondary burial.[112] Still other tombs, however, show signs that offerings were left long after primary and secondary burials took place, well into the late Persian and Hellenistic periods.[113] This interpretative problem is thus related to how scholars define the cult of dead kin and distinguish it from one-time funerary rites. In short, it is unclear how—if at all—the inclusion of food vessels in grave assemblages reflects the practice of an Israelite cult of dead kin.

Funerary inscriptions from Iron Age Judah also belong in a synthesis of material evidence of care for the dead. Because these inscriptions not only invoke the name of the dead but also often promote the protection of the bones and burial site, the construction of such inscriptions reflects the kinds of ritual care of the dead examined throughout this study. Perhaps the most famous example of funerary inscriptions from Iron Age Judah comes from the Tomb of the Royal Steward, noted above, which cautions potential looters against violating the tomb. A striking feature of other Iron Age funerary inscriptions is their invocation of YHWH.[114] For instance, the seventh-century silver amulets from the tomb complex at Ketef Hinnom echo the Priestly blessing of Num 6:24-26: "... For redemption is in him. For Yahweh is our restorer [and] rock. May Yahweh bles[s]

---

111. Amos Kloner and David Davis, "A Burial Cave of the Late First Temple Period on the Slope of Mount Zion," in *Ancient Jerusalem Revealed*, ed. Hillel Geva (Jerusalem: Israel Exploration Society, 1994), 107–10.

112. Suriano, *History of Death*, 48–49, 122, 156.

113. Suriano, *History of Death*, 51 n. 39; Avraham Biran and Rudolph Gophna, "An Iron Age Burial Cave at Tel Ḥalif," *IEJ* 20 (1970): 166–68.

114. Suriano examines such inscriptions in detail (*History of Death*, 98–130, esp. 112–27). See also Seth Sanders, "Naming the Dead: Funerary Writing and Historical Change in the Iron Age Levant," *Maarav* 19 (2012): 11–36.

you and [may he] guard you. [May] Yahweh make [his face] shine…"[115] At Khirbet el-Qôm, an inscription engraved on a pillar near the entrance to the burial cave states: "Uriah the prosperous, his epitaph: Blessed be Uriah by Yahweh. And from his enemies, by his asherah,[116] save him. (Written) by Oniah."[117] The presence of these invocations in a burial setting suggests that, at least for the writers of these inscriptions, YHWH is not excluded from such ritual spaces because of corpse pollution. Indeed, an inscription from Khirbet Beit Lei uses terminology typical of the cult of dead kin (*pqd*) to invite YHWH into the tomb: "Attend [*pqd*] Yah, O gracious God! Acquit Yah, O YHWH!"[118] As we will see in chapter 4, this characterization of YHWH as caregiver for the dead is a potent image that biblical writers use in postexilic depictions of YHWH and Israel.

Due to the issues outlined above, it is difficult to synthesize the textual and material evidence of practices and ideologies concerning the dead in ancient Israel, including the cult of dead kin. In many ways, the material evidence for death-related practices is fraught and eludes conclusive interpretation. In fact, drawing on the work of anthropologist Peter Ucko, Pitard stresses the difficulties in studying death in general, even in contemporary societies, due to the wide range of human responses to it.[119] Ucko, for instance, uses contemporary ethnographic material to demonstrate that the seemingly commonsense interpretations of funerary remains by scholars often fall short of emic interpretations of funerary practices.[120] On this basis, Pitard argues that material evidence—in

---

115. For translation and commentary on the text, see Jeremy D. Smoak, *The Priestly Blessing in Inscription and Scripture: The Early History of Numbers 6:24–26* (New York: Oxford University Press, 2016), 18–19.

116. Other translations render the term *'šrth* in this text as the cult symbol instead of the goddess. For an overview of the problems posed by this term, see Saul M. Olyan, *Asherah and the Cult of Yahweh in Israel* (Atlanta: Scholars Press, 1988), 25–34.

117. This translation closely follows Suriano, *History of Death*, 114.

118. This translation closely follows André Lemaire, "Prières en temps de crise: Les inscriptions de Khirbet Beit Lei," *RB* 83 (1976): 558–68. Previous treatments differ in their reconstructions and translations of this inscription; see further Suriano, *History of Death*, 119 n. 62. If the reconstruction of *pqd* is viable, then it evokes not only an association between YHWH and the cult of dead kin but also, as Suriano notes, the characterization of YHWH in Exod 34:6–7 (*History of Death*, 119–21).

119. Pitard, "Tombs and Offerings," 149.

120. Peter J. Ucko, "Ethnography and Archaeological Interpretation of Funerary Remains," *WA* 1 (1969): 262–80.

the absence of textual evidence—tells us little about ancient belief systems regarding death. A more measured conclusion drawn from Ucko's work, however, might be that scholars must avoid universalizing models of human responses to death. Nevertheless, this difficulty in interpreting the material evidence is one issue among several we must consider in reconstructions of the cult of dead kin in ancient Israel.

Conclusion

This chapter has examined comparative evidence from ancient West Asia of ritual care for the dead. Through an examination of this evidence, some recurring features of the cult emerge: offerings to the dead (food, drink, or other items), the construction of commemorative monuments, invocation of the name of the dead, protection/repatriation of the corpse, and maintenance of the burial site. Ultimately, I would argue that the textual and archaeological evidence cited above reflects the broad cultural pull of the cult of dead kin throughout ancient West Asia, including ancient Israel. When read through this lens, we may get a better sense of how a biblical cult of dead kin fits into the broader landscape of cultic activity, particularly family religion, in the region. Family religion in its many forms is the primary vehicle by which ancient people engage with the divine. It is pervasive and profoundly shapes the social worlds inhabited by its practitioners. Thus, we should be wary of scholarly reconstructions that posit the overthrow of such a fundamental aspect of daily life on the basis of a few biblical texts, which can be construed in very different ways. In chapter 4, I address one of the most problematic assertions about the cult of dead kin—that it is systematically condemned by biblical writers because it is antithetical to the cult of YHWH and the Jerusalem temple. Some of the biblical evidence cited in support of this argument includes the biblical polemics against necromancy, which condemn this divinatory practice in strong terms. However, I argue that we must not conflate necromancy with the cult of dead kin. Though these cultic phenomena share an interest in the dead, they are fundamentally different in terms of sociopolitical context, constitutive rites, participants, and function. Thus, the next chapter examines biblical polemics against necromancy and argues that they should not be interpreted as condemnation of the cult of dead kin, nor an indication of the cult's diminished status in any period.

2

NECROMANCY AND RITUAL CARE
FOR THE DEAD

Previous studies of the cult of dead kin in the Hebrew Bible and ancient Israel have struggled to articulate its relationship with necromancy. Many note that they are separate practices. Yet, due to their common concern for the dead, they are often grouped together, especially in treatments that attempt to theorize death-related rituals more generally or to reconstruct changes in conceptions of these practices over time.[1] Regarding the latter,

---

1. Several studies initially separate these two cultic phenomena only to conflate them later in their analyses. Lewis draws a distinction between cult of the dead and necromancy, which he characterizes as "a form of divination belonging more to the sphere of 'black magic'" (*Cults of the Dead*, 2). Later in his analysis, however, he groups them together: "There was an ongoing battle by the Yahwism which emerges as normative against the practice of necromancy and other death cult rituals such as self-laceration and presenting offerings to the deceased" (176). For a critique of the category of magic, see below. Schmidt initially distinguishes ancestor cult from necromancy (*Israel's Beneficent Dead*, 5 n. 2), but then groups them together in order to reconstruct ancestor cult in Israel because "beliefs associated with necromancy closely approximate those connected with ancestor cult, particularly a belief in the supernatural benevolent power of the dead" (143). This "distinct but together" principle appears again in Van der Toorn's treatment of family religion, in which he draws a distinction between the two practices (*Family Religion*, 233). But then he goes on to group them together based on their concern for the dead: "Necromancy being intimately related with the cult of the dead (it is conceived of as a consultation of the 'ōbôt, the departed fathers, in 1 Samuel 28:3), it could be seen as a form of divination legitimized by the ideology of family religion" (318). Blenkinsopp differentiates between what he calls "death cults," which include disposal of the corpse and rites of commemoration, and "ancestor cult," which assumes that dead kin not only had a postmortem existence but also were able to positively or negatively influence the lives of the living ("Deuteronomy and the Politics," 2–3). As careful as he tries to be about terminology, however, Blenkinsopp's definition of kin-based cult is confused at times. For example, he refers

studies often cite biblical polemics against necromancy as evidence that the biblical writers eventually condemn the cult of dead kin.[2] Many of these scholarly reconstructions posit that cultic interactions with the dead pose a theological problem for biblical writers, specifically that the dead threaten so-called Yahwistic monotheism because of their divine status and polluting nature. Thus, many reconstructions assume that the practices comprising both cult of dead kin and necromancy are condemned by biblical writers. To be sure, the practice of necromancy is strongly condemned in most of the biblical texts in which it appears. However, as I argue in this chapter, we must reconsider the assumption by many that this polemic extends to the cult of dead kin, which itself demonstrates few similarities with the practice of necromancy. Grouping these two cultic phenomena together on the basis of their concern for the dead obscures the fact that the textual evidence—both biblical and cuneiform—treats them differently. By examining these differences, we may better understand the context of necromantic practice, including its setting, participants, and relationship to other forms of cult.

The definition of necromancy varies among scholarly treatments. While some regard necromancy as the attempt to procure information from the dead, others have broadened this definition to include the invocation of the dead in general.[3] I opt for the former, for in my view, the

---

to cult offered to ancestors as "an important integrative element of the social, religious and emotional bond of kinship, and that it took the form of cultic acts offered to them or on their behalf" (3). Yet, in a footnote (n. 6) detailing this interaction, Blenkinsopp cites 1 Sam 28 as the "most familiar example" of such kin-based cult, which ignores the fact that kinship plays no role in that narrative.

2. Such treatments often locate this condemnation of the cult of dead kin in the Persian period. I will review and critique such reconstructions of the cult in ch. 4.

3. "Necromancy, the art or practice of conjuring up the souls of the dead, is primarily a form of divination. The principle purpose of seeking such communication with the dead is to obtain information from them, generally regarding the revelation of unknown causes or the future course of events." See Erika Bourguignon, "Necromancy," *EncRel* 10:345–47. Variations of this definition are commonly used in treatments of necromancy in ancient West Asia. See, e.g., Ann Jeffers: "The purpose of [necromancy] is to obtain directly from the spirits of the dead information concerning the causes of past events or the course of future events." See Jeffers, *Magic and Divination in Ancient Palestine and Syria* (Leiden: Brill, 1996), 167. Schmidt notes that necromancy "involves the communication with the dead for the purpose of retrieving information" (*Israel's Beneficent Dead*, 11). Christophe Nihan regards necromancy as "any form of knowledge obtained by way of consultation of a defunct person." See

dead may be invoked for different reasons and by different means. Conflating these different modes of invocation into a monolithic category, "necromancy," runs the risk of obscuring how these modes function in their particular contexts.[4] Necromancy constitutes one mode of such invocation and focuses particularly on the acquisition of privileged information.[5] It differs in significant ways from other modes of invocation and interaction with the dead, including the practices that comprise cult of dead kin as defined in chapter 1.[6] Thus, I understand necromancy to be

---

"1 Samuel 28 and the Condemnation of Necromancy in Persian Yehud," in *Magic in the Biblical World: From the Rod of Aaron to the Ring of Solomon*, ed. Todd E. Klutz (London: T&T Clark, 2003), 24. Christopher Hays defines necromancy as follows: "Ghosts could be summoned by the living to gain access to knowledge" (*Death in the Iron Age II*, 47). Josef Tropper is one who has broadened the definition of necromancy. See Tropper, *Nekromantie: Totenbefragung im Alten Orient und im Alten Testament* (Neukirchen-Vluyn: Neukirchener, 1989), 14–15.

4. Concerning the cuneiform evidence specifically, JoAnn Scurlock similarly considers necromancy as one of three distinct classes of ghost invocation. See Scurlock, "Magical Means of Dealing with Ghosts in Ancient Mesopotamia" (PhD diss., University of Chicago, 1988), 103. I will examine her categorization of these cultic phenomena further below in the section concerning the cuneiform evidence.

5. By privileged knowledge, I refer to information that the living attain only through divine assistance, such as knowledge of the future.

6. It is important to note that I do not draw this distinction between necromancy and cult of dead kin to assert the separate domains of magic and religion, a conceptually flawed binary that has hindered scholarly interpretation of various cultic practices in the ancient world—especially those deemed illicit by the dominant power structures of any given period and their normative religious discourses. In other words, I understand both necromancy and the cult of dead kin as two different aspects of religion in ancient West Asia in that they both engage with nonobvious beings through ritual. For a discussion of the problems with magic as a category with which to theorize religion, see Jonathan Z. Smith, "Trading Places," in *Relating Religion* (Chicago: University of Chicago Press, 2004), 215–22. Concerning the ancient Mediterranean more specifically, studies such as those of Alan F. Segal and John G. Gager have also treated the problematic separation between magic and religion. See Segal, "Hellenistic Magic: Some Questions of Definition," in *Studies in Gnosticism and Hellenistic Religions*, ed. Roel van den Broek and Maarten J. Vermaseren, EPRO 91 (Leiden: Brill, 1981), 349–75; Gager, "Introduction," in *Curse Tablets and Binding Spells from the Ancient World* (Oxford: Oxford University Press, 1992), 22–25. Such studies note the embeddedness of the category of magic and related concepts (e.g., primitivism) in a predominantly Western discourse whose ways of thinking about non-Western cultures are heavily influenced by imperialist interests and political rhetoric. See, among others, Todd E. Klutz, "Reinterpreting 'Magic': An Introduction," in Klutz, *Magic in the Biblical World*,

the acquisition of privileged information from the dead for the benefit of the living. In this chapter, I examine the references to necromancy in the Hebrew Bible and cuneiform sources to determine any recurring features in these textual depictions of necromantic practice. After outlining these features, I consider the relationship between necromancy and the cult of dead kin in these texts. Ultimately, I argue that these are distinct practices with their own internal logic. Thus, evidence for necromancy, including biblical polemic against it, is not indicative of the status of the cult of dead kin in the ideologies represented in the Hebrew Bible nor, likely, the ways in which ancient Israelite practitioners understood the cult.

It is worth mentioning at the outset that there are relatively few references to necromancy in either the Hebrew Bible or cuneiform sources. Yet, this category of cult looms large in reconstructions of ancient religion. This emphasis is no doubt due in part to the negative portrayal of necromancy in the Hebrew Bible and its association with allegedly foreign cult.[7] Thus,

---

1–9. While noting the problems with *magic* as a term, other studies have attempted to rehabilitate it through more precise definition. See, e.g., Rüdiger Schmitt, "The Problem of Magic and Monotheism in the Book of Leviticus," *JHS* 8 (2008): 7. He defines magic as "performative symbolic acts, which are performed to achieve a certain result by divine intervention." By emphasizing the intervention of deities in these rituals (including YHWH), Schmitt helpfully underscores the similarities between the practices of Mesopotamian exorcists (often construed as magic by modern scholars) and the practices of Israelite priests and prophets. The underlying logic is the same—these rituals are effective because deities addressed by ritual actors make them effective. See also the similar observations of JoAnn Scurlock regarding this problematic binary. See Scurlock, "Magic: Ancient Near East," *ABD* 4:465. Thus, referring to one group of these rituals as magic and the other as religion merely reinscribes the cultic ideology of the biblical writers, which stigmatizes that which is allegedly foreign or non-Yahwistic. See also Stephen D. Ricks, "The Magician as Outsider in the Hebrew Bible and the New Testament," in *Ancient Magic and Ritual Power*, ed. Marvin Meyer and Paul Mirecki, RGRW 129 (Leiden: Brill, 1995), 131 n. 2; Rüdiger Schmitt, *Magie im Alten Testament* (Münster: Ugarit-Verlag, 2004), 368–74; Ann Jeffers, "Magic from before the Dawn of Time: Understanding Magic in the Old Testament: A Shift in Paradigm (Deuteronomy 18.9–14 and Beyond)," in *A Kind of Magic: Understanding Magic in the New Testament and Its Religious Environment*, ed. Michael Labahn and Bert Jan Lietaert Peerbolte (New York: T&T Clark, 2007), 123–32.

7. The association between foreignness and illicit cultic activity is a recurring trope throughout the Hebrew Bible. Some texts, for instance, associate foreigners with various kinds of negatively construed cultic practices. See Christopher T. Begg, "Foreigner," *ABD* 2:829–30, for a brief survey of the terminology and depiction of foreigners in the Hebrew Bible. For a discussion of the Canaanite origins of practices

it is necessary to balance the biblical polemic with the portrayal of necromancy in nonbiblical texts in order to establish recurring characteristics of its practice.[8] Another preliminary consideration is the inherent problem in comparing these texts, which in some cases are separated not only by language but also hundreds of years and thousands of miles. Despite this geographical and chronological disparity, we must work with the material available to us. A persistent danger in doing so, of course, is focusing solely on shared features in the texts and failing to recognize the ways in which they reflect specific, localized concerns. Similarities do emerge among ancient necromantic texts, but the differences between them are equally important, for they may illuminate regional differences, different emphases in particular literary genres, and changes in necromantic practice over time. To combat this methodological problem, I examine not only the

---

such as child sacrifice, Asherah worship, and necromancy, see Schmidt, *Israel's Beneficent Dead*, 138–39, in which he argues that this association is a deliberate distortion by the biblical writers that serves their polemic against such practices. See, similarly, the discussion of "willful confusion" regarding cultic practices in Deuteronomistic polemics in Saul M. Olyan, *Asherah and the Cult of Yahweh in Israel* (Atlanta: Scholars Press, 1988), 11–13. For a broader discussion of the stigmatizing rhetoric against foreigners and foreignness in different biblical texts, see Saul M. Olyan, "Stigmatizing Associations: The Alien, Things Alien, and Practices Associated with Aliens in Biblical Classification Schemas," in *The Foreigner and the Law: Perspectives from the Hebrew Bible and the Ancient Near East*, ed. Reinhard Achenbach, Rainer Albertz, and Jakob Wökrle (Wiesbaden: Harrassowitz, 2011), 17–28.

8. The Ugaritic textual evidence bears no unambiguous witness to necromancy (with the exception, perhaps, of *KTU* 1.124) despite the prevalence of the divine royal dead (*rapi'ūma*) in the Ugaritic texts. However, see Tropper, *Nekromantie*, 151–56, for the interpretation of *KTU* 1.124 as a necromantic text. Egyptian necromancy, however, is a potentially fruitful source of comparison and would be an interesting avenue of future research. See, e.g., Robert Ritner, "Necromancy in Ancient Egypt," in *Magic and Divination in the Ancient World*, ed. Leda Ciraolo and Jonathan Seidel (Leiden: Brill, 2002), 89–96. The practice of necromancy in Hittite texts may also provide useful points of comparison with the biblical evidence, especially as it relates to the use of ritual pits in communicating with the dead. See, e.g., Billie Jean Collins, "Necromancy, Fertility, and the Dark Earth: The Use of Ritual Pits in Hittite Cult," in *Magic and Ritual in the Ancient World*, ed. Paul Mirecki and Marvin Meyer (Leiden: Brill, 2002), 224–38; Gregory McMahon, "Comparative Observations on Hittite Rituals," in *Recent Developments in Hittite Archaeology and History: Papers in Memory of Hans G. Guterbock*, ed. K. Aslihan Yener and Harry A. Hoffner Jr. (Winona Lake, IN: Eisenbrauns, 2002), 132–35.

texts themselves but also (when possible) their individual contexts and the different textual traditions of which they are part.

Necromancy in the Hebrew Bible

The overarching theme in biblical depictions of necromancy is that it is characterized as an illicit, non-Yahwistic form of divination. Texts referring to necromancy include Lev 19:31; 20:6, 27; Deut 18:11; 1 Sam 28:3–19; 2 Kgs 21:6; 23:24; Isa 8:19; 19:3; 29:4; 1 Chr 10:13–14; and 2 Chr 33:6. These texts employ different styles and, sometimes, different vocabulary in their references to necromancy. Such differences may reflect a variety of factors, including social milieu and time period. Yet, their shared features suggest a rough sketch of necromancy in the minds of the biblical writers. For instance, some passages attest to the presence of cult specialists acting as intermediaries between the living and the dead. Others suggest that necromancy is utilized in moments of crisis. Most important, all of these passages lack any reference to the family or the concerns governing care for dead kin; at no point do the texts refer to any of the features of the cult of dead kin outlined in chapter 1. This lacuna reinforces the distinction between necromancy and the cult of dead kin as cultic phenomena because they entail different methods and accomplish different ends. In what follows, I will examine the biblical texts depicting necromancy, discuss the ways in which they overlap and differ from each other, and consider the scholarly debates surrounding their social and historical contexts.

The dating of biblical texts referring to necromancy is highly contested. The debates surrounding the dating of these texts often run along the fault lines of much larger debates within the field regarding source criticism, the dependence of texts on one another, and the direction of that dependence (i.e., if text A and text B are similar, which draws on the other, or do they emerge independently from a common earlier text or shared historical experience?).[9] The recognition of different redactional layers within these necromancy texts inevitably involves these larger interpretive and methodological issues. Indeed, the dating of these texts often entails arranging them and their constitutive parts into a relative chronol-

---

9. For a recent discussion of the difficulty in, first, identifying intertextual allusions in the Hebrew Bible and, second, determining the direction of that influence, see Jeffery M. Leonard, "Identifying Inner-Biblical Allusions: Psalm 78 as a Test Case," *JBL* 127 (2008): 241–65.

ogy based on (1) their context within larger hypothetical sources (e.g., the Deuteronomistic History), which are dated differently by scholars, and (2) how they may reflect the sociopolitical circumstances of Israel and Judah before, during, and after the Babylonian exile. The varying results of these approaches attest to the highly subjective nature of these dating methods. Thus, while I offer some tentative arguments regarding the dating of the biblical necromancy texts cited below, I am aware of the largely speculative nature of both relative and absolute dating of these texts. Furthermore, the contribution of this chapter to the project at hand is an examination of the relationship between necromancy and the cult of dead kin as depicted by different ancient texts with the resulting argument that the phenomena are separate. This distinction between the phenomena seems to be consistent throughout biblical texts; thus, a diachronic analysis of biblical necromancy is unnecessary for the present project but may prove a fruitful avenue of future study.

In a discussion of biblical necromancy, it is perhaps best to begin with our most descriptive account of the practice in the Hebrew Bible, 1 Sam 28:

> As for Samuel, he was dead. All of Israel had lamented for him, and they buried him in Ramah, his city. As for Saul, he had expelled *hāʾōbôt wəʾet-hayyiddəʿōnîm*[10] from the land. The Philistines mustered themselves and came and encamped at Shunem. Saul mustered all of Israel, and they encamped at Gilboa. When Saul saw the encampment of the Philistines, he was afraid and his heart trembled greatly. When Saul inquired of YHWH, YHWH did not answer him—not through dreams, Urim, or prophets. Saul said to his servants, "Seek out a female necromancer[11] for

---

10. I have left this phrase untranslated due to the varying ways in which it is used in different biblical passages, referring either to ghosts and spirits summoned during necromancy or to the necromancers who summon them. The latter sense of the phrase seems to be employed in this particular text; however, leaving the phrase untranslated in this text and those that follow underscores the differences in terminology between biblical necromancy texts and the conceptual differences between their depictions of necromancy. For a discussion of the components of this phrase and their history of interpretation, see Tropper, *Nekromantie*, 189–201, and the more recent discussion in Hays, *Death in Iron Age II*, 170–74. Hays proposes a new etymology of the Hebrew *ʾôb* as deriving from the Egyptian term for an ancestor statue. See also Christopher B. Hays and Joel M. LeMon, "The Dead and Their Images: An Egyptian Etymology for Hebrew *ʾôb*," *JAEI* 1 (2009): 1–4.

11. Concerning the phrase referring to the female necromancer in 28:7, *ʾēšet baʿălat ʾôb*, Mordechai Cogan argues that this construction is a double construct, which

me so that I may go to her and inquire through her." His servants said to him, "There is a female necromancer at En-dor." Saul disguised himself; he dressed in different clothes, and he went with two of his men. They came to the woman at night, and he said, "Divine by means of a ghost for me. Bring up for me whomever I say to you." The woman said to him, "Surely you know what Saul has done, that he has cut off *hā'ōbōt wə'et-hayyiddə'ōnîm*[12] from the land. Why are you laying snares for me to get me killed?" Saul swore to her by YHWH, "As YHWH lives, punishment for this thing shall not befall you." The woman said, "Whom shall I bring up for you?" He said, "Bring up Samuel for me." Then the woman saw Samuel and cried out in a loud voice. The woman said to Saul, "Why have you deceived me? You are Saul!" The king said to her, "Do not be afraid. What do you see?" The woman said to Saul, "I see an *'ĕlōhîm*[13]

"sometimes bears an appositional sense, e.g., *bĕtûlat bat ṣiyôn*, 'the virgin, daughter of Zion' (Isa 37:22)" and should not be understood as a conflation. See Cogan, "The Road to En-dor," in *Pomegranates and Golden Bells: Studies in Biblical, Jewish, and Near Eastern Ritual, Law, and Literature in Honor of Jacob Milgrom*, ed. David P. Wright, David Noel Freedman, and Avi Hurvitz (Winona Lake, IN: Eisenbrauns, 1995), 325. However, Bruce Waltke and Michael P. O'Connor (*IBHS* 9.5.3b) cite the phrase in 28:7 as an example of idiomatic usage of the genitive, often occurring with the terms *'îš*, *ba'al*, *ben*, and their plural and feminine forms to convey the "nature, quality, character, or condition" of a person. Thus, they render the phrase in 28:7 as "a woman, a possessor of a spirit" or "a woman who is a medium." They do not comment on the fact that the phrase includes two genitival forms rather than one; however, that either term is commonly used in this kind of idiomatic construction suggests that the MT may be combining two different versions of this phrase in 28:7. Indeed, as P. Kyle McCarter notes in his commentary, the LXX rendering of the phrase, *gynaika engastrimython*, suggests that the original phrase may have been *'ēšet 'ôb*. See McCarter, *I Samuel: A New Translation with Introduction, Notes, and Commentary* (New York: Doubleday, 1980), 418; see similarly Lewis, *Cults of the Dead*, 107. Thus, my rendering of the phrase agrees with McCarter's assessment that this construction is a conflation of two terms for a female necromancer, *'ēšet 'ôb* and *ba'ălat 'ôb*.

12. Following Lewis, *Cults of the Dead*, 107, I understand the writing of this phrase in 28:9 (*yiddəōnî*) as an instance of haplography in which the final mem of *yiddə'ōnîm* has been lost due to the particle *min* that follows it. Indeed, *yiddə'ōnîm* often accompanies the term *'ōbōt* in this fixed phrase, as in 28:3.

13. Brian Schmidt argues that *'ĕlōhîm* in 28:13 refers not to the ghost of Samuel but to the "gods known to be summoned" in other ancient West Asian necromantic texts. See Schmidt, "The 'Witch' of En-Dor, 1 Samuel 28, and Ancient Near Eastern Necromancy," in Meyer and Mirecki, *Ancient Magic and Ritual Power*, 120–26. This interpretation, he argues, helps account for the fact that the *'ĕlōhîm* in 28:13 takes a plural participle (*'ĕlōhîm rā'îtî 'ōlîm min-hā'āreṣ*), but the *'ĕlōhîm* in 28:15 takes a

ascending from the earth." He said to her, "What is its form?" She said, "An old[14] man is ascending, and he is wrapped in a robe." Saul knew that it was Samuel, and he bowed down with his face to the ground and prostrated himself. Samuel said to Saul, "Why have you disturbed me[15]

---

singular verb (wĕ'lōhîm sār mē'ālay). Schmidt argues that the first 'ĕlōhîm refers to multiple netherworld divinities that accompany the dead person invoked in the ritual, while the second refers to YHWH. Ultimately, this argument is unconvincing. When Saul asks what "his/its form" looks like in 28:14, it seems clear based on the flow of the narrative that Saul is referring to the appearance of the 'ĕlōhîm in the previous verse and thus a singular entity. It would be surprising indeed if a flock of netherworld divinities were to suddenly appear in the narrative and neither Saul nor the supposed post-Deuteronomistic writer (posited by Schmidt) had anything to say about them. Furthermore, 1 Sam 28:13 is not the only place where 'ĕlōhîm, construed as a singular, takes a plural form. In Josh 24:19, for example, 'ĕlōhîm (referring to YHWH) takes both a singular verb (yiśśā') and a plural adjective (qĕdōšîm). Furthermore, Waltke and O'Connor (IBHS 7.4.3d) note that the "honorific plural" is often used for participles referring to YHWH (Job 35:10; Ps 118:7; Isa 42:5) or individual humans (Isa 10:15; Judg 11:35). Thus, the plurality of the participle in this verse need not lead to speculative interpretations of 'ĕlōhîm as referring to any divine being other than the dead Samuel invoked during the necromantic ritual depicted in this text.

14. The LXX version has orthion, "erect," instead of an equivalent term for the Hebrew zāqēn, "old." McCarter prefers the LXX term as the lectio difficilior and argues that the orthography of final nun and pe is easily mistaken (I Samuel, 419). Thus, McCarter argues that the LXX is translating Hebrew zāqēp, "erect," instead of zāqēn. Lewis presents another possible interpretation of this phrase in which the term zāqēp derives from Akkadian zaqāpu, which in the G stem means "to erect" and in the D stem means "to make (hair) stand on end" (CAD 21:54). As Lewis notes, one text (BMS 53:9) even describes an eṭemmu making one's hair stand on end (Cults of the Dead, 116). However, the emphasis on the ghost's appearance in 28:14, which Saul then uses as confirmation of the ghost's identity as Samuel, provides a context in which the age of the ghost seems more relevant than his posture or his imposing presence. Thus, I have translated the MT version of this particular phrase due to its relevance to the surrounding narrative.

15. McCarter notes that this verb appears in the fifth-century epitaph of King Tabnit of Sidon (KAI 13.4, 6, 7), which warns against tomb robbery (I Samuel, 421). See also the discussion of this usage in HALOT 2:1182–83. Suriano also notes the appearance of this verb in multiple funerary inscriptions from the Iron Age Levant, including that of Panamuwa I (KAI 214; see Suriano, History of Death, 163–64). McCarter also posits that Job 12:6 may use this terminology, since "looters" appear in parallel with those who disturb (rgz) an 'ēl. Since the term 'ĕlōhîm may refer to the dead (and 'ēl is a closely related term), it is possible that Job 12:6 is referring to grave robbers disturbing the dead. However, such an interpretation is speculative, especially since the surrounding content of Job 12 contains no reference to the dead and, indeed, refers specifically

by bringing me up?" Saul said, "I am in great distress because the Philistines are waging war against me, but God has turned away from me and will not answer me anymore through prophets or dreams. I summoned[16] you to inform me what I should do." Samuel said, "Why do you ask me? YHWH has turned away from you and is now your adversary.[17] YHWH has acted in accordance with what he spoke through me. YHWH has torn the kingship from your hand and given it to your neighbor, David, because you did not obey YHWH and did not carry out his wrath upon Amalek.[18] Therefore, YHWH has done this thing to you today. In addition, YHWH will deliver Israel with you into the hand of the Philistines. Tomorrow, you and your sons will be with me. YHWH will also deliver the camp of Israel into the hand of the Philistines."

While other biblical texts referring to necromancy are mainly limited to brief prohibitions against its practice or slightly more descriptive references to its inefficacy, the narrative of 1 Sam 28 provides a difficult but descriptive account of the invocation of the dead, which may reflect features of necromantic practice as a historical reality or, at least, its preferred representation in the mind of the biblical writer. First, the list of failed divinatory attempts in verse 6 not only indicates the different methods of divination available to Saul but also suggests that necromancy is a divinatory method of last resort.[19] It is only after failing to receive an answer

to YHWH in 12:9, which suggests that YHWH is the ʾēl or ʾĕlōhîm referred to earlier in the passage. In fact, most attestations of this verb in the *hiphil*, "to cause to quake, disquiet, enrage," refer to the great power of YHWH to shake the earth (Isa 13:13, 23:11; Jer 50:34; Job 2:3). Thus, the reference to robbers shaking or disquieting ʾēl in Job 12:6 may signify a reversal of this normal hierarchy of power, a fundamental disturbance in the ideal relationship between Israel and YHWH (see Ezek 16:43).

16. Lewis notes that the verb of summoning here (qrʾ) is the same used repeatedly in the Ugaritic funerary text (*KTU* 1.161) to summon the *rapiʾūma* (*Cults of the Dead*, 117). However, it is unclear that *KTU* 1.161 entails any necromantic encounter.

17. Following *HALOT* 1:876, I interpret this term ʿār as an Aramaicized form of the Hebrew term ṣār, "adversary." Examples of the Aramaic form appear in Sir 37:5; 47:7. The Akkadian term arû, meaning "enemy," is also attested (*CAD* 1.2:313).

18. This reference to Amalek is clearly an allusion to the narrative in 1 Sam 15, in which YHWH commands Saul to submit the Amalekites to the ban (15:3) by annihilating them and their livestock. However, Saul spares the Amalekite king Agag as well as the livestock (15:9), which leads to YHWH regret his decision to make Saul king (15:11) and to express that regret to Samuel.

19. In this case, that necromancy is Saul's last resort seems related to his earlier prohibition against the practice, to which the narrative alludes in 28:3, 9. It seems

from YHWH through dreams, Urim, and (living) prophets that Saul turns to the necromancer at Endor. Second, the ritual involves three participants—Samuel, Saul, and the necromancer—who, notably, are not related through kinship. In other words, a ritual specialist must intercede on behalf of the living petitioner. Third, although the necromancer invokes the dead Samuel, the text does not refer to the presence of Samuel's corpse. In fact, the notice in verse 3 about his burial in Ramah seems to reinforce the idea that his body is not a necessary component of the ritual. This observation challenges the argument made by some scholars that necromancy poses a threat to Yahwism as expressed in Deuteronomistic ideology because it troubles the binaries of life/purity and death/impurity.[20] The 1 Sam 28 account gives no indication that the summoning of Samuel requires his corpse, nor should we expect Samuel's bones buried in Ramah to suddenly make an appearance at Endor. Therefore, the argument that polemic against necromancy assumes an anxiety about pollution through corpse contact is unsupported by this biblical text. Fourth, the narrative of 1 Sam 28 portrays a successful necromantic encounter,[21] meaning that the

---

that Saul does not want to be caught practicing the type of divination he himself has condemned.

20. See, e.g., Albertz and Schmitt, *Household and Family Religion*, 470; Stephen L. Cook, "Death, Kinship, and Community: Afterlife and the חסד Ideal in Israel," in Dutcher-Walls, *Family in Life*, 119.

21. It is difficult to interpret this encounter as anything but successful. Even though the information Saul receives is not the outcome he desires, the necromancer and her method of divination prove effective. Indeed, compare Samuel's oracle in 1 Sam 28 with the characterization of "true prophecy" in Deut 18:22 ("When a prophet speaks in the name of YHWH and the thing does not happen or come about, then that was not the thing that YHWH spoke. The prophet spoke it in arrogance, and you should not fear him"). By the standards of that text, the necromantic encounter in 1 Sam 28 is an instance of Yahwistic divination. However, as Karen Smelik notes in her study of 1 Sam 28's history of interpretation, many theological treatments of the text have struggled with this aspect of the story, particularly its incompatibility with so-called biblical monotheism. See Smelik, "The Witch of Endor: 1 Samuel 28 in Rabbinic and Christian Exegesis Till 800 A.D.," *VC* 33 (1977): 163–65. Recent work on divination in Israelite religion, however, emphasizes the agency of the necromancer in 1 Sam 28 in her successful summoning of the dead prophet Samuel. See, e.g., Esther J. Hamori, "The Prophet and the Necromancer: Women's Divination for Kings," *JBL* 132 (2013): 827–43; Hamori, *Women's Divination in Biblical Literature: Prophecy, Necromancy, and Other Arts of Knowledge* (New Haven: Yale University Press, 2015). Further, Hamori convincingly argues against the assumption that the necromancer

necromancer succeeds in raising the dead prophet Samuel, who accurately reveals Saul's future. In addition, it portrays necromancy as the source of Yahwistic divination—Yahwistic in the sense that Samuel accurately reports YHWH's condemnation of Saul and its imminent repercussions. Finally, the use of the term 'ĕlōhîm referring to the dead Samuel suggests that the text classes him as a divine being.[22]

While some scholars posit a relatively early date for the composition of 1 Sam 28 in the preexilic period, others argue that its terminology and sociopolitical context are that of Persian Yehud. A common argument among those who posit a preexilic date for 1 Sam 28 is that Saul's encounter with the necromancer is an integral part of the cycle of stories surrounding Saul and David.[23] Furthermore, that the Deuteronomists include the narrative of 1 Sam 28 in the Deuteronomistic History suggests to Lewis that the narrative was already well known at that time, making it impossible to completely suppress.[24] The only recourse, Lewis argues, is to use the narrative to the Deuteronomists' benefit, employing it to depict the downfall of Saul (cultic and otherwise) and the rise of David to the kingship. Other interpreters, such as P. Kyle McCarter, argue that different redactional layers of the text date to different periods, including original, pre-Deuteronomistic narratives, a prophetic redaction in the eighth century, and Deuteronomistic redactions during the reign of Josiah and the Babylonian exile.[25]

Other treatments of 1 Sam 28 place the text in the Persian period due to its use of Deuteronomistic language and its reflection of supposed developments in Israelite religion in this period.[26] For instance, Christophe Nihan argues that 1 Sam 28 belongs to a Persian context because it

---

at Endor is practicing a foreign form of cult. Having summoned a dead Yahwistic prophet to deliver an accurate Yahwistic oracle, there is no indication that the necromancer is engaged in any non-Yahwistic activity (*Women's Divination*, 111–12).

22. See ch. 1 for a discussion of this term as it relates to the dead and my preference for understanding the status of the dead as *divine* beings rather than *preternatural*, *semidivine*, or *supernatural*. For my interpretation of this term as indicating a singular divine being rather than a collective, see my comments in the notes above.

23. E.g., Johnston, *Shades of Sheol*, 418; Cogan, "Road to En-dor," 325; Bill T. Arnold, "Necromancy and Cleromancy in 1 and 2 Samuel," *CBQ* 66 (2004): 199–213.

24. Lewis, *Cults of the Dead*, 117.

25. McCarter, *I Samuel*, 15–18.

26. On Deuteronomistic language, see, e.g., Nihan, "1 Samuel 28," 34–35 n. 50; Schmidt, *Israel's Beneficent Dead*, 111 and passim.

aims to denigrate and undermine the Israelite cult of dead kin—which for Nihan includes necromancy—a cultic development that he argues takes place in the Persian period. His interpretation of the text as an attack on necromancy stems from his interpretation of the text as a demonstration that Saul is unable to manipulate YHWH through necromancy.[27] He makes this argument on the basis of the necromancer's recognition of Saul in verse 12, saying that Saul is unable to remain anonymous to the necromancer. However, Saul's lack of anonymity does not seem relevant in determining the efficacy of the necromantic ritual, so this interpretation is ultimately unconvincing.

In addition, following the arguments of Albertz, Nihan argues that family religion rose in prominence during the exilic and postexilic periods due to the disappearance of "traditional cultic institutions."[28] It was in this context, Nihan argues, that the conflict between "Yahwist orthodoxy" and family religion produced such texts as Isa 8:19–20 and 1 Sam 28. The central issue, he states, is the threat posed by necromancy to "Yahwistic monotheism."[29] One problem with this interpretation, as I note throughout this chapter, is the conflation of necromancy and cult of dead kin. In fact, even Nihan struggles to make sense of the fact that 1 Sam 28 does not depict necromancy as involving kin.[30] Another problem, however, is Nihan's assertion that 1 Sam 28 advocates for Yahwistic monotheism, which I argue is an anachronistic characterization of Israelite religion in any period.[31] More to the point, such a characterization is at odds with 1 Sam 28 itself, since verse 13 refers to Samuel as an ʾĕlōhîm. If we accept Nihan's dating schema, then we must contend with the fact that a Persian-period writer of 1 Sam 28, bent on portraying the sole divine authority and existence of YHWH, explicitly refers to a different divine being who has access to privileged knowledge (about YHWH, no less) and is capable of exerting influence on the living. How does this depiction of the dead

---

27. Nihan, "1 Samuel 28," 51. As I note above, however, it is difficult to view this necromantic encounter as unsuccessful because it accurately informs Saul about YHWH's imminent punishment.

28. Nihan, "1 Samuel 28," 52.

29. Nihan, "1 Samuel 28," 53.

30. Nihan, "1 Samuel 28," 49.

31. For recent discussions of monotheism and its limitations as a category of analysis for Israelite religion, see Levtow, *Images of Others*; Saul M. Olyan, "Is Isaiah 40–55 Really Monotheistic?," *JANER* 12 (2012): 190–201. I expand on this point further in ch. 4.

Samuel support the interests of "Yahwistic monotheism"? In my view, it reflects no such ideological interests. Instead, the usage of *ʾĕlōhîm* in verse 13, which differs from the typical Deuteronomistic terminology used for ghosts and necromancers (e.g., in 1 Sam 28:7, *ʾēšet baʿălat ʾôb*; in Deut 18:11, *šōʾēl ʾôb*), may point to an original pre-Deuteronomistic context rather than a post-Deuteronomistic one. Finally, as I argue in chapter 4, the claim that Yahwistic orthodoxy opposes family religion in the Persian period also has its problems due to the interdependence of centralized and local cultic spheres.

The different redactional layers of 1 Sam 28 (as noted by the scholars cited above) offer the best explanation for (1) the Deuteronomistic language of 1 Sam 28 and (2) the stark differences between it and other biblical texts referring to necromancy. For example, 1 Sam 28 and the Isaiah passages depict the efficacy of necromancy differently. Isaiah 8:19–20 refers to the ignorance and futility (lack of "dawn") in seeking the counsel of ghosts that chirp and mutter.[32] Isaiah 29:4 refers to the lowliness of Jerusalem through comparison with a ghost chirping from the earth. In short, these Isaiah texts do not depict necromancy as particularly effective because of the unintelligibility and powerlessness of the dead, epitomized by their feeble, chirping voices. In stark contrast, 1 Sam 28 depicts necromancy as effective in that Samuel offers an articulate, accurate prediction of the future and communicates the will of the deity (albeit YHWH's great disapproval) to the living petitioner. In no way does it denigrate the dead Samuel or suggest his powerlessness. Therefore, it does not necessarily follow that these texts come from the same conceptual milieu concerning necromancy and its efficacy.

Furthermore, the advocates for a postexilic date of composition for 1 Sam 28 do not offer an adequate explanation of why the supposedly Persian-period writer of 1 Sam 28:3–25 would choose to focus on the figure of Saul when Saul recedes almost entirely from the biblical narrative by the end of the History of David's Rise, after which he is of little interest to the biblical writers.[33] It is unclear why a Persian-period writer would retroject a narrative about necromancy back into the reign of Saul. What seems more likely is that a narrative concerning Saul and necromancy

---

32. See also my treatment of the Isaiah passages later in this chapter.

33. With the exceptions of Pss 18, 52, 54, 57, and 59 as well as the monarchical history in Chronicles. Yet even in Chronicles, the treatment of Saul is minimal. Overall, Saul is a relatively minor figure in this version of Israelite history.

already existed in this period and was then embellished for the purposes of postexilic writers. Nihan's argument that necromancy is the Deuteronomistic epitome of turning away from YHWH ignores the fact that 1 Sam 28 explicitly gives a different rationale for YHWH's abandonment of Saul, his failure to annihilate Amalek (28:18). That Chronicles understands the cause of Saul's downfall to be his use of necromancy indicates a later interpretation of his reign and, perhaps, an interest in repurposing a prior version of 1 Sam 28 depicting Saul's encounter with a necromancer. Thus, it seems plausible that a relatively early version of 1 Sam 28 depicting Saul's necromantic encounter predates the Deuteronomistic polemic against Manasseh's necromantic practice, which is later applied to Saul in the Chronicles account of Israel's history. These developments in biblical depictions of necromancy and its relationship to kingship probably resulted in the Deuteronomistic and post-Deuteronomistic updating of 1 Sam 28 in order to incorporate the preexisting narrative into this broader framework of the rise and fall of kings. However, these redactions do not completely efface some of the earlier narrative features that make 1 Sam 28 distinct from other accounts of necromancy.

Three references to necromancy appear in Leviticus,[34] and these references demonstrate both similarities and differences regarding terminology and emphasis:

---

34. The dating of these passages in Leviticus inevitably involves larger issues of source criticism, including the relationship between the Priestly and Holiness sources and their relative dating. The passages in question fall within the Holiness Code (Lev 17–26), so the most relevant part of these debates for the present study is the provenance of the Holiness source as a whole and Lev 19:31; 20:6, 27 in particular. Israel Knohl argues that the Holiness source is the redactor of the Priestly source and that 95 percent of the Holiness source was composed in the eighth century BCE, while the remaining 5 percent belongs in the exilic period. See Knohl, *Sanctuary of Silence* (Minneapolis: Fortress, 1995), 11–23; see also Jacob Milgrom, "H$_R$ in Leviticus and Elsewhere in the Torah," in *The Book of Leviticus: Composition and Reception*, ed. Rolf Rendtorff and Robert A. Kugler (Leiden: Brill, 2003), 25. Milgrom's rationale for dating the Holiness source to the reign of Hezekiah is partly due to his reconstruction of the development of Israelite religion, particularly the cultic competition between ritual specialists—including priests, prophets, and necromancers—that developed as a result of Assyrian influence and the fall of the Northern Kingdom in the eighth century (Jacob Milgrom, *Leviticus 17–22: A New Translation with Introduction and Commentary* [New York: Doubleday, 2000], 1701). Other commentators argue that, despite its use of older material, the bulk of Leviticus dates to the Persian period due to its relatively late terminology and overall worldview. See, e.g., Erhard S.

Do not turn to *hā'ōbōt wəhayyiddə'ōnîm*; do not seek to be defiled by them. I, YHWH, am your god. (Lev 19:31)

As for the person who turns to *hā'ōbōt wəhayyiddə'ōnîm* in order to whore after them, I will set my face against that person, and I will cut him off from the midst of his people. (Lev 20:6)

As for a man or a woman in whom there is *'ōb 'ô yiddə'ōnî*, he will surely die. They will stone them with stones; their blood will be upon them. (Lev 20:27)

The nature of the material surrounding these passages differs: Lev 19:31 is situated within a long list of negative imperatives, while 20:6, 27 belongs to a passage of conditional statements. In addition, the reference to child sacrifice in Lev 20 (vv. 3–5) is absent in Lev 19.[35] The necromantic termi-

---

Gerstenberger, *Leviticus: A Commentary* (Louisville: Westminster John Knox, 1996), 6; Baruch Levine, "Leviticus: Its Literary History and Location in Biblical Literature," in Rendtorff and Kugler, *Book of Leviticus*, 15–16. I tend more toward this schema of dating the passages in Leviticus. As I will demonstrate in greater detail below, the passages themselves demonstrate significant differences, which may stem from the fact that they come from different writers operating in different periods. I find it plausible that anxiety about necromancers flourished among Israelite cult specialists in the eighth century, especially in the years before and after the downfall of northern Israel; however, this rhetoric continues to be of use in later exilic and postexilic polemic concerning the alleged cultic misdeeds of Judah and Manasseh and the Deuteronomistic rationale for the Babylonian exile.

    35. References to child sacrifice and necromancy also appear in Deut 18:10–12; 2 Kgs 21:6; 2 Chr 33:6. These verses refer to the practice of *mlk* sacrifice, the sacrifice of children attested not only in the biblical text but also Phoenician, Punic, and later classical texts. For the interpretation of Hebrew *mlk* as the proper name of a god Molech, see, e.g., Moshe Weinfeld, "The Worship of Molech and of the Queen of Heaven and Its Background," *UF* 4 (1972): 133–54; John Day, *Molech: A God of Human Sacrifice in the Old Testament* (Cambridge: Cambridge University Press, 1990). For the interpretation of the term as a kind of sacrifice, see Otto Eissfeldt, *Molk als Opferbegriff im Punischen und Hebräischen und das Ende des Gottes Moloch*, BRA 4 (Halle: Niemeyer, 1935). Extrabiblical evidence supports the latter interpretation, including the eighth-century BCE Incirli stela found in southern Turkey and the second-century CE Ngaous inscriptions, both of which refer to types of a *mlk* sacrifice (e.g., *mlk swsm*, "a *mlk* of horses," or *mlk 'mr*, "a *mlk* of a lamb"). Furthermore, Day's argument that the biblical idiom "to play the harlot after" only occurs with a deity (and thus affects our translation of *mlk* as a deity in Lev 20:5) does not adequately consider the use of this idiom in passages that condemn certain divinatory practices, such as Judg 8:27; Hos

nology of 20:27 is noticeably different as well.[36] Unlike the relatively fixed phrase *hāʾōbōt wəhayyiddəʿōnîm*, the two terms are separated by the conjunction *ʾô*, "or," and appear in seemingly singular forms. This variation of the necromancy formula in 20:27 (*ʾôb ʾô yiddəʿōnî*) seems to understand the two terms not as comprising a hendiadys but as synonyms.[37] In addition, the phrase may indicate an underlying principle of necromantic practice—that is, a single entity inhabits the necromancer during the ritual. In other words, an *ʾôb* or *yiddəʿōnî* inhabits the male or female necromancer, which may allow the necromancer to speak for the dead.

A description of the performance of necromantic ritual is almost entirely absent from these passages, which offer no indication of the context in which necromantic divination is sought. However, the Leviticus passages offer some insight regarding the participants in necromantic ritual. The stated audience of Lev 19:2 is "all the congregation of Israel," which provides the most plausible antecedent for the second masculine plural entity addressed in 19:31. Thus, the text is condemning either the practice of necromancy by lay Israelites themselves or the Israelites' patronage of necromancers as cult specialists. Similarly, the stated audience of 20:2 is composed of the Israelites, and this verse goes on to specify that its prohibition against *mlk* sacrifice applies to both the Israelites and resident

---

4:12. If one can be said to play the harlot after the practice of seeking oracles, then the *mlk* may similarly stand for the cultic pursuit of divine favors through human sacrifice. Last, Day argues that verbs of offering (*hʿbr, ntn, śrp*) that appear with the particle *lə* are only followed by a divine name. Therefore, according to his interpretation, the *lə* after these verbs indicates offerings *to* a deity. However, Ezek 23:37 uses this construction (verb of offering + *lə*) without a divine recipient: "and they have even offered up to them *as food*." Thus, it is entirely plausible that this construction (*hʿbr* X *lə-mlk*) may refer to the offering of X as a *mlk*-sacrifice, not the offering of X to a god Molech. For a rebuttal to Weinfeld's arguments, see Morton Smith, "A Note on Burning Babies," *JAOS* 95 (1975): 477–79.

36. Based on the recurrence of the verb *tipnû*, "turn to," in both 19:31 and 20:6, Jacob Milgrom argues that the passages are composed by the same writer. See Milgrom, *Leviticus 17–22*, 1701. This terminology differs from other depictions of necromancy, which employ verbs of seeking (*dāraš*, as in 1 Sam 28:7; Deut 18:11; Isa 8:19; 19:3) or consultation (*šāʾal*, as in 1 Sam 28:6; 1 Chr 10:13). Second Kings 23:24 lacks any verb describing the action of invoking a ghost and rather refers solely to the *ʾōbōt* and *yiddəʿōnîm* themselves. Second Chronicles 33:6 uses the verb *ʿāśâ*, and 1 Sam 28:8 uses the verb *qāsam* to describe divination by necromancy.

37. For the interpretation of this phrase as a hendiadys, see Tropper, *Nekromantie*, 224; Lewis, *Cults of the Dead*, 114; Lewis, "Dead," *DDD* 229–30.

aliens in Israel. Thus, the cultic transgressor in 20:6, *nepeš*, also seems to refer to anyone—Israelite or resident alien—who practices necromancy or hires a necromancer. In Lev 20:27, the text prohibits the cultic activity of both male and female necromancers. Despite this evidence regarding the participants in necromantic ritual, however, none of these passages alludes to the participation of living or dead kin.[38]

In fact, the dead are altogether absent in these Leviticus passages. The focus is not on the inefficacy of necromancy or the powerlessness of ghosts but on the negative outcomes of the practice with respect to Yahwistic cult or legal prohibitions. While all three texts depict negative outcomes for those practicing necromancy, the nuances of these outcomes differ. Two of the outcomes are punitive, including YHWH cutting off the cultic transgressor from the land in Lev 20:6 and death by stoning in 20:27, while Lev 19:31 construes the practice of necromancy as polluting, which interferes with the Israelites' reverence for YHWH and his sanctuary. Leviticus 20:6 uses the imagery of whoring after non-Yahwistic deities, which draws on the rhetoric of covenant disloyalty to YHWH. Leviticus 20:27 lacks any reference to cult and focuses instead on the punishment of necromancers carried out by an unspecified group of people—in this case, not YHWH (see Lev 20:6). Jacob Milgrom argues that the two methods of punishment in 20:6 and 20:27 are meted out to different cultic actors involved in necromancy: "*kārēt* is prescribed for turning to a medium; death, for being one."[39] This interpretation is plausible, yet the differences in terminology

---

38. In fact, Lev 20:5–6 is notable for the different ways in which the family is implicated in cultic misdeeds. In 20:5, for instance, YHWH sets his face against the individual who offers the *mlk* sacrifice as well as his family. However, in 20:6, only the individual who practices necromancy is implicated, and it is he who is cut off from his people. While *mlk* sacrifice involves the family, the individual who resorts to necromancy seemingly acts alone. Being cut off in this context likely refers to the ending of a lineage. The concept of *kārēt* appears elsewhere in the book of Leviticus, including Lev 7:20, 21, 25, 27; 17:4, 9, 10, 14; 19:8; 20:17; 22:3. For a discussion of *kārēt*, see Jacob Milgrom, *Leviticus 1–16: A New Translation with Introduction and Commentary* (New York: Doubleday, 1991), 424–26, 945–46. Milgrom interprets *kārēt* as "a penalty formula found in P, which declares that the person's line will be terminated by God and, possibly, that he will be denied life in the hereafter" (*Leviticus 1–16*, 424).

39. Milgrom, *Leviticus 17–22*, 1739. Milgrom's interpretation of the person in 20:27 as a necromancer finds support in the LXX rendering of the Hebrew phrase *kî-yihyeh bāhem* (literally, "who has in them") as *engastrimythos*, "one who speaks from his stomach." This LXX rendering suggests that the *'ôb* and *yiddə'ōnî* are spirits

and emphasis in these two passages also suggest that they do not originate from the same writer but instead were compiled later due to their thematic consistency.

Deuteronomy 18:11 refers to the practice of necromancy, the consultation of the 'ôb wə-yiddə'ōnî (see the terminology of Lev 20:27) and those who seek the dead (dōrēš hammētîm).[40] This condemnation of necromancy is set before the Israelites' entrance into the land of Canaan, and the text bases its condemnation on the notion that the Israelites must avoid the practices of the Canaanites:

> When you enter the land that YHWH your god is giving to you, you shall not learn to act in accordance with the abominations of those nations. There shall not be found among you one who makes his son or daughter

---

that reside within the necromancer during the invocation ritual (Milgrom, *Leviticus 17–22*, 1765).

40. Interpreters of Deut 18:11 are divided regarding the most plausible historical context for the passage as well as the relationship between this passage and material surrounding it. Some commentators place Deut 18:11 in the context of the eighth or seventh century BCE due to the possible anxiety about Neo-Assyrian cultic influence. See, e.g., Gottfried Seitz, *Redaktiongeschichtliche Studien zum Deuteronomium*, BWANT 93 (Stuttgart: Kohlhammer, 1971), 306. Jack Lundbom places Deut 18:10–12 in this period, arguing that the activity of eighth-century prophets likely expanded the restrictions of the Covenant Code, which only states that a "sorceress" must be put to death, to include cult specialists influenced by cult and divination in the Neo-Assyrian Empire. See Lundbom, *Deuteronomy: A Commentary* (Grand Rapids: Eerdmans, 2013), 554. However, the pervasive similarities between Deut 18:10–11 and 2 Kgs 21:6 suggest to other interpreters that Deut 18:10–12 is an expansion of the latter and composed by an exilic or postexilic writer. See the discussion of these parallels and their implications for dating schemas in Lewis, *Cults of the Dead*, 121–22; Schmidt, *Israel's Beneficent Dead*, 179–83. For bibliography of German scholarship concerning the unity and dating of Deut 18:9–22, particularly the growing tendency to situate it in the exilic or postexilic period, see Tropper, *Nekromantie*, 228–32. Other interpretations of the relationship between Deut 18:11 and 2 Kgs 21:6 understand the latter as an abbreviation of the earlier Deut 18:11 passage (see, e.g., Lewis, *Cults of the Dead*, 102, 123). Such an interpretation then places the depiction of necromancy in Deut 18:11 in the exilic or postexilic period. I tend to prefer the interpretation of this text as an expansion of 2 Kgs 21:6, which places Deut 18:11 in the seventh century at the earliest if we accept (as I do) the Cross school's recognition of a Josianic layer of the Deuteronomistic History. However, as my analysis below will demonstrate, it seems clear that the rhetoric surrounding necromancy continues to be active in later biblical texts.

pass through the fire, one who practices *qsm*, *ʿnn*, *nḥš*, *kšp*, or *ḥbr*,[41] one who inquires of *ʾôb wəyiddəʿōnî*, and one who seeks the dead, because anyone who does these things is an abomination to YHWH. Because of these abominations, YHWH your god is dispossessing them before you.

Verse 11 belongs to a larger passage in 18:10–12 that lists necromancy along with child sacrifice (compare Lev 20:6) and different types of cult specialists as examples of the abominations (*tôʿēbōt*) committed by the Canaanites before Israel's entry into the land. The text characterizes these practices as abominations to YHWH, the consequence of which is the expulsion of the Canaanites from the land (compare the expulsion of those who resort to necromancy in Lev 20:6). Thus, the rhetoric of Deut 18:9 draws on an association between necromancy and Canaanite "foreigners" as well as the threat of expulsion from one's land or community as the result of this practice.[42]

Specific characteristics of necromantic practice are almost entirely absent from this passage. The ambiguity of the phrase *ʾôb wəyiddəʿōnî* (referring either to necromancers or ghosts themselves) makes it difficult to determine whom exactly the passage is condemning as abominations—necromancers or those who hire them. Thus, it is unclear whether the passage has in view cult specialists who hire out their services or lay Israelites

---

41. I leave these specialized terms untranslated, primarily because it is impossible to reconstruct their individual practices or distinguish them from each other with any certainty. The appearance of *qsm* and necromancy in this passage suggests that most of them are methods of divination, while *kšp* (and its Akkadian cognate *kašāpu*) suggests an association with rituals meant to manipulate divine forces for benevolent or malevolent purposes (*CAD* 8:284). For an examination of *nḥš* in biblical contexts and its possible Aramean origin, see Gary A. Rendsburg, *Israelian Hebrew in the Book of Kings* (Bethesda, MD: CDL Press, 2002), 66–67.

42. The similarities between Deut 18:11 and the passages in Lev 20, including the reference to *mlk* sacrifice, expulsion from the land, and the phrase *ʾôb wəyiddəʿōnî*, suggest dependence but are ambiguous regarding the direction of that dependence. Concerning Deut 18:11, Jeffrey Tigay notes that the list of forbidden Canaanite practices is the longest in the Pentateuch, and the various terms in the list may be redundant in some instances. See Tigay, *The JPS Torah Commentary: Deuteronomy* (Philadelphia: Jewish Publication Society of America, 1996), 173. The explanatory note following the phrase *ʾôb wəyiddəʿōnî* suggests that the text is expanding another, perhaps Lev 20:27. Tigay's observation that the list in Deut 18:11 is long and redundant contributes to the impression that this text is drawing on multiple sources to list several prohibited cultic practices and assign them Canaanite origins.

who practice necromancy themselves. However, the broader context of Deut 18 suggests that it is the denigration of illicit cult specialists, including necromancers, in 18:10–11 and 18:14 that is set in opposition to other cult specialists in Israel, including the priests (vv. 1–8) and prophets (vv. 15–16, 18–22). Also missing from this passage is any reference to the dead being invoked or any association between these practices and the concerns of the Israelite family.

Two passages in 2 Kings refer to necromancy in terms of the cultic activity of the Judean kings Manasseh and Josiah:[43]

---

43. Theories about the historical and cultic context of the Deuteronomistic History influence the arguments regarding the date of 1 and 2 Kings and their constitutive passages. Norbert Lohfink outlines the two main approaches to the dating of the Deuteronomistic History: the school of Rudolf Smend, on one hand, and that of Frank Moore Cross, on the other. For a full bibliography of these debates, see Norbert Lohfink, "Recent Discussion on 2 Kings 22–23: The State of the Question," in *A Song of Power and the Power of Song: Essays on the Book of Deuteronomy*, ed. Duane L. Christensen (Winona Lake, IN: Eisenbrauns, 1993), 45–61. The Smend school revises the theory of Martin Noth and maintains his starting point for the composition and redaction of the source in the exilic period and identifies several redactional layers in this and later periods. The Cross school revises the theory of Gerhard von Rad, who critiqued Noth's dating of the source to the exilic period, and posits two major layers— a hopeful strand culminating in the reign of Josiah and a later exilic redaction updating these hopes by responding to the aftermath of the Babylonian exile. More recently, Thomas Römer has cogently argued for compromise between these two schools. See Römer, *The So-Called Deuteronomistic History: A Sociological, Historical, and Literary Introduction* (London: T&T Clark, 2005), 41–43. The redactional layers of the Deuteronomistic History are often cited in attempts to date both 2 Kgs 21:6 and 23:24. Regarding 2 Kgs 21:6, for instance, Burke O. Long notes that many commentators argue that 21:1–7 as well as 21:16–18 originated from a preexilic context and were later redacted during or after the exile in 21:8 and 21:10–15. For a survey of such interpretations, see Long, *2 Kings: The Forms of the Old Testament Literature* (Grand Rapids: Eerdmans, 1991), 247. Determining the compositional setting for 23:24 is similarly difficult because reports of Josiah's reign could originate from different redactional layers. Some commentators argue that 23:24 is part of a larger unit including the rest of ch. 23. This unit, which describes the reign and cultic reforms of Josiah, could belong to a preexilic narrative about Josiah, or it could be part of an exilic writer's vision of Josiah as the enforcer of YHWH's covenant and the Torah in contradistinction to the cultic misdeeds of Manasseh, whom the text ultimately deems responsible for the exile of Judah (2 Kgs 23:26; see, e.g., Lewis, *Cults of the Dead*, 125–26; Long, *2 Kings*, 5). Indeed, the notice in 23:26 that YHWH will punish Israel for Manasseh's cultic misdeeds despite Josiah's loyalty suggests an exilic context.

He made his son pass through the fire, he practiced ʿnn and nḥš, and he had recourse to[44] ʾôb wə-yiddəʿōnîm. He did much evil in the eyes of YHWH, provoking him. (2 Kgs 21:6)

As for hāʾōbōt wəhayyiddəʿōnîm and tərāpîm and "dung balls" [gillûlîm] and all the detestable things that were seen in the land of Judah and in Jerusalem, Josiah expelled them so that he might uphold the words of the instruction written upon the scroll that the priest Hilkiah found in the temple of YHWH. (2 Kgs 23:24)

Burke O. Long describes the list of illicit divinatory methods in 21:6 as "standardized rhetoric," comparing it to Deut 18:10–11.[45] Second Kings 21:2, 9–11 even refer to the expulsion of the nations in their description of Manasseh's transgressions, a striking similarity to the narrative of the Canaanites expelled from the land in Deut 18. In the case of 2 Kgs 21:11, however, the text claims Amorite, not Canaanite, origins for these transgressions. Other features further suggest a close relationship between 2 Kgs 21:6 and Deut 18:11, such as the close association between necromancy and child sacrifice. However, 2 Kgs 21:6 differs from Deut 18:11 in its terminology for necromancy—wəʿāśâ ʾôb wəyiddəʿōnîm, rather than wəšōʾēl ʾôb wəyiddəʿōnî. Lewis posits that the writer of 2 Kgs 21:6 may use the term ʿāśâ to differentiate the sins of Manasseh from the reforms of Hezekiah and Josiah.[46] Thus, Manasseh practiced necromancy in the sense that he reintroduced the practice in Israel.[47] Indeed, Long refers

---

44. Here I follow the interpretation of Mordechai Cogan and Hayim Tadmor, who understand ʿāśâ in the sense of "to have recourse to" (see 1 Sam 8:15), not "to appoint" (as in 2 Kgs 17:32). They argue that this translation better accounts for the fact that the passage is interested in Manasseh's cultic practice, not his appointment of cultic officials. See Cogan and Tadmor, II Kings: A New Translation with Introduction and Commentary (New York: Doubleday, 1988), 267. See my note above regarding ʿnn and nḥš as methods of divination.

45. Long, 2 Kings, 248. Cogan and Tadmor argue that 21:6 is based on Deut 18:11, though "somewhat abbreviated" (II Kings, 267). I prefer interpreting Deut 18:10–11 as an expansion of 2 Kgs 21:6. For further discussion of this interpretation and alternate views, see my comments on Deut 18:11 above.

46. As others have noted, however, the characterization of Hezekiah and Josiah's cultic programs as reform is misleading, since their condemnation of various practices was likely a cultic innovation rather than a return to traditional practice.

47. Lewis, Cults of the Dead, 124. Lewis qualifies this argument, however, by recognizing that "if Manasseh did in fact reintroduce (rather than simply practicing) nec-

to Manasseh as a "structural antagonist" of Josiah, noting that the illicit cultic activities and devices Manasseh uses are overturned later during Josiah's reign (e.g., "foreign" altars, child sacrifice, non-Yahwistic divination, and images of other gods).[48]

Neither 2 Kgs 21:6 nor 23:24 provides much detail regarding the practice of necromancy or the identity of the dead invoked in the ritual. Like the texts discussed above, the recurring theme is that necromancy is opposed to Yahwistic cult (21:6) and violates the tôrâ that legitimates the cultic innovations of Josiah (23:24). An interesting aspect of 21:6, however, is that it suggests that Manasseh either patronizes necromancers or practices necromancy himself. His own practice of necromancy is suggested by the fact that the beginning of the verse clearly accuses him of sacrificing his own son, and the subject of the participles and verbs following this notice does not seem to change. Thus, this passage may suggest that the king himself utilizes necromantic ritual. Furthermore, verse 9 states that Manasseh's use of necromancy leads to its broader practice among the Israelites. Second Kings 23:24 differs from 21:6 in that by associating the hā'ōbōt wǝhayyiddǝʿōnîm with "dung balls" (gillûlîm, or ineffective and supposedly non-Yahwistic divine images), it emphasizes the inefficacy of necromancy. Similar to 21:6, this passage refers to the widespread practice of necromancy throughout Jerusalem and Judah.[49]

While the three references to necromancy in the book of Isaiah situate the practice within the context of extreme distress, they also exhibit interesting differences:

> Surely, they will say to you, "Consult hā'ōbōt wǝhayyiddǝʿōnîm that chirp and mutter, for shouldn't a people consult their gods ['ĕlōhîm],[50] the

---

romancy, we might expect a more explicit wording." Indeed, this interpretation of ʿāśâ as "reintroduce" seems overly speculative.

48. Long, 2 Kings, 249. The argument that the references to child sacrifice and killing of the innocent correspond to different aspects of the Assyrian cult is overly speculative. For an overview of these arguments, see Schmidt, who suggests that killing the innocent in 1 Kgs 21 may correspond to the "substitute king" ritual in Mesopotamia (Israel's Beneficent Dead, 238).

49. For an analysis of the association between necromancy and tǝrāpîm in this passage, see my treatment of the tǝrāpîm further below.

50. Contra Schmidt, Israel's Beneficent Dead, 150, who interprets the 'ĕlōhîm in this passage, as in 1 Sam 28:13, as netherworld deities summoned during necromancy, not the dead.

dead for instruction and a message on behalf of the living?"[51] Surely, they will say such a futile thing.[52] The hard-pressed and hungry will pass by. When they are hungry and angry, they will curse their king and gods. Whether they look above or to the netherworld,[53] they will look and

---

51. For a discussion of the difficulties in distinguishing the quoted speech, speaker, and audience of this passage, see Robert P. Carroll, "Translation and Attribution in Isaiah 8:19f," *BT* 31 (January 1980): 126–34. The division of the passage in this way seems more logical than understanding the phrase "shouldn't a people consult their god(s)" as a negative retort to the people's request for necromantic oracles. Interpreting the phrase as a negative retort would render the passage as follows: "Surely, they will say to you, 'Consult *hā'ōbōt wəhayyiddə'ōnîm* that chirp and mutter.' Shouldn't a people [instead] consult their God ['ĕlōhîm] [rather than] the dead for instruction and a message on behalf of the living? Surely, they will say such a futile thing." Yet, in this division of the passage, it is unclear how the phrase "the dead ... on behalf of the living" fits with the material surrounding it. Indeed, interpreting the *'ĕlōhîm* as YHWH does not account for the apparent parallelism between *'ĕlōhîm* and "the dead." It would not make sense for the biblical writer to refer to YHWH as dead, a characterization reserved for allegedly foreign, non-Yahwistic deities. Instead, the reference to the dead seems to refer back to the *hā'ōbōt wəhayyiddə'ōnîm* earlier in the verse, a reference to the dead invoked in necromantic ritual. Therefore, the dependence of these two phrases suggests that they belong to the same quotation, the people's request for necromantic oracles. Additional support for interpreting the material from "Consult *hā'ōbōt wəhayyiddə'ōnîm*" to "the dead ... on behalf of the living" as a singular quotation comes from the fact that the notice "Surely, they will say such a thing" seems to mark the end of the quotation. For a similar division of this passage, see Joseph Blenkinsopp, *Isaiah 1–39: A New Translation with Introduction and Commentary* (New York: Doubleday, 2000), 242; Schmidt, *Israel's Beneficent Dead*, 148; Van der Toorn, *Family Religion*, 222 n. 70.

52. The phrase *'ăšer 'ên-lô šāḥar* is difficult. The contrast between *šāḥar*, "dawn," and the darkness imagery in 8:22 seems to underscore the ineffectiveness of necromancy in the passage. Other interpretations have emended the MT using the LXX, which has *dōra*, and the Syriac, which has *šuḥda*, both of which seem to be reading *šōḥad*, "bribe," instead of *šāḥar*. Others translate *šāḥar* according to Arabic *saḥara*, "put to forced labor," which would then render the phrase "which has no force." For these and other interpretations of the phrase, see Lewis's survey (*Cults of the Dead*, 132 n. 13). While the meaning of *šāḥar* is unclear, its context indicates that the phrase is meant to emphasize that necromancy is ultimately futile and will not improve the situation of those who seek its aid, which is how I have rendered it above.

53. The use of the term *'ereṣ* here may be a reference to the netherworld, since the passage is concerned with various modes by which the distressed may seek divine assistance, including consultation of the dead.

find distress and darkness, the gloom of anguish and thick darkness. (Isa 8:19–22)[54]

The oracle of Egypt. YHWH is about to ride upon a swift cloud. He will come to Egypt, and the "idols"[55] of Egypt will tremble before him, and the heart of Egypt will melt within it. I will provoke Egyptian against Egyptian, and they will fight among themselves—each man against his brother, each man against his neighbor, city against city, and kingdom against kingdom. The spirit of Egypt shall be emptied[56] within it. I shall

---

54. Commentators on the book of Isaiah posit several layers of redaction, some dating to the reign of Hezekiah in the eighth century and some to the late Persian period. Such debates also characterize the interpretation of Isa 8:19–20 regarding its textual unity and date of composition. Some commentators argue that 8:19–20 is part of a larger textual unit, the Isaianic *Denkschrift*, which spans from 6:1 to 8:18 and is often dated to the eighth century during the Syro-Ephraimite crisis. For instance, Blenkinsopp argues for the preexilic contexts of particular strata, based primarily on their similarities with material in Amos and Hosea (*Isaiah 1–39*, 106–7). Lewis also situates this passage in the context of the Syro-Ephraimite coalition of the eighth century (*Cults of the Dead*, 129). See also Hays, *Death in the Iron Age II*, 272–73 n. 319. Yet, Blenkinsopp and others date Isa 8:19 relatively late compared with the surrounding material based on its loose connection to the verses that precede it, particularly the lack of an antecedent for the verb *yōʾmərû*, "they will say," at the beginning of 8:19 (Blenkinsopp, *Isaiah 1–39*, 244). Other commentators have argued that 8:19–23 comprises at least one addition to the end of the *Denkschrift*, likely added during the exilic or postexilic period (see, e.g., Nihan, "1 Samuel 28," 43–44). For a full bibliography of those who have argued for either the exilic or postexilic addition of these verses, see Hays, *Death in the Iron Age*, 272–73 n. 319.

55. My use of the term *idols* is meant to reflect the polemic of the passage, not my own evaluation of the divine images in question. Lewis argues that the *ʾĕlîlîm* in Isa 19:3 of the MT version may have originally read *ʾĕlōhîm* (*Cults of the Dead*, 133). He bases this argument on the LXX translation of the term as τοὺς θεους, noting that the LXX translates the other attestation of the Hebrew *ʾĕlîlîm* in this passage as τα χειροποιητα, "idols." If Lewis is correct, then this passage constitutes another example of the term *ʾĕlōhîm* as referring to the dead. However, as Schmidt notes, the different translations of *ʾĕlîlîm* in the LXX may be due to the close association between deities and their images, which in some cases may be understood as the deities themselves (e.g., Isa 42:17; Exod 20:23; *Israel's Beneficent Dead*, 158). The comparative biblical evidence suggests that Schmidt's interpretation is the more plausible one. In addition, according to the principle of *lectio difficilior*, the fact that *ʾĕlîlîm* is less common a term than *ʾĕlōhîm* suggests that it is the more likely reading.

56. Following Blenkinsopp, I am emending the MT *wənābəqâ* to read *nəbāqqâ* (*Isaiah 1–39*, 313).

make its counsel void. They will consult "idols," *'iṭṭîm*,[57] and *hā'ōbōt wəhayyiddə'ōnîm*. (Isa 19:3–4)[58]

---

57. The term *'iṭṭîm* is a *hapax*, though it is often interpreted as a reference to the Akkadian *eṭemmu*, "ghost" (see, e.g., *HALOT* 1:37). In the LXX version of this passage, the term is replaced by the phrase τοὺς ἐκ τῆς γῆς φωνοῦντας, "those who speak from the earth." While the term *eṭemmu* appears in Akkadian necromantic texts and thus would make sense in a biblical passage about the *'ōbōt* and *yiddə'ōnîm*, the form of the term is strange. The doubling of the *ṭ* does not reflect the form of the Akkadian term. Furthermore, the appearance of a common root ('-ṭ-m) between *'iṭṭîm* and *eṭemmu* depends on the –*îm* ending of *'iṭṭîm*, which looks suspiciously like a Hebrew masculine plural ending. Another possible (though also problematic) interpretation is that *'iṭṭîm* corresponds to the Akkadian *ittu*, "omen, ominous sign," which occurs in divinatory texts (*CAD* 7:306–8). Admittedly, though, this interpretation does not account for the shift *ṭ* to *t* in the Hebrew term. It is also possible that the term is originally a *qiṭṭēl* form of the verb *'ṭm*, "to stop up (ears)" (*HALOT* 1:37). Thus, the original term might have read *'iṭṭamîm*, "deaf ones," but lost the *mem* of its root to haplography. Such an interpretation would explain the initial short *i*-vowel of the MT form as well as the doubling of the *ṭ*. For a discussion of the *qiṭṭēl* form, see Waltke and O'Connor, who note that this form is associated with "defects, physical or mental" as in the case of *'iṭṭēr*, "disabled," and *'illēm*, "mute" (*IBHS* 5.4.b). Furthermore, emphasizing the disability and, thus, inefficacy, of non-Yahwistic divine beings would fit within the broader context of this passage. However, because of the unresolved difficulty in interpreting the meaning of this term, I have left it untranslated above.

58. Regarding the unity and date of composition for Isa 19:3–4, see the extensive bibliography in Hays, *Death in the Iron Age II*, 282–88. While Blenkinsopp acknowledges that there is no unambiguous historical context alluded to in Isa 19:3–4, he notes that the disorder depicted in 19:2, 4 is "perhaps the most telling clue" and argues that the most plausible period of such disorder would have been the period immediately preceding the Twenty-Fifth (Nubian) Dynasty in the late eighth century BCE (*Isaiah 1–39*, 314). However, it is equally possible that "Egypt" in the text simply represents a major foreign power and does not necessarily reflect Egypt in any particular historical period. Other interpreters emphasize the plausibility that the depiction of Egyptian necromancy reflects actual Egyptian practice and thus suggests an eighth-century context (see, e.g., Hays, *Death in the Iron Age II*, 284). However, the background of crisis in the depiction of necromancy in multiple biblical texts (Deut 18:11; Lev 19:31; 20:6, 27; Isa 19:3; 47:10–12) suggests to Schmidt that these are all instances of exilic or postexilic composition (Schmidt, *Israel's Beneficent Dead*, 154). This method of dating, too, is highly speculative, since a writer's interest in imminent foreign invasion need not reflect historical reality. In fact, the disorder topos is common in other ancient West Asian depictions of cultic misdeeds and how they negatively affect the relationship between different gods and peoples; see, e.g., the Marduk and Shulgi prophecies. In the Hebrew Bible, this topos appears in Mic 7:5–6, and the imagery of infighting in 7:6 ("A son treats [his] father with contempt. A daughter rebels against her mother.

You will be brought low and will speak from the netherworld;[59] your speech will be uttered from the dust. Your voice will be like an *'ôb* from the netherworld; your voice will chirp from the dust. (Isa 29:4)[60]

The text of Isa 8:19 responds to the desire of the Israelite people for necromantic divination and even quotes their request to the prophet. One interesting feature of this passage is the juxtaposition of verses 19–20 and its depiction of necromancy with the reference to signs and portents in verse 18, which may indicate a distinction between—and evaluation of—different methods of divination according to the prophetic writer. Second, the passage denies the efficacy of necromancy, which is reflected in the final phrase of verse 20—literally "what they say will have no dawn." Though the interpretation of this phrase is difficult, it might refer to the darkness of the netherworld and the dismal prospects of the living petitioners who turn to necromancy. Relatedly, the passage depicts those who seek necromantic divination as no better than the dead they invoke, condemned to a world of darkness and distress typified by ancient West Asian depictions of the netherworld.

Like other necromancy texts discussed above, the Isaiah passages do not refer to the practice of necromancy among kin. Instead, Isa 8:19 refers to the participants in necromantic ritual as a "people" seeking instruction from their "gods," perhaps through the prophet or other religious special-

---

A daughter-in-law [rebels against] her mother-in-law. A man's enemies are the men of his house") is strikingly similar to the imagery of Isa 19:2. Therefore, comparative evidence challenges the assumption that the depiction of disorder in Isa 19:3–4 necessarily reflects historical reality and can be used to date the passage.

59. Concerning the pair *'ereṣ*//*'āpār*, see my note above regarding the netherworld references in 8:19.

60. Regarding the historical context of 29:4, Blenkinsopp argues that it is part of a larger oblique allusion (29:1–8) to Jerusalem during the siege of Sennacherib in the late eighth century (*Isaiah 1–39*, 400). Lewis notes that this passage is a woe oracle that is part of a larger collection of oracles against other nations in chs. 13–23, and he argues that it was composed during Sennacherib's siege against Jerusalem in 701 BCE (*Cults of the Dead*, 135). As in the other Isaianic depictions of calamity and imminent destruction by outside forces, it is difficult to determine the historical context for the passage in question. While the siege of Jerusalem by Sennacherib in 701 BCE provides one plausible context for the text's composition, the siege and eventual conquest of Jerusalem by the Babylonians in 586 BCE as well as the looming threat of foreign invasion during the early sixth century also provides equally plausible contexts, if indeed this anxiety reflects historical reality and is not a literary topos.

ists. The use of the term *ʾĕlōhîm* is not surprising given the appearance of the term referring to the dead Samuel in 1 Sam 28:13. However, the term *people* (ʿam) in Isa 8:19 may suggest not a familial context but that of a larger social and cultic unit. The implication may be that the gods invoked in both 1 Sam 28 and Isa 8 are those deemed cultic heroes by the Israelite people. Indeed, the prophet Samuel, known for his Yahwistic prophecy and performance of miracles, would be a prime candidate for this kind of widespread recognition and, perhaps, necromantic intercession.[61] However, since he is the only dead person invoked in necromancy explicitly identified by the biblical text, it is admittedly speculative to reconstruct the nature of the necromantic *ʾĕlōhîm* based on that text alone.

The context provided in Isa 8:21–22 shows that the people request necromantic divination in times of crisis when they are starving and distressed. At such times, according to verse 21, the people will curse their king and their god and, presumably, engage in such divinatory practices. The identities of the multiple speakers and audiences in Isa 8:19 are difficult to determine. First, there is the speaker at the beginning of 8:19 as well as a second-person plurality addressed by a third-person plurality ("surely, they will say to you," *kî-yōʾmərû ʿălêkem*). In the quoted text that follows ("consult *hāʾōbōt wəhayyiddəʿōnîm* that chirp and mutter, for shouldn't a people consult their gods [*ʾĕlōhîm*], the dead for instruction and a message on behalf of the living?"), the speakers seem to be the third-person plurality mentioned previously and the audience the second-person plurality. After the quotation, there is a shift back to the original speaker and audience at the beginning of verse 19, and the third-person plurality mentioned seems to be the "people" of the quotation. Although the chapter contains mul-

---

61. While living, the prophet Samuel has divinely inspired knowledge of the future, which he uses to anoint the early kings of Israel. It is perhaps no accident that Saul later invokes him to foretell the outcome of his imminent battle with the Philistines. Such an association between a prophet's miraculous deeds in life and his ongoing powers after death may similarly underlie the depiction of Elisha's bones in 2 Kgs 13:21, in which physical contact with the prophet's bones revivifies a dead Moabite man. (It is also interesting to note that, in this case, the living and the dead are not kin.) Like Samuel, Elisha exhibits superhuman abilities during his lifetime. Elisha revivifies a dead boy (2 Kgs 4:32–37; 8:5), which may justify the depiction of his bones in 2 Kgs 13:21. The similarities between these two texts, 1 Sam 28 and 2 Kgs 13:21, may help us understand the logic underlying the abilities ascribed to some of Israel's dead. For cultic heroes, such as Elisha and Samuel, the abilities they exhibit in life may be the ones called on after their deaths.

tiple instances of YHWH speaking directly to the prophet (vv. 1, 5, 11), no such introductory notice appears at the beginning of verse 19; thus, it is not clear whether YHWH is speaking to the second-person plurality or whether the prophet himself is the one speaking. To whom YHWH or the prophet is speaking is also ambiguous. Although the relationship between verses 16–18 and verse 19 is unclear, it is possible that the second-person plurality addressed at the beginning of verse 19 includes the prophet's disciples (v. 16) or his children (v. 18). In either case, it is possible that this verse reflects the notion that people may ask prophets to perform necromancy on their behalf. Isaiah 8:19–20 is formulated in such a way as to mock such a request and, perhaps, to separate the practices of the prophet from those of the necromancer.

Isaiah 19:1–3 offers another prophetic critique of necromancy. In this passage, the practice of Egyptian necromancy is depicted as ineffective in the face of YHWH's anger. Although the Egyptians will seek guidance through necromantic divination, YHWH will deliver Egypt into the hands of a harsh enemy. The imagery of verse 2 ("I will provoke Egyptian against Egyptian, and they will fight among themselves—each man against his brother, each man against his neighbor, city against city, and kingdom against kingdom") and the eventual defeat of Egypt in verse 4 suggests that the text considers necromancy as a form of divination used in moments of acute social, military, and political instability. Like the depiction of necromancy in Deut 18:9 and 2 Kgs 21:11, Isa 19:1–4 associates necromancy with a foreign nation, Egypt; unlike these previous passages, however, the Isaiah passage does not claim that the practice originates in that foreign nation. Similar to the depiction of necromancy in 1 Sam 28, Isa 19:3 suggests that necromancy is a divinatory method of last resort after YHWH "swallows up the counsel" of Egypt.[62]

---

62. It is unclear why necromancy would be a divinatory method of last resort in this context. In the case of Mesopotamia, the logic seems to be more explicit. Based on omen literature about seeing or hearing a ghost, descriptions of *namburbî* rituals, and ghost expulsion texts, we know that the dead can be dangerous. Furthermore, that *namburbî* material (that specifically counteracts the effects of a ghost encounter) appears in a necromantic text (K 2779) suggests that the dead were potentially dangerous even when they were intentionally invoked in necromantic ritual. So, we may justifiably posit that Mesopotamian necromancy is used sparingly because of its risks to living practitioners. Of course, the biblical evidence is less clear, and it would be problematic to simply apply the Mesopotamian logic underlying necromancy to biblical or Israelite notions of necromancy. That kind of danger posed by the dead does

A less explicit reference to necromancy appears in Isa 29:4, which compares the distress of Ariel—likely a reference to Jerusalem—to the dismal conditions of the dead in the netherworld. The most relevant aspect of this text is the imagery of the voices of ghosts coming from the netherworld; this imagery is much more elaborate than the brief reference to the "chirping and muttering" of ghosts in Isa 8:19. Although 29:4 is not explicitly an attack on necromancy, its negative depiction of ghosts and their ability to speak from the netherworld suggests a similar bias against the powers of the dead and their ability to communicate effectively with the living.

Two references to necromancy appear in 1 and 2 Chronicles, both of which describe the cultic misdeeds of Judean kings:[63]

---

not appear in the biblical text, and (unlike others) I do not think that anxiety about corpse pollution is related to negative attitudes toward biblical necromancy. Though admittedly speculative, I would posit that reluctance to practice necromancy concerns the value of necromancy in relation to other forms of divination. Since necromancy seems to be used in times of crisis, it is possible that resorting to the dead as sources of information is only necessary and/or appealing when the deity refuses to answer or to provide the desired response. We could speculate that divination through a major deity such as YHWH is more highly valued than divination through the dead, thus reflecting the relative power and authority associated with those two entities. In short, why consult the dead when you can consult a more effective entity? Yet, this explanation is also unsatisfying, since the encounter with the dead Samuel in 1 Sam 28 is, essentially, a successful attempt to divine the will of YHWH and to foretell the future.

63. The provenance of these passages depends on larger discussions of Chronicles and its relationship to other postexilic sources, especially Ezra and Nehemiah. Based on linguistic characteristics shared by these books, some scholars posit that Chronicles was composed by the same writer as Ezra-Nehemiah. See, e.g., Jacob M. Meyers, *II Chronicles* (New York: Doubleday, 1965), xx. For an examination of this view as well as related arguments concerning separate authorship for these books, possible multiple editions, and a Chronistic school, see Gary Knoppers, *1 Chronicles 1–9* (New York: Doubleday, 2003), 96–100. Details within Chronicles as well as its use by later sources suggest that it was composed during the Persian period (539–332 BCE). The detail with which the text speaks of the temple cult suggests to some that the Chronicler was a member of the cult personnel, which places him in Jerusalem in Persian-period Yehud. Textual references to the Babylonian exile and the edict of Cyrus in 539 provide a *terminus post quem* for the text's composition, and the use of Chronicles in the work of later writers, including Sirach and Eupolemos, provides a *terminus ante quem* in the second century BCE. Thus, Knoppers allows a range of dates for Chronicles' composition—from the late fifth century to the mid-third century BCE. For an extensive discussion of the issues related to the dating of Chronicles,

Saul died for his sacrilege [bəmaʿălô] that he committed[64] against YHWH concerning the word of YHWH, which he did not observe, and also for inquiring bāʾôb in order to divine (an oracle). He did not divine by YHWH. (1 Chr 10:13–14)

He made his sons[65] pass through the fire in the valley of Ben-Hinnom. He practiced ʿnn, nḥš, kšp, and he had recourse to ʾôb wayiddəʿōnî, committing evil in the eyes of YHWH and provoking him. (2 Chr 33:6)

The first, 1 Chr 10:13–14, interprets the death of Saul as YHWH's punishment for resorting to necromancy, which is construed as sacrilege by the text. The content of the ritual itself is absent in this passage, but the terminology describing the means of divination (bāʾôb) reflects the language of 1 Sam 28:8 (qosŏmî-nāʾ lî bāʾôb). Yet, the 1 Chr 10:13–14 account also omits information included in 1 Sam 28, including Saul's many attempts to divine YHWH's will through modes of divination considered admissible by the text (1 Sam 28:6). The impetus for Saul's patronage of the necromancer in 1 Sam 28 is that YHWH refuses to reveal himself by any of these divinatory modes prior to the necromantic encounter. However, 1 Chr 10:14 explicitly states that Saul does not attempt to divine through YHWH. This statement may be an attempt to refute the interpretation of 1 Sam 28 as a Yahwistic oracle, an indication that this interpretation persisted in the Persian period.

The second reference to necromancy, 2 Chr 33:6, describes the many cultic transgressions of Manasseh and clearly draws on the narrative of 2 Kgs 21. In fact, the text of 2 Chr 33:6 reproduces the narrative of 2 Kgs 21 regarding the reign of Manasseh almost verbatim. According to the Chronicles passage, his cultic misdeeds include rebuilding the high places

---

see Knoppers, *1 Chronicles 1–9*, 101–17. Other analyses of Chronicles posit multiple redactional layers. For a discussion of these redactional schemas, see Ralph W. Klein, *2 Chronicles: A Commentary* (Minneapolis: Fortress, 2012), 11–13. For the purposes of the present analysis, I accept the consensus view that Chronicles is a Persian-period composition; furthermore, the references to necromancy in 1 Chr 10:13–14 and 2 Chr 33:6 likely reflect relatively late conceptions of necromancy in the Hebrew Bible.

64. For the range of uses of the term maʿal, see Knoppers, *1 Chronicles 1–9*, 523–24. Like other instances of this term, the punishment for transgressors is severe. In the case of 1 Chr 10:13–14, the punishment for Saul's sacrilege is death.

65. It is interesting to note that the version of Manasseh's cultic misdeeds in 2 Chr 33 expands his *mlk* sacrifices to include multiple sons, rather than the one son mentioned in 2 Kgs 21:6. This expansion may reflect the desire of the Chronicler to exaggerate these cultic transgressions.

destroyed by Hezekiah; worshiping Baal, Asherah, and the host of heaven; sacrificing children; engaging in illicit forms of divination (including necromancy); and placing a non-Yahwistic image in the sanctuary. The only additional item that appears in this list—and not 2 Kgs 21—is *kāšap*, which also appears in Deut 18:11. As Ralph Klein suggests, this addition is probably due to a dependence on Deut 18:11, which lists these three cultic activities together.[66] Indeed, like Deut 18:11 (as well as Lev 20:3–5; 2 Kgs 21:6), this text places child sacrifice alongside necromancy. Unlike the punishment suffered by Saul in 1 Chr 10:13–14, however, this text does not prescribe violent punishment or death for the necromantic activity of Manasseh, despite the fact that it construes his activity as sacrilege.[67]

Two other biblical texts, Isa 28:7–22 and 65:4, require brief mention because some interpreters have argued that they, too, refer to necromancy. However, I have chosen to exclude them from the discussion of biblical evidence above. First, Van der Toorn argues that Isa 28:7–22 is a polemic against necromancy practiced among priests and prophets.[68] As support for this argument, he cites the covenant between Isaiah's opponents and

---

66. Klein, *2 Chronicles*, 480.

67. In light of Chronicles' dependence on the Deuteronomistic History and its emphasis on necromancy as a sacrilegious activity, it is interesting to note that this passage excludes the reference in 2 Kgs 23:24 to Josiah eventually expelling necromancers from the land. Schmidt reasons that this omission may be due to the fact that 2 Chr 33:10–20 gives an alternate account of Manasseh and his later cultic reforms unattested in any other text (*Israel's Beneficent Dead*, 220–21). In this account, Manasseh shows remorse for his cultic misdeeds and expels foreign gods from the land (33:15). Because Schmidt understands necromancy as the invocation of gods who then summon the ghosts of the dead, he argues that Manasseh's expulsion of foreign gods in the Chronicler's account has already rid the land of necromancy, thus rendering Josiah's annihilation of necromancy redundant. However, Schmidt's interpretation of necromantic ritual as involving netherworld deities is problematic, making this interpretation of the Josianic lacuna in Chronicles unsatisfying. See my discussion of this interpretation in the notes above.

68. Karel van der Toorn, "Echoes of Judean Necromancy in Isaiah 28,7–22," *ZAW* 100 (1988): 199–217. Though Van der Toorn has become one of its more recent proponents, this interpretation is not new. Previous scholars who have advocated for this reading of Isa 28:7–22 include George W. Wade, *The Book of the Prophet Isaiah* (London: Methuen, 1911), 180; Samuel Daiches, "Isaiah and Spiritualism," *JC* supplement (July 1921): 6; Eduard König, *Das Buch Jesaja* (Gütersloh: Bertelsmann, 1926), 254; Baruch Halpern, "'The Excremental Vision': The Doomed Priests of Doom in Isaiah 28," *HAR* 10 (1986): 109–21.

both death (*māwet*) and the netherworld (*šə'ôl*) mentioned in verses 15, 18, both of which suggest to Van der Toorn that Isaiah's opponents engage in necromancy. Van der Toorn further argues that the unintelligible speech in verses 10, 13 mimics the bird-like utterances of the dead. For support, he notes that the dead are depicted as bird-like in several ancient West Asian texts, including the Epic of Gilgamesh, Ištar's Descent, and the Myth of Nergal and Ereškigal.[69] While it is possible that the repetitive sounds of the words in these lines (*ṣaw lāṣāw ṣaw lāṣāw qaw lāqāw qaw lāqāw zəʿêr šām zəʿêr šām*) are meant to be onomatopoeic of bird calls, much like the *pilpel* form of *ṣpp*, "chirp, peep" (Isa 8:19; 10:14; 29:4; 38:14), there is no reference to birds in this passage, nor is there any indication that this line concerns death-related ritual.

Indeed, there are a few problems that stand in the way of including Isa 28:7–22 as evidence of necromancy in this chapter. Van der Toorn's interpretation assumes that the covenant with death and Sheol should be taken at face value—that is, we should interpret that covenant as reflecting the necromantic (or otherwise death-related) activity of Isaiah's opponents. Instead, this imagery appears to be a polemical characterization of Isaiah's opponents and their political or cultic affiliations, depicting them as ineffective as the dead in Sheol.[70] Other features of verse 15 support this interpretation. After all, it is unlikely that Isaiah's opponents would say of themselves: "We have made a lie [*kāzāb*] our refuge, and we have hidden ourselves in deceit [*šeqer*]." Read instead through the lens of polemic against Isaiah's opponents, the imagery of aligning oneself with death and Sheol becomes another way of expressing the futility of affiliation with deities other than YHWH. Indeed, we see the contrast between the life-giving powers of YHWH and the powerlessness of "dead" deities elsewhere in the Hebrew Bible. For example, in Jer 10:10, YHWH is referred to as the "living god" (*'ĕlōhîm ḥayyîm*), while the images of deities other than YHWH (and, likely, the deities themselves) are described as "nothingness" (*hebel*) in Jer 10:15.[71] Moreover, the appearance of both death and Sheol in opposition to the salvific power of YHWH in Hos 13:14 further suggests that the use of these entities in Isa 28:15, 18 is intended to set up a

---

69. Van der Toorn, "Echoes," 201, 211.

70. Other biblical references to the weakness and inefficacy of the dead appear in Isa 14:4–21; 26:14; Job 14:21; Ps 88:5, 11; Qoh 9:5, 10.

71. This term, *hebel*, is associated with the images of deities other than YHWH elsewhere in Jeremiah (e.g., Jer 16:18–19; 51:18).

contrast with YHWH, not to suggest death-related ritual. Therefore, the imagery of this passage (*māwet, šəʾôl, kāzāb, šeqer*) is likely polemical, not an indication of the supposed necromantic activity of Isaiah's opponents. While Van der Toorn's interpretation is somewhat intriguing, it does not demonstrate with any certainty that Isa 28:7–22 is evidence of biblical necromancy. More important, it is unclear that verse 9 is connected in any way with death or death-related imagery.

Similarly, the interpretation of Isa 65:4 as an example of necromancy through dream incubation is possible, but ultimately speculative. Recent proponents of this interpretation include Theodore Lewis, Phillip Johnston, and Francesca Stavrakopoulou, who argue that those who "sit among graves [*qəbārîm*] and spend the night [*yālînû*] in secret places [*nəṣûrîm*]" are seeking oracles from the dead through incubation in tombs.[72] This interpretation of the passage even appears in the LXX, which reads: ἐν τοῖς μνήμασι καὶ ἐν τοῖς σπηλαίοις κοιμῶνται δι᾽ ἐνύπνια, "they lie down in tombs and caves for the sake of dreams." Yet, it is also possible that the MT passage merely refers to the pollution resulting from physical contact with corpses and their tombs. This emphasis on the presence of corpses and tombs actually deviates from depictions of necromancy in the Hebrew Bible, which do not attest to the presence of corpses in necromantic ritual. For instance, as I note above, 1 Sam 28 explicitly notes the location of Samuel's corpse in Ramah, which is far removed from the site of his necromantic invocation in Endor.

While it is possible that Isa 65:4 refers to invoking the dead through incubation, this method is otherwise unattested in the biblical text and thus difficult to reconstruct here. However, if it is indeed a reference to necromancy,

---

72. Lewis, *Cults of the Dead*, 159; Johnston, *Shades of Sheol*, 54, 160–61. Francesca Stavrakopoulou argues that the places depicted in Isa 1:29–30; 65:3–5; 66:17 are mortuary gardens associated with the cult of dead kin. See Stavrakopoulou, "Exploring the Garden of Uzza: Death, Burial, and Ideologies of Kingship," *Bib* 87 (2006): 1–12. However, see Tropper, *Nekromantie,* 326, for discussion regarding the problems with this interpretation, including the fact that no extant depictions of ancient West Asian dream incubation are set in or near tombs. Like Tropper, I do not altogether reject the interpretation of Isa 65:4 as an example of necromancy. However, there simply is not enough evidence to indicate that this is the best reading of the passage, especially when alternate interpretations are equally plausible. Susan Ackerman points out the similarities between dream incubation and necromancy but maintains that they are distinct practices. See Ackerman, *Under Every Green Tree: Popular Religion in Sixth-Century Judah* (Atlanta: Scholars Press, 1992), 200, 202.

it is interesting to note that it demonstrates the similar ways in which deities and the dead are treated in cultic settings. For instance, as Susan Ackerman notes, other ancient West Asian attestations of dream incubation mostly involve deities, and biblical texts even depict YHWH himself as appearing to people in dreams (1 Kgs 3:4–15 // 2 Chr 1:1–13).[73] Among these attestations, however, only one text depicts the dead speaking to the living through dreams: the dream of Nabonidus, in which the dead king Nebuchadnezzar appears to him instead of a deity.[74] Therefore, while the interpretation of Isa 65:4 as an instance of necromancy through dream incubation is appealing in some ways, the text is not explicit enough to be included among the evidence for biblical necromancy examined in this chapter.[75]

---

73. Ackerman, *Under Every Green Tree*, 195–201.

74. For a discussion and translation of this text, see A. Leo Oppenheim, *The Interpretation of Dreams in the Ancient Near East* (Philadelphia: American Philosophical Library, 1956), 191, 250. I will address the similar cultic treatment of deities and the dead further below.

75. For similar reasons, I have excluded Qoh 9:3b–7. Despite Aron Pinker's argument that Qoh 9:3b–7 should be considered another example of necromancy, his interpretation of this passage is ultimately unconvincing. See Pinker, "Qohelet 9:3b–7: A Polemic against Necromancy," *JJS* 63 (2012): 218–37. His argument relies a great deal on interpreting the difficult phrase wə'aḥărāyw 'el mētîm at the end of 9:3 as a reference to invoking the dead. Pinker emends the phrase to read wə'ôrəḥāyw 'el mētîm ("his paths are to the dead"). While Pinker rightly notes that the phrase 'el mētîm appears in other biblical attestations of necromancy (Deut 18:11; Isa 8:19), the verb accompanying the phrase (drš) in these passages is lacking in Qoh 9:3. The use of the term 'ōraḥ, "way, path," with reference to invoking the dead is unattested in any biblical text about necromancy. Furthermore, the emendation itself is problematic, for it lacks the ending –ôt we would expect to see on a plural form of 'ōraḥ (e.g., 'ōrəḥōtāyw in Isa 2:3; 'orəḥôtāy in Job 13:27; and 'orəḥôtām in Prov 9:15). Choon-Leong Seow's revision of the text further challenges the interpretation that the passage refers to necromancy: "This is the evil in all that is done under the sun: that there is one fate for all. So, too, the mind of human beings is full of evil { }; irrationality is in their mind when they are alive. Indeed, who is the one who chooses? Unto all the living there is certitude, {and unto the dead is finality}." See Choon-Leong Seow, *Ecclesiastes: A New Translation with Introduction and Commentary*, AYB 18C (New Haven: Yale University Press, 1997), 296. Here Seow is reading w'ḥry <> 'l-hmtym, "unto the dead is finality/the end," instead of w'ḥryw 'l-hmtym, "after it unto the dead." His interpretation of 'ḥry as "finality, the end" is based on cognates in Ugaritic (uḫ-ra-a-yi, w'uḫry) and Arabic ('uhrāy). See Seow, *Ecclesiastes*, 300–301, for a more detailed analysis of these cognates. While it is clear that the surrounding text in Qoh 9 emphasizes the powerlessness and ignorance of the dead, it is not clear that 9:3b–7

Necromancy and the Cult of Dead Kin in the Hebrew Bible

Admittedly, the biblical passages that refer to necromancy are different in style and focus: 1 Sam 28 is a narrative depiction of necromantic ritual, while Deut 18:11 and Lev 19:31; 20:6, 27 are set within collections of proscriptive statements regarding various practices. Second Kings 21:6 and 23:24 refer to necromancy in terms of the broader history of kings and their cultic activity, and the passages in Chronicles mirror this treatment. The prophetic references to necromancy, Isa 8:19; 19:3; and 29:4, are similarly set within polemics about Israel's failure to uphold YHWH's laws. Yet, taken together, these biblical passages demonstrate certain patterns regarding the practice of necromancy. All of these texts depict necromancy as an illicit form of divination, either prohibiting it or emphasizing its allegedly non-Yahwistic nature. Leviticus 19:3 construes it as polluting; Lev 20:6 depicts it in terms of cultic disloyalty; Deut 18:10–12 refers to it as an abomination to YHWH; both 2 Kgs 21:6 and 2 Chr 33:6 consider it "evil" in the eyes of YHWH; and 1 Chr 10:13–14 construes it as "sacrilege." Necromancy is often associated with other cult practices considered illicit by the biblical writers, such as other methods of divination and child sacrifice (Deut 18:11; Lev 20:6; 2 Kgs 21:6; 23:24; 1 Chr 10:13; 2 Chr 33:6). Some passages suggest that people turn to necromancy in moments of acute crisis (1 Sam 28; Isa 8:19–22, 19:2–4). Others associate necromancy with foreign nations (Deut 18:9; 2 Kgs 21:2; Isa 29:4). A few of these texts emphasize the powerlessness of the dead and the inefficacy of necromancy (Isa 8:19–22; 19:3–4; 29:4). More important, the concerns that underpin the cult of dead kin do not appear in any of these passages. There are no references to offerings to the dead, tomb maintenance, or commemoration through invocation of the name or commemorative monuments. In fact, the reference to Saul disturbing Samuel in 1 Sam 28:15 uses language (*rgz*) that can be construed as antithetical to caring for the physical remains of the dead.[76] The biblical passages referring to necromancy never mention

---

has necromancy in view. Thus, I have omitted it from the evidence for biblical necromancy in this study.

76. For a discussion of other terms associated with ideal and nonideal treatment of the dead, see Saul M. Olyan, "Some Neglected Aspects of Israelite Interment Ideology," *JBL* 124 (2005): 606–7. As Olyan notes, the verb *šlk*, "cast," is associated with dishonorable forms of burial, while the verb *nwḥ*, "set at rest," is associated with honorable burial.

the family and do not suggest that those involved in the practice are kin, nor do they indicate that these cultic actors intend to care for the dead they invoke.

Instead of situating necromancy within the realm of the family, some of these texts seem to place it in the context of competition among religious specialists. Some clearly attest to the presence of a specialist in necromancy (1 Sam 28; Lev 20:27), even if we limit the rendering of *hāʾōbōt wəhayyiddəʿōnîm* exclusively to "ghosts and spirits" and not those who invoke them. If we accept that the phrase does refer to necromancers in some cases, then a reference to such cult specialists is likely in 2 Kgs 23:24 and possible in Lev 19:31; 20:6; 2 Kgs 21:6; and Isa 19:3–4. Indeed, some texts set up an implicit contrast between the work of necromancers and that of priests and prophets. In 1 Sam 28, for example, Saul only resorts to necromancy after he has failed to divine YHWH's will through dreams, priests (who use the Urim), and living prophets. The narrative of 2 Kgs 23:34 says that Josiah must rid the land of necromancy in accordance with the scroll found by Hilkiah, a priest. A contrast between the deeds of the prophet and the necromancer also seems to appear in Isa 8:19–20, which cautions (the prophet?) against heeding the people's request for necromantic divination. By alienating necromancers through such polemic, the biblical writers may aim to help rival cult specialists—specifically Yahwistic priests and prophets—secure religious authority and patronage. Thus, I argue that cultic competition is at stake in these polemical references to necromancy, which attempt to alienate it from normative Yahwism.[77] Necromancy provides an alternate means of petitioning YHWH for information, and this service may threaten priests and prophets in their roles as intermediaries between the Israelites and the divine. Recourse to the dead as conduits of privileged knowledge (i.e., of the future) compete with Urim and other oracles. Polemic against necromancy makes sense in this context, as it seeks to undermine not only the practices of these rival religious specialists but also the efficacy of the dead themselves. The persistence of

---

77. Indeed, both Bloch-Smith and Smith argue that polemics against consulting the dead through intermediaries date to the Hezekiah and Josiah reforms of the eighth century BCE and were later incorporated into Deuteronomic legal material, the Holiness Code, and the writings of Isaiah (Bloch-Smith, *Judahite Burial Practices*, 146–47; Smith and Bloch-Smith, "Death and Afterlife," 281). Bloch-Smith attributes these changes to the influx of refugee cultic personnel from the north and the threat they posed to Judahite cultic and political figures.

people and kings in seeking necromantic oracles, as depicted in biblical texts, suggests that they understand necromancy to be an effective means of divination, and the cult specialists who invoke the dead likely view necromancy as legitimate within Yahwistic cult. In fact, 1 Sam 28 strongly suggests that necromancy is a means of divining a Yahwistic oracle, an interpretation that seems to persist in the Persian period, as indicated by the refutation of that claim in 1 Chr 10:14.

Therefore, I argue that necromancy be excluded from reconstructions of the cult of dead kin in the Hebrew Bible and ancient Israel, as several others have suggested.[78] A weakness in some previous studies of the cult of dead kin stems primarily from the conflation of these two distinct forms of interaction with the dead.[79] Both phenomena refer to the dead, but their purposes and participants are different. While necromancy belongs to the realm of religious specialists, whose practices may pose a threat to the priestly and prophetic circles that polemicize against them, the cult of dead kin belongs in the realm of family religion. Moreover, their conflation in previous scholarship has led to hasty conclusions asserting the presence of polemics against the cult of dead kin and family religion more generally in certain strands of the biblical text. If we excise polemics against necromancy from the biblical evidence for the cult of dead kin, then we are left with the impression that the biblical text is largely uninterested in practices meant to commemorate and care for the dead. However, the biblical writers are very interested in protecting the interests of priests and prophets whom they consider the legitimate Yahwistic intermediaries.

---

78. See, e.g., Schmitt, "Problem of Magic," 11; Albertz, "Family Religion in Ancient Israel," 99. Albertz emphasizes that, besides 1 Sam 28, no biblical text referring to necromancy situates it within a domestic context (Albertz and Schmitt, *Household and Family Religion*, 470). A similar argument appears in the work of Johnston: "Necromancy and the cult of dead kin are obviously related in their preoccupation with the dead.... Nevertheless, they are distinct practices, and one can occur without the other, as in modern spiritism. Thus it is useful to look at them separately" (*Shades of Sheol*, 154).

79. This conflation has also led to the speculative etymology of Sheol as deriving from *šāʾal*, "to ask," referring to necromancy. See, e.g., Theodore J. Lewis, "Dead, the Abode of the," *ABD* 3:102. For examples of studies that conflate these cultic phenomena, see my comments above.

The Role of the *Tərāpîm* in Israelite Family Religion

To adequately treat the problem of necromancy and its relationship to the cult of dead kin, we must conclude this section with an examination of scholarship on the nature of the *tərāpîm*. What are these objects?[80] Are they used in necromancy? Do they belong in the realm of family religion? Over the past twenty years, the interpretation of the *tərāpîm* as ancestor figurines used in necromancy has gained some acceptance in the field.[81] However, as I argue below, there are some problems with this interpretation. By far, the most pervasive aspect of the *tərāpîm* in the Hebrew Bible is their association with divination (1 Sam 15:23; 2 Kgs 23:24; Ezek 21:26; Zech 10:2), although this feature does not appear in Gen 31 or 1 Sam 19.[82] Despite the divinatory function depicted in the majority of these texts and the appearance of necromancy in 2 Kgs 23:24 alongside the *tərāpîm*, no biblical text directly refers to the use of the *tərāpîm* in necromancy. Instead, this interpretation depends on speculative analogy with extra-

---

80. There is some scholarly disagreement about whether to refer to the *tərāpîm* as a singular or plural entity. Although the *tərāpîm* are treated as a singular object in 1 Sam 19, I will refer to the *tərāpîm* as a plural entity due to the plurality of these objects in other biblical texts and the plural form of the term itself.

81. See, e.g., Oswald Loretz, "Die Teraphim als 'Ahnen-Götter-Figur(in)en' im Lichte der Texte aus Nuzi, Emar und Ugarit," *UF* 24 (1992): 134–78; Rainer Albertz, *History of Israelite Religion in the Old Testament Period* (Louisville: Westminster John Knox, 1994), 1:38; Jeffers, *Magic and Divination*, 225, 229; Meindert Dijkstra, "Women and Religion in the Old Testament," in *Only One God? Monotheism in Ancient Israel and the Veneration of the Goddess Asherah*, ed. Bob Becking et al., BibSem 77 (London: Sheffield Academic, 2001), 164–88; Benjamin D. Cox and Susan Ackerman, "Micah's Teraphim," *JHS* 12 (2012): 1–37; Susan Ackerman, *Women and the Religion of Ancient Israel* (New Haven: Yale University Press, forthcoming).

82. Both of these texts depict women (Rachel and Michal) using the *tərāpîm*, though not for divinatory purposes. Susan Ackerman has recently argued that this lacuna in Gen 31 and 1 Sam 19 is due to the general exclusion of women from practices of the Israelite cult of dead kin (Ackerman, *Women and the Religion of Ancient Israel*, manuscript 25). According to this argument, the texts do not depict the women as divining by means of the *tərāpîm* because such divination, constitutive of the cult of dead kin, is off limits to women. In ch. 3, I will examine this argument that women are excluded from the Israelite cult of dead kin. In short, I argue that other biblical texts suggest a more significant role for women in the cult of dead kin. For instance, reading Isa 56:6 as a reference to cult of dead kin typically offered by sons *and* daughters challenges the argument that women were altogether excluded from the cult.

biblical evidence and supposed parallels between cultic terms in different biblical texts.

Most scholarly treatments of the term *tərāpîm* offer one of two interpretations: the *tərāpîm* are figurines representing either household gods or ancestors.[83] The former argument relies on translations of *tərāpîm* in the LXX (*eidolon*, "image/idol," or *glyptos*, "carving") and Targumim (*ṣalmānayyā'*, "statue," or *dəmā'în*, "likeness"), which reflect later interpretations of the *tərāpîm* as depicting supposedly illegitimate images of gods. Furthermore, two biblical texts (Gen 31:30, Judg 18:24) refer to the *tərāpîm* as *ʾĕlōhîm*. The use of this term alongside the *tərāpîm* has led to speculation on possible parallels between the Nuzi *ilānu*, "gods," and the biblical *tərāpîm*/*ʾĕlōhîm*. Although this interpretation of the *tərāpîm* as household gods once dominated scholarly conversations about the *tərāpîm*, it seems to have largely fallen out of favor.

More recent treatments have argued that the *tərāpîm* are ancestor figurines used in necromancy. These interpretations also cite extrabiblical evidence and offer contextual readings of different attestations of the *tərāpîm* to create a coherent image of the *tərāpîm* as ancestor figurines. First, the location of the *tərāpîm* in the household in some biblical texts (Gen 31:19–35; 1 Sam 19:11–17, Judg 17–18)[84] and their depiction as roughly anthropomorphic in form (1 Sam 19:11–17) have encouraged some scholars to envision them as representations of ancestors. Second, Harry Hoffner argues that *tərāpîm* is a loan word from the Hittite *tarpi(š)*, meaning "a spirit which can on some occasions be regarded as protec-

---

83. Household gods: Sidney Smith with Cyril J. Gadd, "Tablets of Kirkuk," *RA* 23 (1926): 127; Anne E. Draffkorn, "ILANI/*ʾĕlōhîm*," *JBL* 76 (1957): 216–24. Ancestors: Karel van der Toorn and Theodore J. Lewis, "תרפים," *TDOT* 15:777–89; Lewis, "Teraphim," *DDD* 1588–1601; Van der Toorn, "The Nature of the Biblical Teraphim in the Light of the Cuneiform Evidence," *CBQ* 52 (1990): 203–22. In his treatment of divination in ancient Israel, Frederick H. Cryer attempts to reconcile these two views of the *tərāpîm*, arguing that Mesopotamian divination often entails the presence of the deity; thus "it is conceivable that the Old Testament conjunction of teraphim=idol and teraphim=oracle-instrument are merely two sides of the same coin." See Cryer, *Divination in Ancient Israel and Its Near Eastern Environment* (Sheffield: JSOT Press, 1994), 273.

84. Van der Toorn goes even further and posits that the bedchamber may have been the preferred location within the household where the *tərāpîm* were situated ("Nature of the Biblical Teraphim," 209).

tive and on others as malevolent."[85] Third, extrabiblical parallels between gods and the dead are cited as evidence of a potential parallel between the *tərāpîm* and the dead; in addition to the Nuzi evidence, Lewis notes that the parallel appears in the Old Babylonian story of Etana, texts from Emar, and both Old and Neo-Assyrian texts.[86]

Van der Toorn further argues that the association between *tərāpîm* (ancestor figurines) and *qsm* in Ezek 21:26; 1 Sam 15:23; and Zech 10:2 suggests that consultation of the *tərāpîm* was a type of necromancy. Although *qsm* is often translated as the more general term "divination," Van der Toorn argues that the term is more specifically associated with necromancy in texts such as Deut 18:10–14; 1 Sam 28; and Mic 3:6, 11.[87] However, this reading overstates what these texts say about this particular aspect of *qsm*. In the case of Deut 18:10–14, *qsm* appears with those who practice child sacrifice and many terms associated with diviners, including terms for necromancers. Nothing in the passage indicates that *qsm* is a form of necromancy, however. It is only one of several practices deemed illicit by the text. Furthermore, the use of *qsm* at the beginning of this list suggests to some commentators that it is meant to be an inclusive term for the items that follow it.[88] The use of *qsm* in 1 Sam 28:8 clearly refers to necromancy (*qosŏmî-nā' lî bā'ôb*), but the inclusion of the means by which the necromancer divines this oracle—*bā'ôb*—suggests that the term *qsm* denotes divination in general, not necromancy in particular. Thus, it does not support Van der Toorn's argument that *qsm* by itself is a term for necromancy.

Finally, Mic 3:6, 11 do not include any reference to the dead, ghosts, or necromancy. Instead, the parallel between *qsm* and *ḥāzôn* in 3:6 suggests

---

85. Harry A. Hoffner, "Hittite Tarpiš and Hebrew Terāphim," *JNES* 27 (1968): 66. Though, as Van der Toorn himself notes, etymology is not very reliable in determining the use of this term among biblical writers ("Nature of the Biblical Teraphim," 204). Indeed, we must not rely on the etymology of a cultic term to determine its function.

86. Lewis, "Teraphim," 1591–92.

87. Van der Toorn, "Nature of the Biblical Teraphim," 215. On the translation "divination," see BDB, 890. The *HALOT* entry for the term includes "prediction, survey of future events" and "decision (by means of an oracle)" (2:1115–16).

88. "Arguments for understanding *qsm* as a very general term are based on (1) the Deuteronomistic tendency to list a general term first in a series with subsequent terms providing clarification and nuance, (2) on comparative etymology, and (3) on uses of *qsm* elsewhere in the Hebrew Bible (cf. Num 23:23; 1 Sam 15:23; 2 Kgs 17:17; Mic 3:6)." See Joanne K. Kuemmerlin-McLean, "Magic (OT)," *ABD* 4:468.

that *qsm* is once again associated with divination in general, not necromancy in particular. The use of *qsm* in Mic 3:11 demonstrates that the term may be used to refer to the divinatory practices of both prophets and necromancers. However, the polemics against necromancy aim to alienate necromancy from other forms of divination, thus creating a distinction between allegedly licit, Yahwistic divination performed by priests and prophets and illicit, non-Yahwistic divination performed by necromancers. Therefore, the appearance of the *tərāpîm* with *qsm* in Ezek 21:26; 1 Sam 15:23; and Zech 10:2 indicates that the *tərāpîm* are associated with some kind of divinatory practice, *qsm*, but not necessarily necromancy specifically. In fact, Ezek 21:26 seems to nicely illustrate this conclusion: the verse states that the king of Babylon stands at the head of two roads to perform divination (*liqsom qāsem*) before listing several different divinatory methods, including belomancy, consultation of *tərāpîm*, and extispicy.[89]

Van der Toorn cites another parallel, 2 Kgs 23:24 // Deut 18:11, as evidence of the necromantic function of the *tərāpîm*. The former text refers to those expelled from the land by Josiah, including those who utilize necromancy, the *tərāpîm*, and allegedly illicit cult images (*wəgam et-hā'ōbôt wə'et-hayyiddə'ōnîm wə'et-hattərāpîm wə'et-haggillūlîm wə'ēt kol-haššiqqūṣîm*). According to Van der Toorn, Deut 18:11 contains similar wording (*wəhōbēr ḥāber wəšō'ēl 'ôb wayiddə'ōnî wədōrēš 'el-hammētîm*) with the substitution of *tərāpîm* with "the dead" (*hammētîm*), thus indicating that Deut 18:11 understands the *tərāpîm* to be ancestor figurines used in necromancy.[90] The weakness of this argument is its reliance on the phrase *'ôb wayiddə'ōnî* to constitute a parallel between these two verses. While both verses list allegedly illicit cultic practices and practitioners and may be similar on a broadly conceptual level, they list different terms and practices—with the sole exception of *'ôb wayiddə'ōnî*. Furthermore, the terms *'ôb* and *yiddə'ōnî* (or their variants) often appear together (Deut

---

89. In her study of divination terminology, Ann Jeffers argues that this term may be cognate to Arabic *qsm*, which means "to cut into pieces," which would suggest that *qsm* as a divinatory term is associated with the casting of lots. However, Jeffers notes that its use in multiple biblical texts (Num 23:23; Mic 3:6; Prov 16:10; 1 Sam 28:8) indicates that the term refers to divination more generally (*Magic and Divination*, 96–98). See also Arnold's comments on 1 Sam 28:8: "Saul's imperative to the woman … involves a *terminus technicus* for divination generally, which is not limited to necromancy but includes all forms of divination" ("Necromancy and Cleromancy," 201).

90. Van der Toorn, "Nature of the Biblical Teraphim," 215.

18:11; Lev 19:31; 20:6, 27; 1 Sam 28:3, 9; 2 Kgs 21:6; 23:24; Isa 8:19; 19:3; 2 Chr 33:6),[91] which suggests that their co-occurrence in 2 Kgs 23:24 and Deut 18:11 does not constitute a parallel between these two passages as much as the use of a set phrase to denote the same cultic phenomenon. Thus, the argument that *tərāpîm* and *hammētîm* are in parallel in these two passages is unconvincing.

For some, the relationship between necromancy and the cult of dead kin hinges on the interpretation of the *tərāpîm* as ancestor figurines. Based on the evidence cited above, I find the ancestor-figurines argument unconvincing. However, if indeed the *tərāpîm* were ancestor figurines used in necromancy, and necromancy were a facet of the cult of dead kin, then we must still struggle to make sense of the fact that biblical polemic against necromancy chooses to focus on this particular facet of the cult of dead kin while largely ignoring others, such as feeding or invoking the name of the dead.[92] The rationale for this omission may either be that (1) the biblical writers polemicizing against necromancy understand it to be separate from other practices constitutive of the cult of dead kin or (2) they are creating this distinction through their polemic because necromancy alone poses an ideological threat to the brand of Yahwism they advocate—presumably because it rivals divination performed by priests and prophets. At present, however, I am unconvinced that the *tərāpîm* are ancestor figurines used in necromancy or that necromancy is a facet of the biblical cult of dead kin. What does seem relatively clear based on the evidence cited above is that the *tərāpîm* are objects used in divination (1 Sam 15:23; 2 Kgs 23:24; Ezek 21:26; Zech 10:2) and that they or the entities they represent are construed as divine (Gen 31:30, 32; Judg 18:24). It seems plausible that the *tərāpîm* are—or, at least, represent—divine beings capable of delivering oracles to those who possess them. The appearance of the *tərāpîm* in domestic spaces (Gen 31:19–35; 1 Sam 19:11–17; Judg 17–18) further suggests that this mode of divination is associated with Israelite family religion. To say much more than that, however, is overly speculative.

---

91. Notable exceptions include 1 Sam 28:7, 8, in which *'ôb* appears by itself and either designates the woman at Endor as a necromancer or specifies the means by which one performs divination (see also 1 Chr 10:13–14a).

92. Indeed, previous treatments have struggled to make sense of the fact that the biblical writers do not condemn care for dead kin (see, e.g., Schmidt, *Israel's Beneficent Dead*, 275; Albertz and Schmitt, *Household and Family Religion*, 433).

Necromancy in Cuneiform Evidence from Mesopotamia

Much has been made of the Mesopotamian influence on biblical necromancy, and previous studies often give the impression of a vast corpus
of extant cuneiform texts detailing necromantic practice. Considering
the number of cuneiform texts that survive from ancient Mesopotamia,
relatively few depict or even mention necromancy. This dearth of texts
may suggest the rarity of necromancy as a practice. However, the fact that
these texts are attested over a broad chronological and geographical span
suggests that necromancy persists at least as a concept for many centuries in cuneiform literature. The final section of this chapter examines the
cuneiform evidence for necromancy in order to evaluate any parallels with
biblical depictions of its practice. The texts most often cited as evidence
for necromancy include: (1) Lu, a professions list, which includes different terms often translated as "necromancer," the *ša eṭemmi*[93] and *mušēlû
eṭemmi*, and the *mušēlītum*, who is able to *šūlû ša eṭemmi*, "raise a ghost;"[94]
(2) the Sumerian composition Gilgamesh, Enkidu, and the Netherworld
and its later adaptation in tablet XII of the Standard Epic of Gilgamesh,
which depict deities raising the dead Enkidu from the netherworld in
order to speak to Gilgamesh; (3) an Old Assyrian letter from Kültepe
(ancient Kanesh), which refers to the consultation of ghosts (TCL 4 5 ll.
4–7); (4) a Neo-Assyrian letter from Kuyunjik, which concerns the crown
prince of Assyria and a ghost (*LAS* 132); (5) a Neo-Assyrian petitionary
diagnostic text (*LKA* 139:28–30); (6) an excerpt from the Babylonian
wisdom poem Ludlul bēl nēmeqi, which refers to seeking information
from a *zaqīqu*; (7) a late Babylonian tablet from Babylon that prescribes
the acts and incantations necessary for necromantic ritual (BM 36703); (8)
a Neo-Babylonian tablet from Kuyunjik that demonstrates parallels with
BM 36703 but includes additional apotropaic material (K 2779); and (9) a
third- or fourth-century BCE text detailing the concoction of an ointment
used in the invocation of a ghost (*SpTU* 2:20). In addition, I will discuss
the dream report of Nabonidus, in which the dead king Nebuchadnezzar appears to the Neo-Babylonian king Nabonidus, and its similarities
with other cuneiform texts about necromancy. In some cases, the parallels
between the cuneiform and biblical evidence are quite striking—necro-

---

93. *CAD* 4:401.
94. *CAD* 10:265.

mancy is utilized in moments of crisis; an intermediary aids the living petitioner in contacting the dead; and women as well as men may act as necromancers. However, some important differences between the two corpora also emerge. Unlike biblical polemic against necromancy, the cuneiform texts do not condemn its practice or those who utilize it. Overall, the cuneiform texts are much more detailed in their depiction of the practice itself, especially in later ritual texts. Moreover, while there is an overall lack of concern for the cult of dead kin in necromantic ritual, the family does play a role in some cuneiform texts referring to necromancy. Therefore, unlike the biblical evidence, the cuneiform evidence suggests that necromancy may, perhaps, be considered an aspect of family religion in ancient Mesopotamia. However, the cuneiform evidence still treats necromancy as separate from the cult of dead kin.

The least descriptive references to necromancy appear in versions of the lexical list Lu, which provides the names of various professions. In both second- and first-millennium versions of the list, terms appear that seem to denote a necromancer, including the *ša eṭemmi*, *mušēlû eṭemmi*, and the *mušēlītum*. The equation [búr] = *šūlû ša eṭemmi*, which also appears, is often interpreted "to raise, said of a ghost."[95] However, Schmidt argues against interpreting the *mušēlû eṭemmi* as a necromancer: "The š causative of elû might signify 'to remove,' cf. *CAD* 4 (1958): 134, #11c, in which case the *mušēlû eṭemmi* = lú sag-bulug-ga would be an exorcist, not a necromancer." Schmidt similarly argues against interpreting the *šūlû ša eṭemmi* = bur₂ as a necromancer: "So, the question arises, is the meaning 'to free from a ghost' or 'to free a ghost'?"[96] However, the imagery of bringing up appears in other necromantic texts (BM 36703 and K 2779) depicting the role of Šamaš in invoking the dead (*at-ta-ma la-iṭ-su-nu* ᵈUTU DI.KU₅ *šá e-la-a-ti ana šap-la-a-ti*),[97] not performing exorcism. Thus, it seems plausible that these lexical texts similarly refer to the invocation of ghosts. Unfortunately, the texts do not provide any further details about the practice of necromancy, such as the reasons for invocation, the identity of the dead invoked, or constitutive ritual elements. However, it is worth noting that the appearance of necromancers in this professions list suggests that

---

95. *CAD* 4:397; Irving L. Finkel, "Necromancy in Ancient Mesopotamia," *AfO* 29 (1983): 1.

96. Schmidt, *Israel's Beneficent Dead*, 118 n. 25.

97. Here I follow Finkel's edition of these texts. See Finkel, "Necromancy in Ancient Mesopotamia," 11.

we are dealing with cult specialists, not lay practitioners. Furthermore, the term *mušēlītum* suggests that women could function as necromancers.

Tablet XII of the Standard Gilgamesh Epic is an Akkadian translation of the second half of the Sumerian composition Gilgamesh, Enkidu, and the Netherworld.[98] This Sumerian text, along with others,[99] was probably composed in the Ur III period, although the earliest extant copies date to the Old Babylonian period, the period in which the Akkadian epic took shape. After incorporating elements from these Sumerian poems, the epic attained a fairly static form by the end of the Middle Babylonian period in the last half or quarter of the second millennium. Andrew George argues that the translation of Gilgamesh, Enkidu, and the Netherworld in tablet XII and its inclusion in the epic probably occurred around the time that the Standard Babylonian version was redacted by a Middle Babylonian editor.[100] The passage most relevant to a discussion of necromancy includes lines 238–243 of the Sumerian narrative, in which the gods Enki and Utu help Gilgamesh invoke his dead friend Enkidu:

> Father Enki supported him (Gilgamesh) in this matter.
> He spoke to the valiant warrior Utu, the son whom Ningal bore:
> "Now after you yourself have opened a chink in the Netherworld,
> Send his servant up to him from the Netherworld!"
> He (Utu) opened a chink in the Netherworld,
> By means of his (Utu's) gust of wind, he sent his (Gilgamesh's) servant up from the Netherworld.[101]

---

98. For the relationship between Gilgamesh, Enkidu, and the Netherworld and tablet XII of the Standard Babylonian version of the Gilgamesh Epic, see Aaron Shaffer, "The Sumerian Sources of Tablet XII of The Epic of Gilgamesh" (PhD diss., University of Pennsylvania, 1963), 26–44; Samuel Noah Kramer, *History Begins at Sumer* (Philadelphia: University of Pennsylvania Press, 1981), 258–60, 270–74; Jeffrey Tigay, *The Evolution of the Gilgamesh Epic* (Philadelphia: University of Pennsylvania Press, 1982), 26–35; Andrew George, *The Babylonian Gilgamesh Epic: Introduction, Critical Edition, and Cuneiform Texts* (New York: Oxford University Press, 2003), 47–54, 743–77; and Susan Ackerman, *When Heroes Love: The Ambiguity of Eros in the Stories of Gilgamesh and David* (New York: Columbia University Press, 2005), 43–46.

99. E.g., Gilgamesh and the Land of the Living, The Death of Gilgamesh, and possibly Gilgamesh and the Bull of Heaven. This reconstruction of the development of the epic follows the analysis of Tigay, *Evolution*, 241–50.

100. George, *Babylonian Gilgamesh Epic*, 49.

101. This excerpt follows the translation from Alhena Gadotti, *"Gilgamesh,*

These lines are preserved in ten surviving manuscripts, eight of them associated with Nippur.[102] In the reunion that follows this invocation, Enkidu describes the conditions of different ghosts who populate the netherworld, the overarching theme being that one's fate in the netherworld depends on whether that person has living descendants to provide care. In fact, Enkidu's speech in tablet XII ends with the observation that the ghost who has no *pāqidu*, or cultic custodian,[103] must eat scraps in the netherworld. Although Enkidu's message includes this reference to the cult of dead kin, Gilgamesh, Enkidu, and the Netherworld does not associate it with the necromantic ritual itself.

Schmidt argues against using this mythological text as the basis for reconstructing actual necromantic practice, since it may depict an exceptional case, not typical invocation of the dead. Furthermore, he questions whether the summoning of Enkidu even qualifies as necromancy: "Enkidu is not explicitly identified as a ghost or *eṭemmu*, but as 'servant' subur-a-ni or 'demon' *utukku* in the Akkadian."[104] Despite Schmidt's objections, it seems unnecessary to exclude the text as evidence of necromancy simply because Enkidu is not referred to as an *eṭemmu*. The context itself indicates that he is brought up from the netherworld in the manner of a ghost invoked in a necromantic ritual. Furthermore, the features of the practice shared by this epic material and extant ritual texts, which I examine further below, suggest that the portrayal of necromancy in the epic is not so exceptional. In fact, the necromantic practice depicted in Gilgamesh, Enkidu, and the

---

Enkidu, and the Netherworld" and the Sumerian Gilgamesh Cycle (Boston: de Gruyter, 2014), 159.

102. For a treatment of different manuscript traditions of this composition, see Gadotti, *Gilgamesh, Enkidu, and the Netherworld*, 129–51. Unfortunately, the findspots of these manuscripts from Nippur—many of them discovered during the Babylonian expeditions of 1888–1900—are unknown. Fragments of Gilgamesh, Enkidu, and the Netherworld discovered in the third campaign are attributed to House F in "Tablet Hill" at Nippur. Eleanor Robson dates the texts found in House F to the beginning of Samsu-iluna's reign (1749–1712 BCE). See Robson, "The Tablet House: A Scribal School in Old Babylonian Nippur," *RA* 95 (2001): 39–66. The other surviving manuscripts of lines 238–43 of Gilgamesh, Enkidu, and the Netherworld include one from Ur, whose provenance is unknown, and an entirely unprovenanced text known as the Schøyen manuscript (or X1 in Gadotti's treatment).

103. See my discussion of the *pāqidu* and its relevance to the cult of dead kin in ch. 1.

104. Schmidt, *Israel's Beneficent Dead*, 118 n. 25.

Netherworld shares multiple elements with the portrayal of necromancy in other genres: a living petitioner seeks privileged information from the dead, the invocation of the dead involves a third-party intermediary, the dead person invoked speaks directly to the living petitioner, and the sun god (Utu, in this case) plays a role in the ritual.[105] Another recurring element shared by this depiction of necromancy and many others is that the ritual does not involve living and dead kin. Yet, there are also differences between the necromantic encounter in Gilgamesh, Enkidu, and the Netherworld and other texts. Unlike later ritual texts, Gilgamesh, Enkidu, and the Netherworld does not contain a detailed account of a living petitioner invoking the dead through various incantations or the application of ointments, nor does it involve apotropaic elements reflecting the potentially dangerous nature of interacting with ghosts. These differences, however, may be due in large part to change in necromantic practice over time as well as the fact that the actors in Gilgamesh, Enkidu, and the Netherworld are divine or semidivine, unlike the human actors depicted in the prescriptive ritual texts.

An Old Assyrian letter from ancient Kanesh (TCL 4 5 ll. 4–7) provides further details about necromantic practice. The letter reads: "We inquire of female dream interpreters [šāʾilātim], female diviners [bāriʾātim], and ghosts [eṭemmē], and Aššur continues to attend to you."[106] The writer consults three different methods of divination before going on to implore the letter's recipient to return to Aššur and pay homage to the god Aššur. This letter is one of many sent from wives of merchants in Aššur to their husbands working in Kanesh in Asia Minor.[107] Although the text is brief,

---

105. In fact, three of the texts examined in this section (Gilgamesh, Enkidu, and the Netherworld, *LKA* 139, and BM 36703) depict a solar deity as the one who intercedes between the living and the dead, by either speaking to the dead on behalf of the living (*LKA* 139) or raising the dead from the netherworld (Gilgamesh, Enkidu, and the Netherworld, BM 36703).

106. See also the interpretation of this text in JoAnn Scurlock, "Ghosts in the Ancient Near East: Weak or Powerful," *HUCA* 68 (1997): 106 n. 32. For other textual attestations of the female dream interpreter, see *CAD* 17.1:110. For other attestations of the female diviner, see *CAD* 2:112.

107. Because the Old Assyrian residential level has not been found in Aššur, we only have letters from the Aššur wives sent to Kanesh. In the *karum* at Kanesh, archaeologists have discovered intramural burials within domiciles in the residential areas of the two main phases of habitation in the lower village by the merchants of Aššur. Although many of the tombs were looted in antiquity, those left undisturbed

some details emerge regarding the relationship of necromancy to other forms of divination, the participants in necromantic ritual, and what information it procures. In the text, necromancy is one of three modes of divination listed, which indicates that it may be utilized in conjunction with these other methods or when one or all of them have previously failed. Since the text does not refer to a necromancer or any other third-party intermediary in the necromantic encounter, it is unclear whether the writer of the letter hired the services of a necromancer or questioned the ghosts herself. If the latter, this text is another example of women performing necromancy. If the former, the text shows that women could hire the services of cult specialists who could perform the ritual for them. In either case, the feminine forms of two other kinds of cult specialists (*šā'ilātim* and *bāri'ātim*) in this text suggest that the necromancer(s) might also be female. The information gleaned from this necromantic encounter concerns the cultic responsibilities of the letter's recipient to the god Aššur. Unfortunately, the textual corpus contains no further information regarding the performance of the ritual itself.[108] The text is silent regarding the identity of the dead invoked in the ritual, and it lacks any reference to the family or care for dead kin.

Some scholars argue that the practice of necromancy became more widespread during the Neo-Assyrian period.[109] However, a text often cited in support of this argument, a letter from Kuyunjik dating to the reign of Esarhaddon (*LAS* 132.1–11), does not seem to conform to the definition of necromancy as inquiry of the dead for the purpose of procuring privileged information:

---

contain jewelry, dishware, and other objects. In her analysis of this text and its corpus, Céline Michel examines the relationship between the women who composed such letters and the dead they write about. Interestingly, Michel notes that the women in these letters often invoke the spirits of the dead alongside both major and family deities. See Michel, "Femmes et ancêtres: Le cas des femmes d'Aššur," *Topoi* supplement 10 (2009): 1027–39.

108. Oppenheim suggests that another letter from this corpus, Lewy KTS 25a, refers to necromancy and the divine status of the dead (*Interpretation of Dreams*, 221–22). However, it is not clear that the *ilum* in this text refers to the dead. On the multivalence of *ilum* and cognate terms in ancient West Asia, see my discussion in ch. 1.

109. See, e.g., Nihan, "1 Samuel 28," 28; Schmidt, *Israel's Beneficent Dead*, 117, 141, passim; Tropper, *Nekromantie*, 103.

In accordance with her [the queen mother's][110] loyalty [*kinūtu*], Aššur (and) Šamaš have ordained me as crown prince of the land of Aššur. Her ghost blesses him to the extent that he cares for [*palāḫu*] the ghost [*eṭemmu*]. "May his descendants rule over the land of Assyria!" Care [*palaḫ*] for the gods begets kindness. Care [*palaḫ*] for the Anunnaki increases life. [May the king, my lord] establish order.[111]

While the text refers to the invocation of the dead, the *eṭemmu* (likely Ešarra-ḫamât, the queen mother) does not provide any privileged information to the living. Instead, the text seems to indicate that the gods will ensure the kingship of her son Assurbanipal in exchange for the queen mother's piety toward them, which is indicated by the term *kinūtu*, "loyalty, reliability."[112] Whether she offers this cult while she is alive or continues to do so in the netherworld is unclear. This cultic reciprocity appears again in the statement that the queen mother blesses the crown prince in proportion to his care for her ghost. Interestingly, the term used for this care (*palāḫu*) also appears in familial contexts, including adoption and marriage contracts, in which one party swears to care for another.[113] The

---

110. Although she is not explicitly identified in the text, Simo Parpola argues that the female figure in this text is Esarhaddon's main wife, Ešarra-ḫamât, and the mother of Assurbanipal. See Simo Parpola, *Letters from Assyrian Scholars to the Kings Esarhaddon and Assurbanipal*, AOAT 5/2 (Kevelaer: Butzon & Bercker, 1983), 120. Parpola further argues that this text was likely composed soon after the coronation of Assurbanipal (comparing it to *Letters from Assyrian Scholars* no. 129), which itself took place only a few months after the death of the queen mother. The use of the term *palāḫu*, which often appears in reference to the care offered to dead kin, further suggests that the crown prince offers this care to his recently deceased mother.

111. My translation of the text closely follows that of Parpola, *Letters from Assyrian Scholars* nos. 132, 107. As Parpola notes, the last few lines of this excerpt concerning the reciprocity between gods and the pious are drawn from the Counsels of Wisdom (*BWL* 104; see *Letters from Assyrian Scholars*, 120).

112. *CAD* 8:396.

113. *CAD* 12:45–46. For a discussion of the similarities and differences in the care offered to gods and dead kin, see also Karel van der Toorn, "Gods and Ancestors at Emar and Nuzi," *ZA* 84 (1994): 38–59; Daniel Fleming, "The Integration of Household and Community Religion in Ancient Syria," in Bodel and Olyan, *Household and Family Religion*, 40–43. Van der Toorn argues that this term is associated with care for the dead ("Nature of the Biblical Teraphim," 218). However, Van der Toorn's interpretation of this text as an example of necromancy is problematic: "The fact that the maternal ghost is reported to have responded verbally to filial piety implies, it seems, a form of necromancy" (218). First, the text does not explicitly mark the speaker of

term appears later in this text when it refers to the care for the gods, thus underscoring the conceptual overlap between the cultic care of gods and the dead.[114]

Other translations of the text indicate the different ways in which the dynamic between the living and the dead depicted in it may be interpreted. Due in part to the broken nature of the text, it is sometimes unclear how its different parts fit together. The translation I have offered above requires minimal insertion of additional material to make sense of the extant text, especially in comparison to other translations, which require a great deal of reconstructed material.[115] It is this added material, not the extant text, that is explicitly necromantic in nature. Therefore, while this text refers to the reciprocity inherent in both the cult of gods and the cult of dead kin,[116] it is not an example of necromancy.

Attributed to Neo-Assyrian Aššur, the ninety-five-line text *LKA* 139 mainly concerns the alleviation of a human petitioner's suffering. It opens with the various troubles of the petitioner (ll. 1–13) before moving on to a prayer to Šamaš (ll. 14–31) and Girra (ll. 40–64), then detailing the ritual actions performed by the petitioner (ll. 65–78), then another prayer to the gods (ll. 79–89), and ending with the final ritual acts of the petitioner (ll. 90–95). Other texts share certain sections of *LKA* 139, but only one (K2583+10409) shares its reference to necromancy in lines 28–30:

---

the line "May his descendants rule over the land of Assyria!" Second, even if the queen mother speaks this line, it is unclear that the overall episode is a necromantic encounter. If we interpret "May his descendants rule over the land of Assyria!" as a wish rather than a declarative statement of what the future holds, then the queen mother does not divulge privileged information to the crown prince in this text but instead articulates the blessing referred to in the previous sentence.

114. For a discussion of this overlap and its implications in theorizing the cult of dead kin, see my discussion in ch. 1.

115. A different interpretation of this text appears in *CAD* 4:397: "I shall show to the king [a tablet with the prophecy of a *šā'iltu*-necromancer] as follows: in the truth of Aššur (and) Šamas they (the spirits) have told me (that he will be) the crown prince of Assyria, her (the dead queen's?) ghost blesses him (and says) as (the prince) has shown reverence to the ghost, 'His descendants shall rule over Assyria!'" However, as Finkel notes, this translation is "highly interpretative" ("Necromancy in Ancient Mesopotamia," 1).

116. Indeed, this reciprocity between the living and the dead is a pervasive characteristic in cuneiform depictions of cult of dead kin: "But if he (behaves) like a good family ghost, then on the day which is the lot of humankind, death of his god, rites will be set up for him on his grave" (see Alster, "Incantation to Utu," 76).

Šamaš, speak to the ghost[s] of my family,
so that they may reveal to me and explain to me
the way of the misfortune[s] of humanity that I have experienced.[117]

The purpose of inquiring of the ghosts of one's family is to determine what the petitioner has done to warrant his current ailments. Although the text is broken in line 6, the implication seems to be that other types of divination have failed to diagnose and relieve the ailments of the petitioner: "Seven times his problem [could not be solved by ritual expert, nor] by dream-interpreter."[118] Two major deities—first Šamaš, the sun god, and later Girra, the god of fire—act as intermediaries for the petitioner, seeking to find the cause of his ailments from the angry personal god and goddess. As Van der Toorn notes, it is possible that Šamaš is the intercessor during the day, while Girra takes over this role at night (ll. 34, 58–59).[119] Indeed, the text treats them in similar ways, and the invocation of the deities is identical (ll. 18–20, 54–56). However, while line 28 explicitly refers to Šamaš inquiring of the ghosts of the petitioner's family, the text is broken in line 60, where Girra might perform the same kind of inquiry. Thus, lines 28–30 comprise the only extant reference in the text to necromancy.

Notable features of necromancy in this text include the appearance of Šamaš as the intermediary between the living petitioner and the dead. More important, the living petitioner explicitly invokes his dead kin for the purpose of divining information. The information procured during this necromantic encounter is diagnostic and concerns the alleviation of the petitioner's suffering. Despite the invocation of one's family ghosts in this ritual, there is no indication in the text that care of dead kin is associated with this encounter between the living and the dead. Thus, while this text may represent a facet of family religion insofar as it concerns ritual interaction between living and dead kin, it does not address the practices or concerns central to the cult of dead kin, such as the nourishment or commemoration of the dead.

---

117. My translation closely follows that of Karel van der Toorn, *Sin and Sanction in Israel and Mesopotamia* (Assen: Van Gorcum, 1985), 153. See also Werner Mayer, *Untersuchungen zur Formensprache der Babylonischen Gebetsbeschwörungen*, StPohl 5 (Rome: Biblical Institute Press, 1976), 264; Scurlock, "Ghosts in the Ancient Near East," 91.

118. [KI LÚ.DINGIR *u* ˡ]ú EN.ME.LI *di-en-šú* EN 7°-[*šú* NU SI.SÁ]. This reconstruction of the text appears in Van der Toorn, *Sin and Sanction*, 147, 152.

119. Van der Toorn, *Sin and Sanction*, 147.

The Babylonian wisdom poem Ludlul bēl nēmeqi ("I will praise the Lord of Wisdom") glorifies the god Marduk by depicting the suffering and eventual restoration of one man, Šubši-mešrê-Šakkan. In lines 4–9 of Tablet II, Šubši-mešrê-Šakkan attempts to diagnose and alleviate his suffering through multiple methods of divination, including necromancy:

> I called to my god, but he did not show his face.
> I inquired of my goddess, but she did not raise her head.
> The diviner has not determined the cause through divination.
> The dream interpreter has not cleared up my case through libanomancy [maššakku].[120]
> I beseeched [bâlu] a spirit [zaqīqu], but it did not inform me.
> The exorcist could not dispel the divine wrath (against me) through ritual.[121]

Several extant manuscripts, dating to the first half of the first millennium, preserve different parts of the poem.[122] The prevalence of these manuscripts is partly due to the use of the poem as a scribal training exercise, as indicated by the shape and format of some of the manuscripts.[123] Six of these manuscripts preserve the lines quoted above, including the reference to the zaqīqu in line 8. Three of these originate from Nineveh, while the remaining three are associated with Sultantepe, Babylon, and Sippar.

The interpretation of this text as referring to necromancy depends on one's rendering of zaqīqu in line 8. Wilfred Lambert's translation of line 8 reads: "I sought the favor of the zaqīqu-spirit, but he did not enlighten me."[124] Although Lambert leaves zaqīqu untranslated, compounding it

---

120. For the interpretation of the term maššakku (or its variant muššakku) as indicating a form of divination using incense, see CAD 10.1:279.

121. My translation closely follows that of Cogan, "Road to En-dor," 324. These lines also correspond to Amar Annus and Alan Lenzi's tablet II ll. 5–9 in their edition of the poem. See Annus and Lenzi, Ludlul bēl nēmeqi: The Standard Babylonian Poem of the Righteous Sufferer (Helsinki: Neo-Assyrian Text Corpus Project, 2010), 6, 19, 35. Although they identify relatively new manuscript fragments of tablet II, these fragments only provide duplicate material; thus, they note that their tablet II differs only slightly from Wilfred G. Lambert's earlier critical edition of the poem. See Lambert, Babylonian Wisdom Literature (Oxford: Clarendon, 1960), 21–62.

122. Annus and Lenzi, Ludlul bēl nēmeqi, ix.

123. Annus and Lenzi, Ludlul bēl nēmeqi, ix.

124. Lambert, Babylonian Wisdom Literature, 39.

with "spirit" suggests its association with a ghost, not a deity.[125] This translation differs from that of Amar Annus and Alan Lenzi, who render the term as "the dream god."[126] The semantic range of *zaqīqu* is broad,[127] and its interpretation depends largely on context. However, the association of *zaqīqu* with ghosts is well established, and the verb *bâlu*, "to beseech, pray to," is used not only for gods but also human agents.[128] Furthermore, as the other references to necromancy cited in this chapter suggest, necromancy often appears alongside other forms of divination, especially when they have failed. For instance, Mordechai Cogan notes a parallel between the different modes of divination initially used by Saul in 1 Sam 28 and the failed divinatory attempts in Ludlul. In both cases, the supplicant attempts to obtain information through different methods of divination—by dreams, Urim, and prophets in Saul's case, and by deities, extispicy, and dreams in Ludlul. According to Cogan, these cases may suggest that necromancy is used as a last resort in obtaining information through divination.[129] Therefore, the translation of line 8 as a reference to necromancy is plausible and perhaps preferable to the translation of *zaqīqu* as "dream god," especially since the divine determinative does not precede the term.

The text's depiction of necromancy demonstrates both similarities and differences with other cuneiform texts. Like *LKA* 139, the dead person is supposed to reveal privileged diagnostic information to the living petitioner concerning the alleviation of his current suffering. Unlike later ritual texts, it lacks extensive prescriptions for apotropaic ointments and

---

125. However, in his discussion of the term and its range of usage, Oppenheim notes that the use of the term in Ludlul remains a crux: "Here, the word obviously refers to some specific avenue of communication with the god, an avenue which failed the unfortunate. It is possible, though rather unlikely, that *zaqīqu* designates here messages conveyed in dreams; one could think of what we are used to term glibly, 'inspiration'" (Oppenheim, *Interpretation of Dreams*, 235).

126. Here they draw on the work of Oppenheim, who examines the different names for the Mesopotamian dream god, including dMamu, dAN.ZAG.QAR (variant dAN.ZAG.GAR), and dZaqiqu (variant dZiqiqu). See *Interpretation of Dreams*, 232–37. See also "*zaqīqu*," *CAD* 21:59, which refers to the term's usage as "referring to a specific manifestation of the deity."

127. See, e.g., *CAD* 21:59–60; Oppenheim, *Interpretation of Dreams*, 234; Sol Cohen and Victor Avigdor Hurowitz, "הבל הוא חקות העמים (Jer 10:3) in Light of Akkadian Parṣu and Zaqīqu Referring to Cult Statues," *JQR* 89 (1999): 287–90.

128. *CAD* 2:2.

129. Cogan, "Road to En-dor," 325.

rituals. In addition, there is no reference to an intermediary (neither deity nor cult specialist) who intercedes between the living and the dead. Most important, the relationship between the living petitioner and the spirit invoked in the ritual is unclear in this text. Yet, there is no indication that this interaction between the living and the dead concerns the family or the cult of dead kin.

In her examination of ghost-summoning rituals in cuneiform texts, JoAnn Scurlock argues that necromancy is one of three types of these rituals, the other two being ghost-assistance prescriptions ("prescriptions in which appeals for assistance of a general nature are made to ghosts") and ghost-substitution prescriptions ("prescriptions in which a ghost is asked to act as substitute for the patient, taking ills or sins down to the underworld with him"). Although necromantic texts share some characteristics with these other ghost-related rituals, Scurlock draws some fundamental distinctions between them. For instance, she notes that in necromancy texts, there is only one practitioner, offerings are made to certain gods (such as the Anunnaki and Pabilsag), and the central ritual is the concoction of an ointment that is applied to the face of the living petitioner so that he can see and speak with the ghost.[130] Additional material in these texts often concerns the protection of the living petitioner from the adverse effects of this encounter with a ghost, which is construed as highly dangerous in omen texts.

The Late Babylonian text BM 36703 and the Neo-Babylonian K 2779, first published by Irving Finkel, demonstrate these characteristics outlined by Scurlock very well.[131] The first obverse column of BM 36704 is rather broken, but the extant text suggests a scenario in which a living petitioner concocts an ointment before reciting an incantation seven times, at which point the petitioner anoints his eyes before Šamaš. In what follows, the petitioner recites an incantation. The necromantic nature of the text becomes clear in obverse column ii, in which Šamaš summons a ghost who then inhabits a skull.[132] At this point, the text states: "May he [Šamaš]

---

130. Scurlock, "Magical Means," 103, 107.

131. Finkel, "Necromancy in Ancient Mesopotamia," passim.

132. Rather than interpreting column ii lines 2′–3′ as referring to Šamaš raising a ghost from the netherworld, Scurlock argues that the dust and tendons are being addressed directly here ("Magical Means," 323). However, this interpretation does not account for the direct address to Šamaš in lines 5′–6′: "May he who is within the skull answer [me], Šamaš, opener of the darknes[s]." Even if Scurlock is correct that the

bring up a ghost of the darkness....[133] I summon [you], skull.[134] May the one within the skull answer!" (ll. 3′–5′). The lines that follow prescribe the preparation of another ointment, although its usage goes unstated.

The following lines of BM 36703 (ll. 11′–23′) are duplicated almost exactly in K 2779 (ll. 1–9). This shared section of text is almost unintelligible until the notice, "Recite the incantation three times. Anoint your eyes. You will see a ghost, and it will speak with you" (BM 36703 ll. 21′–23′ // K2779 ll. 8–9). From there, K 2779 and BM 36703 diverge. BM 36703 includes a broken notice about an incantation before the rest of the column disappears altogether. K 2779, on the other hand, goes on to include *namburbî* material, a ritual for counteracting evil omens. Lines 10–18 of K 2779 prescribe the ritual means of averting the evil omen caused by contact with a ghost, well-known from the Šumma Alû omen series, and include offerings and incantations to Šamaš. The text then seems to depict an offering to Šamaš, though lines 21–22 are quite broken, and the text disappears completely in line 23.

Both BM 36703 and K 2779 are notable for their elaborate descriptions of the ritual elements of the necromantic encounter. Like other necromancy texts, Šamaš plays a major role in facilitating communication

---

dust and tendons are being addressed directly, the overall sense of the passage seems to be that Šamaš is a necessary intermediary for this manipulation of the dead. In fact, K 2779 explicitly refers to Šamaš as such an intermediary: "You are the one who keeps them (the ghosts) in check.... (You bring) the things below; you bring the things below above" (ll. 13–14).

133. I have chosen to omit the next sentence in the text because of its opacity. Finkel has interpreted UZU.SA UG₇ as "sinews of a dead man," which is plausible ("Necromancy in Ancient Mesopotamia," 9). However, the accompanying verb in this sentence is altogether reconstructed by Finkel, making interpretation of the overall sentence far too speculative.

134. The text has two variants of this term (*gulgul, gulgullat*), seemingly in construct form, one after the other. See *CAD* 5:127–28 for attestations of these forms. This noun is treated as masculine or feminine, depending on the text. The first term appears to be the construct form of the masculine *gulgullu*, while the second appears to be the construct of feminine *gulgullatu*. Translating both of the construct forms is awkward, since the second term is followed by a verb, not a governing noun. It is possible that a noun in this position is missing. In light of this awkward iteration of the same term, I have chosen to translate it only once, as opposed to Finkel's translation "skull of skulls" ("Necromancy in Ancient Mesopotamia," 9). Finkel has reconstructed the second masculine or feminine singular accusative pronominal suffix on the verb *ašassi*, "I summon," which I follow here.

between the living and the dead. In addition, the living petitioner is able to speak directly to the dead. The nature of the relationship between the living and the dead is unclear; however, there is no indication in the texts that the living and the dead are kin. Because these texts merely prescribe ritual components and do not report an actual performance of the ritual, they do not report what kinds of information are divulged in the ritual. Unlike other textual attestations of necromancy, BM 36703 and K2779 both stress the importance of the ointment applied to the living petitioner, which either helps the petitioner see the ghost or protects him from the adverse effects of the encounter itself.

An interesting aspect of K 2779—and one that differs from other necromancy texts—is its reference to the *kispu* in its *namburbî* section (ll. 10, 16). The *kispu* seems to have been part of the apotropaic rituals prescribed in this section of K 2779, perhaps to counteract the negative effects of a successful necromantic invocation. This reference to the *kispu* in a necromantic context suggests that the text does associate necromancy with the cult of dead kin or, at least, its constitutive rituals if not its central concerns. It seems that the use of the *kispu* in this context is meant to placate the dead and in doing so alleviate the threat of the ghost's presence. Yet, the focus is not on regular care for dead kin, and nothing in the texts suggests that petitioners sought information from dead kin through necromancy.

The majority of the third- or fourth-century text *SpTU* 2 no. 20 concerns the many plants and processes involved in making an ointment, the application of this ointment, and the repeated recitation of an incantation.[135] The necromantic nature of the ritual is clear in the statements that the ghost will speak to the one invoking him (ll. 18', 5, 24) and that the ghost will make a decision (l. 22). Furthermore, the notice "incantation to make a man's *namtaru* speak" in line 15' also suggests that this is a necromantic invocation. After all, as Scurlock notes, the term *namtaru* is often associated with death or fate and could be associated with specific people.[136] *SpTU* 2 no. 20 shares some characteristics with BM 36703 and K 2779; the text describes incantations urging the dead to speak to the living

---

135. For a critical edition and brief discussion of this text, see Egbert von Weiher, *Uruk: Spätbabylonische Texte aus dem Planquadrat U 18. Teil IV* (Mainz am Rhein: von Zabern, 1993), 100–104. Scurlock places this text in the context of third- or fourth-century Uruk ("Magical Means," 342).

136. *CAD* 11.1:247–49; Scurlock, "Magical Means," 333.

(ll. 11′–20′), accompanied by the making of the ointment (ll. 16′–19′). The application of this ointment is also similar to that in BM 36703 and K 2779—applied between the eyes of the living petitioner so that he may speak to a ghost and the ghost may respond. Like K 2779, *SpTU* 2 no. 20 also includes a final line that refers to the performance of a *namburbî*. However, this line, the one preceding it, and those following it are too broken to reconstruct the content of this *namburbî* ritual.

Scurlock also notes parallels between *SpTU* 2 no. 20 and two other texts, *BAM* III 215.44–63 and a cuneiform document translated by Jean-Marie Durand, number 336: 1′–10′, lines 44–58, both of which similarly refer to an incantation to be used when one wants "to see a ghost in order to make a decision."[137] The three texts contain almost identical language concerning the creation of an ointment to rub on the petitioner's face, the application of which seems to coincide with recitation of the incantation recorded in the texts. The association Scurlock proposes between *BAM* III 215.44–63 and the Muššu'u incantation series, which was likely

---

137. INIM.INIM.MA GIDIM IGI.DU$_8$ EŠ.BAR TAR-si (*SpTU* 2 no. 20, l. 22). *BAM* III 215 is part of a library collection discovered in a private house in Aššur. The collection contains catalogues, such as the titles of various series and groups of texts, including the Muššu'u, of which *BAM* III 215 is part. See Olof Pedersén, *Archives and Libraries in the City of Aššur: A Survey of the Material from the German Excavations*, part 2 (Uppsala: Almqvist & Wiksell, 1986), 41–76. The archive, N4, was located in the eastern part of the city of Aššur and dates to the Neo-Assyrian period. Unlike other libraries discovered in the city during this period, N4 was owned privately by a family of exorcists and comprises the largest collection of texts found in the city. Assigning ownership of the texts to a family of exorcists stems from the fact that almost a third of the texts contain colophons ascribing ownership individuals with the title MAŠ.MAŠ. Most of the texts in this collection, totaling about 631 in number, date to the Sargonid period, though some date to the Middle Assyrian period or are copies of Middle Assyrian texts. According to the colophon, the scribe responsible for writing *BAM* III 215 is Nabu-zer-Aššur-ukin, an "Assyrian scribe" (*ṭupšaruu aššurû*), who is the son of Bel-Kundi-ilaja, the "chief scribe and scribe of the Aššur temple" (*rab ṭupšarri u ṭupšar bīt Aššur*). For a critical edition and analysis of Muššu'u, see Barbara Böck, *Das Handbuch Muššu'u "Einreinbung": Eine Serie Sumerischer und Akkadischer Beschwörungen Aus Dem 1. JT. Vor Chr* (Madrid: Consejo Superior de Investigaciones Científicas, 2007). Scurlock places Jean-Marie Durand, *Documents Cunéiformes de la ive Section de l'École pratique des Hautes Études* (Paris: Librairie Droz, 1982), n. 336: 1′–10′, ll. 44–58, in Aššur during the Neo-Assyrian period. See JoAnn Scurlock, "Ritual 'Rubbing' Recitations from Ancient Mesopotamia (A Review of Barbara Böck, *Das Handbuch Muš̌'u 'Einreibung': Ein Serie sumerischer und akkadischer Beschwörungen aus dem 1.Jt vor Chr*. Biblioteca del Próximo Oriente Antiguo, 3," *Or* 80 (2011): 88.

used in the context of therapeutic massage, provides another example of ritual attempts to alleviate the adverse effects of successful necromantic encounters. Scurlock argues that these Muššu'u incantations would arm the living petitioner in the necromantic ritual against the effects of contact with ghosts: "No harm would come to the necromancer if the diseases caused by the spirits with whom he was seeking contact had already been warded off by the recitation of the appropriate spells."[138] Since the application of ointments in necromantic encounters seemingly takes place before the ghost appears, this application relies on a notion of preventative care—not just palliative care—in Akkadian medical discourse. Otherwise, the application of this ointment might only aid the process of seeing the ghost in the first place, not necessarily to alleviate the effects of that encounter.

Another text that must be considered along with the evidence for Mesopotamian necromancy is a dream report of Nabonidus:[139]

> I am the legitimate representative [našparšunu dannu] of Nebuchadnezzar and Neriglissar, kings who preceded me. Their armies are entrusted to me. I do not neglect their orders. I make them happy. Awēl-Marduk, son of Nebuchadnezzar, and Lābâši-Marduk, son of [Neri]glissar....[140] I became worried about the close approach of the Great Star and Sîn. A young man stood by my side and told me, "There are no evil signs in the conjunction." In that dream, Nebuchadnezzar, a prior king, and an attendant [girsequ] were standing on a chariot. The attendant said to Nebuchadnezzar, "Speak with Nabonidus. Let him report to you that dream which he had." Nebuchadnezzar listened to him and said to me, "Tell me what favorable signs you have seen." I answered him and said, "In the dream, the Great Star, Sîn, and Marduk were high in the midst of the heavens. I carefully examined them. He/it called me by my name."[141]

---

138. Scurlock, "Ritual 'Rubbing' Recitations," 88.

139. My translation closely follows that of Beaulieu, *Reign of Nabonidus*, 110–15. For a different rendering of the text, see *ANET*, 309–10. For previous discussions of the text, see Hayim Tadmor, "The Inscriptions of Nabunaid: Historical Arrangement," in *Studies in Honor of Benno Landsberger*, ed. Hans G. Güterbock and Thorkild Jacobsen, AS 16 (Chicago: University of Chicago Press, 1965), no. 8; Paul-Richard Berger, *Die neubabylonischen Königsinschriften*, AOAT 4/1 (Neukirchen-Vluyn: Neukirchener Verlag, 1973), 384–86 (Stelen-Fragment XI); Beaulieu, *Reign of Nabonidus*, 20–22.

140. The next few lines are quite choppy, making reconstruction of their content overly speculative. Thus, I have chosen to omit them from the translation above.

141. I have produced this text in its entirety above because it is not usually included in discussions of necromancy. Yet, as I argue below, it features significant

This report appears in column V, lines 14–34, and VI, lines 1–36, of an inscription found on a stela in the royal palace of Babylon. It is one of several surviving inscriptions from the reign of Nabonidus, including other dream reports in which the deities Marduk and Sîn appear to the king. Although the text in question is broken, it is of interest here because it nevertheless demonstrates characteristics consistent with necromantic encounters. The content of the text consists of the following: in a dream, the dead king Nebuchadnezzar II appears to the usurper king Nabonidus. Within that dream, Nabonidus relates to Nebuchadnezzar a previous dream consisting of astronomical phenomena, presumably so that Nebuchadnezzar would interpret these phenomena for him. Unfortunately, the broken text does not preserve the response of Nebuchadnezzar, which would likely entail the interpretation of these phenomena and their revelation to Nabonidus.[142] The text seems to depict the only extant example of dream incubation in which a dead person appears to the living incubant.[143]

This method of invoking the dead through dream incubation, of course, is quite different from that depicted in necromantic ritual texts. In addition, there is no reference to apotropaic ritual, neither the manufacture of ointments nor the offering of the *kispu*, to avert the dangers of encountering a ghost. Another important difference between this text and many necromancy texts cited above is that the dead person is not only identified by the text but also a well-known figure. That Nebuchadnezzar appears to Nabonidus in the dream is no doubt apologetic, intended to legitimize the reign of the usurper Nabonidus, who ascended to the throne following the violent deaths of three other kings.[144] Only two other ancient West Asian necromancy texts, Gilgamesh, Enkidu,

---

parallels with cuneiform necromancy texts and thus must be considered alongside them.

142. Beaulieu notes that the text following the break likely consists of Nebuchadnezzar's reply, based on the presence of the verb *ilsanni* and *–me*, the particle marking direct speech (*Reign of Nabonidus*, 113). However, the masculine singular subject of this verb is ambiguous, especially since the preceding lines refer to both Sîn and Marduk.

143. For a discussion of this text and its relationship to other attestations of ancient West Asian dream interpretation, see Oppenheim, *Interpretation of Dreams*, 202–6.

144. This emphasis on the legitimacy of Nabonidus's reign and its apologetic tone suggest to Beaulieu that the inscription was composed soon after the accession of Nabonidus (*Reign of Nabonidus*, 22).

and the Netherworld and 1 Sam 28, explicitly identify the dead person invoked in the ritual. Interestingly, in all of these texts, including the dream report of Nabonidus, the living petitioners are kings (Nabonidus, Gilgamesh, Saul) interacting with the named dead (Nebuchadnezzar, Enkidu, and Samuel). Furthermore, if we take the inscription of Nabonidus's mother, Adad-guppi,[145] at its word that Nabonidus was personally acquainted with Nebuchadnezzar during his lifetime, then all three of these necromantic encounters involve people who knew each other in life. The dream report shares other features with the necromancy texts from Mesopotamia as well. The dead and the living petitioner are not kin, and the report of Nabonidus's dream demonstrates no interest in caring for the dead Nebuchadnezzar through the rites characteristic of the cult of dead kin. Another shared feature is the presence of an intermediary between the living and the dead. In the dream report, an attendant (*girsequ*)[146] of Nebuchadnezzar intercedes between the two kings before they speak to each other directly. However, the text does not refer to the *girsequ* as a necromancer or any other kind of religious specialist.

Conclusion

The cuneiform texts referring to necromancy demonstrate patterns in the ways in which the practice is depicted. Almost all of the texts refer to privileged information divulged by the dead to the living petitioner, especially in cases where the living petitioner is suffering (Ludlul, *LKA* 139, *SpTU* 2 no. 20). Some texts refer to the use of an ointment in necromantic invocation, its application, and the accompanying recitation of incantations (BM 36703, K 2779, *SpTU* 2 no. 20). This ointment may be one method of protecting the living petitioner against the adverse effects of the necromantic encounter. Multiple texts refer to the role of a divine intermediary, especially Šamaš (= Sumerian Utu), in invoking the dead (Gilgamesh, Enkidu, and the Netherworld; BM 36704; K 2779; *LKA* 139).[147] When necromancy is listed among other types of divination, it appears last or

---

145. For a discussion of Adad-guppi and this text, see Beaulieu, *Reign of Nabonidus*, 67–79, as well as my treatment in ch. 3.

146. Beaulieu, following Oppenheim, suggests that the *girsequ* is a eunuch based on the similar imagery depicting eunuchs in Assyrian iconography (*Reign of Nabonidus*, 112).

147. Indeed, the presence of a solar deity in necromancy and the cult of dead kin

relatively late in the list, which may indicate that necromancy is a divinatory method reserved for times of acute crisis (TCL 4 5, Ludlul). Two texts suggest that women could function as necromancers (Lu, TCL 4 5). The appearance of the ghosts of one's family in *LKA* 139 suggests that there may be some overlap between family religion and necromancy. However, in this text and others, there is an overall lack of concern for the care of dead kin; there are no references to nourishment of the dead or commemoration. While dead kin may be invoked, it is for the purpose of obtaining information from them, not commemorating or caring for them. In fact, the use of a skull in K 2779 suggests the disturbance of bones (compare *rgz* in 1 Sam 28) rather than their preservation and care. While some texts refer to the *kispu* (Gilgamesh, Enkidu, and the Netherworld; K 2779), it is not part of the necromantic ritual itself. Instead, these references complement the necromantic encounter, either by explaining the fate of those in the netherworld (Gilgamesh, Enkidu, and the Netherworld) or averting the negative effects of the ghost's presence (K 2779). This lack of concern for the care of the dead suggests that necromancy and the cult of dead kin must be considered separate cultic phenomena, even when they appear together in a cuneiform text.

This lack of concern for the commemoration and care for the dead is also a fundamental feature of the biblical representation of necromancy. Unlike the single attestation of dead kin in *LKA* 139, the family is entirely absent from depictions of necromancy in the Hebrew Bible. The biblical references to necromancy focus instead on the religious specialist or laypeople who perform the necromantic ritual, who are then negatively portrayed by the biblical writers and contrasted with other, allegedly legitimate cult specialists, particularly prophets and priests. In our most detailed biblical description of necromancy, 1 Sam 28, kinship does not determine who among the dead is invoked in the ritual. Thus, while the cult of dead kin is minimally present in cuneiform depictions of necromancy, it is entirely lacking in biblical depictions of necromancy.

Reconstructions of Israelite religion tend to conflate death-related phenomena. Such a conflation is likely due in large part to the scant nature of the extant evidence.[148] However, rituals related to the dead need not be

---

constitutes one similarity between textual depictions of the two phenomena. I will further examine the role of this solar deity in depictions of care of dead kin in ch. 4.

148. Pitard articulates some of the methodological problems that arise from this limited data set: "I believe that the study of Israelite concepts of death and afterlife

synthesized into a single coherent system of cultic practices and related ideologies, especially when the extant evidence treats them differently. The cult of dead kin and necromancy may exist separately alongside each other and have their own systems of logic and practice. Frederick Cryer articulates this principle with respect to modern ethnographic studies: "Comparison of the ancient Near Eastern cult of dead kin with similar practices in existing traditional societies might [serve] as a useful safeguard against the tendency to assume that, where veneration of the ancestors may be safely assumed, it may be likewise assumed that one invariably attempts to derive information from them."[149] It is also true that death-related practices do not always rely on a well-articulated or widely accepted rationale for those practices. For example, present-day mourners may leave items at a gravesite, but this practice does not necessarily inform, nor is it informed by, ideologies about afterlife, ghosts, or care for the dead. As Levi Rahmani notes, "The incentives for our own actions are often a composite of a number of different motivations, often conflicting and seldom completely reconciled."[150] More recently, Thomas Laqueur has expressed a similar sentiment concerning the seemingly contradictory nature of attitudes toward the dead body:

> [The dead body] matters in disparate religious and ideological circumstances; it matters even in the absence of any particular belief about a soul or about how long it might linger around its former body or about what might become of it after death; it matters across all sorts of beliefs about an afterlife and God. It matters in the absence of such beliefs. It matters because the living need the dead far more than the dead need the living. It matters because the dead make social worlds. It matters because we cannot bear to live at the borders of our mortality.[151]

---

has often suffered from a tendency to overinterpret one's evidence, overgeneralize from limited data, overrely on meagre and weak evidence in drawing up complex reconstructions of systems of practice and belief, and to overuse cultural parallels from neighboring or more distant societies for interpreting unattested or ambiguous aspects of Israel's thought" ("Tombs and Offerings, 147).

149. Cryer, *Divination in Ancient Israel*, 182–83.

150. Levi Y. Rahmani, "Ancient Jerusalem's Funerary Customs and Tombs: Part One," *BA* 44 (1981): 172.

151. Thomas W. Laqueur, *The Work of the Dead: A Cultural History of Mortal Remains* (Princeton: Princeton University Press, 2015), 1.

Different death-related practices and their respective rationales may coexist with seemingly little cognitive dissonance among practitioners.

In closing, both the biblical and cuneiform evidence suggests that we must consider necromancy as separate from the cult of dead kin in ancient West Asia. Both cultic phenomena refer to the dead, but their purposes, principles, and participants are distinctly different. The cult of dead kin is not concerned with divination but with the commemoration and care of the dead. Thus, while biblical necromancy involves rival religious specialists, care for dead kin belongs in the realm of family religion. Unlike the competition posed by necromancers in the Hebrew Bible, ritual actors involved in care for the dead do not pose a threat to priestly or prophetic circles, which may explain the appearance of biblical polemic against necromancy but the relative lack of polemic against cult of dead kin. Moreover, the conflation of these practices in previous scholarship has led to hasty conclusions regarding polemics against certain practices pertaining to the dead in strands of the biblical text. Once we recognize a distinction between necromancy and the cult of dead kin, it becomes clear that there is no systematic condemnation of commemoration and care for the dead in the Hebrew Bible.

3

Women in the Israelite Cult of Dead Kin

In the preceding chapters, I have outlined the contours of the cult of dead kin both in and outside ancient Israel, examined its relationship with other forms of death-related ritual, and highlighted its place within the broader landscape of family religion in ancient West Asia. In order to understand the scope and influence of the cult of dead kin, one must appreciate the deep embeddedness of the cult within the life of the family. The cult of dead kin mediates the ongoing relationship between the living and the dead, thus expanding the boundaries of the family unit to include not only living members but also the dead who continue to receive care from them. In biblical studies, the increased interest in family religion has also coincided with, and likely been encouraged by, close consideration of the social roles of women in the ancient world.[1] Rituals concerning offspring, especially those surrounding pregnancy, childbirth, and nursing, are particularly associated with women in biblical scholarship.[2] Thus, women have a great deal of influence over these central moments in the life cycle of the family. However, the participation of women in the opposite end of that life cycle, the rituals comprising the cult of dead kin, continues to be a source of disagreement among biblical scholars. Some studies have argued that women are largely excluded from these rituals, as both offerers and recipients.[3]

---

1. Albertz and Schmitt offer a recent examination of these overlapping developments in biblical studies (*Family and Household Religion*, 8–11).

2. Meyers, *Households and Holiness*, 17; Olyan, "What Do We Really Know," 64–65. Olyan draws a further distinction concerning rites related to childbirth, however, and argues that ancient West Asian evidence does indicate that men as well as women were likely involved in rituals concerning fertility and conception ("What Do We Really Know," 60–61).

3. E.g., Van der Toorn, *Family Religion in Babylonia*, 229; Ackerman, "Cult Centralization," 19–40; Ackerman, *Women and the Religion of Ancient Israel*, manuscript

To be sure, most textual depictions of ancestors and the cult of dead kin in ancient West Asia, including the Hebrew Bible, idealize patrilineal descent and relationships between men. The focus on the patriarchs as the fathers or progenitors of Israel in the Torah and elsewhere no doubt influences the scholarly tendency to construe ancestors as male. Other biblical references to dead predecessors as ʾābôt (lit. "fathers") include the burial notices of the kings of Israel and Judah throughout the Deuteronomistic History and the description of the conquered city of Jerusalem in Neh 2:3, 5 as the place of "the graves of my ʾābôt."[4] Most important, one of our most

---

25. The argument that the Israelite cult of dead kin is solely the realm of men, however, is not new. In fact, this argument already appears in nineteenth-century examinations of the cult. See Immanuel Benzinger, *Hebräische Archäologie* (Leipzig: Mohr, 1894), 140; Wilhelm Nowack, *Lehrbuch der hebräischen Archäologie* (Leipzig: Mohr, 1894), 154, 348, cited in Phyllis A. Bird, *Missing Persons and Mistaken Identities* (Minneapolis: Fortress, 1997), 81 n. 3. Concerning the Mesopotamian evidence, Bayliss draws a similar distinction, stating that women could "take responsibility for the funerary cult, though not necessarily participate in it" ("Cult of Dead Kin," 119).

4. Hebrew grammar tends to obscure the inclusion of women in groups of mixed gender: the verbs and pronouns used for such groups are always masculine. For this reason, it can be difficult to determine whether women are included in these groups and participate with men in certain activities. This feature of Hebrew grammar also applies to the use of certain kinship terms. For instance, the banê-yiśrāʾēl, literally "the sons of Israel," more often refers to the Israelites as a whole, including both men and women. Therefore, it is possible that the term ʾābôt (lit. "fathers") may function in a similar way, referring to a collective of both male and female predecessors. Some texts explicitly use the term to refer to the patriarchs, Abraham, Isaac, and Jacob (Exod 3:13, 15; Deut 1:8, 11, 21), in which cases the term clearly refers to male predecessors. Other texts use the term to refer to predecessors, but the gender is more ambiguous. The ʾābôt who resided in Egypt (Gen 46:34; Exod 10:6; 1 Sam 12:6, 7, 8, 15), for instance, are not named, nor given any gendered markers. References to the burial of the kings of Israel and Judah (1 Kgs 1:21; 2:10; 11:21, 43; 14:20, 22, 31; 15:8, 24; 22:40; 2 Kgs 8:24; 15:7, 22, 38; 16:20; 20:21) often use the set phrase "PN slept with his fathers" (šākab PN ʿim-ʾăbōtāyw). While these passages focus on the activities of kings, it is not clear that the burial notices in them refer exclusively to the tombs of kings. While the idiom of burial uses the masculine kinship term ʾābôt, it may obscure the fact that wives and mothers of kings were also buried in those tombs. In fact, Gen 49:29–31 refers to the burial of Jacob in the cave at Machpelah, where Abraham, Sarah, Isaac and Rebekah, and his own wife Leah had been buried previously. In this passage, Jacob instructs his sons regarding his burial: "As for me, I will be gathered to my people. Bury me with my ʾābôt in the cave in the field of Ephron the Hittite." Epigraphic evidence also shows this idiom used in the context of a woman's death. The sarcophagus inscription of Yabâ includes the notice that she "went the way of her fathers" in Akkadian. See

descriptive texts for the cult of dead kin in ancient Israel, 2 Sam 18:18, specifically refers to the relationship between a son and his dead father: "In his lifetime, Absalom took and set up for himself a stela [*maṣṣebet*], which is in the Valley of the King, because he said, 'I do not have a son to commemorate my name.' He called the stela by his own name, and it is called the Monument [*yād*] of Absalom to this day." The gendered language here is unambiguous; Absalom lacks a *son*. The text assumes that a son would typically act as Absalom's cultic caregiver, erecting a *maṣṣebet* or stela and invoking his father's name, thus commemorating his dead father.

However, there are problems with the argument that women are altogether excluded from this cult, especially if we consider ancestor cult, or the care for one's dead elders, as one facet of a broader category, cult of dead kin.[5] As I have defined it in this study, the cult of dead kin includes offerings of food and drink (and sometimes other items, such as incense), the construction of commemorative monuments, invocation of the name of the dead, and the protection and (when necessary) repatriation of human remains. In this chapter, I examine biblical texts that depict women either offering or receiving such ritual care, thus challenging the widespread argument that women are excluded from the cult of dead kin in ancient Israel. Many of these biblical texts are absent from previous discussions of the cult because these studies have overlooked some constitutive rituals of the cult.

Abdulilah Fadhil, "Die Nimrud/Kalḫu Aufgefundene Grabinschrift der Jabâ," *BaghM* 21 (1990): 464. Another instance—not involving burial—where the term *'ābôt* may include a woman is 1 Kgs 15:12, which depicts the cultic reforms of Asa: "He [Asa] turned away the consecrated ones [*qədēšîm*] from the land and removed all of the *gillûlîm* [lit. "dung balls," referring to allegedly illegitimate divine images] that his *'ābôt* had made." The next verse goes on to say that Asa also removed his mother, Maacah, from the position of queen mother because she had made an image for the goddess Asherah. Reading these verses together, it seems plausible that Maacah is included in the *'ābôt* of 15:12 and their construction of illegitimate cult images. Nevertheless, the use of a masculine kinship term to refer to ancestors of mixed gender further demonstrates the emphasis on patrilineal descent in Israelite family religion, including the cult of dead kin. It is perhaps this patrilineal focus in the terminology related to the cult of dead kin that has led biblical scholars to overlook the participation of women in the cult as well. Thus, the gender-obfuscating nature of Semitic languages, including Hebrew, may affect the ways in which we reconstruct the cultic activities of men and women. For a more thorough analysis of the idiom of dead predecessors as *'ābôt*, see Suriano, *Politics of Dead Kings*, passim.

5. I understand *ancestor* here as an elder predecessor. For a more detailed discussion of my preferred terminology for the cult, see the introduction.

As we recognize a growing range of ritual acts and imagery closely associated with the care of the dead in ancient Israel, we see a growing number of biblical attestations in which women offer or receive that care.

In addition, I argue that women in these texts participate both directly and indirectly in the cult, meaning that they may receive or offer care themselves or they may create opportunities for others to do so. Thus, the roles that women play in the cult of dead kin are complex and influenced by various factors. In fact, recent studies of the Israelite family similarly recognize the patrilineal ideal of the biblical text, while pointing out several examples in which descent and inheritance are mediated by women. For instance, in her study of "socially marked women and maternally identified kin" in the Hebrew Bible, Cynthia Chapman challenges the prevailing notion in biblical studies that kinship is exclusively patrilineal. In order to understand the Israelite family at all, Chapman argues, we must consider the different ways in which kinship is articulated and how different texts deploy such terms and concepts: "Instead of 'domaining' women and matrilineal kin out of the treatments of political and social structures, we need to theorize all relationships within one lens, 'as part of one integral system.'"[6] Jacqueline Vayntrub makes a similar point in her analysis of Gen 27 and the Ugaritic Aqhat Epic:

> In this story, the mere existence of a son who performs acts of filial devotion is not sufficient to ensure survival of the trans-generational line: alternative strategies may be necessary. Unconventional acts of devotion by a female family member keep the family line intact. Father-to-son transmission is held up as an ideal, so long as it can be achieved successfully. In its extant form, the story appears to challenge this ideal in asking whether filial succession alone is reliable as a strategy for preserving the family across generations.[7]

The goal of this chapter is to hold these two aspects of the cult of dead kin in tension: the patrilineal ideal of commemoration and care and, at the same time, the prevalence of women mediating both.

Another problem we face in discussing the cult of dead kin in general and the role of women in particular is that most of the extant evidence

---

6. Cynthia R. Chapman, *The House of the Mother: The Social Roles of Maternal Kin in Biblical Hebrew Narrative and Poetry* (New Haven: Yale University Press, 2016), 11.

7. Jacqueline Vayntrub, "Like Father, Like Son: Theorizing Transmission in Biblical Literature," *HBAI* 7 (2018): 512.

depicts royal cults of dead kin in texts and commemorative monuments. Thus, the view of the cult we get from this evidence is inevitably skewed toward the royal sphere, which may differ in significant ways from the practices of nonroyal families. If, for instance, an ancient West Asian queen receives cult from her living descendants, to what extent can we extrapolate a broader familial practice from that ritual? Of course, this is a perennial problem in the reconstruction of most ancient practices: the evidence left by elites and their practices tend to survive, while residues of nonelite practices tend to disappear from the textual and material records. In addition, ancient texts, including the Hebrew Bible, often omit the mundane in favor of the unusual and exceptional. Such is the case for death and the rituals surrounding it. For instance, we have no biblical text prescribing the liturgy of a typical funeral and only one describing a funeral itself (that of Abner in 2 Sam 3:31–37), but we have many references to corpse exposure and abuse in various forms (e.g., Deut 21:22–23; Josh 8:28–29; 1 Sam 31:6–13; 1 Kgs 14:10–11; Jer 8:1–3; 16:1–19). Similarly, we do not find prescriptive texts or literary accounts depicting the ideal performance of the cult of dead kin. Instead, we find nonideal scenarios in which the dead either lack kin to care for them or suffer some other kind of hardship, such as dislocation from one's ancestral land. These depictions of nonideal death are particularly relevant to a discussion of women because these are the cases in which women tend to play a more prominent role in the cult of dead kin throughout ancient West Asia, at least as it is represented in texts.[8]

Where and how are women depicted in textual representations of the cult of dead kin? What roles do they play? Are they, as some argue, excluded from the cult? If so, in what ways? Are women only depicted as participants in the cult of dead kin when men are absent? Is the performance of the cult by men always preferred? Is the participation of women in this cult only a last resort? In general, the role of women in the cult of

---

8. Jo Ann Hackett similarly notes the more prominent roles of women in patriarchal societies (and, perhaps, their heightened visibility to the modern scholar) in times of crisis: "Interestingly, and perhaps not surprisingly, periods of what has been termed social dysfunction are actually periods when women's status is relatively higher than in settled times.... In periods of severe dysfunction, centralized institutions might give way to more local handling of affairs, a situation we have already seen to be often conducive to women's participation." See Hackett, "In the Days of Jael: Reclaiming the History of Women," in *Immaculate and Powerful*, ed. Clarissa W. Atkinson, Constance H. Buchanan, and Margaret R. Miles (Boston: Beacon, 1985), 19.

dead kin is more pervasive than previous studies have posited. That role is particularly well attested in moments of crisis when social and political order is disrupted in various ways. Though the cult of dead kin is fundamentally patriarchal and concerned primarily with male actors, women do occupy an important position within this cult, one that has been largely overlooked in the Hebrew Bible and cognate literatures.

Women in the Cult of Dead Kin outside Israel

Before considering biblical depictions of women in the cult of dead kin, it is important to contextualize their treatment within the broader ancient West Asian cultural landscape. Indeed, evidence from various sites and time periods shows that women could function as both participants in and recipients of the cult of dead kin, though their roles in associated rituals are not as well attested as those of men. For instance, several cuneiform texts from different sites and periods attest to the roles of women in the cult. Piotr Michalowski notes that two women, Geme-ninlila and Šulgi-simti, receive libation offerings along with King Šulgi in a text from Drehem in the Ur III period.[9] Another text from the same period (and, perhaps, the same site)[10] refers to provisions for the libation place (KI.A.NAG) of Takum-matum, wife of King Šu-Sîn. This designation as the wife of the king suggests that Takum-matum receives cult because of her marriage and affiliation with the king. In fact, many Sumerian administrative texts refer to the sacrificial offerings and care offered to dead royal women.[11] Alfonso Archi examines a text from Ebla in which sacrificial offerings are listed for prominent dead women in the royal court as well as former sovereigns.[12] Previous studies have also noted the practice of sacrificing to dead Hittite kings and queens.[13] Though depictions of nonroyal cult of

---

9. Piotr Michalowski, "The Death of Šulgi," *Or* 46 (1977): 222.

10. Grant Frame, "A New Wife for Šu-Sîn," *ARRIM* 2 (1977): 3–4. Frame notes that the tablet was purchased on the antiquities market and that its provenance cannot be determined with certainty.

11. Jean-Jacques Glassner, "Women, Hospitality and the Honor of the Family," in *Women's Earliest Records*, ed. Barbara S. Lesko (Atlanta: Scholars Press, 1989), 89.

12. Alfonso Archi, "The High Priestess, dam-dingir, at Ebla," in *"Und Mose schrieb dieses Lied auf": Studien zum Alten Testament und zum Alten Orient,* ed. Manfried Dietrich and Ingo Kottsieper (Münster: Ugarit-Verlag, 1998), 48.

13. A concise survey of this Hittite scholarship appears in Hallo, "Royal Ancestor Worship," 383.

dead kin are relatively rare, Miranda Bayliss notes that one text seems to list the full range of potential participants in the nonroyal cult: "Whether (you be) one who has no brother or sister, or one who has no family or relatives, or one who has no son or daughter, or one who has no heir to make libations of water."[14] The inclusion of the sister and daughter in this list assumes that women could participate, at least as caregivers in the cult. The text implies that these women offer care to those in their natal family, but it does not state whether these women are married. Thus, it is unclear whether they would be able to offer this care to members of their natal families if they were married.

In fact, other texts suggest that the inclusion of women in certain rites of the cult of dead kin, such as invocation of the name of the dead, may largely depend on their marital status. Examining this issue, Karel van der Toorn analyzes an Old Babylonian genealogical list, commissioned by Sîn-nāṣir, that includes wives of men in the genealogy as well as their unmarried daughters.[15] The genealogy takes the form of a prayer to the moon god Sîn, who is able to mediate the food and drink offerings between the living family members of Sîn-nāṣir and those who have died. The text refers explicitly to the bread and water offered to the dead kin of Sîn-nāṣir, a characteristic of the *kispu*. In addition, the recitation of this genealogy may have been a mode of invoking the names of the dead, another component of the cult of dead kin. Thus, those included in the genealogy may be understood as recipients of both modes of care described in the text. Mothers of descendants appear in this list, though they are sometimes only named as "wife of PN," and daughters who serve as a *nadītum*, a woman dedicated to a deity,[16] not only appear but are also named (e.g., "Amat-aya, *nadītum* of Šamaš, his [Išme-Ea's] daughter").

Van der Toorn offers a plausible explanation for the inclusion of the *nadītum* in the family genealogy: these women do not leave their natal family in the same way as a married daughter, who becomes integrated into the family and genealogy of her husband. Thus, if this text demonstrates a broader pattern of women's inclusion in the cult of dead kin, it appears that their inclusion depends on their affiliation with men in a particular lineage, especially a father or husband. If a woman cannot claim

---

14. Bayliss, "Cult of Dead Kin," 118–19.

15. Van der Toorn, *Family Religion*, 54.

16. This woman is often unmarried and childless. See *CAD* 11.1:63–64 for further discussion.

affiliation through a male family member and the social stability it entails, then she becomes a particularly marginalized member of society. In fact, Paula Hiebert argues that the Akkadian term *almattu*, a cognate of Hebrew *'almānâ*, refers to a woman "without males who are responsible for supporting her."[17] Such support would likely include ritual care for the dead.

A Neo-Assyrian text in which the dead queen mother blesses the crown prince Assurbanipal (*LAS* 132.1–11) is an example of a royal woman both receiving the cult of dead kin from her son and offering him a blessing in return:[18]

> In accordance with her [the queen mother's] loyalty [*kinūtu*], Aššur (and) Šamaš have ordained me as crown prince of the land of Aššur. Her ghost blesses him to the extent that he cares for [*palāḫu*] the ghost [*eṭemmu*]. "May his descendants rule over the land of Assyria!" Care [*palaḫ*] for the gods begets kindness. Care [*palaḫ*] for the Anunnaki increases life. [May the king, my lord] establish order.

As I argued in chapter 2, the terminology used in this text suggests that it refers to the rituals and underlying principles of the cult of dead kin, not necromancy. The principle of reciprocity is particularly clear: Assurbanipal cares for (*palāḫu*) his dead mother, who then blesses his reign and that of his descendants. Another interesting aspect of the text is its close association between cult of dead kin and loyal service to the gods. Indeed, it uses the same term (*palāḫu*) to refer to care for the dead queen mother and the gods. Furthermore, the queen mother's ability to bestow the blessing seems related to the loyalty she herself has shown the gods, in life or death. The reference to her loyalty (*kinūtu*) immediately before the statement that Aššur and Šamaš ordain the coronation of Assurbanipal suggests that she is able to intercede with these deities on behalf of her son. This reciprocity between the gods and the king seems to provide the rationale for the generalization: "Care [*palaḫ*] for the gods begets kindness. Care [*palaḫ*] for the Anunnaki increases life. [May the king,

---

17. Paula S. Hiebert, "'Whence Shall Help Come to Me?': The Biblical Widow," in *Gender and Difference in Ancient Israel*, ed. Peggy L. Day (Minneapolis: Fortress, 1989), 128.

18. My translation and treatment of this text appear in ch. 2 in the discussion concerning the alleged relationship between this text and Mesopotamian necromancy. I have reproduced the text here to emphasize its relevance to a discussion of the cult of dead kin, particularly the role of women in the cult.

my lord] establish order." Care, in this context, includes both the cult of dead kin and the cult of the gods. In this case, the mode of care for the dead queen mother is not specified by the text. However, its association with care for the gods suggests that it may similarly entail material offerings and invocation.[19]

In a commemorative inscription, Adad-guppi, mother of the Neo-Babylonian king Nabonidus, claims to offer the *kispu* to the dead kings Nebuchadnezzar and Neriglissar.[20] There are two copies of this inscription, discovered in 1906 and 1956, at Harran. The stelae on which the text is inscribed were likely set up in the vicinity of the temple dedicated to Sîn at Harran. The bulk of the text translated below is missing at the end of column II in one version of the text, but the inscription resumes after the break in column III. There was originally a relief sculpture atop one stela, but only the bottom edge of the scene has been preserved, making it difficult to decipher.[21]

> In the 21 years of Nabopolassar, king of Babylon, 43 years of Nebuchadnezzar, son of Nabopolassar, and 4 years of Neriglissar, king of Babylon (the kings reigned continuously for 68 years), I[22] served them with all my heart and was dutiful toward them. I presented Nabonidus, my son and offspring, before Nebuchadnezzar, son of Nabopolassar, and Neriglissar, king of Babylon. Day and night, he served them dutifully and consistently did what pleased them. He established my excellent name

---

19. Karel van der Toorn argues that *palāḫu* entails material offerings on the basis of a text from Emar (Emar VI no. 213.10–13), in which the term refers to the payment of a living family member's debts. See Van der Toorn, "The Domestic Cult at Emar," *JCS* 47 (1995): 38 n. 34.

20. For collations and more extensive treatments of the text, see Beaulieu, *Reign of Nabonidus*, 68–79; Hanspeter Schaudig, *Die Inschriften Nabonids von Babylon und Kyros' des Großen: Samt den in ihrem Umfeld entstandenen Tendenzschriften* (Münster: Ugarit-Verlag, 2001), 500–513; Benno Landsberger, "Die Basaltstele Nabonids von Eski-Harran," in *Halil Edhem Hâtira Kitabi* (Ankara: Türk Tarih Kurumu Basimevi, 1947), 115–51; Tsukimoto, *Untersuchungen zur Totenpflege (kispum)*, 122–23.

21. For images of the stelae, see Cyril J. Gadd, "The Harran Inscriptions of Nabonidus," *AnSt* 8 (1958): 41, 44–48.

22. Although the inscription is written in the first-person voice of Adad-guppi, Beaulieu argues that it is more likely that Nabonidus commissioned the inscription after her death, perhaps at the same time as the rebuilding of Eḫulḫul, the temple of Sîn in Ḫarran (Beaulieu, *Reign of Nabonidus*, 68 n. 1). See, similarly, Tremper Longman III, *Fictional Akkadian Autobiography* (Winona Lake, IN: Eisenbrauns, 1991), 101–3.

before them. They elevated me[23] as a daughter, their own offspring [*kīma*
DUMU.SAL *ṣīt libbišunu*]. Later, they died. No one among their sons and
none of their kin [*nišu*] or their elite officials whose goods and property
they increased when they elevated them [*rēšišunu ullû*] offered incense
to them. Every month without ceasing, dressed in fine clothes, I offered
all of the *kispu*: fattened sheep, bread, beer, wine, oil, honey, and fruit.
I regularly established *kispu* offerings of good, fragrant incense, and I
continuously set them in their presence. (col II., ll. 40–60–col. III, ll. 1–4)

Explicitly using the terminology of the *kispu* (*akassapšunūtima*, "I established *kispu* rites for them"), the text lists the different items Adad-guppi
offers. Notably, the text also describes her prior relationship with the kings
in kinship terms. In fact, the text does not say that Adad-guppi simply
acted like a daughter to the kings but that the kings themselves exalted
her as though she were their biological daughter (*kīma* DUMU.SAL *ṣīt
libbišunu*, ll. 49–50). The implication in the text seems to be that this
exalted status is the result of the service she renders to them during their
lifetimes; however, Adad-guppi's claim to this status is further supported
by the service she renders them in death, offering them care when their
own descendants and courtiers have failed to do so. No one who has prof-
ited from the kings during their reigns—including their own sons, kin,
and other elite officials of the court—offers incense to them when they are
dead. Interestingly, it seems at times that offering incense is a synecdoche
for the full range of rites constitutive of the cult of dead kin. In fact, the
text refers to the offering of incense as if it is the quintessential rite of the
kispu in column II, lines 56–57 and column III, lines 1–3. In the absence of
such care, Adad-guppi claims, she becomes the sole caregiver for the dead
kings, showing them the same loyalty in death as she had in life.

This text depicts a crisis scenario in which dead kings lack a cultic
caregiver from their own families and a woman with no kinship ties (by
birth) to the dead becomes the sole administrator of the cult of dead kin.
However, the claim made in the text is not that the dead kings lack sons
who can offer the *kispu* but rather that their sons fail to do so. Thus, the
crisis depicted in the text concerns lack of cultic piety, not lack of off-

---

23. The idiom here (*ullû rēšiya*) refers to the elevation of one's status, often used
in the context of leadership roles such as kingship (*CAD* 4:126). In fact, this idiom also
appears in ll. 54–55 of the inscription, which describe the sons and officials who fail to
offer incense to the dead Neo-Babylonian kings.

spring. The implication is that Adad-guppi and her son Nabonidus would restore proper piety to the kingship. Of course, this is a valuable rhetorical strategy: Adad-guppi is able to claim or (if we accept the rhetoric of the inscription) affirm her status as daughter to the dead kings through performance of the cult, thus bolstering the legitimacy of the kingship of Nabonidus. In this way, Adad-guppi's inscription and its depiction of the cult of dead kin seems to alleviate the political rupture caused by the ascent of Nabonidus, who had no dynastic claim to the throne. Through performance of the cult, Adad-guppi grafts herself and, by extension, her son onto the family tree of the previous dynasty. Such rhetoric tacitly argues that the reign of Nabonidus is legitimate not through blood relations but through loyal service to the kings, both in life and death. Through this service, both Adad-guppi and Nabonidus effectively become the kin of well-established royalty. For the purposes of this chapter, it is noteworthy that this inscription casts Adad-guppi as the ritual actor who forges such bonds of kinship.

Gender fluidity plays a particularly fascinating role in texts from Emar and Nuzi, where fictive maleness is sometimes bestowed on women in the context of inheritance and care for the dead.[24] In fact, when wives or daughters appear as heirs in inheritance documents from Emar, the texts explicitly refer to these women as men in the context of that inheritance.[25] Thus, mothers are both "father and mother," and daughters are "male and

---

24. See, e.g., Gary Beckman, "Family Values on the Middle Euphrates," in *Emar: The History, Religion, and Culture of a Syrian Town in the Late Bronze Age*, ed. Mark W. Chavalas (Bethesda, MD: CDL, 1996), 58; Van der Toorn, "Gods and Ancestors." Andrew C. Cohen similarly examines gender fluidity in the context of death rituals in early dynastic southern Mesopotamia (ca. 2900–2350 BCE). In his study, Cohen analyzes the GALA, a mourning specialist, who occupies "a liminal status in the binary structure of gender roles." See Cohen, *Death Rituals, Ideology, and the Development of Early Mesopotamian Kingship: Toward a New Understanding of Iraq's Royal Cemetery of Ur* (Leiden: Brill, 2005), 54–55. Cohen posits that the ambiguous ways in which cuneiform texts gender the GALA reflect the boundary-crossing nature of death and death ritual.

25. For textual references and further examination of this phenomenon at Emar, see Katarzyna Grosz, "Daughters Adopted as Sons at Nuzi and Emar," in *La femme dans la Proche-Orient antique*, ed. Jean-Marie Durand (Paris: Éditions Recherche sur les Civilisations, 1987), 81–86; Zairira Ben-Barak, "The Legal Status of the Daughter as Heir in Nuzi and Emar," in *Society and Economy in the Eastern Mediterranean (c. 1500–1000 B.C.)*, ed. Michael Heltzer and Edward Lipiński (Leuven: Departement Oriëntalistiek, 1988), 87–97.

female." Two of these texts include care for the dead among the duties of the daughter who inherits her father's estate:[26]

> Unara, my daughter, I have established as female and male. Let her invoke my gods and my dead [DINGIR.MEŠ-*ia ù me-te-ia lu-ú tù-na-bi*].[27]

> Al-ḫati, my daughter, I have established as female and male. Let her invoke my gods and my dead.

In fact, Pitard argues that the use of the terms *kunnû*, "to attend to," and *nabû*, "to invoke," in these texts suggest that the offering of food and drink and the invocation of the name were important aspects of this care for the dead.[28] An inheritance text from Nuzi describes a similar situation in which daughters are referred to as sons of their father and given the responsibility of caring for the dead:[29] "Whoever among my daughters holds my fields and houses (and) is dwelling in my house shall serve [*i-pal-la-aḫ*][30] the gods and my ghosts [DINGIR.MEŠ *ù e-ṭe₄-em-mi-ia*]." Thus, texts from Emar and Nuzi depict the legal fiction of turning female kin

---

26. For an analysis of these texts, see John Huehnergard, "Five Tablets from the Vicinity of Emar," *RA* 77 (1983): 13–19, texts 1 and 2.

27. Some interpreters of these texts argue that this phrase is a hendiadys and thus that the dead are divine at Emar. See, e.g., Van der Toorn, "Gods and Ancestors," 38–59, Tsukimoto, *Untersuchungen zur Totenpflege (kispum)*, 104–5. In a more recent argument, however, Van der Toorn posits that the terms 'ilī and *mētē* refer to images of the dead and their corpses, respectively. See Karel van der Toorn, "Second Millennium West Asian Family Religion," in Bodel and Olyan, *Household and Family Religion*, 27. For the most part, Fleming accepts this interpretation ("Integration of Household," 40–43). For the argument against this interpretation, see Wayne Pitard, "Care of the Dead at Emar," in Chavalas, *Emar*, 127–29. In this discussion about the role of women in the cult of dead kin, however, the debate is largely beside the point. The relevant point here is that women are depicted in this context as primarily responsible for the care of dead kin, a responsibility closely regulated by legal documents.

28. Pitard, "Care of the Dead at Emar," 129.

29. For further analysis of this text, see Ernest R. Lacheman and David I. Owen, "Texts from *Arrapḫa* and from Nuzi in the Yale Babylonian Collection," in *Studies on the Civilization and Culture of Nuzi and the Hurrians*, ed. Martha A. Morrison and David I. Owen (Winona Lake, IN: Eisenbrauns, 1981), 1:386–87.

30. This text also challenges Pitard's argument that the term *palāḫu*, "to serve, honor," refers to the care for living recipients, not the dead ("Care of the Dead at Emar," 127).

into men so that they may inherit the household and participate in the cult of dead kin.

However, the fictive maleness depicted in these texts begs the question: What can we do with this evidence? Are these examples of women taking part in the cult of dead kin, even though the texts explicitly classify them as male? Are they male only in the context of inheritance but not cult—that is, must these daughters be sons only so that they can inherit property but not necessarily to care for the dead? Another lingering question is the status of these fictive males relative to nonkin males. Are these daughters/sons tacitly considered better cultic substitutes than nonkin males in these texts? If so, then these texts seem to value certain kinds of kinship more than others, regardless of gender. Unfortunately, the evidence does not allow us to definitively answer such questions. Instead, these texts contribute to the overall complexity of women's roles in the cult of dead kin in ancient West Asia.

The evidence from the Levant contains fewer references to women actors in the cult of dead kin. However, a few attestations are relevant to our discussion. In the Ugaritic Funerary Text (*KTU* 1.161), Queen Tharyelli participates in the ceremony praising the *rapi'ūma*, divine dead kings of Ugarit. As I have argued in chapter 1, the exchange of sacrifice for blessing in this text strongly suggests the kind of reciprocity inherent in the cult of dead kin. Since the *rapi'ūma* are the ones bestowing blessings on living members of the royal family, the text is a cogent piece of evidence for the royal cult of dead kin at Ugarit. It is also interesting to note that the queen, Tharyelli, is explicitly mentioned in the text as a recipient of blessing alongside the king:

> Peace, peace to Ammurapi
> And peace to his sons!
> Peace to Tharyelli!
> Peace to her house!
> Peace to Ugarit!
> Peace to its gates![31]

That Tharyelli is mentioned by name in the text suggests that she may have had a prominent role in the ritual. The participation of Tharyelli in the coronation ceremony at Ugarit is also interesting because it demonstrates

---

31. *KTU* 1.161, ll. 31–34.

that the cult of dead kin may help support claims to the Ugaritic kingship; in this case, invoking the *rapi'ūma* in the context of King Ammurapi's coronation legitimates his nascent reign. She may also be the same Tharyelli who commissions a commemorative stela near the temple of Dagan (*KTU* 6.13),[32] in which case the queen might participate in the cult of dead kin in a variety of ways.[33]

Although extant texts from Sam'al do not focus on the participation of women in the cult of dead kin, the iconographic depiction of women on commemorative stelae suggests that women were, at least, recipients of such cult. Bonatz has catalogued the different iconographic depictions of mortuary feasting on commemorative stelae from Sam'al and the nearby site of Marash, noting several instances in which a woman is depicted as the recipient of commemoration and offerings.[34] Many of the scenes depicting women share the same iconographic tropes as those depicting men. In fact, the banquet scene prevalent among these stelae is remarkably consistent: an individual sits on a raised chair and lifts a cup in one hand. A table full of food is positioned in front of the chair. In many of the scenes, an attendant stands next to the table and waves a fan in the direction of the seated individual.[35] In another scene, a man and woman appear together, sitting on either side of a full table.[36] The depiction of these individuals with ample food and drink suggests that care for the dead ideally entails such offerings.

Despite variations in geography and time period, some recurring themes emerge from these attestations of women participating in the cult of dead kin. Almost all of these women are members of royal or elite families within their respective cultures, which should not surprise us, considering uneven patterns of preservation among elite and nonelite material culture. Modes of care depicted include offerings of food, drink, and incense; invocation of the name of the dead; and the construction of a commemorative monument. Interestingly, the extant evidence does not depict women protecting the corpse, preserving the burial site, or repatri-

---

32. See my discussion of this text and its interpretative difficulties in ch. 1.

33. See my discussion of this evidence in the introduction.

34. For images of these scenes, see Bonatz, *Das syro-hethitische Grabdenkmal.* These women are sometimes featured alone (B4, C46, C51), as part of a gendered pair (B9, C21), or as a family (C62).

35. Bonatz, *Syro-hethitische Grabdenkmal*, C46, C35.

36. Bonatz, *Syro-hethitische Grabdenkmal*, C21.

ating the physical remains of the dead. However, preservation of the burial site may be implied in the cases of Emar and Nuzi, since the burial site may be understood as part of the dead father's estate inherited by his daughter. The evidence from Sam'al constitutes our only iconographic depictions of women in the cult of dead kin, though the *pgr* stela from Ugarit (*KTU* 6.13) may also have been meant for public display as a commemorative monument for Queen Tharyelli. While Ur III and Old Babylonian texts refer to women in the form of lists (offering or genealogical, respectively), the texts referring to the queen mothers provide more context for the offering of care to the dead. In the depictions of Assurbanipal's mother and Adad-guppi, the performance of the cult of dead kin coincides with the legitimation of their sons' ascent to the throne. The piety shown by both mothers and their sons thus bolsters the legitimacy of their reigns. The participation of Tharyelli in the coronation ceremony at Ugarit similarly uses the cult of dead kin to secure the nascent kingship of Ammurapi, her husband. Thus, the theme of social rupture or discontinuity becomes increasingly apparent in these cases. Such is the case for the inheritance texts of Emar and Nuzi as well: the lack of a son to inherit the father's estate is a threat to continuity of ownership and, relatedly, care for the dead. Thus, daughters are made into sons so that both proprietary and cultic continuity may be preserved. In short, it is perhaps in these moments of social, political, and cultic rupture or discontinuity that women could and would play a more prominent role in the cult of dead kin.

Women in the Cult of Dead Kin in the Hebrew Bible

The extent of women's roles in the biblical cult of dead kin has often been overlooked or minimized in previous studies. However, multiple biblical texts depict women as either recipients or offerers of the cult. Taken together, some recurring patterns emerge in these instances of women's participation, many of which are similar to the participation of women in the cult elsewhere in ancient West Asia. Most striking, women are often depicted as participants in the cult during moments of crisis, especially instances of nonideal death. In these cases, nonideal death often entails sudden, violent death or the threat of dying without offspring who may commemorate or care for the dead. Biblical women act on behalf of the dead by performing different elements of the cult of dead kin, such as sacrifice to the dead, preservation of the name, construction of commemorative monuments, and protection of human remains. It is interesting to note, however, that women are never depicted in the biblical text repatriating the remains of the dead, which is another parallel with the evidence from ancient West Asia discussed above. In addition to biblical texts in which women participate in the cult, other texts referring to women as matriarchs of Israel, though not cultic, are also relevant to understanding the status of women as ancestors. The biblical texts depicting care for the dead performed by women include Ps 106:28 (and its interpretation of Num 25:2); 2 Sam 14:7; Isa 56:3–5; Num 27:1–11; and 2 Sam 21:10. Instances in which dead women receive cultic care include Gen 35:19–20; 2 Kgs 9:34–37; and perhaps Deut 5:16 // Exod 20:12.[37] Noncultic references to women as ancestors in ancient Israel include 2 Sam 19:38; Ruth 4:11; Isa 51:2; and Jer 31:15.

Genesis 35:19–20 suggests that women could be recipients of care in the cult of dead kin. In this text, Jacob erects a stela (*maṣṣēbâ*) for his wife Rachel upon her death: "Rachel died and was buried on the road of Ephratah,[38] which is Bethlehem. Jacob set up a stela next to her grave. It is the stela of Rachel's grave to this day." The passage suggests that a husband may offer care to his dead wife. The construction of a *maṣṣēbâ* at her burial site and the text's explicit reference to the ongoing presence of the monument at the site suggests the continued significance of Rachel to the living, perhaps as an ancestor or cultural hero. Although the passage does not refer to any inscription on the stela, such as the name of Rachel herself, the association between it and Rachel is somehow preserved throughout generations and may indicate that her burial is considered a pilgrimage site. The *maṣṣēbâ* appears elsewhere in the Hebrew Bible as a marker for the presence of deities (e.g., the *maṣṣēbâ* Jacob erects at Bethel in Gen

---

37. Of course, the argument that Deut 5:16 // Exod 20:12 refers to the cult of dead kin is somewhat speculative because honoring one's father and mother can also take place when they are living. Multiple texts refer to the honoring of living persons (Num 22:17, 37; 24:11; 1 Sam 2:29, 30; 15:30). The metaphor of honoring one's living father or master also appears in Mal 1:6, describing the honor due YHWH. However, this does not exclude the possibility that one may honor the dead as well as the living. In other biblical texts, the term *kabbēd* is used for honoring the dead (2 Sam 10:3 = 1 Chr 19:3). Indeed, the duties of the ideal son in the Ugaritic Aqhat Epic include acts both before and after the death of the father; see my discussion of these duties in ch. 1.

38. Genesis 48:7 uses "road of Ephrat," but Mic 5:1 places Ephratah in apposition to Bethlehem in the vocative, where no directional *he* makes sense. I have chosen to use the latter rendering of the city name in the translation above.

38:18)[39] and in Rachel's case may similarly mark a ritual locus where rites of invocation and material offerings could be made to the dead, though such ritual activity is absent from this text and therefore speculative.

It is also interesting to note that Rachel's death is nonideal in several ways. She dies suddenly and violently in childbirth, which itself is severely polluting according to the Priestly writers (Lev 12). Furthermore, she dies while traveling and thus removed from the domicile and the land associated with her family. Because of this dislocation, she is not buried in the family tomb but instead on the road to Bethlehem. Several biblical texts depict burial in the family tomb as an ideal form of interment. In fact, there is evidence that wives were typically buried in their husbands' family tombs.[40] Unlike other biblical figures, such as Joseph, Rachel's bones are not repatriated at a later time. Yet, Rachel's nonideal burial does not exclude the possibility that she could receive cult. In fact, comparative evidence from Mesopotamia suggests that the dead could receive *kispu* offerings even if the location of the corpse was physically removed from familial property and from the offerings themselves. For example, a letter from King Hammurabi of Babylon to Sin-iddinam refers to the *kispu* offered by a father to his son who has gone missing.[41] Without the corpse or even assurance of his son's fate, the father makes offerings to this absent son as if he were dead. Another example of this long-distance care appears in the Old Babylonian version of the Gilgamesh Epic, in which Gilgamesh pours

---

39. The stelae found in the cultic niche of the Arad temple provide archaeological evidence for this practice as well. For a discussion of the temple and stelae at Arad, see Yohanan Aharoni, "Arad: Its Inscriptions and Temple," *BA* 31 (1968): 18–19; Aharoni, "Israelite Temples in the Period of the Monarchy," *PWCJS* 1 (1969): 69–70; Ruth Amiran, Ornit Ilan, and Wolfgang Helck, *Arad: Eine 5000 Jahre alte Stadt in der Wüste Negev, Israel* (Neumünster: Wachholtz, 1992), 84–94. Tryggve Mettinger argues that the stelae in the temple at Arad are the "clearest example of all" of an Iron II period "masseboth cult" in Israel in which such monuments are a licit form of representing deities. See Mettinger, *No Graven Image? Israelite Aniconism in Its Ancient Near Eastern Context* (Stockholm: Almqvist & Wiksell, 1995), 143–49.

40. For instance, in her examination of the social location of the biblical ʾalmānâ (often translated "widow"), Hiebert argues that an Israelite wife continues to be under the protection of her husband's family even after her husband's death ("Whence Shall Help," 128–29). See also the discussion of Ruth's ongoing affiliation with her dead husband's family in Saul M. Olyan, *Friendship in the Hebrew Bible* (New Haven: Yale University Press, 2017), 64–69.

41. See my discussion of this material in the introduction.

out libations for his dead father, Lugalbanda, while he is en route to the Cedar Forest. These cases, among others, demonstrate that the corpse is not always a necessary component in making offerings to one's dead kin, at least in cuneiform sources. While it is notable that Rachel's remains are not transported to the family tomb in Machpelah for burial (as were the remains of Jacob in Gen 50), it may not necessarily prevent her from receiving care from living kin after her death. Indeed, the monument erected by Jacob may facilitate this ongoing care.

In 2 Sam 14:7, a woman is responsible for indirectly ensuring the preservation of her dead husband's name through their son. In this text, a widow from Tekoa brings a dilemma before King David. Although the scenario she presents is a falsehood meant to encourage David's forgiveness of Absalom, it assumes some aspects of the cult of dead kin. One of her two sons has killed the other, and now the community wants to execute the remaining son for the crime. Doing so, however, will leave her and her dead husband without any living offspring. She describes the imminent execution of her only surviving son as follows: "They will extinguish my coal that remains [gaḥaltî ʾăšer nišʾārâ] so that my husband has neither name nor remnant [šēm ûšəʾērît] upon the face of the land." This close association between the existence of a son and the preservation of her dead husband's name suggests that the son would preserve his name in some way, perhaps through ritual invocation of that name or by bearing that name himself.[42] The relevance of this text to the present discussion is that here we find a woman acting on behalf of her dead husband, ensuring the preservation of his name and memory through their son. Although the son is the one who effects this preservation, it is the man's wife who osten-

---

42. For a discussion of this mode of commemorating the dead in the Mesopotamian cult of dead kin, see Bayliss, "Cult of Dead Kin," 117. Yet, onomastic evidence elsewhere in ancient West Asia demonstrates the prevalence of papponymy rather than patronymy in naming patterns. See, e.g., Frank Moore Cross, "A New Aramaic Stele from Taymāʾ," CBQ 48 (1986): 387–94. However, Cross's argument that papponymy is also practiced among the high priests in the Persian period has been challenged by more recent work and largely discarded. See Cross, "A Reconstruction of the Judean Restoration," JBL 94 (1975): 4–18; James C. VanderKam, "Jewish High Priests of the Persian Period: Is the List Complete?," in Priesthood and Cult in Ancient Israel, ed. Gary A. Anderson and Saul M. Olyan (Sheffield: Sheffield Academic, 1991), 67–91. In any case, it is perhaps preferable to interpret this reference to preserving the name of the father in 2 Sam 14:7 as referring to ritual invocation rather than naming a son after his father.

sibly brings the matter to David and thus allows her son to do so. In this way, she indirectly provides the necessary care for her dead husband. It is also possible, though not certain, that the woman's description of her son as "my ember" or "my coal" (*gaḥaltî*) refers to the care and commemoration he provides for her as well. After all, in Mesopotamian family religion, a brazier was closely associated with the presence of heirs and the longevity of a household, and the Akkadian phrase *kinūnu bilû*, "extinguished brazier," is a metaphor used for the extinction of a household that lacks heirs to maintain it.[43] Therefore, 2 Sam 14:7 depicts the threat of cultic discontinuity due to the lack of an heir, a threat counteracted by the intervention of a woman.

In 2 Sam 21:10, Riṣpah, one of Saul's concubines, protects the exposed corpses of her sons and other Saulides who have been executed by the Gibeonites. In this passage, she protects the remains of her dead kin from further spoliation: "Riṣpah, the daughter of Ayyah, took sackcloth and spread it out for herself upon the rock. From the beginning of the harvest until water was poured out upon them from the heavens, she did not allow birds of the sky to settle upon them during the day or beasts of the field during the night." When the corpses of these Saulides are left exposed by the Gibeonites, Riṣpah steadfastly fends off wild animals and birds so that their remains do not suffer further abuse and shame. Thus, she prevents the kind of spoliation described in biblical curse formulae (e.g., Deut 28:26). This protection of human remains is an element of the cult of dead kin, yet one that has been largely ignored in previous treatments of the cult. Yet, in this text, we see a woman offering that kind of care for her dead kin. In fact, her actions on behalf of the dead in this passage serve as a model for David in the verses that immediately follow. Indeed, in verses 11–14 of the same chapter, David hears of Riṣpah's actions and subsequently brings the bones of Saul and Jonathan back from Jabesh-Gilead to the land of Benjamin and buries them in the tomb of Kish, Saul's father, along with the remains of the executed Saulides. Riṣpah, then, is a model of loyal care for the dead. Yet, the depiction of Riṣpah's care for the dead does not include transportation or burial of the remains. Instead, her role is only to protect the corpses, not to repatriate them.

---

43. See *CAD* s.v. "*belû*," 2:191; s.v. "*balû*," 2:72; s.v. "*kinūnu*," 8:394–95; Van der Toorn, *Family Religion*, 130.

The text of Ps 106:28, its allusion to Num 25:2, and its reference to sacrifices for the dead is difficult but potentially illuminating. If we accept—as some scholars do[44]—that Ps 106:28 is a reference to care for the dead in the form of sacrifice, then its adaptation of Num 25:2 also suggests the participation of women in that care. Numbers 25:1–3 states: "Israel dwelled in Shittim, and the people began to whore around with daughters of Moab. They [the daughters of Moab] invited the people to the sacrifices of their gods [zibḥê 'ĕlōhêhen], and the people ate and bowed down to their gods ['ĕlōhêhen]. Israel joined itself to Baal Peor, and the anger of YHWH burned against Israel." Psalm 106 retells the narrative of Num 25 and Israel's stubbornness and apostasy in the wilderness period, including the Baal Peor incident: "They joined themselves to Baal Peor and ate sacrifices of the dead." The Ps 106 version of the narrative thus replaces "sacrifices of their gods" (zibḥê 'ĕlōhêhen) in Num 25:2 with "sacrifices of the dead" (zibḥê mētîm), interpreting 'ĕlōhîm as "the dead." Furthermore, it is important to note that women—not men—are the practitioners of this cult in Num 25. Not only do women offer these sacrifices, but the gods themselves also receive the feminine plural possessive suffix, 'ĕlōhêhen. Thus, Ps 106:28 seems to interpret Num 25:1–3 as a reference to care for the dead offered exclusively by Moabite women. While this passage refers explicitly to the practices of the Moabites and is primarily interested in polemicizing against them as non-Yahwistic, it may still reflect assumptions about women's participation in care for the dead. It is important to note, at least, that this polemic imagines that women could offer such sacrifices to the dead.

Another text, Isa 56:3–5, depicts the intercession of YHWH on behalf of the eunuch who has no offspring to care for him after his death:

Do not let the eunuch say, "Now I am a dry tree." For thus says YHWH regarding the eunuchs who keep my Sabbaths and choose that which

---

44. Lewis prefers reading Ps 106:28 as a reference to sacrifices for the dead and notes that the LXX rendering of the passage explicitly refers to these offerings as thysias nekron, "sacrifices of the dead" (Cults of the Dead, 167 n. 6). Lewis further argues that nowhere else does the biblical text refer to images of foreign deities as mētîm or "dead" (Cults of the Dead, 167, 176). In contrast, Schmitt interprets the reference to the dead in this passage as a pejorative epithet for illicit deities. Thus, he dismisses the passage as a reference to food offerings to the dead, since it seems to refer to the dead gods of Num 25:2. He argues that the term dead is polemical in this context, used to denigrate the power of other gods, and does not refer to the care of the literal dead (Albertz and Schmitt, Household and Family Religion, 456).

pleases me and hold fast to my covenant: "I will give in my house and within my walls a commemorative monument [*yād wā-šēm*] better than sons and daughters. I will give him an everlasting name [*šēm ʿôlām*][45] that will not be cut off [*yikkārēt*]."

Instead of allowing the eunuch, who seemingly has no hope of producing offspring, to fade into obscurity following his death, YHWH provides him with a *yād wā-šēm*, a "commemorative monument."[46] It is likely that this reference to a *yād wā-šēm* "better than sons and daughters" (*ṭôb mibbānîm ûmibbānôt*) can be construed in multiple ways. First, it assumes the construction of a commemorative monument for the dead, typically erected by one's offspring, which serves as a locus for invocation of the name and, perhaps, offerings. Second, the passage asserts that YHWH himself will offer a better memorial than one provided by living descendants because it will endure forever in the temple itself. The imagery of a name being cut off (*yikkārēt*) is similar to the language of separation from YHWH during the exile, separation from YHWH in death, and the fate of those who lack offspring.[47]

---

45. This emphasis on the eternal status of the eunuch's name suggests the ongoing nature of his relationship with YHWH, his divine caregiver—a relationship I will explore more thoroughly in ch. 4. Claims to the eternal status of one's relationship with YHWH, such as the "eternal covenant loyalty" (*ḥesed ʿôlām*) shown by YHWH in Isa 54:8, are characteristic of anxiety surrounding the exile and its implications for that relationship. For an examination of different biblical views concerning the exile and its effect on YHWH's covenant with Israel, see Saul M. Olyan, "The Status of the Covenant during the Exile," in *Berührungspunkte: Studien zur Social- und Religionsgeschichte Israels und seiner Umwelt: Festschrift für Rainer Albertz zu seinem 65. Geburtstag*, ed. Ingo Kottssieper, Rüdiger Schmitt, and Jakob Wöhrle (Münster: Ugarit-Verlag, 2008), 333–44.

46. This phrase is probably best rendered as a hendiadys meaning "commemorative monument." See my discussion of the phrase in ch. 1.

47. For a discussion of this language and its resonances in an exilic context, see Saul M. Olyan, "'We Are Utterly Cut Off': Some Nuances of נגזרנו לנו in Ezek 37:11," *CBQ* 65 (2003): 43–51. Psalm 88:6 describes those in the underworld as those who are "cut off" (*nigzārû*) from the hand of YHWH and are no longer remembered by him. Similarly, Ps 6:6 states that the dead do not remember YHWH and cannot praise him, while Ps 28:1 refers to those in the netherworld as those to whom YHWH no longer listens. The imagery of these texts indicates significant overlap in their notions of death, remembrance, and separation from YHWH: being in the netherworld constitutes separation from YHWH that prevents commemoration of or by him. Other biblical texts, however, emphasize that YHWH can access the netherworld. For a dis-

Another way of interpreting the *yād wā-šēm* in relation to offspring is that the commemorative monument acts as a substitute for sons and daughters. In any of these interpretations, it is important to note that this text assumes that both sons and daughters could commemorate the dead; they may offer care for their dead father through the construction of a commemorative monument or physically embody his memory. Thus, a possible reading of Isa 56:5 is that YHWH provides the eunuch with better commemoration than that offered by both sons *and daughters*—meaning that both men and women are typically expected to offer this kind of commemoration, at least according to this writer. The passage takes for granted the participation of women in the cult of dead kin and draws no distinction between their participation and that of their brothers. Isaiah 56:3–5 is also another attestation of the cult of dead kin in which lack of progeny is a central concern because it negatively affects one's commemoration after death.

The inclusion of the Jezebel and Jehu narrative (2 Kgs 9:34–37) in a discussion of the cult of dead kin presents some challenges, as I have noted previously in chapter 1. After the remains of Jezebel are violently trampled by horses following her execution at Jehu's command, Jehu nevertheless orders his men to care for (*piqdû*) and bury her (*qibrûhā*). After all, he says, "She is a king's daughter." It would seem that, despite her status as an enemy of Jehu, the fact that Jezebel is royalty affords her the requisite rites of care and burial following her death.[48] If it is Jezebel's royal status that necessitates this treatment, then the care offered to her in this passage may not be indicative of the cult offered to women more generally but rather women who are affiliated with royal houses. More specifically, Jehu refers not to Jezebel's royal status as queen of Israel but as the daughter of the king of Tyre. Thus, Jezebel's right to burial is attributed to her affiliation with her royal father, possibly because he is still alive,

---

cussion of such texts, see Olyan, "We Are Utterly Cut Off," 46 n. 9. The 2 Sam 14:7 narrative juxtaposes the name of the father with "remnant" (*šēm ûšəʾērît*). Similarly, the description of levirate marriage in Deut 25:5–6 refers to the name of a childless man being blotted out (*yimmāḥeh*). In both cases, the imagery suggests an anxiety about the childless dead being forgotten.

48. Lewis makes a similar observation of her royal status and how it may afford her death-related rites (*Cults of the Dead*, 121). For support, Lewis cites a Neo-Assyrian text in which the spirits of dead queens are summoned to bury a recently deceased queen (*Cults of the Dead*, 121 n. 56). See *CAD* 13:202a = Wolfram von Soden, "Aus einem Ersatzopferritual für den assyrischen Hof," *ZA* 45 (1939): 44, ll. 40–41.

unlike her husband, Ahab. It is also possible that rendering proper rites to the daughter of this king is politically motivated, meant to lessen any tension caused by the coup. Indeed, by offering Jezebel proper rites, Jehu may intend to reestablish political ties with Tyre or, at least, reduce the possibility of negative diplomatic consequences for the death of Jezebel. It does not, however, indicate that women in general were allotted such consideration after death.

Yet, the death of Jezebel is nonideal in every sense. She suffers a violent death followed by corpse exposure and is ultimately denied proper burial and commemoration because her corpse has been mutilated to the point of nonrecognition. When Jehu's men seek out her remains, they find only her skull, feet, and palms, which they report back to Jehu. The episode ends with Jehu repeating the prophecy of Elijah the Tishbite: "In the allotment of Jezreel, the dogs will eat the flesh of Jezebel, and the corpse of Jezebel will be like dung upon the face of the field in the allotment of Jezreel so that they will not say, 'This is Jezebel.'" Thus, the name of Jezebel cannot even be invoked. This depiction is strikingly similar to the imagery used to describe men who lack a cultic caregiver. In fact, it is possible that Jezebel's fate is like that described in 2 Sam 14:7, the extermination of one's name and remnant, or in Deut 25:5–6, the blotting out of one's name. Furthermore, the retelling of the prophecy implies that, despite the commands of Jehu, his men do not give Jezebel proper burial rites because her corpse is unrecognizable. Thus, the text explicitly states that no one will be able to mark the site where her remains lie.[49] Though Jehu uses the terminology of the cult of dead kin (*piqdû*) in his command, the end result is that Jezebel receives none of that care. Thus, it seems as though the use of cultic terminology here is ironic in the sense that, rather than receiving care, Jezebel's fate is the cultic opposite of that care—utter annihilation and lack of commemoration.

If we accept Brichto's argument that the commandment of Deut 5:16 // Exod 20:12 refers to care for dead kin, then its inclusion of both the father

---

49. The implication that Jehu's men cannot give Jezebel proper burial because of the deteriorated state of her corpse is unlike other biblical accounts of burial. For instance, Eshbaal's head is buried in Abner's tomb (2 Sam 4:12), and Saul's headless corpse is buried in Jabesh (1 Sam 31:9; 2 Sam 21:12–14). These texts suggest that body parts or corpses missing body parts can receive burial. Nevertheless, the reference in 2 Kgs 9:34–37 to Jezebel's corpse being like dung in the field implies that she does not receive such burial rites.

and mother is notable and relevant to the present discussion. Brichto argues that the close association between honoring one's parents and longevity in the land assumes a *quid pro quo* relationship between the living and the dead, mediated by cult:[50]

> Honor [*kabbēd*] your father and your mother just as YHWH your god commanded you so that your days may be long and so that it may be good for you upon the land that YHWH your god is giving to you. (Deut 5:16)

> Honor [*kabbēd*] your father and your mother so that your days may be long upon the land that YHWH your god is giving to you. (Exod 20:12)

This interpretation of the commandment to honor one's parents as a reference to the cult of dead kin assumes that dead parents could bestow rightful ownership of property and blessings on their descendants in return for that care, a reciprocity between the living and dead that is never explicitly stated in the biblical text.[51] Of course, that respect need not be limited to their postmortem existence. After all, one's claim to ancestral land no doubt depended on one's performance of duties during one's parents' lives and after their deaths. This notion of respect shown to parents while they are alive and after they die also appears in the duties of the ideal son listed in the Aqhat Epic from Ugarit. Thus, if Exod 20:12 // Deut 5:16 does refer to care for one's parents (living or dead), it is interesting to note that the mother is mentioned along with the father.

The narrative of Num 27:1–11 concerns similar issues to those found in the inheritance texts from Emar and Nuzi. The passage explains the laws of inheritance should a man die without a male heir. The daughters of Zelophehad bring their case before Moses at the entrance of the tent of meeting and argue that they should inherit their dead father's property. After consulting YHWH, Moses agrees that they should receive the inheritance. The passage is relevant to the present discussion because of its reference to the father's "name" and its close association with the inheritance of his property. The daughters of Zelophehad say to Moses: "Why should

---

50. Brichto, "Kin, Cult, Land," 31.

51. This assumption of cultic reciprocity and its relevance to land claims is a central point in other treatments of the cult of dead kin, including that of Stavrakopoulou (*Land of Our Fathers*, passim).

the name of our father be diminished among his family because he has no son? Give us a possession among our father's brothers" (v. 4). This episode is also reminiscent of the dilemma of Absalom in 2 Sam 18:18, who lacks a son to invoke his name. In the case of Num 27, it seems that female kin assert their ability and right to inherit their father's property and perpetuate his name. If perpetuating the name of the father includes ritual invocation of that name, then this passage is another biblical attestation of women acting as caregivers for the dead in the absence of male cultic actors. Like the cases at Emar and Nuzi, it is also possible that inheriting their father's property entails preservation of the family tomb. The matter of Zelophehad's daughters appears again in Num 36 and clearly refers to the ruling of Moses in Num 27. The primary concern of Num 36 is the possible marriage of the daughters into another tribe and thus the transfer of their inheritance into the possession of a tribe other than Manasseh. In order to prevent this transfer, Moses rules that the daughters may only marry within the tribe of Manasseh, thus ensuring continuity of ownership for that property.

This focus on the name of the father and its preservation in the absence of male descendants also calls to mind the institution of levirate marriage in Deut 25:5–6.[52] In such a situation, the concern is not only that a man's name will be "blotted out" but also that his property may be taken outside his tribe should his widow remarry:

> If brothers dwell together and one of them dies (and he has no son), the wife of the dead man shall not be married to an outsider who is not kin. Her husband's brother will come to her and take her as his wife and perform his duty as her husband's brother. The first-born whom she bears will rise up in the name [*yāqûm ʿal-šēm*] of his dead brother so that his name is not blotted out [*yimmāḥeh*] of Israel.

Like the case of Zelophehad's daughters, the focus in this passage is on the preservation of the dead father's name. In this case, however, there are no children, sons or daughters, to preserve it. Thus, the only way to keep the name of the dead father from fading into oblivion is to perpetuate his line

---

52. For a discussion of scholarly debates concerning the relative chronology of biblical depictions of levirate marriage, see Susan Niditch, "Legends of Wise Heros and Heroines," in *The Hebrew Bible and Its Modern Interpreters*, ed. Douglas A. Knight and Gene M. Tucker (Chico, CA: Scholars Press, 1985), 452–53.

via one of his living brothers. Presumably, this practice of levirate marriage also ensures that any inheritance of the dead man will remain within his tribe.

Related to these instances of women participating in the cult of dead kin in the Hebrew Bible are explicit references to women as matriarchs of Israel. Though these texts do not mention care for the dead, they do contribute to an overall understanding of women as ancestors. For instance, Ruth 4:11 refers to multiple matriarchs in its description of Ruth and her future role in the house of Boaz:

> All the people in the gate and the elders were witnesses and said, "May YHWH make the woman who is coming to your [Boaz's] house like Rachel and Leah, the two of whom built the house of Israel. Act valiantly ['ăśēh-ḥayil] in Ephrathah! Invoke the name [qərā'-šēm] in Bethlehem![53] May your house be like the house of Perez, whom Tamar bore to Judah, from the seed which YHWH will give to you from this young woman."

Rachel and Leah are not only referred to by name but are explicitly credited with establishing Israel through bearing children. The term used here, bānâ, "to build," is striking because it is so often associated with the duties

---

53. The two masculine singular imperatives in 4:11 are addressed to Boaz. The first, "act valiantly," is an idiom that appears in only a few places in the Hebrew Bible. In one instance, it appears in the context of military action, Saul smiting the Amalekites in 1 Sam 14:48. In another instance, it describes the ideal wife, who earns the praise of her husband for her actions and wisdom in Prov 31:29. In both cases, the idiom seems to refer to actions taken by someone in the proper fulfillment of his or her duties, whether a king or a wife. This valence may also underlie the appearance of the idiom in Ruth 4:11, since Boaz is being commanded to provide the proper commemoration for Mahlon through his marriage to Ruth. The second imperative, "invoke the name," seems to be a clear reference to the cult of dead kin. The preceding verse makes it clear that the name in 4:11 is that of Mahlon: "I have also acquired Ruth the Moabite, wife of Mahlon, as a wife in order to raise up the name of the dead [ləhāqîm šēm-hammēt] upon his inalienable inheritance [naḥălātô] such that the name of the dead will not be cut off from his brothers and the gate of his place." The idiom of raising the name of the dead is similar to that which appears in Deut 25:5–6 above, though the verb qwm appears in different verbal stems. It is also interesting to note that Boaz is the one expected to invoke the name of the dead, though he may do so only after taking Ruth as his wife. Thus, this passage is another instance in which a woman indirectly provides rites of commemoration for her dead husband.

of great men, especially kings, in ancient West Asia.[54] Here, however, the building of Israel is attributed to two women.[55] In addition to Rachel and Leah, the passage goes on to invoke the narrative of Tamar, who bore the descendants of Judah. This particular reference may also draw on the fact that, like Ruth, Tamar must resort to a form of levirate marriage in order to secure an heir for her dead husband. As I argue above, this tradition of levirate marriage is closely related to concerns about lack of progeny and commemoration.[56] All of these allusions to biblical matriarchs underscore the role of women in the continuation and strengthening of biblical lineages.

This emphasis on childbirth also appears in Isa 51, which addresses the people of Israel and refers back to many elements of the patriarchal narratives. Verse 2 states, "Look to Abraham your father and to Sarah who bore you. Though he was only one, I called him and blessed him and made him numerous." Though the focus of the verse is on Abraham, the explicit

---

54. See, e.g., various essays in Mark J. Boda and Jamie Novotny, eds., *From the Foundations to the Crenellations: Essays on Temple Building in the Ancient Near East and Hebrew Bible* (Münster: Ugarit-Verlag, 2010); Ömür Harmanşah, *Cities and the Shaping of Memory in the Ancient Near East* (Cambridge: Cambridge University Press, 2013).

55. Chapman also notes the use of such building imagery in biblical descriptions of matriarchs, including Sarai (Gen 16:2; *House of the Mother*, 150–57).

56. The depictions of levirate marriage in these texts vary, however. In Gen 38, Tamar uses deception so that Judah, the father of her dead husband Er, will procreate with her. She must do so after Judah's son Onan refuses to act as a *levir* with her and thus "raise seed for your brother" (*hāqēm zeraʿ ləʾāḥîkā*). In addition, Judah refuses to offer his remaining son, Shelah, as a husband to her. While Judah publicly acknowledges that he is the father of Tamar's unborn child, the text states that he never engages in intercourse with her after that. Thus, the text does not seem to depict a levirate marriage as it appears in Deut 25:5–10. In the Deuteronomy passage, only brothers who dwell together are mentioned as potential spouses for their brother's widow. Deuteronomy 25:5 explicitly states that a brother will take his brother's widow as a wife. If the brother refuses to do so, 25:9–10 describes the public shaming of that man by the widow, a scenario that does not appear in Gen 38. The depiction of levirate marriage in Ruth does not involve brothers of the dead; indeed, Naomi explicitly bemoans the fact that she cannot provide her daughters-in-law with any sons as husbands (Ruth 1:11–13). Boaz, a kinsman (*gōʾēl*) of Ruth's and Naomi's dead husbands, takes Ruth as a wife after a closer kinsman refuses to do so. The terminology for these relationships differs between the texts as well. While both Gen 38 and Deut 25:5–10 use the verb *yibbēm* in reference to levirate marriage, the narrative in Ruth uses the verb *gāʾal* (and its participial form *gōʾēl*).

reference to Sarah as a mother is notable. The context of this passage is the promise of hope and salvation for the Israelites in exile. It reminds the people that YHWH created them and the earth itself; he has saved them in the past and will redeem them in the near future. Thus, the reference to Sarah appears in a moment of crisis when all hope seems lost. The prophetic oracle thus alludes to Sarah as matriarch in order to bolster the hope of the Israelites in exile.

Rachel's status as an ancestor is particularly well attested. As noted above, Rachel is buried with a commemorative monument in Gen 35:20, and her burial place is referenced explicitly in other biblical texts. In Jer 31:14, she mourns for the Israelites: "A voice is heard in Ramah—lamentation and bitter weeping—Rachel weeping for her children [lit. 'sons']. She refuses to be comforted concerning her children because they are not." This passage depicts the matriarch as the inconsolable mourner who wails at the death of Israel, construed here as her children. Much like the reference to Sarah in Isa 51:2, this allusion to Rachel appears in a context of crisis for the Israelites. Finally, the figure of Rachel appears once more in a slightly different context, though no less indicative of her status as a matriarch of Israel. In 1 Sam 10:2, immediately after anointing Saul as the king of Israel, Samuel gives him directions using the tomb of Rachel as a landmark: "When you leave me today, you will find two men next to the tomb of Rachel on the border of Benjamin at Zelzah." This reference to the tomb of Rachel assumes that the site is a well-known feature of the landscape, which further suggests that its physical structure and association with the matriarch persisted in the period when the text was composed.[57]

Although the passage does not refer to the matriarchs of Israel, 2 Sam 19:38–40 is also relevant to a discussion of women as ancestors. In this text, Barzillai asks to return to his city so that he can be buried near the grave of his father and mother: "Let your servant return so that I may die in my city beside the grave of my father and mother.... The king kissed Barzillai and blessed him, and he returned to his place [māqôm]." This passage sug-

---

57. For an analysis of the location of Rachel's tomb and its relationship to ancestral landholding, the nature of Rachel's death during childbirth, and concerns about corpse pollution, see Benjamin D. Cox and Susan Ackerman, "Rachel's Tomb," *JBL* 128 (2009): 135–48. For an examination of Rachel's tomb in the Hebrew Bible as well as later religious traditions, see Fred Strickert, *Rachel Weeping: Jews, Christians, and Muslims at the Fortress Tomb* (Collegeville, MN: Liturgical Press, 2007).

gests that the common phrase "tomb of the ancestors [*'ābôt*]"[58] is not the only way of conceptualizing burial with one's kin in the Hebrew Bible. In this instance, the family tomb of Barzillai is not simply defined in terms of male kin but with reference to both his mother and his father. While it is true that women are typically depicted as socially mobile in the sense that they may change kinship affiliation when they marry, this reference to Barzillai's mother suggests that the family tomb may be defined in terms of its female occupants as well. In addition, the reference to the "place" of Barzillai is another instance in which such a term is closely associated with the burial site.[59] The association between one's city and the graves of one's parents is also similar to the language of Neh 2:5, in which Nehemiah refers to Jerusalem as the "city of my ancestors' graves" (*'îr-qibrôt 'ăbōtay*).[60]

A common theme that emerges among these biblical attestations of women offering or receiving the cult of dead kin is that they are often set in nonideal circumstances, which could disrupt ideal performance of the cult. Rachel dies in childbirth while traveling. Riṣpah must defend the corpses of the Saulides, including her sons, from spoliation by wild animals and birds. The corpse of Jezebel is ravaged by animals to the point that she is unrecognizable. The widow from Tekoa bemoans the fact that she and her husband will have no remaining heirs to remember them. The eunuch has neither son nor daughter to remember him. Zelophehad has no sons to inherit his property following his death.

Despite the attestations of women involved in the biblical cult of dead kin, women are never depicted performing some ritual acts constitutive of the cult. Women may receive commemorative monuments, offer sacrifices to the dead, protect the physical remains of the dead, and preserve their names, but they are never depicted repatriating those remains. Although, as noted above, maintaining the burial site may be implied when one inherits the family estate, as in the case of Zelophehad's daughters, it is not stated explicitly. Similarly, we have no explicit depiction of women's bones being repatriated after dying abroad. Rachel, for instance, is buried in the spot where she dies, not transported to the family tomb

---

58. See my discussion about translating *'ābôt* as "ancestors" rather than "fathers" above.

59. See also the association between the burial site and the place of the dead in the Aqhat Epic and Late Babylonian funerary inscription in ch. 1.

60. This version of the phrase appears in Neh 2:5. In 2:3, it appears as "house of my ancestors' graves" (*bêt-qibrôt 'ăbōtay*).

in Machpelah. Perhaps this lack of repatriation is due to the well-known existence of a monument to Rachel at the time in which the narrative was composed, but such an explanation is ultimately speculative. Jezebel is another case in which the corpse is not repatriated, but this is a particularly nonideal case in which the corpse is left unrecognizable after trampling and spoliation by animals. We do see in the case of Barzillai's parents in 2 Sam 19:38 that a mother and father could be buried together and that the family tomb could be referred to as the dwelling place of both dead parents. The ongoing reverence for the tomb of Rachel also suggests that her burial place was maintained and held in high esteem, perhaps as a site of pilgrimage. Another possible interpretation is that these narratives reflect gendered division of labor within the cult of dead kin, with women and men associated with different rites and duties involved in the cult. However, the paucity of evidence depicting repatriation and tomb maintenance prevents us from arguing definitively for any particular gendered pattern.

Finally, a brief word on the Israelite onomasticon is necessary, since it has been cited as supporting evidence for women's exclusion from the cult of dead kin in previous scholarly treatments. Such studies have argued that women are excluded from ancestor status based in part on the fact that no female kinship terms are compounded with theophoric elements in Israelite personal names: "In Hebrew anthroponymics there is not one feminine kinship term used as a theophoric element, in spite of the veneration of certain women such as Rachel (1 Samuel 10:2; Jeremiah 31:15). The ancestor cult was therefore apparently concerned primarily with patrilineal ancestors."[61] This argument depends on the interpretation of these theophoric elements as referring to the divinity of deceased family members, not the assigning of familial terminology to a deity. Such an argument works well in names with the −'ēl theophoric element, but it does not sufficiently explain the meaning of names with a Yahwistic one. For example, if Abiel ('ābî'ēl) means "my father ['ābî] is a god ['ēl]" following his death, it is difficult to imagine that Abijah should similarly be interpreted to mean that my father ('ābî) has attained the status of YHWH (yāh) upon his death. The parallel structure of these names suggests that the theophoric elements serve similar functions in denoting the proper names of deities. Indeed, we have plenty of evidence for the parallels

---

61. Van der Toorn, *Family Religion*, 229.

between YHWH and the Canaanite god El.[62] If the theophoric element in a personal name such as Abiel refers instead to the proper name of a male deity ("El is my father" in the case of Abiel), then we should not be surprised that these Israelite personal names contain no feminine kinship terms to describe them. After all, El or Yahweh is construed as a male deity by biblical writers.[63] Furthermore, the rarity of goddess names in the Israelite onomasticon in general provides another reason for this absence of feminine kinship terminology.[64] Thus, the lack of female kinship terms in personal names follows this general pattern—goddesses rarely appear in personal names, so personal names lack female kinship terms with which to describe them. Therefore, the Israelite onomasticon may not be a reliable indicator of men or women's identification as ancestors, nor the exclusion of women from the cult of dead kin.

---

62. See, e.g., Frank Moore Cross, *Canaanite Myth and Hebrew Epic* (Cambridge: Harvard University Press, 1997), 44–46 and passim. In fact, Cross notes instances in which the name YHWH appears with an El epithet in the biblical text, especially in the patriarchal narratives (e.g., Gen 14:22 [*'ēl 'elyôn*]; 16:13 [*'ēl rō'î*]; 17:1 [*'ēl šadday*]; 21:33 [*'ēl 'ôlām*]).

63. However, the Moabite personal name *qaus'immī* is an exceptional case in which a male national deity (Qaus) is juxtaposed with a feminine kinship term (*'immī*). See further discussion of this name below.

64. See, e.g., Jeffrey Tigay, *You Shall Have No Other Gods: Israelite Religion in the Light of Hebrew Inscriptions*, HSS 31 (Atlanta: Scholars Press, 1986), 13–14, 18–20. No attested personal names from Israel feature female kinship terms in juxtaposition with divine names. Instead, these female kinship terms often appear in apposition to other (male) kinship terms (e.g., *'immî'ah, 'ahî'ēm, 'ahî'immōh*). In a few instances from surrounding cultures, the maternal kinship term is juxtaposed with the proper name of a deity (*'immî'aštart, qaus'immī*). Albertz and Schmitt propose that one attested Hebrew name, *'ahīmalkâ* ("the Queen [of Heaven] is my brother"), juxtaposes a masculine kinship term with a goddess title, but this interpretation of the word *malkâ* is speculative (*Family and Household Religion*, 364). For further analysis and bibliography on these attestations, see Albertz and Schmitt, *Family and Household Religion*, 363–67, 577, 580. Furthermore, Olyan argues that there is no correlation between the prevalence of goddess names in personal names and the prominence of these goddesses in Israel, Ammon, Ugarit, New Kingdom Egypt, and the Punic West (*Asherah and the Cult*, 35–37). Even in cases where goddesses appear in narrative texts, offerings lists, or dedicatory stelae, the names of these goddesses rarely appear in the personal names of their respective cultures for reasons we do not understand.

Conclusion

In sum, it is problematic to exclude Israelite women entirely from the cult of dead kin and the status of ancestors, despite the prevalence of men as ancestors and cultic actors in biblical and comparative evidence. The evidence cited above suggests that women could be participants in the cult of dead kin as both caregivers and recipients of that care. Thus, Jacob cares for his wife Rachel by erecting a *maṣṣēbâ*; the eunuch in Isa 56 lacks sons *and daughters* to commemorate him; Riṣpah defends the exposed remains of her dead sons and other Saulides; Ps 106 interprets the cultic activity of Moabite *women* in Num 25:2 as sacrifices for the dead; a widow from Tekoa indirectly preserves the name of her dead husband in 2 Sam 14:7; and the daughters of Zelophehad both inherit their father's property and preserve his name in Num 27:1–11. The relevance of many of these texts to the cult of dead kin and the roles of women within it has been overlooked by previous studies. Furthermore, the biblical references to the matriarchs of Israel suggest that such women could achieve an elevated status as cultural heroes and ancestors. Based on this evidence, the preceding analysis suggests that women may indeed have played a vital role in the care of dead kin. When we consider that ancient Israel was a patriarchal society focused on patrilineal descent and that the language of the Hebrew Bible itself obscures the presence of women in groups of mixed gender, then the texts examined here become all the more striking and worthy of ongoing investigation.

To what extent can the biblical evidence for women's participation in the cult of dead kin indicate the regular roles of women in such rituals? One could argue that these biblical attestations depict exceptions to the rules governing the cult rather than its typical performance. Again, we must confront the limitations of our evidence. For the most part, the biblical passages examined above do not depict ideal instances of care for the dead performed by or for women. Almost every passage depicts circumstances that somehow deviate from ideal performance of the cult of dead kin—instances of corpse exposure, for instance, or lack of offspring. However, we may make similar observations regarding the biblical depiction of men in the cult of dead kin: in most cases, the depictions of the cult being performed by or for men are not ideal, either. Indeed, the same issues appear in those passages—lack of descendants (2 Sam 18:18; Isa 56:3–5), death outside familial territory (Gen 49:29–32; 50:12–14; Josh 24:32; Judg 16:31; 2 Sam 2:31; 21:12–14), and neglect of human remains

(Neh 2:3, 5). Therefore, biblical depictions of both men and women in the cult of dead kin utilize the same narrative topoi concerning nonideal death. While biblical attestations involving women depict exceptional, nonideal circumstances, it does not necessarily follow that the performance of the cult by and for women was itself exceptional in the view of our authors.

The familial context in which women receive or perform the cult of dead kin in ancient West Asia varies. While some texts depict women as recipients or participants in the cults of their natal families, others depict their activity in the cults of families into which they marry. In his analysis of the Sîn-nāṣir genealogy, Van der Toorn argues that unmarried women participated in the cult of their natal families, while married women participated in the cult of their husbands' families. In the Ur III period, Takum-matum, the wife of King Šu-sîn, receives libations. This designation as the wife of the king suggests that Takum-matum receives cult because of her marriage and affiliation with the king. In other texts,[65] both sisters and daughters are referred to as possible caregivers, making libations for the dead. This description implies that these women offer care to those in their natal family, but it does not state whether these women are married. Thus, it is unclear whether they would be able to offer this care to members of their natal families if they were married. The mother of Assurbanipal receives care from her son, the crown prince. The inscription of Adad-guppi is different from these other cases: while it compares Adad-guppi to a daughter, it does not say that she is kin of the dead. Nevertheless, she offers cultic care to the dead Neo-Babylonian kings who preceded her son Nabonidus. At Emar and Nuzi, daughters become fictive sons to inherit the property of their fathers and assume care for the dead. It is unclear whether these daughters are married. In the Ugaritic Funerary Text, Queen Tharyelli participates in the coronation ceremony of her husband Ammurapi, which coincides with the commemoration of royal ancestors.

Concerning the biblical evidence, women are depicted performing the cult in either their natal families or the families into which they marry—with a few exceptions. Some texts suggest that women could receive or provide cultic care in the context of their natal families. Although Jeze-

---

65. E.g., Wilfred G. Lambert, "An Address of Marduk to the Demons: New Fragments," *AfO* 19 (1959/1960): 117 ll. 7–10.

bel has become part of the Israelite royal family through her marriage to Ahab, Jehu refers to burying her in 2 Kgs 9:34–37 as the right due to her status as a king's daughter. This observation suggests that care for the dead Jezebel reverts back to her natal family and that Jehu and his men must facilitate that care by burying her. The daughters of Zelophehad are able to preserve the name of their father in Num 27:1–11. The reoccurrence of this narrative in Num 36 and its concern about the intermarriage of Zelophehad's daughters with outsiders may suggest that inheriting their father's property and preserving his name relies either on their being unmarried or married to someone within the tribe.

Other biblical texts depict women receiving or providing cultic care for the dead in the families into which they marry. Rachel receives commemoration from her husband (Gen 35:20). The woman from Tekoa (2 Sam 14:7) indirectly participates in the ongoing care for her dead husband by ensuring that their last living son offers that care. As I note above, the text may imply that the son also offers care to his mother. The practice of levirate marriage and its preservation of the name of a dead man demonstrate that a woman may indirectly preserve his name by conceiving with his kinsman and providing him with offspring (Gen 38; Deut 25:5–6; Ruth 4:11). Other texts are less clear about their familial contexts. The reference to the Moabite women's sacrifices to the dead (Ps 106:28), for instance, does not say in what context the sacrifices take place. The commandment of Deut 5:16 // Exod 20:12 assumes that the mother will be honored by her offspring, presumably both sons and daughters, though the grammatical form of the imperative in both texts is masculine singular. Isaiah 56:3–5 also implies that the son and daughter would offer commemoration to their father, perhaps through invocation and/or a commemorative stela. However, it is not clear whether the text assumes that the daughter who cares for her dead father still resides with her natal family or has married into another household. Therefore, the familial context for women participating in the cult of dead kin is inconsistent both in and outside the Hebrew Bible.

However, comparative evidence shows that other features of women's participation in the cult of dead kin are rather consistent throughout ancient West Asia and the Mediterranean. This topos of women acting as caregivers for the dead in times of crisis is particularly prevalent in ancient literature. Two well-known ancient narratives, the Isis and Osiris myth and Sophocles's *Antigone*, offer detailed depictions of women performing rites characteristic of the cult of dead kin. The foundational story of Osiris, the Egyptian god of the underworld, includes the intervention of his sister and wife, Isis, after he is killed and dismembered by their brother Seth. It is only after Isis gathers the remains of Osiris and offers them proper care that Osiris may take up his place as god of the underworld. *Antigone* features another classic example of a woman offering care for her dead brother who has been killed in battle and whose corpse lies exposed on the battlefield. In this case, Antigone defies a royal decree by giving her brother proper burial rites. The play explicitly juxtaposes the law of the land, which states that her treasonous brother cannot receive these rites, and the law of the gods, which requires that the dead be buried. In both narratives, the dead suffer violent deaths followed by corpse exposure. The methods of care for these corpses take different forms in the narratives but correspond to Egyptian and Greek customs of burial and commemoration. What is most significant about them for the purposes of our discussion is that these women offer care to the dead in moments of crisis when the dead seemingly have no one else to care for them. These famous stories thus suggest an even broader cultural landscape in which similar narratives about women acting as caregivers for the dead may have flourished and resonated with their audiences.

4

The Status of the Dead
in the Postexilic Period

The trauma and ideological crisis caused by the Babylonian exile led to a variety of responses. The loss of the Jerusalem temple and the Davidic monarchy in Judah required the biblical writers to reconsider such fundamental principles of Israelite society as the status of Israel's covenant with YHWH and the relationship between Israelites and non-Israelites. In addition to such national concerns, scholarly treatments have also focused on the impact of the exile on family religion. These studies have posited the development of biblical polemic against the cult of dead kin and a decline in its practice in the exilic and postexilic periods. Such reconstructions draw heavily on the notion that Deuteronomistic ideology from the seventh century onward drastically altered the nature of family religion in Israel by centralizing the cult at the temple in Jerusalem and condemning more local forms of cult, including the practices of care and commemoration for the dead.[1] According to such reconstructions, Deuteronomistic ideology rendered the cult of dead kin incompatible with Yahwistic cult and led to biblical polemic against certain death rituals. A fundamental assumption of this reconstruction is a paradigm in which the cult of dead kin and other forms of local cult must be viewed in opposition to forms of centralized cult, including that of the Jerusalem temple, and to Yahwistic ideology as articulated by biblical writers.

---

1. See, e.g., Halpern, "Jerusalem and the Lineage"; Van der Toorn, *Family Religion*; Joseph Blenkinsopp, "The Family in First Temple Israel," in Perdue et al., *Families in Ancient Israel*, 48–103; Blenkinsopp, "Deuteronomy and the Politics"; Lewis, *Cults of the Dead*; Herbert Niehr, "Changed Status," 136–55; Stavrakopoulou, *Land of Our Fathers*.

Close analysis of the biblical evidence, however, challenges this reconstruction of cult. In this chapter, I examine exilic and postexilic texts that suggest, instead, the ongoing significance of the cult of dead kin in biblical depictions of YHWH and the Jerusalem temple. The use of the imagery and individual practices of the cult of dead kin in these depictions suggests that the cult not only continued to be practiced by Israelites in this period but was also embraced rather than rejected by the biblical writers who produced these texts. For instance, the depiction of YHWH as divine caregiver in prophetic texts reflects a broader tradition of care for the dead in ancient West Asia—that is, in times of acute crisis when the dead have no one to care for them, a nonkin actor may offer that care.[2] Indeed, in cuneiform sources, we see both kings and gods fulfill this role. In none of these instances do scholars posit the overthrow of the cult of dead kin; rather, its performance by Mesopotamian kings and gods seems to underscore not only the significance of the cult but also its role in affirming social relationships between the dead and those who care for them. Thus, YHWH as divine caregiver in texts such as Isa 56:3–5 and Ezek 37:11–14 is not a strike against the cult of dead kin, but rather an indication of its ongoing importance in family religion and Yahwistic ideology in postexilic Yehud.

The Supposedly Reduced Status of the Cult of Dead Kin

The supposedly reduced status of the cult of dead kin appears in several reconstructions of the cult, though it is located by scholars in different periods and attributed to different factors: the influx of exiled Israelites to Judah in 721 BCE, the cultic reforms of Hezekiah and Josiah in the eighth and seventh centuries, the Babylonian exile, and the return of some of the exiles to the land of Judah in the sixth century. In each of these recon-

---

2. YHWH also appears as a comforter to mourners in Zion (Isa 66:10–11, 13) and commands that other divine beings comfort Jerusalem (Isa 40:1). The comforter, who may be a family member or close affiliate of the deceased, signals the end of the mourning period. YHWH himself marks the end of the mourning period in texts such as Jer 31:12: "Then the maiden shall rejoice with dance as well as young men and old men together. I will turn their mourning into joy. I will comfort them [niḥamtîm], and I will make them rejoice out of their sorrow." Saul M. Olyan outlines other actions of the comforter in the context of mourning: to join the mourner in mourning rites (Job 2:11; Isa 51:19), to mark the end of the mourning (Gen 37:35), and to offer consolation (Job 16:5; 42:11; Lam 1:16) See Olyan, *Biblical Mourning: Ritual and Social Dimensions* (New York: Oxford University Press, 2004), 47–48.

structions, however, the marginalization of the cult of dead kin is understood in terms of its incompatibility with Deuteronomistic ideology and the supposedly normative Yahwism espoused by the biblical writers. In Van der Toorn's reconstruction of Israelite family religion, he argues that the establishment of Israelite monarchy during Saul's reign introduced an ongoing tension between the religion of the state and religion of the family. For instance, he cites the prohibition against necromancy and the lack of "regard for the sacral value of the family inheritance" among other official policies that supposedly diminished the scope of family religion.[3] He further argues that the disintegration of the Northern Kingdom led to the development of an ideology that privileged national or centralized cult above local forms of cult. In this reconstruction, the former inhabitants of the Northern Kingdom, cut off from their ancestral lands and former cult places, developed new ideas about Israel's relationship to its national deity, and these concepts formed the basis of the Deuteronomistic ideology that emerged later in Judah. In short, according to Van der Toorn's reconstruction of Israelite religion, the imported ideology of the exiled northerners subverted the fundamental principles of family religion and found wide acceptance among elite Judahite circles that similarly experienced exile from their ancestral lands and cult places in 586 BCE. Thus, family religion, including the cult of dead kin, was replaced by what Van der Toorn characterizes as "familial participation" in a national Yahwistic religion.[4]

Other reconstructions locate the supposedly reduced status of the cult of dead kin in the late eighth and seventh centuries, arguing that the cultic ideology of the Deuteronomistic reformers, including Hezekiah and Josiah, attacked and limited the cult of dead kin. In this reconstruction, Deuteronomistic circles intentionally undermined care of the dead in order to ensure centralization of the cult, the deterioration of old kinship ties, and the development of new ideologies of kinship.[5] Joseph Blenkinsopp, for example, characterizes the relationship between royal forms of cult and household cult as adversarial, arguing that the intent of cultic reforms, such as the Deuteronomistic centralization of the cult, was to divert resources and allegiance away from local cultic structures and redirect them toward the state cult.[6] The prohibition of both the cult of dead

---

3. Van der Toorn, *Family Religion*, 181–82.
4. Van der Toorn, *Family Religion*, 378.
5. See, e.g., Halpern, "Jerusalem and the Lineage," passim.
6. Blenkinsopp, "Family in First Temple Israel," passim. Unlike Blenkinsopp,

kin and necromancy thus intended to "loosen the spiritual bonds of kinship in general, and especially the link between kinship and land tenure,
by removing one of the principal reasons for inalienability, namely, the
ancestral plot, as locus of ancestral burial and attendant rites."[7] Blenkinsopp also suggests that the psalms describing the oblivion of the dead (e.g.,
Pss 6:6; 30:10; 88:6; 115:17) indirectly oppose older, more popular notions
of the dead in which they continue to interact with the living. Lewis also
posits an adversarial relationship between what he calls "normative Yahwism" and "care for the dead,"[8] a position similar to Klaas Spronk's earlier
argument that Yahwism and ancestor cult were incompatible due to the
"monopolizing" tendencies of the former.[9] Albertz also emphasizes a fundamental disjunction between the beliefs and practices of family religion
and forms of centralized cult—until the seventh century, when Deuteronomistic reform tried to integrate the two.[10]

However, there are some problems with this understanding of the
impact of Deuteronomistic ideology on the cult of dead kin. In fact, certain features of the biblical text caution against reconstructing an adversarial relationship between the cult of dead kin and this ideology. First,
one of the refrains within the Deuteronomistic History is that a recently
deceased king "lies with his ancestors" (1 Kgs 2:10; 11:43; 14:20, 31; 15:8,
24).[11] A similar refrain appears in the Priestly material, where one is "gathered to one's kin" (Gen 25:8, 17; 35:29; 49:29, 33; Num 20:24, 26; 27:13;
31:2; Deut 32:50).[12] The Deuteronomistic phrasing assumes the ritual
ideal of common burial within the family tomb.[13] If the Deuteronomists

---

Niehr argues that such a stance against lineage systems could only emerge after the
demise of the monarchy, since royal families also utilize the rhetoric of kinship and
landholding ("Changed Status," 151).

7. Blenkinsopp, "Family in First Temple Israel," 89.

8. Lewis, *Cults of the Dead*, 2.

9. Spronk, *Beatific Afterlife in Ancient Israel*, 42.

10. Albertz, "Family Religion in Ancient Israel," 104–5.

11. See my discussion and translation of ʾābôt as "ancestors" in ch. 3.

12. Lewis also notes epigraphic parallels to this burial imagery in the Tel Dan
Aramaic inscription ("my father lay down, he went to his [ancestors]"; "How Far Can
the Texts," 173 n. 14).

13. For a thorough treatment of these biblical burial notices, see Suriano, *Politics
of Dead Kings*. Integrating biblical and archaeological evidence, Suriano argues that
these burial notices not only evoke the imagery of collective burial in the Levant but
also help construct the monarchical histories of Israel and Judah by marking the death

were so invested in dismantling ideologies of lineage and their connection to care for the dead, we should not expect to see this phrase repeated over and over again in the text's depiction of royal burial and succession. In addition, some of the most compelling biblical evidence for ritual care for the dead comes from the Deuteronomistic History (Deut 26:14; 1 Sam 19; 2 Sam 2:31; 14:7; 18:18; 21:10, 12–14).[14] Most important, although the Deuteronomists condemn several aspects of temple cult, they are remarkably silent about care for the dead and family religion in general. As we have already observed, the reference to food offerings for the dead in Deut 26:14 does not assume a general proscription in all circumstances and, notably, assumes that the activity takes place. As I argue in chapter 2, although the Deuteronomistic History contains multiple polemics against necromancy, such prohibitions are not aimed at ritual care for the dead.[15]

Deuteronomistic polemic against the *tərāpîm* and *maṣṣēbôt* does not seem related to the cult of dead kin either. For instance, 2 Kgs 23:24 states that Josiah removes *tərāpîm* as well as *ʾōbôt* and *yiddəʿōnîm*,[16] and *gillûlîm* from the land of Judah: "Also, Josiah turned away those who divined by spirits [*hāʾōbôt wəhayyiddəʿōnîm*], *tərāpîm*, illegitimate cult images [*haggillûlîm*, lit. 'dung balls'], and all of the detestable things that were found in the land of Judah and Jerusalem." The text views all of these cultic objects or offices as illicit. Yet, as I argue in chapter 2, necromancy and the cult of dead kin are separate cultic phenomena, and it is unclear that the *tərāpîm* are associated with the cult of dead kin. Therefore, 2 Kgs 23:24 is not a clear polemic against the cult of dead kin. Although the Deuteronomistic History praises Josiah for destroying *maṣṣēbôt* (2 Kgs 23:14), I understand this instance of the term to refer to stelae marking local sanctuaries that could pose an economic and political threat to the Jerusalem temple. The

---

and succession of individual kings (*Politics of Dead Kings*, 41–50). Suriano's study is particularly helpful here because it illuminates biblical writers' persistent use of imagery associated with funerary and mortuary practice in order to articulate social and political ideologies.

14. See my discussion of these individual texts throughout ch. 1.

15. For a more detailed analysis of this distinction, see ch. 2. Albertz himself denies that necromancy was part of family religion (Albertz and Schmitt, *Family and Household Religion*, 99). Bloch-Smith further argues that these polemics against necromancy are mainly directed at cultic specialists who challenged the authority claimed by priests and prophets (*Judahite Burial Practices*, 150).

16. In this case, this phrase seems to refer to those who communicate with the dead, not the dead themselves.

pairing of the *maṣṣēbôt* with *ʾăshērîm* in this passage suggests that the term refers to cult objects set up in a sanctuary. Furthermore, it is unlikely that these *maṣṣēbôt* refer to commemorative stelae marking burial sites (as in Gen 35:20) because this text goes on to say that Josiah fills their sanctuaries (*məqômām*, lit. "places") with human bones.[17] This act seems to be intentionally ritually defiling and thus aims to render these cult places polluted and defunct, which does not make sense if the *maṣṣēbôt* in this passage are burial markers where human remains are already in close proximity.[18] Although some aspects of family religion probably took place at such local sanctuaries,[19] the Deuteronomistic condemnation of these sanctuaries and the *maṣṣēbôt* that mark them is not an attack on family religion itself.

For some scholars, the loss of ancestral lands during the exilic period also contributed to the end of the Israelite cult of dead kin. In Van der Toorn's reconstruction, the ideologies of the exiled northern Israelites, which later developed into Deuteronomistic ideology, reinterpreted the relationship between Israel and its national deity and thus attacked family religion as incompatible with supposedly normative Yahwism. When Judahite circles experienced exile from ancestral lands and cult places in 586 BCE, these principles gained wider acceptance. His analysis argues that the physical separation of the exiled Israelites from the Jerusalem temple as well as their ancestors' tombs contributed to their willingness to accept such a new religious paradigm.[20] This argument assumes the primacy of tombs as the locus for cultic care for the dead and the relative immobility of the dead themselves, an interpretation that ignores biblical evidence for the portability of human remains and the construction of commemorative

---

17. Indeed, Theodore J. Lewis emphasizes the multivalence of *maṣṣēbôt* in the biblical text, pointing out that they may indicate the presence of a deity, mark a tomb, be boundary markers, be tribal markers, and be surrogates for male heirs. See Lewis, "Divine Images and Aniconism in Ancient Israel," *JAOS* 118 (1998): 41. Thus, it is problematic to assume that all *maṣṣēbôt* are equal in the eyes of the Deuteronomists.

18. A possible counterargument, however, is that these are *maṣṣēbôt* in the style of Absalom's monument in 2 Sam 18:18, which is not necessarily set up in close proximity to a burial site. However, the pairing of this term with *ʾăshērîm*, cult objects indexing the presence of a particular deity, suggests that the *maṣṣēbôt* of this passage function in a similar way.

19. Albertz notes that the fulfillment of vows takes place at public sanctuaries (2 Sam 15:8; 1 Sam 1:21; 2:19), as does the "annual sacrifice" of 1 Sam 20 ("Family Religion in Ancient Israel," 100, 114–15).

20. Van der Toorn, *Family Religion*, 362.

stelae in loci outside a burial context. As noted in chapter 1, comparative evidence from Mesopotamia also suggests that the dead could receive care in places outside the burial site.[21]

More recent reconstructions of the supposed marginalization of the cult of dead kin locate this development in the postexilic period.[22] For instance, Herbert Niehr argues for a drastically reduced status of the dead in this period, and he cites the following evidence as indicative of the changing status of the dead: the attitude toward the royal cult in Ezek 43:7–9; condemnation of the *marzēaḥ* (Jer 16:5–8; Amos 6:7); prohibition of certain mourning rites, such as shaving or self-laceration (Deut 14:1; Lev 19:28; 21:5); prohibition of necromancy (Deut 18:9–12; Lev 19:31; 20:6, 27); and the supposed suppression of household gods in the Decalogue (Exod 20:3–5 // Deut 5:7–9). Among the ideological causes of this alleged shift, Niehr cites a priestly interest in the holiness of Jerusalem (Neh 11:1, 18) and the influence of the Deuteronomistic ideology. However, Niehr's analysis relies on some problematic assumptions about the nature of family religion and overlooks biblical evidence that challenges his reconstruction. The thoroughness of his reconstruction makes it an illustrative example of similar analyses that posit the diminished status of the cult of dead kin in the postexilic period, so I will address the different features of his argument below.

The polemic in Ezek 43:7–9, which both Niehr and Stavrakopoulou claim indicates a widespread program of demoting the status of the Israelite dead, focuses on the dangers of corpse pollution, including the threat it poses to the Jerusalem temple.[23] The text states that the close proximity of the temple and the corpses of Judahite kings leads to the defilement of YHWH's holy name:

---

21. These texts include the Old Babylonian letter from King Hammurabi of Babylon to Sin-iddinam in which a father offers the *kispu* to his missing son, whom he presumes has died; Gilgamesh pouring libations to his father, Lugalbanda, en route to the Cedar Forest in the Gilgamesh Epic; and the Genealogy of the Hammurapi Dynasty, in which the king makes *kispu* offerings to those who have died abroad on military campaign.

22. See, e.g., Niehr, "Changed Status," 136–55; Nihan, "1 Samuel 28," 23–54; Nathan MacDonald, "The Hermeneutics and Genesis of the Red Cow Ritual," *HTR* 105 (2012): 351–71.

23. Stavrakopoulou accepts Niehr's analysis on this point (Stavrakopoulou, *Land of Our Fathers*, 117–20). For arguments against this interpretation, see Albertz and Schmitt, *Family and Household Religion*, 456.

He said to me, "Human, (this is) the place of my throne and the place of the soles of my feet, where I will dwell in the midst of the Israelites forever. The house of Israel shall no longer pollute my holy name—neither they nor their kings—through their whoring, through the corpses[24] of their kings, (through) their high places,[25] or by setting their threshold beside my threshold so that their doorpost was next to my doorpost and a wall was between me and them. They polluted my holy name through their abominations that they committed, and I will consume them in my anger. Now they shall remove their whoring and the corpses of their kings from me so that I may dwell in their midst forever."

For Niehr, the separation of the royal cult from the temple indicates that "the royal death cult is idolatry incompatible with the worship of YHWH."[26] However, this text seems more concerned about the defiling nature of corpses than about providing a general rebuke against cultic activity concerning the dead. In fact, the detailed way in which the passage describes the proximity of the royal corpses to the threshold of the temple ("setting their threshold beside my threshold so that their doorpost was next to my doorpost and a wall was between me and them") suggests that its primary concern is corpse contact, that is, with proximity rather than practice. In fact, the image of corpses defiling the temple occurs elsewhere in Ezekiel, such as Ezek 9:7, in which YHWH himself orders that the temple be defiled with corpses. Since defilement is one explanation for the departure

---

24. Other commentators argue that this text refers not to royal tombs but to memorial monuments or offerings to the royal dead. See, e.g., David Neiman, "PGR: A Canaanite Cult Object in the Old Testament," *JBL* 67 (1948): 55–60; Jürgen H. Ebach, "PGR = (Toten-)opfer? Ein Vorschlag zum Verständnis von Ez. 43,7.9," *UF* 3 (1971): 365–68. I opt here for the more widely accepted interpretation of Hebrew *peger* as "corpse."

25. The translation of this word (*bāmôtām*) is difficult to integrate into the rest of the passage. Its form in the MT looks like a plural form of *bamâ*, "high place," although it lacks the instrumental *bet* preposition attached to other nouns in this series. Other translators understand this word to be a form of the verb *mût*, "to die," which would change the meaning of the phrase to something like "the corpses of their kings at their death." In his commentary on the text, Walther Zimmerli also posits that this word may be the result of scribal error, influenced by the infinitive construct that follows it (*batittām*). See Zimmerli, *Ezekiel* (Philadelphia: Fortress, 1983), 2:409. Following Zimmerli, I prefer either omitting the word altogether or translating it as a plural of *bamâ*, which is less awkward than the redundant phrase "through the corpses of their kings at their death."

26. Niehr, "Changed Status," 139.

of a deity from its sanctuary, this image in Ezekiel offers one interpretation why YHWH would abandon Jerusalem during the Neo-Babylonian siege and allow his people to go into exile. Therefore, Niehr's argument that this text represents a shift in biblical attitudes toward the dead mischaracterizes the evidence. Much like Deut 26:14, which I discuss further below, the concern here is with corpse pollution and its possible defilement of both the sanctuary and offerings to YHWH. Anxiety about corpse pollution is not equivalent to condemnation of cultic care for the dead. In fact, ethnographic studies may offer helpful comparative models for the coexistence of concepts of corpse pollution and ongoing interest in care of the dead. For instance, two case studies, Maurice Bloch's examination of the Merina and James Watson's examination of modern Cantonese communities,[27] describe contexts in which societies may accept both at the same time. Although these societies demonstrate anxieties about corpse pollution, they do not seek to undermine the care of the dead. Instead, pollution may reflect sensory response to the realities of death or social transitions occasioned by the removal of a person from a social group. Therefore, pollution ideology is more concerned with the continuity of the community, composed of both the living and the dead, than undermining practices surrounding the dead.

Similarly, the biblical polemic against the *bêt marzēaḥ* is not indicative of a condemnation of the cult of dead kin, and Niehr's characterization of the *marzēaḥ* in Jer 16:5 as a "house where the wailing, the funeral repast and the nourishment of the dead take place" invites revision.[28] Rather than the cult of dead kin, this text seems to focus on the care provided by comforters to the living who mourn for the dead. One role of the "comforter" (*mənaḥēm*) in the biblical text is to help mourners end their period of mourning and reintegrate themselves into society and cult.[29] In fact, the technical term for this kind of ritual comforting appears in Jer 16:7 ("They shall not break bread in mourning in order to comfort him [*lənaḥămô*] on account of the dead. They shall not give them a cup of comfort [*kôs*

---

27. Bloch, "Death, Women, and Power," 211–29; James L. Watson, "Death Pollution in Cantonese Society," in Bloch and Parry, *Death and the Regeneration of Life,* 55–86.

28. Niehr, "Changed Status," 143.

29. Gary A. Anderson, *A Time to Mourn, a Time to Dance: The Expression of Grief and Joy in Israelite Religion* (University Park: Pennsylvania State University Press, 1991), 19–58, 60–97; Olyan, *Biblical Mourning,* 57–59.

tanḥûmîm] on account of his father or his mother"). The phrase "in order to comfort him on account of the dead" (lənaḥămô ʿal-mēt) does not refer to comfort offered to the dead but rather to those who mourn them. Since fasting can be one aspect of mourning activity (e.g., 2 Sam 1:12), the offering of food and drink to those who mourn is possibly an example of the comforter marking the end of the mourning period. However, in the broader context of this passage, YHWH instructs Jeremiah not to enter the bêt marzēaḥ or to engage in this comforting behavior, perhaps because the imminent calamity that will overtake the land will obliterate the distinction of such ritual states: many will die violently, corpse exposure will be rampant, and no one will observe typical mourning rituals.[30]

Yet, Niehr argues that the supposed "condemnation" of food offerings to the dead in Deut 26:14 and the portrayal of the marzēaḥ in Jer 16:5 indicate further limitation of care for the dead. Concerning the alleged prohibition against food offerings for the dead in Deuteronomy, Niehr states, "So Deut 26:14 establishes a clear-cut division between YHWH and the persons under his protection and mourning and the dead, which are separated from the divine realm."[31] However, like Ezek 43, this text seems to be more concerned with the ritual purity of the tithe than with banning care for the dead. The negative confession in Deut 26:14 states: "I have not eaten any of [the tithe] while in mourning, nor have I put any of it away while unclean. I have not given any of it to the dead." The passage assumes that one in mourning would be ritually unclean, presumably due to corpse contact or through close proximity or contact with a tomb. Giving some of the tithe to the dead would render one unclean through corpse or tomb contact. More important, it would threaten the tithe's

---

30. Ezekiel 24:16–17 also describes the cessation of typical mourning behavior: "Human, I am about to take from you the desire of your eyes with a stroke. You shall not lament or weep. Your tears shall not flow. Sigh in silence. You shall not mourn for the dead. Bind your turban upon yourself. Put your sandals on your feet. You shall not cover your lip. You shall not eat the bread of men [leḥem ʾănāšîm]." Some translations render leḥem ʾănāšîm as "the bread of mourners," based on the context of the passage and its focus on mourning practices. In addition to not mourning the dead, the audience of this passage is directed not to uncover their heads and feet, nor to cover their lip in mourning. Eating the "bread of men" or the "bread of mourners" also seems to be constitutive of mourning behavior. However, it is unclear whether this term refers to the food eaten by mourners during the mourning period or the food offered by comforters when that period has ended.

31. Niehr, "Changed Status," 142.

holiness (Deut 26:13). Although Deut 26:14 is often cited as evidence for a widespread Deuteronomistic polemic against feeding the dead, this argument mischaracterizes the text and then applies this flawed interpretation to Deuteronomistic ideology as a whole.[32] The fact is that there is simply no prohibition in this text against offering nontithed food to the dead. Furthermore, a similar concern about corpse pollution and sacrifices to YHWH appears in Hos 9:4, which suggests that this anxiety about corpse pollution is not a new development in the postexilic period.[33] Hosea 9:4 compares the sacrifices of the Israelites to the bread of mourners (*leḥem ʾônîm*). Anyone who eats this bread of mourners will be made unclean by it. The implication is that the bread of mourners is polluted and polluting, presumably because it has been in contact with a corpse. Thus, this passage refers to the pollution of food through corpse contact in order to express YHWH's rejection of the Israelites' sacrifices: they are as unacceptable to YHWH as bread polluted by corpse contact during mourning.

---

32. On the basis of Deut 26:14, Lewis argues that "it seems safe to infer that any offerings to the dead would have been considered offensive to Deuteronomistic theology" (*Cults of the Dead*, 172 n. 2). However, other scholars have argued against this view, such as Albertz and Schmitt (*Household and Family Religion*, 455–56).

33. For a discussion of this text and its parallels in Deut 26:14, see Matthew J. Suriano, "Breaking Bread with the Dead: Katumuwa's Stele, Hosea 9:4, and the Early History of the Soul," *JAOS* 134 (2014): 385–405. Though dating any biblical text based on its possible allusions to contemporary historical events is fraught with problems, the majority scholarly opinion on the date of the book of Hosea depends a great deal on this kind of analysis. The references to the kings of Israel and Judah (1:1), including "the house of Jehu" (1:4), suggest to many scholars that the prophetic message dates to the reign of Jeroboam II in the eighth century BCE. The repeated references to Assyria and Egypt further suggest that the international political context for the book is the Assyrian period prior to the fall of northern Israel in 721 BCE. For analyses that date Hosea's prophetic message to this period, see Brad E. Kelle, *Hosea 2: Metaphor and Rhetoric in Historical Perspective* (Atlanta: Society of Biblical Literature, 2005), 20; Francis I. Anderson and David Noel Freedman, *Hosea: A New Translation with Introduction and Commentary* (New York: Doubleday, 1980), esp. 40–52; Graham I. Davies, *Hosea* (Sheffield: Sheffield Academic, 1993), 14–15; Hans Walter Wolff, *Hosea: A Commentary on the Book of the Prophet Hosea* (Philadelphia: Fortress, 1974), xxi; James Luther Mays, *Hosea: A Commentary* (Philadelphia: Westminster, 1969), 3–5. More recent studies posit a sixth-century context for the final shaping of the book and its message. See, e.g., James M. Trotter, *Reading Hosea in Achaemenid Yehud* (London: Sheffield Academic, 2001), passim.

Another argument for the supposedly diminished status of the cult of dead kin states that the prohibition of certain mourning rites, such as self-laceration and shaving (Deut 14:1; Lev 19:28; 21:5), developed during the exilic and postexilic periods as a result of Deuteronomistic separation of YHWH from the realm of the dead.[34] Niehr accepts the analysis of Van der Toorn, who claims that these mourning rites attempted to reinvigorate the dead with symbols of vitality, such as blood and hair.[35] According to Niehr, the biblical prohibition of these rites condemns the establishment of this ritual bond between the living and the dead. Yet, this characterization of these mourning rituals—both their function and the logic underlying their prohibition—is flawed. There is no indication in the text that these rituals aim to revivify the dead in any way, and the argument that they function in this way is entirely speculative. Thus it is unlikely that revivification of the dead is the reason for biblical polemic against these practices.

Instead, I would argue that such prohibitions should be interpreted in light of biblical mourning rites and what they communicate about the place of mourners in cult and society.[36] Although Van der Toorn's arguments concerning ritual communion and potential revivification of the dead are overly speculative, the mourning processes of the living do seem to mirror the status of the recently deceased; for instance, mourners may sit on the ground and cover their heads with dust.[37] This dirty, dejected state is similar to many depictions of the dead and the netherworld in ancient West Asian texts, which often portray the netherworld as dusty, dark, and unpleasant, and its denizens as mourners.[38] However, this imitation of the

---

34. Although Niehr notes that Jer 16:1–5 mentions these rites without critique, he does not mention other noncondemnatory attestations in the biblical text. A more detailed list of such attestations (Isa 15:2; 22:12; Jer 41:4–5; 47:5; Amos 8:10; Ezra 9:3) appears in Olyan, *Biblical Mourning*, 113–14.

35. Niehr, "Changed Status," 144–45.

36. Olyan, *Biblical Mourning*, 35.

37. See, e.g., the description of Jacob mourning for his son Joseph in Gen 37:34–35. Jacob explicitly states that he will descend to the netherworld with his son: "Jacob tore his robes, put sackcloth on his loins, and mourned for his son for many days. All of his sons and daughters rose to comfort him, but he refused to be comforted. He said, 'I will descend to Sheol mourning my son.' His father wept for him."

38. See, e.g., tablet XII of the Akkadian Gilgamesh Epic. For a critical edition of the text with commentary, see George, *Babylonian Gilgamesh Epic*. After Gilgamesh loses two wooden toys when they roll down into the netherworld, Enkidu, his loyal friend, offers to go down into the netherworld to retrieve them. Gilgamesh advises Enkidu on

dead need not indicate an attempt to revivify them, an idea that is nowhere supported by the biblical evidence. Mourning processes fulfill many social, political, and personal needs, and identification between mourners and the recently deceased may help establish an ongoing, mutually beneficial relationship between the living and the dead.[39] Concerning the logic underlying the prohibition of these rites in Deuteronomy and the Holiness Code, I accept Olyan's view that shaving and self-laceration are markers of mourning that are not easily reversible, in contrast to such mourning practices as sitting on the ground, weeping and wailing, and strewing dirt and ashes on one's head. Therefore, after the period of mourning has passed, these markers of mourning remain on the cultic actor, potentially mixing the antithetical ritual states of mourning and praising YHWH.[40] If shaving and self-laceration are potential violators of mutually exclusive ritual states, the prohibitions in Deut 14:1 and Lev 19:28; 21:5 have nothing to do with Niehr's radical shift in biblical conceptions of the dead.

Some studies invoke monotheism as the underlying reason for the biblical polemic against certain death rituals. Like Niehr, Stavrakopoulou argues that the biblical condemnation of such practices (Lev 19:28; Deut 14:1; 18:9–12; 26:14; Isa 8:19–20; 57:3–13; 65:1–5; Ps 106:28) was a response to the threat the powerful dead pose to "emergent monotheisms," which emphasized "centralized, exclusive preferences of the biblical YHWH."[41] Yet, the status of the dead as divine, semidivine, supernatural, or impotent beings is unclear, unstated, or inconsistent in the biblical text.[42] At no point do the biblical writers explicitly position care for the dead in opposition to the worship of YHWH. In fact, it is unclear that the Deuteronomistic History has any conception of this supposed rivalry. Furthermore, Stavrakopoulou argues that the supposed demotion of the dead in Israelite households in the postexilic period mirrored the growing intolerance toward divine beings in YHWH's pantheon, which coincided with this "emergent monotheism."[43]

---

how he should dress and behave in the netherworld so as to elude capture and imprisonment there. In order to blend in among the inhabitants of the netherworld, Enkidu must be filthy, downcast, and unadorned with ornamentation or weapons.

39. Olyan, *Biblical Mourning*, 44–45.
40. Olyan, *Biblical Mourning*, 118–23.
41. Stavrakopoulou, *Land of Our Fathers*, 19.
42. See my discussion of this interpretative problem in ch. 1.
43. Stavrakopoulou, *Land of Our Fathers*, 143–44.

Monotheism as a concept looms large in scholarly reconstructions of ancient Israel, yet it is unclear that monotheism accurately characterizes biblical Yahwism or Israelite religion. Mark Smith defines Israelite monotheism as "the worship and belief in Yahweh and disbelief in the reality of other deities."[44] However, he notes elsewhere the problem with attributing "beliefs" or "internal attitudes" to Israelite religion, because the Hebrew Bible is primarily concerned with practice. Baruch Halpern attempts to redefine monotheism; for example, he refers to YHWH's absorption of other deities' characteristics as "affective monotheism" because it is an expression of devotion to that god.[45] Konrad Schmid describes a similar process in the "Priestly concept of monotheism," which attempted to synthesize traditions of the God of the ancestors, the God of the exodus, and YHWH the god of Israel.[46] This terminology is misleading, however, because this process (which Smith calls "convergence") occured in other cultures to which scholars do not ascribe monotheistic tendencies. In fact, Schmid posits that the characterization of Marduk in the Enuma Elish may have influenced the Priestly synthesis of God during the exilic period.[47] The use of *monotheism* to describe this phenomenon in Israelite religion seems inherently teleological and points toward what Halpern describes as the "self-conscious monotheism" or "philosophical monotheism" in the exilic and postexilic periods.[48] Yet, it is unclear that monotheism accurately describes Yahwism in these periods, either.

More recent work on biblical evidence from the exilic and postexilic periods has challenged the interpretation that such texts reflect the emergence of an Israelite monotheism. In his study of icon polemics in ancient West Asia, Nathaniel Levtow challenges the association between biblical aniconism and the supposed development of monotheism during the exile. Instead of reading passages such as Isa 40:6–20 as evidence for aniconic theology, Levtow argues that such polemics participate in a broad ancient

---

44. Smith, *Early History of God*, 1.

45. Baruch Halpern, "'Brisker Pipes Than Poetry': The Development of Israelite Monotheism," in *Judaic Perspectives on Ancient Israel*, ed. Jacob Neusner, Baruch A. Levine, and Ernest S. Frerichs (Philadelphia: Fortress, 1987), 80.

46. Konrad Schmid, "The Quest for 'God': Monotheistic Arguments in the Priestly Texts of the Hebrew Bible," in *Reconsidering the Concept of Revolutionary Monotheism*, ed. Beate Pongratz-Leisten (Winona Lake, IN: Eisenbrauns, 2011), 271–89.

47. Schmid, "Quest for 'God,'" 288.

48. Halpern, "Brisker Pipes Than Poetry," 100.

West Asian discourse in which one group dishonors the icons of another group as a strategy of sociopolitical subversion. By emphasizing the creation of divine images by human hands (Isa 44:9–20; Jer 10:4–16), these texts undermine the work of Mesopotamian mouth-opening and mouth-washing rituals, which attempt to disassociate the image from its production and materiality.[49] The icon parodies of the Hebrew Bible confer shame on the cultic images and practices of the Neo-Babylonians, which inverts the expected relationship of suzerain-vassal relations between Babylon and Judah. The exilic polemic against divine images, thus, does not signal an emergent monotheistic ideology among biblical writers but instead participates in a much older and broader tradition of icon polemics.

Although biblical scholars often argue that Second Isaiah (Isa 40–55) bears unequivocal witness to a new, radical monotheism, Olyan challenges this argument by focusing on assumptions about the existence of divine beings other than YHWH.[50] For example, Isa 40:1–8, 25–26; and 45:12 recognize the existence of the heavenly host, and Isa 51:9–11 alludes to the conflict myth in which YHWH defeats the sea dragon. Olyan notes that the divine host in Second Isaiah is similar to the host in texts such as Judg 5:20; Hab 3:5; and Ps 68:18.[51] Therefore, we must read the statement of Isa 45:5, "besides me there is no god," in light of these passages. Instead of interpreting this verse as a theological statement about the nonexistence of other deities, we may consider it among the other biblical passages, such as Exod 15:11, that describe the incomparable nature—not sole existence—of YHWH. In fact, Olyan emphasizes the similarities in depictions of YHWH and Marduk with regard to incomparability; both YHWH and Marduk (in the Enuma Elish) assert their dominance over the host, their defeat of the sea dragon, and their creation of the earth and humanity. In short, Isa 45:5 may not reflect a new, radical understanding of YHWH's sole existence, but rather a hyperbolic statement characteristic of rhetoric about divine incomparability.[52] The characterization of exilic and postexilic Yahwistic ideologies as "emergent monotheisms" mischaracterizes the relationship between YHWH and other divine beings; further, the supposed emergence of monotheism does not support the claim that Yahwistic ideology was at odds with the cult of dead kin in the postexilic period.

---

49. Levtow, *Images of Others*, 26–27, 97.
50. Olyan, "Is Isaiah 40–55," 190–201.
51. Olyan, "Is Isaiah 40–55," 195 n. 18.
52. Olyan, "Is Isaiah 40–55," 197, 200.

The first two commandments in the Decalogue (Exod 20:3–5 // Deut 5:7–9) also appear in discussion of the cult of dead kin and its status in the postexilic period. Niehr argues that these commandments—the prohibition against worshiping other gods before YHWH and creating cult images for these deities—originally referred to the worship of household gods, not allegedly foreign deities. It is unclear, however, how Niehr reconciles this argument with the inclusion of the commandment to honor one's father and mother (Exod 20:12 // Deut 5:16). In fact, he argues that this commandment originally referred to care for one's living parents and dead ancestors; however, in the present state of the text "all post mortem aspects of honouring one's parents are intentionally removed from view."[53] Despite this supposed suppression of custodial responsibility toward the dead, it has long been claimed that this commandment reflects these aspects of family religion.[54] If the first two commandments are originally intended to prohibit care for the dead and the third commandment is originally intended to support it, then Niehr fails to account for how these "original" meanings coexist at any point. His argument that "the prohibition of the ancestor cult in the first commandment forced the authors of the Decalogue to minimize the care of the dead elders" seems to assume that the commandment in Exod 20:12 // Deut 5:16 in its original form is earlier than the first two commandments.

Regardless, this argument is overly speculative. Furthermore, it misinterprets the nature of the first commandment as a prohibition against the worship of other gods. The phrase ʿal pānāy, "before me," however, suggests that the worship of any other gods must be subordinate to the worship of YHWH, the national god of Israel.[55] Again, this is a matter of incomparability, not existence. The use of the preposition pǝnê seems

---

53. Niehr, "Changed Status," 141–42.

54. Brichto, "Kin, Cult, Land," 30–31. To support his argument that the Hebrew term kabbēd may include funerary and mortuary aspects, Brichto cites Akkadian texts in which an adopted son must honor (palāḫu) his adoptive parents by burying and mourning them (31 n. 49).

55. The scholarly debate over the most plausible translation of this phrase is extensive. Though others have argued that this phrase refers to the denial of the existence of other deities besides YHWH, in his commentary on the text, William H. Propp notes the spatial aspect of this phrase, "occupying the same time and/or space.... So one possible meaning is that no other deities may be worshiped in Yahweh-shrines." See Propp, Exodus 19–40 (New York: Doubleday, 2006), 167. Moshe Weinfeld's interpretation of the commandment also favors this translation of the phrase: "You shall have no

to indicate hierarchy: YHWH is always first, and all others follow after him. The use of this phrase to indicate hierarchy appears elsewhere in the Hebrew Bible, including Deut 21:16, which depicts a father's preference for one son over another: "On the day that [a father] bequeaths his property to his sons, he will not be able to make the son of the beloved [wife] the first-born instead of [ʿal pənê] the son of the hated [wife], who is the firstborn." In this text, the phrase indicates the relative status of the two sons and prohibits the elevation of the preferred son over the rightful heir. In the context of Exod 20:3–5 // Deut 5:7–9, the phrase similarly prohibits the elevation of other gods over YHWH. Therefore, even if the commandment in Exod 20:3–5 // Deut 5:7–9 does refer to household gods or dead ancestors, it still is not a blanket prohibition against their care.

Niehr also argues that the reference to Jerusalem in Neh 11:1, 18 as the ʿîr haqqōdeš ("city of the sanctuary," "city of holiness," or "holy city") suggests a priestly concern with ritual purity, specifically the separation of the ritually pure city from the realm of the dead.[56] Indeed, this concern with separating the unclean from the holy city of Jerusalem is clear in Isa 52:1, which states: "Awake, awake, put on your strength, Zion! Put on your beautiful garments, Jerusalem, the holy city [ʿîr haqqōdeš], for the uncircumcised [ʿārēl] and the unclean [ṭāmēʾ] shall never again enter you." His citation of Nehemiah as evidence for a stark separation between these two realms is strange, however, because of the references to Jerusalem as the "city of my ancestors' graves" in Neh 2:3, 5. The "graves of David" also appear in Neh 3:16 without any negative connotation. Rather than condemning the existence of these graves, Nehemiah's appeal to Artaxerxes explicitly states that he will go to Jerusalem in order to rebuild them along with the rest of the city (Neh 2:1–5), though the text does not specify where these graves are located in relation to the city. Therefore, if one were to characterize care for the dead in Nehemiah, these texts seem to be clear examples of an explicitly positive outlook. Nehemiah's dismay at the deteriorated state of his ancestors' graves implies an ongoing concern for

---

other gods in my presence." See Weinfeld, *Deuteronomy 1–11* (New York: Doubleday, 1964), 275.

56. "The Temple formed the centre of the city, and the place of YHWH's dwelling in the midst of his people. This place is characterized by order, justice and ritual purity. Outside the city was the place of the necropoleis and the desert, which had the connotation of anti-order, as forming the habitat of enemies, nomads, wild beasts, and demons" (Niehr, "Changed Status," 148–49).

the dead and their burial sites in the postexilic period. It is unclear how the biblical writers reconcile the holiness of the city with this concern for graves. Perhaps the graves were located outside the city; however, the text does not explicitly state this. In any case, the concern for the state of the graves is clear in these texts.

Finally, Niehr also cites a sharp distinction between YHWH and the realm of the dead as further indication of the changing status of the dead. He cites several passages that separate YHWH from the dead and the netherworld. For instance, there is no memory of YHWH in death, and the dead cannot praise YHWH in Ps 6:5. Similarly, YHWH refuses to listen to the dead in the netherworld in Ps 28:1. Psalm 88:4–6 refers to the dead in the netherworld as those who are cut off from YHWH and whom YHWH no longer remembers. Psalm 115:17 also states that the dead do not praise YHWH in Sheol, and Isa 38:18 states that Sheol and death cannot praise YHWH. However, there is biblical material that challenges this notion of the dead as entirely cut off from YHWH. Both Amos 9:2 and 1 Sam 2:6 depict YHWH as intervening in the realm of Sheol, either to punish or to save. Similarly, Ps 139:8 states that YHWH is in Sheol, just as he is present in other faraway realms. Other texts use the image of YHWH rescuing someone from the "Pit" of the netherworld (Pss 16:10; 30:4–5; 40:2), and the imagery of Ezek 37:11–14 demonstrates that YHWH himself may physically interact with the realm of the dead in order to act on their behalf.

These are two persistent threads running through biblical conceptions of death, and we may posit a couple of explanations for their coexistence in the text. It is plausible, for instance, that these contrasting views of Sheol offer us a glimpse into the diversity of thought in Israelite religion, a tradition capacious enough to accommodate different ideas about death and afterlife. It is also possible that this emphasis on YHWH's access to the netherworld may have developed as the result of postexilic anxieties about the status of Israel's covenant with YHWH.[57] As I argue further below, such texts use the image of YHWH interceding on behalf of the dead in order to express the hope that YHWH will similarly rescue the figuratively dead exiles and affirm the covenant between them. In other words, it is possible that these two threads represent different sides of a theological debate during the exile: between those who believed that the covenant was

---

57. Olyan argues that these depictions of YHWH's relationship with the netherworld may have developed as a response to anxieties about the exile and its cultic implications ("We Are Utterly Cut Off").

invalid and the exiles were cut off from YHWH and those who held out hope that the deity would restore them.

In summary, the arguments for a drastically reduced status of the dead in the postexilic period are unconvincing. This mischaracterization of certain texts, however, provides us with an opportunity to further reexamine common assumptions regarding Israelite family religion and its relationship to Deuteronomistic ideology. The reconstructions cited above share the view that the cult of dead kin was incompatible with supposedly normative Yahwistic ideology. They locate this opposition between cultic spheres in preexilic, exilic, or postexilic contexts, but the underlying cause for this tension in any period is that the dead pose a threat to YHWH's cult and temple. However, the evidence cited in support of this central thesis does not clearly depict the reduced status of the cult of dead kin in any period. In fact, a lot of this evidence is unrelated to the cult, much less a polemic against it.

YHWH as Divine Caregiver and the Cult of Dead Kin in the Postexilic Period

Contrary to the reconstructions cited above, I argue that biblical texts from the postexilic period indicate that the cult of dead kin is compatible with Yahwistic ideology as depicted by the biblical writers. In fact, previous studies have overlooked the depiction of YHWH as divine caregiver of the dead in these postexilic texts, and its relevance to reconstructions of the cult of dead kin in this period. Two texts in particular, Ezek 37:11–14 and Isa 56:3–5, vividly depict YHWH in this way, offering the dead the kinds of ritual care typically offered by living kin. What do these texts indicate about the status of the cult of dead kin in the postexilic period and its relationship to Yahwistic cult and the Jerusalem temple? I argue that they reflect two important realities: first, the ongoing significance of the cult of dead kin in this period and, second, the compatibility of the cult with biblical conceptions of Yahwistic cult and the Jerusalem temple. Further, these texts challenge scholarly reconstructions that posit the marginalization of the cult of dead kin in the postexilic period. Instead of condemning the cult, the biblical writers depict YHWH as the cultic caregiver par excellence. This depiction does not undermine the cult of dead kin but instead draws on a broader motif in ancient West Asia of a benevolent god or king acting as caregiver for the marginalized, including the untended dead.

Although previous studies have recognized the "beneficent tomb opening" and repatriation of bones in Ezek 37:11–14,[58] none has examined these acts as belonging to the realm of the cult of dead kin. Viewed through this interpretative lens, however, the depiction of YHWH exhuming and repatriating the dead in this passage is a striking example of a deity performing ritual care for the dead.[59] In this famous text, YHWH shows the prophet Ezekiel a valley of dry bones, which represent the Israelites in exile:

> He said to me—Human, these bones are all the house of Israel. They say, "Our bones are dry, and our hope is lost. We are utterly cut off." Therefore, prophesy and say to them, "Thus says my lord YHWH, 'I am about to open your graves and raise you from your graves, my people. I will bring you to the land of Israel. You will know that I am YHWH when I open your graves and raise you from your graves, my people.'"

As I have argued throughout this study, the protection and repatriation of human remains are constitutive practices of the cult of dead kin. YHWH's actions in Ezek 37:11–14 thus depict YHWH as divine caregiver for the figuratively dead Israel. Similar to the dead depicted in the Genealogy of the Hammurapi Dynasty, the remains of the dead in Ezek 37:11–14 lie in a foreign land. Thus, in verses 12–13, YHWH declares that he will open their graves and raise them from their graves, and in verse 14 repatriate them. The text draws on the topos of protection and repatriation of bones to depict YHWH's ongoing relationship with Israel, despite the trauma and cultic upheaval of the exile.

Other biblical texts refer to the similar protection and repatriation of bones by human kin. In some cases, the transportation of human remains occurs immediately after death. For instance, Gen 49:29–32 and 50:12–14

---

58. E.g., Olyan, "Unnoticed Resonances," 491–501.

59. For a more detailed treatment of the imagery in this passage, see Olyan, "We Are Utterly Cut Off," 43–51. The depiction of the exiled Israelites as "dead" in Ezek 37:1–14 likely refers to their covenantal relationship with YHWH. This metaphor relies on some notion of the dead as cut off from YHWH, an idea reflected in passages such as Pss 6:5; 28:1; 88:4–6; 115:17; Isa 38:18. In order to challenge the interpretation that the exile has invalidated the covenant and that the Israelites are thus "dead" to YHWH, Ezek 37:11–14 uses the imagery of the cult of dead kin to demonstrate that YHWH is still the divine caregiver of Israel. This performance of the cult indicates that the covenant between YHWH and Israel is still valid.

refer to Jacob's sons transporting their father's corpse after his death so that it may be buried in his ancestral tomb. In Judg 16:31, Samson's kinsmen transport his corpse from the Philistine city of Gaza to the tomb of his father Manoah. In 2 Sam 2:32, Joab and the servants of David bring back the corpse of Joab's brother, Asahel, from battle in Gibeon to be buried in his father's tomb in Bethlehem. Other texts refer to the disinterment, transportation, and reburial of human remains. The biblical depiction of Joseph's burial (Gen 50:25; Exod 13:19; Josh 24:32) also suggests that his bones are first buried in Egypt, then disinterred, transported, and reburied in Shechem.[60] In 2 Sam 21:12–14, David disinters the bones of Saul and Jonathan from their initial burial in Jabesh-Gilead and transports them to their ancestral tomb in Benjamin. In several ways, Ezek 37:11–14 mirrors the circumstances of 2 Sam 21:12–14. Exhuming the bones of the dead exiles allows YHWH to return them to their homeland. By performing this care, YHWH (like David) asserts his bond with the dead.

Outside the Hebrew Bible, the eighth-century Barrākib grave inscription from Sam'al also refers to the benevolent transportation of the remains of Barrākib's father, Panamuwa II, following his death on military campaign.[61] This care, including the construction of a commemorative monument and transportation of his corpse, is performed by the Assyrian king Tiglath-pileser III, who is Panamuwa's suzerain. This text is relevant to a discussion of Ezek 37:11–14 not only for its portrayal of a nonkin actor performing the rites constitutive of the cult of dead kin but also because it follows the pattern demonstrated by the Genealogy of the Hammurapi Dynasty and hymns to Šamaš, which I will discuss further below. In the absence of living descendants to offer care for the dead, a suzerain (either a king or god) may offer that care and, in doing so, may affirm and perpetuate the sociopolitical relationship between himself and the dead.

The imagery of a deity restoring the literal and figuratively dead from the grave also appears in cuneiform texts depicting the god Marduk. A broken Akkadian hymn from Ugarit, called The Righteous Sufferer (RS

---

60. Although the biblical text does not explicitly state that Moses disinters the bones of Joseph in Exod 13:19, the passage of time between the death of Joseph in Gen 50:25 and the exodus narrative suggests that his body was buried at some point in Egypt. The bones of Joseph remain in transport until the death of Joshua in Josh 24:32, when they are reburied in Shechem.

61. For a discussion of this inscription, see *KAI* 215; Josef Tropper, *Die Inschriften von Zincirli*, 98–131; *COS* 2:158–60.

25.460), describes the god Marduk as one who restores the human speaker from death: "the lord lifted my head, reviving me from the dead (ll. 13′– 16′)."[62] The text goes on to describe Marduk's restoration of the sufferer by evoking the imagery of burial and inverting it: "He took the spade from the hand of the one who wished to bury me, he opened my eyes" (ll. 43′–44′).[63] In the Babylonian wisdom poem Ludlul bēl nēmeqi ("I will praise the Lord of Wisdom"), Marduk is repeatedly described as the one who revives the dead: "Marduk is able to restore from the grave" (tablet IV, l. 75).[64] This comparative evidence suggests that the depiction of YHWH as divine caregiver in Ezek 37:11–14 draws on both of these broader traditions—the benevolent repatriation of one's dead kin and divine restoration from the grave. The combined rhetorical force of these themes helps Ezekiel articulate his view that the covenant between Yahweh and the exiles is still valid. In fact, YHWH's actions seem to contradict the assertion in verse 11 ("Our bones are dry, and our hope is lost. We are utterly cut off") by demonstrating that YHWH may indeed maintain relations with the figuratively dead exiles through the manipulation of bones. The allusion in Ezek 37:11–14 to the constitutive rituals of the cult of dead kin also suggests its currency among biblical writers and consumers of the text. This text, which clearly comes from an exilic or postexilic context, does not demonstrate cultic anxiety about separating YHWH from the supposedly polluting realm of the dead.[65] Instead, it uses the cult of dead kin to articulate the ongoing covenantal relations between YHWH and Israel.

The image of YHWH as divine caregiver for the dead also appears in Isa 56:3–5, in which YHWH promises an "everlasting name" and "commemorative monument" (*yād wā-šēm*)[66] for the childless eunuch:

---

62. Yoram Cohen, *Wisdom from the Late Bronze Age*, WAW 29 (Atlanta: Society of Biblical Literature, 2013), 167. Cohen examines the parallels between this text and Ludlul bēl nēmeqi, including their use of the "righteous sufferer" motif.

63. Cohen, *Wisdom from the Late Bronze Age*, 169.

64. Annus and Lenzi, *Ludlul bēl nēmeqi*, 44.

65. I examine this phenomenon more closely in Kerry Sonia, "'In My House and within My Walls': The Shared Space of Yahweh and the Dead in Israelite Religion," in *With the Loyal You Show Yourself Loyal: Essays on Relationships in the Hebrew Bible*, ed. T. M. Lemos et al., AIL (Atlanta: SBL Press, forthcoming).

66. For a discussion of the phrase *yād wā-šēm*, see Dwight W. Van Winkle, "The Meaning of *yād wāšēm* in Isaiah LVI 5," *VT* 47 (1997): 378–85; Gnana Robinson, "The Meaning of *jd* in Isa 56,5," *ZAW* 88 (1976): 282–84; Sara Japheth, "*jd wšm* [Isa. 56:5]—A Different Proposal," *Maarav* 8 (1992): 69–80; Izaak J. de Hulster, *Iconographic Exegesis*

Let not the alien who has joined himself to YHWH say, "YHWH will surely separate me from his people." Let not the eunuch say, "I am a dry tree." For thus said YHWH, "To the eunuchs who keep my sabbaths, choose that which pleases me, and hold fast to my covenant, I will give in my house and within my walls a commemorative monument [*yād wā-šēm*] better than sons and daughters. I will give him an everlasting name that will not be cut off."

Much like Ezek 37:11–14, this passage depicts YHWH as a cultic substitute for the eunuch's kin, offering the kind of care and commemoration ideally expected of one's descendants. As I have demonstrated above, this is a well-attested trope in depictions of ancient West Asian royalty, who effectively make kinship bonds through performance of this cult. For instance, Seth Sanders identifies this cultic phenomenon in a ritual text from Mari, in which Zimri-Lim offers the *kispu* to two legendary kings, Sargon and Naram-Sin, to whom Zimri-Lim is not related: "By assuming this ritual role of caretaker [*pāqidu*] the Amorite king demonstrates that he is not only the heir of powerful ancestors and population groups, but a dutiful one."[67] Much like Zimri-Lim, the Old Babylonian king Ammiṣaduqa uses the *kispu* to claim lineage from previous kings and people groups in

---

and Third Isaiah (Tübingen: Mohr Siebeck, 2009), 147–51. De Hulster notes the different resonances of both terms, *yād* and *šēm*, in the Hebrew Bible. The term *yād*, for instance, refers not only to the hand of YHWH (Isa 59:1; 60:21; 62:3; 64:7; 65:2; 66:2, 14) but also to a physical monument in 2 Sam 18:18, where it appears in parallel to the term *maṣṣebet*. The term *yād* can also mean "penis," as it does in Isa 57:8, 10, which is similar to the usage of *raglāyim*, "feet," to refer to genitalia (e.g., 1 Sam 24:4; Isa 6:2; 7:20). This resonance is particularly relevant to Isa 56:3–5 and its description of the eunuch. After all, the point of the passage is that YHWH will act as divine caregiver for the eunuch, whose altered genitalia prevent him from procreating and thus securing living descendants to offer him care. Thus, the use of *yād* to refer to a commemorative monument seems to play on these different resonances of the term—YHWH offers the eunuch a *yād* as a substitute for that which he lacks. In fact, Hayim Tadmor makes a similar point concerning this verse: "The pun here is on the word 'name' (*šēm*) which in Akkadian meant a 'male successor', in conjunction with the word used for 'perish' (*yikkārēt*), the very verb that defines castration in Deut 23:1." See Tadmor, "Was the Biblical *sārîs* a Eunuch?," in *Solving Riddles and Untying Knots: Biblical, Epigraphic, and Semitic Studies in Honor of Jonas C. Greenfield*, ed. Ziony Zevit, Seymour Gitin, and Michael Sokoloff (Winona Lake, IN: Eisenbrauns, 1995), 331–32. In many biblical texts, the term *šēm* is closely associated with commemoration (2 Sam 14:7; 18:18; Isa 14:22; Prov 10:7).

67. Sanders, "Naming the Dead," 29.

the Genealogy of the Hammurapi Dynasty. As I discuss in chapter 3, this strategic use of the *kispu* in Babylonian cult persisted into the reign of Nabonidus, whose mother Adad-guppi is also depicted as dutifully offering care to the dead kings of the previous dynasty. In the eighth-century inscription Barrākib erects for his father at Sam'al, Tiglath-pileser III also assumes the role of cultic custodian by caring for the corpse of his dead vassal, Panamuwa II, while on military campaign. Viewed in this context, YHWH's behavior in Isa 56:3–5 becomes a clear example of a deity assuming the role of cultic custodian for the eunuch.

In fact, the reference to a commemorative monument "better than sons and daughters" in Isa 56:5 further underscores the nature of YHWH as the ideal cultic caregiver. Unlike the commemoration offered by living descendants, which may lapse over time and fall out of use, the commemoration provided by YHWH will endure forever. This statement is affirmed by the placement of this memorial. The reference to the "house" of YHWH in verse 5, its parallelism with "house of prayer" in verse 7, and the explicit references to sacrifices on the altar of YHWH in verse 7 suggest that the memorial is placed within the Jerusalem temple. Indeed, there is evidence elsewhere in ancient West Asia of commemorative monuments placed in or near sanctuaries dedicated to major deities, presumably to ensure the ongoing care of the dead.[68] Thus, the placement of the memorial for

---

68. Other interpreters of this passage have emphasized the placement of a monument in a sanctuary with the intention of better preserving the memory of the dead and to offer continual service to a deity: "In interpreting the stelae inside a temple (court), it was concluded that they either represent a deity or a living or dead person who or whose relatives guarantee(s) the presence of this person in the presence of a deity" (de Hulster, *Iconographic Exegesis*, 168). Comparative examples of this practice may also include the *pgr* stelae at Ugarit, both of which were found in a temple precinct. The stela erected for the *'il'ibu* in the Aqhat Epic is also located in the sanctuary (*bqdš*). The epigraphic evidence from Sam'al also demonstrates that care for the dead often overlaps with the cultic care for deities. See, e.g., my discussion of the Hadad inscription as well as the Katumuwa stela. Although it does not depict the erection of stones in a sanctuary, Num 17:17–25 similarly depicts the inscription of the names of the twelve tribes of Israel onto sticks, which are then placed in the tent of meeting. On the next day, the stick on which Aaron's name is inscribed buds and flowers, which signifies the chosenness of the tribe of Levi among the other tribes. Though the monuments in this text are wood, not stone, the recurring image of the dry or flowering tree is strikingly similar in both Num 17:23 and Isa 56:3. In both cases, the tree that bears fruit is indicative of divine blessing.

the eunuch in the Jerusalem temple ensures that his memory will endure under the ongoing care of YHWH.[69]

Stavrakopoulou concedes that the imagery of the *yād wā-šēm* draws on the cult of dead kin; however, because the text asserts that YHWH is the one who commemorates the eunuch, she argues that the temple has usurped the role of the cultic custodian, extending the control of the temple to include commemoration of the dead. According to this argument, YHWH effectively absorbs the functions of the cult of dead kin in the postexilic period, rendering the performance of the cult by living descendants redundant. Stavrakopoulou cites the oracle in Isa 56:3–5 as evidence of this development:

> The ideological thrust of this oracle represents a polemical double-strike against kinship contexts of ancestral cults.... In asserting that the YHWH temple can offer the community the regenerative and memorializing functions of the ancestral cult, the dead are rendered redundant, and the mortuary rituals associated with the household are appropriated and subsumed within the cultic control of the "central" sanctuary.[70]

According to this interpretation, that YHWH offers this cult to the eunuch effectively undermines the cult itself.[71]

---

69. Other interpreters of Isa 56:3–5 have noted the use of imperial imagery in the passage, particularly land grants bestowed on loyal servants by Assyrian kings. See, e.g., Jacob L. Wright and Michael J. Chan, "King and Eunuch: Isaiah 56:1–8 in Light of Honorific Royal Burial Practices," *JBL* 131 (2012): 99–119. While this analysis privileges the king-servant dynamic of the passage over that of father-son, I do not view these approaches are mutually exclusive but rather complementary. After all, we often find such overlapping metaphors in biblical depictions of YHWH, who is both king and father.

70. Stavrakopoulou, *Land of Our Fathers*, 125.

71. This reading of the text is not entirely new. In fact, previous interpreters have argued that this passage signals a shift in ideologies of community, a shift that juxtaposes the bodily and the spiritual and involves a rather supersessionist reading of the text. In his commentary on the text, Claus Westermann states, "But here in Trito-Isaiah, the physical and the spiritual have ceased to be necessarily united in this way. The name may live on without descendants born of one's body.... The new community is on the way to a new form of association which is no longer identical with the old concept of the chosen people. As early as here we find present important elements of the New Testament's concept of community." See Westermann, *Isaiah 40–66* (Philadelphia: Westminster, 1969), 314.

However, there are two problems with this interpretation. First, it is hard to imagine that any biblical writer would polemicize against a particular cultic practice by depicting YHWH as its ideal actor. The performance of the act by YHWH himself would seem to legitimize rather than undermine it. In fact, we may compare this performance of cult by the deity himself to biblical texts in which YHWH voices his approval or condemnation of certain cultic behaviors and practices. In this same passage, for instance, YHWH explicitly states that foreigners who join themselves to him and observe his Sabbaths are acceptable to him (Isa 56:3–7). Biblical writers are thus able to articulate their normative views about participation in the cult using both rhetorical devices. Second, this passage does not depict YHWH's care for those with living descendants but for those who lack them, which does not suggest that YHWH is usurping anyone's duties toward their dead kin. Instead, this text suggests a thoroughgoing concern for care of the dead, a concern so well established that the text would depict YHWH as caring for those who have no kin to commemorate them. Instead of allowing the eunuch, who ostensibly has no hope of producing offspring, to fade into obscurity following his death, YHWH provides him with a commemorative monument, thereby reinforcing the importance of commemoration in the cult of dead kin and expanding the boundaries of the Israelite community to include both eunuchs and foreigners.[72] The argument that this depiction undermines the cult of dead kin ignores the possibility that Isa 56:3–5 may actually authorize this cult by making YHWH the practitioner par excellence in the absence of living custodians—providing the eunuch with a commemorative monument in the temple itself and thus an everlasting name. Furthermore, we may ask ourselves why a biblical text would depict YHWH as the practitioner of a cult it seeks to eradicate. If this is an attack on care for the dead, it is perhaps the subtlest polemic of its kind in the Hebrew Bible, a text otherwise

---

72. In his commentary on this passage, Joseph Blenkinsopp uses the lens of cognitive dissonance to describe the social and political circumstances surrounding the production of this text. In the wake of disappointed hopes about political and cultic dominance, he argues, anxieties about group identity become particularly pronounced in the biblical text. Isaiah 56:3–5 and its surrounding material reflect this anxiety, and this passage in particular shows one reaction to this problem: expanding the boundaries of the community and admitting those whose participation may have been otherwise questioned, such as the foreigner and the eunuch. See Blenkinsopp, *Isaiah 56–66* (New York: Doubleday, 1964), 135–41.

replete with explicit, violent condemnations of supposedly illegitimate cult practices.

Viewed in broader comparison with ancient West Asian material, however, the role of YHWH as divine caregiver in Isa 56:3–5 becomes more apparent. In fact, the depiction of care for the untended dead in attestations of the Mesopotamian *kispu* may provide instructive parallels to the characterization of YHWH in Isa 56:3–5. In the Genealogy of the Hammurapi Dynasty, the king offers the *kispu* to different groups who lack someone to care for them, such as those who have died while abroad on military campaign.[73] Through this care for the untended dead, the king demonstrates his beneficence—and perhaps his interest in preserving order and preventing the malevolent behavior of restless ghosts—by standing in for absent cultic custodians. To my knowledge, no scholar argues that this performance of the *kispu* by the king in the Genealogy of the Hammurapi Dynasty indicates the cessation of these practices among nonroyal groups or that the text advocates for this cessation. Rather, the performance of the *kispu* by the king suggests the ongoing importance of the cult of dead kin in both the royal and nonroyal spheres. The offering of food and drink to the dead does not threaten the sovereignty of the king; instead, the king actually uses this care to demonstrate the qualities of an ideal ruler, thus bolstering his cultic and political authority. These conclusions equally apply to other previously cited examples of royalty offering the cult of dead kin to nonkin, including Zimri-Lim, Tiglath-pileser III, and Adad-guppi.

Biblical depictions of YHWH caring for the dead may well draw on a widespread understanding of deities, particularly solar deities, caring for the dead, especially the dead who lack human caregivers. This image of the ideal ruler also appears in hymns to the Mesopotamian sun god Šamaš, who provides the *kispu* to the roving ghost and invokes the name of the deceased. In one case, the text specifies that Šamaš aids those who have received no proper burial, including those whose corpses were devoured by wild animals in the steppe.[74] In another text, Šamaš is the "helper of the roving ghost who is not entrusted with virility."[75] Smith also notes that the sun god Istanu is associated with care for the dead in a second-millennium

---

73. Finkelstein, "Genealogy of the Hammurapi Dynasty."

74. *SpTU* 3, no. 67 ii.47–50, iii.31–38, quoted in Scurlock, "Ghosts in the Ancient Near East," 79.

75. Adam Falkenstein, in *Vorläufiger Bericht über die von der Deutschen Forschungsgemeinschaft in Uruk-Warka unternommenen Ausgrabungen*, vol. 15, by Hein-

Hittite text: "Thou, Istanu, art father and mother of the oppressed, the lonely (and the) bereaved person."[76] As with the eunuch in Isa 56:3–5, this text suggests that the deity must take care of the man who dies without offspring. Thus, the role of solar deities in administering proper care for the dead is another striking parallel to Isa 56:3–5 in its depiction of a deity caring for the untended dead.[77] Also striking is the lack of any negative assessment of this divine care. Therefore, contrary to the interpretation of Isa 56:3–5 as indicating the diminishment of the cult of dead kin, YHWH's performance of cultic care for the eunuch suggests the ongoing significance of the postexilic cult of dead kin, which could be performed by actors other than living descendants, including YHWH himself.

In fact, rather than understanding YHWH's role as divine caregiver as an altogether new development in the postexilic period, we may view it as an extension of a more pervasive biblical trope in which YHWH cares for those who are particularly marginalized in Israelite society. For instance, YHWH acts as divine caregiver for the living orphan (Ps 10:14) and the widow (Prov 15:25). In multiple texts, the orphan and widow appear together in this depiction of Yahwistic care (Exod 22:22; Ps 68:6; Isa 1:17; Jer 49:11). In some instances, this concern extends to other marginalized groups as well, such as the *gēr* or "resident alien" (Pss 94:6; 146:9; Jer 7:6; Deut 10:18; 27:19; Mal 3:5) and the poor (Job 29:12; Ps 82:3). This trope is similar to the role of YHWH in the cult of dead kin because here he is also caring for those who have no kin to do so. Psalm 94 is particularly interesting in this regard because it combines both solar imagery and YHWH's intervention on behalf of the widow, foreigner, and orphan:

> YHWH is the god of vengeance. God of vengeance, shine forth [*hôpia'*].
> Lift yourself up, judge of the earth. Return recompense to the proud.

---

rich von Lenzen (Berlin: Akademie, 1959), 36.10, quoted in Scurlock, "Ghosts in the Ancient Near East," 80.

76. Mark Smith, *The Origins of Biblical Monotheism: Israel's Polytheistic Background and the Ugaritic Texts* (New York: Oxford University Press, 2001), 91.

77. While the eunuch in Isa 56:3–5 is not necessarily dead, the focus of the passage seems to be his cultic fate after death, which explains the emphasis on lack of offspring and the ritual elements of the cult of dead kin. A similar concern appears in 2 Sam 18:18, in which Absalom erects a commemorative stela for himself because he has no son to commemorate his name (presumably after his death). Due to this focus on the postmortem fate of the eunuch in Isa 56:3–5, the text belongs in a discussion of care for the untended dead.

YHWH, how long will the wicked, how long will the wicked triumph? They pour forth; they speak arrogance. All those who commit iniquity act proudly. YHWH, they crush your people and afflict your inalienable inheritance [naḥălātəkā]. They slay a widow and a foreigner, and they murder orphans.

Like the widow, orphan, and resident alien, one who dies without a living caregiver is also a vulnerable member of Israelite society. Just as YHWH advocates for protection of the poor, widow, orphan, and resident alien in the texts cited above, YHWH also acts on behalf of the untended dead in Ezek 37:11–14 and Isa 56:3–5. These depictions of YHWH do not signify a biblical polemic against the cult of dead kin but rather demonstrate the beneficence of YHWH for those who occupy marginalized spaces in Israelite society.[78]

Indeed, the image of YHWH as the redeemer of Israel draws on similar idioms of kinship, designating YHWH as the close associate or kinsman of those he redeems. This redeemer imagery becomes particularly prevalent in Second Isaiah. For instance, YHWH is referred to as the gōʾēl or "redeemer" of Israel in Isa 41:14; 44:6, 24; 47:4; 48:17; 49:26; 54:5; 59:20; 63:16; Jer 50:34; Pss 19:15; 78:35; and 103:4. Other biblical texts use a form of the verb gʾl (Isa 43:1; Pss 77:16; 106:10; Mic 4:10; Lam 3:58; Jer 31:10) to depict the actions of YHWH on behalf of Israel, and Israel is referred to as "the redeemed of YHWH" (gəʾûlê YHWH) in Isa 62:12 and Ps 107:2. In addition to Israel, YHWH appears as the redeemer of individuals, including the orphan in Prov 23:11 and Job in Job 19:25. In these instances, the redeemed individuals lack close human intimates to act on their behalf. YHWH acts on behalf of those who have no one to support them, as he does in Ezek 37:11–14 and Isa 56:3–5. Further, the kinship dimension of the human gōʾēl is particularly clear in biblical texts that depict the redemption of property (Lev 25:25; Num 5:8; Deut 19:6, 12), vengeance for murder (Num 35:12, 19, 21, 24, 26, 27; Josh 20:2, 5; 2 Sam 14:11), and the practice of levirate marriage (Ruth 2:20; 3:9, 12, 13; 4:1, 3, 6, 8, 14). The passage in 1 Kgs 16:11 also lists the gōʾēl along with male offspring (maštîn

---

78. In fact, Suriano suggests that a bowl found in Tomb 8 at Beth Shemesh, inscribed with "your brother," might have originally been used for charitable donations but was later repurposed to feed the dead. Suriano argues that the appearance of this bowl in the repository in Tomb 8 "strongly suggests that offering food for those in need could overlap with offering food for the dead" (*History of Death*, 161).

bəqîr) and friends of Baasha (*rēʿēhû*). Thus, the attribution of this position to YHWH fits into the overall picture of YHWH as one who acts on behalf of those who lack kin to care for and commemorate them.

While some biblical texts emphasize YHWH's role as cultic caregiver for the dead, other texts depict the exact opposite. In Jer 49:10, YHWH seems to deprive an enemy of Israel, Esau, of the cult of dead kin by disturbing his tomb and annihilating his progeny and close associates. Thus, the text supports the argument that the cult of dead kin continues to have sociopolitical currency in the postexilic period because biblical writers use it to articulate YHWH's relationships with both treaty partners and enemies. In this passage, the description of Esau, who represents the Edomites, recalls the imagery of "malevolent tomb opening" and the curses against it found in Iron Age funerary inscriptions from the Levant. In this case, however, it is YHWH himself who exposes the grave of Esau: "Indeed I will strip Esau bare.[79] I have uncovered [*gillêtî*] his hiding places [*mistārāyw*], and he cannot conceal[80] himself. His offspring,[81] brothers, and neighbors are destroyed. He is no more. Leave your orphans. I indeed will keep them alive. As for your widows, let them trust in me." The imagery of this passage is strikingly similar to the judgment of YHWH against Esau in Obad 6, though the terminology is different: "How Esau is searched out [*nehpəśû*]! How his hidden treasures [*maṣpūnāyw*] are discovered [*nibʿû*]!"

The language of Jer 49:10 is similar to the Ahiram sarcophagus inscription examined in chapter 1. In this inscription, Ahiram's son, Ittobaʿl, refers to the sarcophagus as his father's "eternal dwelling-place" (*kšth bʿlm*)

---

79. Following Jack R. Lundbom, I translate this verb (*ḥāśaptî*) as a prophetic perfect. See Lundbom, *Jeremiah 37–52* (New York: Doubleday, 2004), 331. This verb (*ḥśp*), meaning "to strip bare," also appears in the context of uncovering the shame and iniquity of Judah in Jer 13:26–27 and the pillaging of Esau in Obad 6. The use of the verb in Jer 49:10 likely draws on both of these nuances of shame and violation.

80. Following Lundbom and William Holladay, I emend this *niphal* participle (*wənehbâ*) to an infinite absolute (*wənaḥbōh*). See Lundbom, *Jeremiah 37–52*, 332; Holladay, *Jeremiah 2: A Commentary on the Book of the Prophet Jeremiah 26–52* (Minneapolis: Fortress, 1989), 370.

81. Holladay prefers to emend the MT with the LXX, changing *zarʿô*, "his offspring," to *zərôaʿ*, "his arm" (*Jeremiah 2*, 370). Holladay argues, " 'offspring' and 'brothers' is a curious parallel" (371). However, viewed in the context of the cult of dead kin, all three of these categories could be potential caregivers for Esau—offspring, brothers, and neighbors. By eliminating all of them, YHWH is depriving Esau of any cultic caregivers in the afterlife.

and curses those who would open (*wygl*) it. Jeremiah 49:10 also uses this verb (*glh*) to depict the violent uncovering of Esau's "hiding places." In addition, the term *mistār*, "hiding place," often refers in other biblical texts to dark, subterranean places where treasure is stored (Pss 10:9; 17:12; Isa 45:3; Jer 23:24; Lam 3:10).[82] Judahite tombs often appear in hillsides and below ground, which further suggests that these deep, dark places in Jer 49:10 may be tombs. In fact, YHWH exhorts the Edomites in Jer 49:8 to "flee, turn back, and dwell deep" within the earth. Thus, both the imagery and context of this passage suggest that the hiding places of Esau may refer to ancestral tombs. Furthermore, the uncovering of these hiding places (or tombs) coincides with the extirpation of Esau's offspring and close associates, both of whom could offer cultic care to Esau in death. Indeed, the inscriptions of the Ahiram sarcophagus as well as those of Tabnit and Eshmunazar II of Sidon refer to lack of progeny as a curse against those who violate a burial site. Such curses likely mimic the fate of the one whose grave is disturbed: such a disturbance likely prevents one's offspring from providing proper care for the dead in the afterlife. In fact, the Tomb of the Royal Steward inscription from Silwan expresses a similar anxiety about corpse and tomb disturbance, explicitly telling whoever reads the inscription that no treasure is buried in the tomb with the dead.[83] This comparative evidence suggests that Jer 49:10 may refer to an instance of corpse disturbance and lineage extirpation by YHWH himself, the result being that Esau is deprived of cult from his descendants and close associates (offspring, brothers, and neighbors) such that all memory of him dies. In fact, the statement in verse 10 that Esau "ceases to exist" (*'ênennû*) is similar to the description of Jezebel's trampled corpse in 2 Kgs 9:37 (*lō'-yōmərû zō't 'îzābel*): "They may not say, 'This is Jezebel.'" Both of these texts, 2 Kgs 9:37 and Jer 49:10, depict figures that the biblical writers vehemently condemn, and both figures may ultimately suffer for their misdeeds with the spoliation of their physical remains and, perhaps, lack of commemoration in death. Verse 11 in the Jer 49 passage is also interesting for its depiction of YHWH's care for Esau's orphans and widows.[84] This reference to care for the orphan and widow is in stark contrast to YHWH's violent punish-

---

82. Lundbom interprets this term as referring to caves, such as the Wadi ed-Daliyeh and Wadi *Murabba'at* caves, where people on the run could hide (*Jeremiah 37–52*, 331–32).

83. See my discussion of this inscription in ch. 1.

84. Both Lundbom and Walter Brueggemann call this particular verse strange

ment of Esau and may serve to emphasize his role as divine caregiver for the marginalized and unaffiliated.[85]

This possible reference to YHWH depriving Esau of the cult of dead kin demonstrates the inverse of YHWH's care for the eunuch in Isa 56:3–5 and the "dead" Israel in Ezek 37:11–14. Instead of affirming and perpetuating sociopolitical relations by performing the cult, YHWH signals the termination of such a relationship with Esau (and the Edomites) because Edom has violated its treaty relations with Judah, which we may infer from the depiction of Edom in several biblical texts (Isa 21:11–12; 34:5–6; 63:1–6; Ezek 25:12–14; 32:29; 35:15; Amos 1:11–12; Mal 1:2–5; Obad 6; Ps 137:1, 7; Lam 4:21–22), including its role in the destruction of Jerusalem in 586 BCE.[86] The depiction of YHWH in Jer 49:10 as the opposite of a cultic custodian for the dead further suggests the ongoing significance of the cult of dead kin in the postexilic period. After all, if the cult were not socially and politically significant, the biblical writers would not depict its violent disruption by YHWH. Here again, we must not interpret YHWH's suppression of Esau's cult of dead kin as an attack on the practice of the cult itself. Rather, the fact that the biblical writers choose the imagery of the cult of dead kin to articulate the violent punishment of Edom underscores the ongoing symbolic value of the cult and the conditions surrounding an ideal death.

In fact, YHWH's exhumation of the bones of his enemies is a more pervasive biblical motif. For instance, in Ezek 6:4–5, YHWH declares that he himself will scatter the bones of those who utilize supposedly

---

in the context of the passage. See Lundbom, *Jeremiah 37–52*, 2004; Brueggemann, *A Commentary on Jeremiah* (Grand Rapids: Eerdmans, 1998), 457.

85. In this regard, I disagree with Robert P. Carroll's assessment that this depiction of YHWH's care for the orphans and widows in 49:11 "suggests a lack of serious hostility towards Edom." See Carroll, *Jeremiah: A Commentary* (Philadelphia: Westminster, 1986), 803.

86. For a discussion of a possible treaty relationship between Judah and Edom, see Elie Assis, "Why Edom? On the Hostility towards Jacob's Brother in Prophetic Sources," *VT* 56 (2006): 1–20; Jason C. Dykehouse, "An Historical Reconstruction of Edomite Treaty Betrayal in the Sixth Century BC. Based on Biblical, Epigraphic, and Archaeological Data" (PhD diss., Baylor University, 2008). Such a political relationship between the two nations would help explain the patriarchal narratives depicting the kinship of Esau and Jacob. For a discussion of this kinship language, see Bert Dicou, *Edom, Israel's Brother and Antagonist: The Role of Edom in Biblical Prophecy and Story* (Sheffield: JSOT Press, 1994).

illicit altars and divine images: "I will cast your slain before your illicit cult images [gillûlîm, lit. 'dung-balls']. I will put the corpses of the Israelites before their illicit cult images [gillûlîm], and I will scatter your bones around your altars." The persistent use of the first person in this passage emphasizes that YHWH is the one who performs this corpse disturbance and exposure. Leviticus 26:30 depicts a similar scene in which YHWH himself commits corpse abuse. Like his acts against Esau in Jer 49:10, this disturbance is targeted at those who have angered YHWH by supposedly violating covenant relations. In Jer 49:10, this covenant concerns treaty relations between Judah and Edom, while Ezek 6:4–5 concerns the violation of Israel's exclusive covenant with YHWH.[87] The narrative depicting Josiah's destruction of the altar at Bethel in 2 Kgs 23:15–18 also uses this trope of corpse disturbance as punishment for allegedly illicit forms of cultic worship. After destroying the altar and high place (bāmâ) at Bethel, Josiah exhumes bones buried in the tombs on the mountain and burns them on the altar (which was supposedly already destroyed in the previous verse).[88] Some interpreters have suggested that this treatment of the bones at Bethel is an act of ritual violence intended to deny the dead Bethel elite care in the afterlife.[89] In fact, the next verse depicts the opposite of this

---

87. The imagery of Jer 8:1–2 is similar to this passage in that it also depicts YHWH encouraging the exhumation and exposure of Israelite corpses as a result of their illicit forms of worship. Unlike Ezek 6:4–5, this text does not depict YHWH himself as the one who performs these acts. Other texts, such as Jer 16:2–8; 34:20; 1 Kgs 14:10–11; and Deut 28:26, also depict corpse exposure as the punishment for Israelites who worship deities other than YHWH. However, they do not refer to exhumation of those bodies, nor to YHWH as the agent of that corpse abuse.

88. Burning the bones of one's enemies also appears in Amos 2:1, which condemns Moab for burning the bones of the king of Edom to lime. Comparative evidence from Mesopotamia also suggests that burning the body could be negatively construed. In the Sumerian narrative Gilgamesh, Enkidu, and the Netherworld, the ghost of one who burned to death is not even present in the netherworld. Variants of this statement include "His ghost is not there" (MSS HVDDSS); "His ghost does not dwell in the Netherworld" (MS ll); "His ghost [is not] in the Underworld" (MS qq); and "His ghost has no place (there)" (MS rr; see George, Babylonian Gilgamesh Epic, 776). The burning of bones is not always construed negatively, however. In 1 Sam 31:12, the men of Jabesh-Gilead take the exposed corpses of Saul and his sons, burn them, and bury them. The text does not explain the rationale for this treatment of the corpses, but it is possible that burning them is construed positively in this case because of the abuse and shame they have already endured at the hands of the Philistines in 31:9–10.

89. Stavrakopoulou, Land of Our Fathers, 84–88.

malevolent behavior—the protection of the burial site of the man of God who had previously prophesied Josiah's retributive acts against Bethel. When Josiah learns of the commemorative monument marking this burial site, he declares, "Let him rest. Let no one move his bones." Thus, 2 Kgs 23:15–18 depicts the performance of cultic care for the dead, protection of the burial site, as well as its opposite, exhumation and destruction of human remains. In this way, biblical writers use these acts of care or violation to signify either adherence to or deviation from supposedly licit forms of Yahwistic cult.[90]

Indeed, the actions of YHWH in Jer 49:10 and Josiah in 2 Kgs 23:15–18 reflect the retributive violence of kings depicted in cuneiform texts. In his analysis of Ezek 37:1–14, Olyan notes the depiction of "malevolent tomb opening" in an inscription detailing the conflict between Assurbanipal and Elam. By exhuming the bones of the Elamite kings and transporting them far from their burial contexts, Assurbanipal boasts that he has deprived their ghosts of *kispu* rites and imposed restlessness on them. The threat of similar actions by Sennacherib against his enemy Merodach-Baladan is also implied in the Nebi Yunus inscription, as noted by Olyan.[91] In short, both kings and gods use the cult of dead kin to reward or punish. To loyal servants, they grant commemorative monuments and care for their physical remains. Yet, they obliterate any memory of their enemies by attacking such monuments and violating both human remains and burial sites. Such violation assumes and strategically uses the cult of dead kin as a rhetorical framework. It does not signal the overthrow of that cultic framework.

Thus, postexilic texts, such as Ezek 37:11–14 and Isa 56:3–5, depict YHWH as divine caregiver for the dead and metaphorically dead, while Jer 49:10 depicts him as one who sabotages the care of his human enemies. These texts use the imagery and practices of the cult of dead kin to signify one's status in relation to YHWH, either as loyal servant or enemy. Far from undermining the cult, these texts suggest the ongoing significance of the cult of dead kin in the postexilic period. Moreover, these depictions of the cult are consistent with other ancient West Asian depictions of care for

---

90. For other resonances of the ritual violence and defilement in 2 Kgs 23, see Lauren A. S. Monroe, *Josiah's Reform and the Dynamics of Defilement: Israelite Rites of Violence and the Making of a Biblical Text* (New York: Oxford University Press, 2011); Mark Leuchter, "Between Politics and Mythology: Josiah's Assault on Bethel in 2 Kings 23:15–20," in Olyan, *Ritual Violence*, 67–91.

91. Olyan, "Unnoticed Resonances," 495–97.

the dead performed by both royalty and gods, who may act as benevolent caregivers for those who lack kinship ties, such as orphans, widows, and the childless dead. Indeed, this aspect of YHWH as the divine caregiver for the poor, orphan, widow, and resident alien is a pervasive biblical motif, and his beneficence toward the dead and metaphorically dead in Ezek 37:11–14 and the eunuch in Isa 56:3–5 is a logical extension of this motif. In fact, this image of YHWH as the champion of the oppressed and the caregiver for the marginalized would have been particularly meaningful in the exilic and postexilic periods, when the status of the covenant between YHWH and Israel was uncertain. Rather than being cut off from YHWH, these texts demonstrate that YHWH affirms his ongoing relationship with the Israelites by offering protection and care to those relegated to the social and political margins.

Conclusion

What are the grounds for reconstructing care for the dead in the postexilic period? Biblical texts such as Isa 56:4–5; Ezek 37:11–14; Neh 2:3, 5; and Jer 49:10 suggest that custodial care for the dead remained significant in this period. Concerning archaeological evidence for Israelite burial practices, Schmitt points out the continuity of burial assemblages through the late Second Temple period.[92] Bloch-Smith's analysis of Iron Age burials supports this assessment: based on a sample of hundreds of interments from the tenth through sixth century, she argues that Judahite conceptions of the dead or, at least, material residues of these ideologies remained consistent throughout the Iron Age.[93] However, the preceding analysis does not claim that care for the dead remained entirely static throughout Israel's history, including the postexilic period. While I challenge the assumption that the exile *must* have ended or drastically altered care for the dead, it is conceivable that separation from ancestral lands and tombs during the exile elicited a variety of responses regarding the relationship between the living and the dead.

Biblical texts give us some indication of the theological debates that emerged following the exile, such as the status of Israel's covenant with YHWH and YHWH's status with respect to the gods of the conquering

---

92. Albertz and Schmitt, *Family and Household Religion*, 457.
93. Bloch-Smith, *Judahite Burial Practices*, 147–48.

Neo-Babylonians.[94] The former debate particularly pertains to the present analysis because it indicates that the exiles were renegotiating their relationship with the national deity, whom the biblical text associates so closely with the land of Judah. If some aspects of care for the dead rely on ties to ancestral landholding, then we should expect a similar range of responses to the crisis of exile. On this point, however, it is important to note that the majority opinion of the extant biblical text assumes either a continuous or renewed relationship between YHWH and Israel, no doubt influenced by the eventual return of the exiles to the land of Judah. By analogy, care for the dead may be subject to various interpretations during the exilic period, but the resettlement of the exiles could provide a feasible context in which the relationship between the living and the dead is reaffirmed if, indeed, it is ever drastically altered.

The recognition of the passages cited above as reflecting the cult of dead kin also sheds further light on the phenomenon of nonkin using rites constitutive of the cult of dead kin to create, affirm, or alter sociopolitical relationships in this period. In Isa 56:3–5 and Ezek 37:11–14, YHWH offers care for the untended dead in order to assert his covenantal relationship with those who receive his care. We may plausibly situate this rhetoric in the context of the exile and its ideological aftermath when the status of Israel's covenant with YHWH was uncertain. Thus, by offering to commemorate the eunuch and repatriate the bones of Israel, YHWH is demonstrating not only that he is capable of offering such care[95] but also that covenantal relations between them are still valid. The imagery of

---

94. The eternal covenant of Gen 17 and the new covenant of Jer 31 imply two different interpretations of the covenant during the exilic period. The former assumes that the covenant between YHWH and Israel is still valid after 586 BCE, while the latter assumes that the prior covenant is void and a new one must be made. For an examination of the status of the covenant in this exilic and postexilic periods, see Olyan, "Status of the Covenant," 333–44. The rhetoric of texts such as Isa 44:6–8, 9–20 and Jer 10:1–16 uses praise of YHWH's incomparability and icon polemics against foreign gods to depict YHWH as superior to the gods of Babylon, thus subverting the political realities of the Israelites in exile. For an analysis of the rhetoric of icon polemics in the Hebrew Bible and ancient West Asia, see Levtow, *Images of Others*, passim.

95. Interestingly, the Hebrew Bible itself is divided on the issue of YHWH's efficacy in the underworld, some texts asserting his ability to save from the grips of Sheol (1 Sam 2:6; Isa 26:19–21; Pss 30; 139:7–13; Amos 9:2) and others claiming that the dead are beyond his help (Pss 6:1–5; 28:1; 88; 115:16–18; Isa 14:3–11, 12–20; Job 10:18–22; Prov 15:11; 27:20; Qoh 9:1–12). Ezekiel 37:11–14 seems to assert the former,

malevolent tomb opening in Jer 49:10 also uses this rhetorical strategy to assert the opposite. Because Edom contributed to the downfall of Judah in 586 BCE, Jer 49:10 depicts YHWH as violently disturbing Esau's tomb and annihilating his offspring and close associates, which may indicate the termination of Esau's cult of dead kin.

Finally, biblical and comparative evidence urges us to reexamine the supposed reduced status of the cult of dead kin in the postexilic period. Both Isa 56:3–5 and Ezek 37:11–14 depict YHWH himself as divine caregiver, performing the rituals that comprise the cult—erecting a commemorative monument, preserving the name of the dead, and repatriating the physical remains of the dead. These texts are part of a broader tradition in ancient West Asia of royalty and gods caring for the dead in times of crisis, especially when the dead have no one else to care for them. Therefore, the depiction of YHWH as divine caregiver does not undermine the cult of dead kin in the postexilic period but rather affirms its importance to the Israelite family as well as biblical articulations of Yahwistic covenant. This analysis of the cult of dead kin in the postexilic period also encourages us to reconsider the relationship between cultic spheres more generally.[96] Rather than understanding locally based forms of cultic authority as inherently antithetical to more centralized forms of authority, we must instead appreciate the overlap and reciprocity between these spheres.

---

thereby participating in this ideological debate by depicting YHWH as the cultic caregiver of the dead Israel.

96. Other evidence from ancient Israel further suggests a pervasive overlap between centralized and local forms of cult. For instance, the onomasticon of Israel exhibits a large percentage of personal names with Yahwistic theophoric elements, which indicates an orientation toward the national deity. See Saul M. Olyan, "Family Religion in Israel and the Wider Levant of the First Millennium BCE," in Bodel and Olyan, *Household and Family Religion*, 117–18. The invocation of YHWH in epigraphic evidence from burial contexts also suggests the overlap between national and family religion (Suriano, *History of Death*, 116).

Conclusion

This study began by considering the tension between memory and forgetfulness. How is memory constructed and preserved? Can it endure through monuments, inscriptions, and ritual care for the dead? Indeed, the biblical notice of Absalom's monument in 2 Sam 18:18 suggests such an anxiety. Because he lacks a son to commemorate his name, Absalom must erect a monument for himself while he is still living. Whether an embodiment of the dead or a marker for future offerings, this stela is Absalom's way of safeguarding his memory. This is just one example of the ways in which ancient people recognized the materiality of memory and hoped to prolong it through monuments and ritual. Throughout this study I have argued that such commemoration and care for the dead were pervasive phenomena throughout ancient West Asia, including the Hebrew Bible and ancient Israel. Evidence from Mesopotamia, Ugarit, and Sam'al offers striking parallels to depictions of care for the dead in the Hebrew Bible. In addition, epigraphic evidence from ancient Israel suggests that at least some of the practices depicted in the biblical text reflect the cultic activity of ancient Israelites. Previous studies have examined some recurring aspects of the cult of dead kin in the biblical and comparative evidence: providing the dead with food, drink, and other items; construction of a commemorative monument; and invoking the name of the dead. As I argue in chapter 1, we may expand the ritual repertoire of the cult to include other acts of care for the dead, particularly rituals that preserve the integrity of human remains. Such rituals include the protection and repatriation of bones as well as protection of the burial site. We see these aspects of the cult reflected in both the biblical evidence and cuneiform sources.

As we expand the definition of the cult of dead kin to include more practices concerned with care for the dead, we also see an expansion of who could participate in this cult. Chapter 3 argues that this expansion included women, who could be participants in the biblical cult of dead kin as both caregivers and recipients of that care. Thus, Jacob cares for his wife Rachel by erecting a *maṣṣēbâ* in Gen 35:20; the eunuch in Isa 56:5 lacks sons *and daughters* to commemorate him; Riṣpah defends the exposed remains of her dead sons and other Saulides in 2 Sam 21:10; Ps 106:28 interprets the cultic activity of Moabite *women* in Num 25:2 as sacrifices for the dead; a widow from Tekoa indirectly preserves the name of her dead husband in 2 Sam 14:7; and the daughters of Zelophehad both inherit their father's property and preserve his name in Num 27:1–11. The full relevance of these texts to the cult of dead kin—and the roles of women within it—has been overlooked by the scholarly discourse on conceptions of death in Israelite religion. Further, biblical references to the matriarchs of Israel suggest that such women could achieve an elevated status as cultural heroes and ancestors. Based on this evidence, this study argues that women did indeed play vital roles in the ritual care of the dead and the construction of biblical lineages.

The evidence for the cult of dead kin—both in and outside Israel— also encourages us to reconsider some underlying assumptions about this cult and its relationship to other cultic phenomena that concern the dead. In chapter 2, I argue that the conflation of death-related practices in previous studies has led to problematic assumptions about the development of Israelite religion. Biblical polemic against necromancy, for instance, is often misconstrued as polemic against the cult of dead kin. However, both the biblical and most of the cuneiform evidence suggests that we must consider necromancy as separate from the cult of dead kin in ancient West Asia. Both cultic phenomena concern the dead, but their purposes, principles, and participants are different. For instance, the cult of dead kin is not concerned with divination, the acquisition of privileged knowledge, but with the commemoration and care of the dead. Further, while biblical necromancy involves ritual specialists, such as the necromancer at Endor in 1 Sam 28, care for the dead is performed by kin and, in some cases, close associates. The threat posed by necromancers to other ritual specialists, including priests and prophets, may explain the appearance of biblical polemic against necromancy and the relative lack of polemic against the ritual care of the dead. This recategorization of the cult of dead kin and necromancy has serious implications concerning the reconstruction of the supposedly reduced status of the dead and the cult of dead kin in the postexilic period. That some exilic and postexilic texts assume the existence of the cult and draw heavily on its imagery suggests that the cult of dead kin not only continued to be an important feature of Israelite society in this period but also that it was compatible with biblical articulations of Yahwistic ideology.

As I argue throughout this study, the constitutive rituals of the cult of dead kin signify affiliation between the living and the dead and help structure current political, social, and economic landscapes in terms of the past, particularly through claims of lineage and loyalty. Because of their highly significant value, these rituals are potent tools in discourses about power and authority in the biblical text and cognate literatures. In the Hebrew Bible, the cult of dead kin signifies the positive or negative relationships between the living and the dead. For this reason, it may be used strategically to affirm or challenge these relationships. Thus, as I argue in chapter 4, this use of the cult is particularly prevalent in times of crisis—when certain power structures are upset by various circumstances. In both biblical and cuneiform sources, for instance, performing the cult of dead kin may help mediate the tensions surrounding an abrupt shift in political power, such as the usurpation of a dynasty. By claiming to offer care for the dead, a new dominant political power may minimize this disruption and instead graft itself onto the lineage of the previous dynasty. In this way, performing the cult of dead kin effectively makes nonkin into fictive kin of the dead.

This strategy of making kin through cult is particularly relevant in reconstructions of Israelite religion in the postexilic period. During this period, the trauma of the exile cast doubt onto preexisting ideologies, such as the covenant between YHWH and Israel and the inviolability of Jerusalem and its temple. The exile of Judahite elites to Babylon further challenged these concepts and begged the question whether YHWH had been defeated by a foreign power. If not, why would the national god of Israel willfully abandon his people? Biblical texts even question whether the Israelites may continue to worship YHWH in a foreign land. Two prophetic texts from the postexilic period, Ezek 37:11–14 and Isa 56:3–5, respond to these anxieties with the imagery of the cult of dead kin and cast YHWH in the role of the nonkin caregiver of the dead. By depicting YHWH in this way, these texts show that the covenant between YHWH and Israel is still valid. Both the dead exiles and the childless eunuch, who seemingly have no hope of receiving commemoration and care, are still under the power and protection of YHWH.

Previous studies of the cult of dead kin in ancient Israel have overlooked the relevance of these prophetic passages to the question of the cult's viability in the postexilic period. The recognition of these passages as drawing on the practices of the cult of dead kin challenges previous reconstructions that posit a reduced status for the cult in this period. Rather than indicating the subversion of the cult of dead kin in the postexilic period, these texts suggest instead that biblical writers assume the existence of the cult and evaluate it positively—to such an extent that YHWH himself is portrayed as the practitioner par excellence. In light of such observations, we must also reconsider the paradigm assumed by many of these reconstructions in which centralized cult and local forms of cult, such as the cult of dead kin, must be in opposition. As I note in the introduction to this study, Ackerman traces the origins of this paradigm to Weber's *Ancient Judaism*, in which he argues that the Deuteronomistic program of cult centralization seeks to erode kin-based communities.[1] However, the depiction of YHWH as divine caregiver for the dead in the postexilic period troubles this central-versus-local binary. In fact, it shows that the biblical writers draw heavily on the imagery and practices of family religion to articulate their ideologies about the national deity.

Examining the supposedly reduced status of the biblical cult of dead kin is also useful because it illuminates the influence of modern theological concepts on reconstructions of Israelite religion. As I note in chapter 4, this analysis is prevalent among treatments of the cult of dead kin and appears in different configurations. While some locate the marginalization of the cult in the preexilic, exilic, or postexilic periods, they all understand it to be opposed to forms of centralized cultic authority. Thus, they all try to identify when and why the cult of dead kin became obsolete. A common assumption underlying these reconstructions is that Israelite religion eventually developed into what modern theologians would call monotheism during the postexilic period. Some treatments go so far as to relate this emergent religious outlook to later Christian ideologies about community and cult. In this way, reconstructions of the "reduced status" of the cult of dead kin may depend on a teleological understanding of Israelite religion that seeks to trace a trajectory from more supposedly primitive practices, such as the cult of dead kin, to more modern practices and ideologies that resemble those of rabbinic Judaism and early Christianity.

In short, the preceding analysis is both an examination of the underlying ritual logic of the Israelite cult of dead kin and an argument for the usefulness of a paradigm shift away from the Weberian model of central-

---

1. Ackerman, "Cult Centralization," 19–40.

ized authority in favor of models that better account for the often symbiotic relationship between cultic spheres. More generally, this study contributes to a better understanding of the relationship between Israelite family religion, epitomized by the cult of dead kin, and its relationship to the Jerusalem temple and the supposedly normative Yahwism espoused by biblical writers. After all, both the family and the state are in a constant process of making and unmaking themselves, always losing and gaining new members. It is the ongoing project of both social groups to maintain some degree of continuity in spite of this constant change. This project of maintaining social cohesion greatly depends on rhetorical strategies that treat that cohesion as natural, self-evident, something taken for granted rather than asserted or overtly challenged. As Catherine Bell argues, ritual "is designed to do what it does without bringing what it is doing across the threshold of discourse or systematic thinking."[2] Ritual, then, is a particularly potent tool in this discourse. The rituals constitutive of the cult of dead kin offer deeply resonant ways to create, affirm, or contest affiliations in different spheres of Israelite society—from inheritance rights among siblings to the politics of kings to the relationship between Israel and its national deity. This understanding of the cult of dead kin and its use by nonkin actors helps us understand the role of the cult not only in Israelite family religion but also in articulations of Yahwistic temple cult. Indeed, it demonstrates how interdependent these cultic spheres actually are.

---

2. Bell, *Ritual Theory, Ritual Practice*, 93.

Bibliography

Abusch, Tzvi. *Babylonian Witchcraft Literature*. Atlanta: Scholars Press, 1987.

Ackerman, Susan. "Cult Centralization, the Erosion of Kin-Based Communities, and the Implications for Women's Religious Practices." Pages 19–40 in *Social Theory and the Study of Israelite Religion: Essays in Retrospect and Prospect*. Edited by Saul M. Olyan. Boston: Brill, 2012.

———. "Household Religion, Family Religion, and Women's Religion in Ancient Israel." Pages 127–58 in *Household and Family Religion in Antiquity*. Edited by John Bodel and Saul M. Olyan. Oxford: Blackwell, 2008.

———. *Under Every Green Tree: Popular Religion in Sixth-Century Judah*. Atlanta: Scholars Press, 1992.

———. *When Heroes Love: The Ambiguity of Eros in the Stories of Gilgamesh and David*. New York: Columbia University Press, 2005.

———. *Women and the Religion of Ancient Israel*. New Haven: Yale University Press, forthcoming.

Aharoni, Yohanan. "Arad: Its Inscriptions and Temple." *BA* 31 (1968): 18–32.

———. "Israelite Temples in the Period of the Monarchy." *PWCJS* 1 (1969): 69–74.

Albertz, Rainer. "Family Religion in Ancient Israel and Its Surroundings." Pages 89–112 in *Household and Family Religion in Antiquity*. Edited by John Bodel and Saul M. Olyan. Oxford: Blackwell, 2008.

Albertz, Rainer, and Rüdiger Schmitt. *Household and Family Religion in Ancient Israel and the Levant*. Winona Lake, IN: Eisenbrauns, 2012.

Albright, William F. *Archaeology and the Religion of Israel*. 5th ed. Garden City, NY: Doubleday, 1968.

———. *History of Israelite Religion in the Old Testament Period*. Vol. 1. Louisville: Westminster John Knox, 1994.

————. *Yahweh and the Gods of Canaan: A Historical Analysis of Two Contrasting Faiths*. London: Athlone, 1968.

Alster, Bendt. "Incantation to Utu." *ASJ* 13 (1991): 27–96.

Amiran, Ruth, Ornit Ilan, and Wolfgang Helck. *Arad: Eine 5000 Jahre alte Stadt in der Wüste Negev, Israel*. Neumünster: Wachholtz, 1992.

Anderson, Francis I., and David Noel Freedman. *Hosea: A New Translation with Introduction and Commentary*. New York: Doubleday, 1980.

Anderson, Gary A. *A Time to Mourn, a Time to Dance: The Expression of Grief and Joy in Israelite Religion*. University Park: Pennsylvania State University Press, 1991.

Annus, Amar, and Alan Lenzi. *Ludlul bēl nēmeqi: The Standard Babylonian Poem of the Righteous Sufferer*. Helsinki: Neo-Assyrian Text Corpus Project, 2010.

Archi, Alfonso. "The High Priestess, dam-dingir, at Ebla." Pages 43–53 in *"Und Mose schrieb dieses Lied auf": Studien zum Alten Testament und zum Alten Orient*. Edited by Manfried Dietrich and Ingo Kottsieper. Münster: Ugarit-Verlag, 1998.

Arnold, Bill T. "Necromancy and Cleromancy in 1 and 2 Samuel." *CBQ* 66 (2004): 199–213.

Assis, Elie. "Why Edom? On the Hostility towards Jacob's Brother in Prophetic Sources." *VT* 56 (2006): 1–20.

Assmann, Jan. *Religion and Cultural Memory: Ten Studies*. Translated by Rodney Livingstone. Stanford: Stanford University Press, 2006.

Avigad, Nahman. "The Epitaph of a Royal Steward from Siloam Village." *IEJ* 3 (1953): 137–52.

Avishur, Yitzhak. "The 'Duties of the Son' in the 'Story of Aqhat' and Ezekiel's Prophecy on Idolatry (Ch. 8)." *UF* 17 (1985): 49–60.

Baker, Jill L. "Form and Function of Mortuary Architecture: The Middle and Late Bronze Age Tomb Complex at Ashkelon." *Levant* 42 (2010): 5–16.

————. "The Funeral Kit: A Newly Defined Canaanite Mortuary Practice Based on the Middle and Late Bronze Age Tomb Complex at Ashkelon." *Levant* 38 (2006): 1–31.

Bayliss, Miranda. "The Cult of Dead Kin in Assyria and Babylonia." *Iraq* (1973): 115–25.

Beaulieu, Paul-Alain. *The Reign of Nabonidus, King of Babylon 556–539 B.C.* New Haven: Yale University Press, 1989.

Beckman, Gary. "Family Values on the Middle Euphrates." Pages 57–79 in

Emar: The History, Religion, and Culture of a Syrian Town in the Late Bronze Age. Edited by Mark W. Chavalas. Bethesda, MD: CDL, 1996.

Begg, Christopher T. "Foreigner." *ABD* 2:829–30.

Bell, Catherine. *Ritual Theory, Ritual Practice.* New York: Oxford University Press, 1992.

Ben-Barak, Zairira. "The Legal Status of the Daughter as Heir in Nuzi and Emar." Pages 87–97 in *Society and Economy in the Eastern Mediterranean (c. 1500–1000 B.C.).* Edited by Michael Heltzer and Edward Lipinski. Leuven: Departement Oriëntalistiek, 1988.

Benzinger, Immanuel. *Hebräische Archäologie.* Leipzig: Mohr, 1894.

Berger, Paul-Richard. *Die neubabylonischen Königsinschriften.* AOAT 4/1. Neukirchen-Vluyn: Neukirchener Verlag, 1973.

Berlejung, Angelika, and Bernd Janowski, eds. *Tod und Jenseits im alten Israel und in seiner Umwelt.* Tübingen: Mohr Siebeck, 2009.

Biran, Avraham, and Gophna, Rudolph. "An Iron Age Burial Cave at Tel Halif." *IEJ* 20 (1970): 151–69.

Bird, Phyllis A. *Missing Persons and Mistaken Identities.* Minneapolis: Fortress, 1997.

Blenkinsopp, Joseph. "Deuteronomy and the Politics of Post-mortem Existence." *VT* 45 (1995): 1–16.

———. "The Family in First Temple Israel." Pages 48–103 in *Families in Ancient Israel.* Edited by Leo G. Perdue, Joseph Blenkinsopp, John J. Collins, and Carol Meyers. Louisville: Westminster John Knox, 1997.

———. *Isaiah 1–39: A New Translation with Introduction and Commentary.* New York: Doubleday, 2000.

———. *Isaiah 56–66.* New York: Doubleday, 1964.

Bloch, Maurice. "Death, Women, and Power." Pages 211–30 in *Death and the Regeneration of Life.* Edited by Maurice Bloch and Jonathan Parry. Cambridge: Cambridge University Press, 1982.

Bloch, Maurice, and Jonathan Parry, eds. *Death and the Regeneration of Life.* Cambridge: Cambridge University Press, 1982.

Bloch-Smith, Elizabeth. "Death in the Life of Israel." Pages 139–43 in *Sacred Time, Sacred Place.* Edited by Barry M. Gittlen. Winona Lake, IN: Eisenbrauns, 2002.

———. "From Womb to Tomb: The Israelite Family in Life as in Death." Pages 122–31 in *The Family in Life and in Death: The Family in Ancient Israel; Sociological and Archaeological Perspectives.* Edited by Patricia Dutcher-Walls. New York: T&T Clark, 2009.

———. *Judahite Burial Practices and Beliefs about the Dead*. JSOTSup 123. Sheffield: Sheffield Academic, 1992.

Böck, Barbara. *Das Handbuch Muššu'u "Einreinbung": Eine Serie Sumerischer und Akkadischer Beschwörungen Aus Dem 1. JT. Vor Chr.* Madrid: Consejo Superior de Investigaciones Científicas, 2007.

Boda, Mark J. "Ideal Sonship in Ugarit." *UF* 25 (1993): 9–24.

Boda, Mark J., and Jamie Novotny, eds. *From the Foundations to the Crenellations: Essays on Temple Building in the Ancient Near East and Hebrew Bible*. Münster: Ugarit-Verlag, 2010.

Bodel, John, and Saul M. Olyan. "Introduction." Pages 1–4 in *Household and Family Religion in Antiquity*. Edited by John Bodel and Saul M. Olyan. Oxford: Blackwell, 2008.

Boer, Rients de. "A Babylonian Funerary Cone." Pages 42–47 in *Annual Report*. Edited by Jesper Eidem. Leiden: Netherlands Institute for the Near East, 2012.

Bonatz, Dominik. *Das syro-hethitische Grabdenkmal: Untersuchungen zur Entstehung einer neuen Bildgattung in der Eisenzeit im nordsyrisch-südostanatolischen Raum*. Mainz: von Zabern, 2000.

———. "The Iconography of Religion in the Hittite, Luwian, and Aramaean Kingdoms." Pages 1–29 in *Iconography of Deities and Demons in the Ancient Near East*. 2nd ed. Edited by Jürg Eggler and Christoph Uehlinger. Leiden: Brill, 2000.

———. "Katumuwa's Banquet Scene." Pages 39–44 in In Remembrance of Me: Feasting with the Dead in the Ancient Middle East. Edited by Virginia Rimmer Herrmann and J. David Schloen. Chicago: Oriental Institute of the University of Chicago, 2014.

Bordreuil, Pierre, and Dennis Pardee. "Le rituel funéraire ougaritique RS. 34.126." *Syria* 59 (1982): 121–28.

Borger, Rykle. *Beiträge zum Inschriftenwerk Assurbanipals: Die Prismenklassen A, B, C = K, D, E, F, G, H, J, und T sowie andere Inschriften*. Wiesbaden: Harrassowitz, 1996.

Bourguignon, Erika. "Necromancy." *EncRel* 10:345–47.

Brichto, Herbert Chanan. "Kin, Cult, Land and Afterlife—A Biblical Complex." *HUCA* 44 (1973): 1–54.

Brody, Aaron J. "Late Bronze Age Intramural Tombs." Pages in vol. 1 of *Ashkelon I: Introduction and Overview (1985–2006), Final Reports of the Leon Levy Expedition to Ashkelon*. Edited by Lawrence E. Stager, J. David Schloen, and Daniel M. Master. Winona Lake, IN: Eisenbrauns, 2008.

———. "New Perspectives on Levantine Mortuary Ritual: A Cognitive Interpretative Approach to the Archaeology of Death." Pages 123–41 in *Historical Biblical Archaeology and the Future: The New Pragmatism*. Edited by Thomas E. Levy. London: Equinox, 2010.

Brueggemann, Walter. *A Commentary on Jeremiah*. Grand Rapids: Eerdmans, 1998.

Carroll, Robert P. *Jeremiah: A Commentary*. Philadelphia: Westminster, 1986.

———. "Translation and Attribution in Isaiah 8:19f." *BT* 31 (January 1980): 126–34.

Carsten, Janet. "Introduction: Cultures of Relatedness." Pages 1–36 in *Cultures of Relatedness: New Approaches to the Study of Kinship*. Edited by Janet Carsten. Cambridge: Cambridge University Press, 2000.

Chapais, Bernard. "From Biological to Cultural Kinship." Pages 48–59 in *Primeval Kinship: How Pair-Bonding Gave Birth to Human Society*. Cambridge: Harvard University Press, 2008.

Chapman, Cynthia R. *The House of the Mother: The Social Roles of Maternal Kin in Biblical Hebrew Narrative and Poetry*. New Haven: Yale University Press, 2016.

Cogan, Mordechai. "The Road to En-dor." Pages 319–26 in *Pomegranates and Golden Bells: Studies in Biblical, Jewish, and Near Eastern Ritual, Law, and Literature in Honor of Jacob Milgrom*. Edited by David P. Wright, David Noel Freedman, and Avi Hurvitz. Winona Lake, IN: Eisenbrauns, 1995.

Cogan, Mordechai, and Hayim Tadmor. *II Kings: A New Translation with Introduction and Commentary*. New York: Doubleday, 1988.

Cohen, Andrew C. *Death Rituals, Ideology, and the Development of Early Mesopotamian Kingship: Toward a New Understanding of Iraq's Royal Cemetery of Ur*. Leiden: Brill, 2005.

Cohen, Sol, and Victor Avigdor Hurowitz. "חקות העמים הבל הוא (Jer 10:3) in Light of Akkadian Parṣu and Zaqīqu Referring to Cult Statues." *JQR* 89 (1999): 277–90.

Cohen, Yoram. *Wisdom from the Late Bronze Age*. WAW 29. Atlanta: Society of Biblical Literature, 2013.

Collins, Billie Jean. "Necromancy, Fertility, and the Dark Earth: The Use of Ritual Pits in Hittite Cult." Pages 224–38 in *Magic and Ritual in the Ancient World*. Edited by Paul Mirecki and Marvin Meyer. Leiden: Brill, 2002.

Connerton, Paul. *How Societies Remember*. New York: Cambridge University Press, 1989.

Cook, Stephen L. "Death, Kinship, and Community: Afterlife and the חסד Ideal in Israel." Pages 106–21 in *The Family in Life and in Death: The Family in Ancient Israel; Sociological and Archaeological Perspectives*. Edited by Patricia Dutcher-Walls. New York: T&T Clark, 2009.

Cox, Benjamin D., and Susan Ackerman. "Micah's Teraphim." *JHS* 12 (2012): 1–37.

———. "Rachel's Tomb." *JBL* 128 (2009): 135–48.

Cradic, Melissa S. "Embodiments of Death: The Funerary Sequence and Commemoration in the Bronze Age Levant." *BASOR* 377 (2017): 219–48.

Cross, Frank Moore. *Canaanite Myth and Hebrew Epic*. Cambridge: Harvard University Press, 1997.

———. "A New Aramaic Stele from Taymāʾ." *CBQ* 48 (1986): 387–94.

———. "A Reconstruction of the Judean Restoration." *JBL* 94 (1975): 4–18.

Cryer, Frederick H. *Divination in Ancient Israel and Its Near Eastern Environment*. Sheffield: JSOT Press, 1994.

Daiches, Samuel. "Isaiah and Spiritualism." Supplement, *JC* (July 1921): 1–4.

Davies, Graham I. *Hosea*. Sheffield: Sheffield Academic, 1993.

Day, John. "The Development of Belief in Life after Death in Ancient Israel." Pages 231–57 in *After the Exile: Essays in Honor of Rex Mason*. Edited by John Barton and David James Reimer. Macon, GA: Mercer University Press, 1996.

———. *Molech: A God of Human Sacrifice in the Old Testament*. Cambridge: Cambridge University Press, 1990.

Dever, William G. "The Silence of the Text: An Archaeological Commentary on 2 Kings 23." Pages 143–68 in *Scripture and Other Artifacts: Essays on the Bible and Archaeology in Honor of Philip J. King*. Edited by Michael D. Coogan, J. Cheryl Exum, and Lawrence E. Stager. Louisville: Westminster John Knox, 1994.

Dicou, Bert. *Edom, Israel's Brother and Antagonist: The Role of Edom in Biblical Prophecy and Story*. Sheffield: JSOT Press, 1994.

Dijkstra, Meindert. "Women and Religion in the Old Testament." Pages 164–88 in *Only One God? Monotheism in Ancient Israel and the Veneration of the Goddess Asherah*. Edited by Bob Becking, Meindert Dijkstra, Marjo C. A. Korpel, and Karel J. H. Vriezen. BibSem 77. London: Sheffield Academic, 2001.

Dijkstra, Meindert, and Johannes C. de Moor. "Problematic Passages in the Legend of Aqhatu." *UF* 7 (1975): 171–215.

Draffkorn, Anne E. "ILANI/ʾělōhîm." *JBL* 76 (1957): 216–24.

Durand, Jean-Marie. *Documents Cunéiformes de la ive Section de l'École pratique des Hautes Études.* Paris: Librairie Droz, 1982.

Dutcher-Walls, Patricia. "The Clarity of Double Vision: Seeing the Family in Sociological and Archaeological Perspective." Pages 1–15 in *The Family in Life and in Death: The Family in Ancient Israel; Sociological and Archaeological Perspectives.* Edited by Patricia Dutcher-Walls. New York: T&T Clark, 2009.

Dykehouse, Jason C. "An Historical Reconstruction of Edomite Treaty Betrayal in the Sixth Century BC. Based on Biblical, Epigraphic, and Archaeological Data." PhD diss., Baylor University, 2008.

Ebach, Jürgen H. "PGR = (Toten-)opfer? Ein Vorschlag zum Verständnis von Ez. 43,7.9." *UF* 3 (1971): 365–68.

Eissfeldt, Otto. *Molk als Opferbegriff im Punischen und Hebräischen und das Ende des Gottes Moloch.* BRA 4. Halle: Niemeyer, 1935.

Fadhil, Abdulilah. "Die in Nimrud/Kalḫu Aufgefundene Grabinschrift der Jabâ." *BaghM* 21 (1990): 461–70.

Faust, Avraham, and Shlomo Bunimovitz. "The Judahite Rock-Cut Tomb: Response at a Time of Change." *IEJ* 58 (2008): 150–70.

Finkel, Irving L. "Necromancy in Ancient Mesopotamia." *AfO* 29 (1983): 1–17.

Finkelstein, Jacob J. "The Genealogy of the Hammurapi Dynasty." *JCS* 20 (1966): 95–118.

Fleming, Daniel. "The Integration of Household and Community Religion in Ancient Syria." Pages 37–59 in *Household and Family Religion in Antiquity.* Edited by John Bodel and Saul M. Olyan. Oxford: Blackwell, 2008.

———. *Time at Emar: The Cultic Calendar and the Rituals from the Diviner's House.* Winona Lake, IN: Eisenbrauns, 2000.

Foster, Benjamin R. "Late Babylonian Schooldays: An Archaizing Cylinder." Pages 79–87 in *Festschrift für Burkhart Kienast: Zu seinem 70. Geburtstage dargebracht von Freunden, Schülern und Kollegen.* Münster: Ugarit-Verlag, 2003.

Frame, Grant. "A New Wife for Šu-Sîn." *ARRIM* 2 (1977): 3–4.

Franklin, Norma. "The Tombs of the Kings of Israel: Two Recently Identified Ninth Century Tombs from Omride Samaria." *ZDPV* 119 (2003): 1–11.

Gadd, Cyril J. "The Harran Inscriptions of Nabonidus." *AnSt* 8 (1958): 35–92.

Gadotti, Alhena. *"Gilgamesh, Enkidu, and the Netherworld" and the Sumerian Gilgamesh Cycle*. Boston: de Gruyter, 2014.

Gager, John G. "Introduction." Pages 3–41 in *Curse Tablets and Binding Spells from the Ancient World*. Oxford: Oxford University Press, 1992.

George, Andrew. *The Babylonian Gilgamesh Epic: Introduction, Critical Edition, and Cuneiform Texts*. New York: Oxford University Press, 2003.

Gerstenberger, Erhard S. *Leviticus: A Commentary*. Louisville: Westminster John Knox, 1996.

Gibson, John C. L. *Canaanite Myths and Legends*. 2nd ed. London: T&T Clark, 2004.

———. *Phoenician Inscriptions, Including Inscriptions in the Mixed Dialect of Arslan Tash*. Vol. 3 of *Textbook of Syrian Semitic Inscriptions*. Oxford: Oxford University Press, 1982.

Glaim, Aaron. "Reciprocity, Sacrifice, and Salvation in Judean Religion at the Turn of the Era." PhD diss., Brown University, 2014.

Glassner, Jean-Jacques. "Women, Hospitality and the Honor of the Family." Pages 71–90 in *Women's Earliest Records*. Edited by Barbara S. Lesko. Atlanta: Scholars Press, 1989.

Gray, John. "Social Aspects of Canaanite Religion." Pages 170–92 in *Volume du Congres Geneve*. VTSup 15. Leiden: Brill, 1966.

Grosz, Katarzyna. "Daughters Adopted as Sons at Nuzi and Emar." Pages 81–86 in *La femme dans la Proche-Orient antique*. Edited by Jean-Marie Durand. Paris: Éditions Recherche sur les Civilisations, 1987.

Hackett, Jo Ann. "In the Days of Jael: Reclaiming the History of Women." Pages 15–38 in *Immaculate and Powerful*. Edited by Clarissa W. Atkinson, Constance H. Buchanan, and Margaret R. Miles. Boston: Beacon, 1985.

Haelewyck, Jean-Claude. "The Phoenician Inscription of Eshmunazar: An Attempt at Vocalization." *BABELAO* 1 (2012): 77–98.

Hallo, William W. "Royal Ancestor Worship in the Biblical World." Pages 381–401 in *Shar'arei Talmon: Studies in the Bible, Qumran, and the Ancient Near East Presented to Shemaryahu Talmon*. Edited by Michael Fishbane and Emanuel Tov. Winona Lake, IN: Eisenbrauns, 1992.

Hallote, Rachel. *Death, Burial, and Afterlife in the Biblical World: How the Israelites and Their Neighbors Treated the Dead*. Chicago: Dee, 2001.

———. "Mortuary Archaeology and the Middle Bronze Age Southern Levant." *JMA* 8 (1995): 93–112.

———. "'Real' and Ideal Identities in Middle Bronze Age Tombs." *NEA* 65 (2002): 105–11.

———. "Tombs, Cult, and Chronology: A Reexamination of the Middle Bronze Age Strata of Megiddo." Pages 199–214 in *Studies in the Archaeology of Israel and Neighboring Lands in Memory of Douglas L. Esse*. Edited by Samuel R. Wolff. SAOC 59. Chicago: Oriental Institute of the University of Chicago, 2001.

Halpern, Baruch. "'Brisker Pipes Than Poetry': The Development of Israelite Monotheism." Pages 77–115 in *Judaic Perspectives on Ancient Israel*. Edited by Jacob Neusner, Baruch A. Levine, and Ernest S. Frerichs. Philadelphia: Fortress, 1987.

———. "'The Excremental Vision': The Doomed Priests of Doom in Isaiah 28." *HAR* 10 (1986): 109–21.

———. "Jerusalem and the Lineages in the Seventh Century BCE: Kinship and the Rise of Individual Moral Liability." Pages 11–107 in *Law and Ideology in Monarchic Israel*. Edited by Baruch Halpern and Deborah W. Hobson. Sheffield: JSOT Press, 1991.

Hamori, Esther J. "The Prophet and the Necromancer: Women's Divination for Kings." *JBL* 132 (2013): 827–43.

———. *Women's Divination in Biblical Literature: Prophecy, Necromancy, and Other Arts of Knowledge*. New Haven: Yale University Press, 2015.

Haran, Menahem. "The Bas-Reliefs on the Sarcophagus of Ahiram King of Byblos in Light of Archaeological and Literary Parallels from the Ancient Near East." *IEJ* 8 (1958): 15–25.

Harmansah, Ömür. *Cities and the Shaping of Memory in the Ancient Near East*. Cambridge: Cambridge University Press, 2013.

Hays, Christopher B. *Death in the Iron Age II and in First Isaiah*. Tübingen: Mohr Siebeck, 2011.

Hays, Christopher B., and Joel M. LeMon. "The Dead and Their Images: An Egyptian Etymology for Hebrew *'ôb*." *JAEI* 1 (2009): 1–4.

Healey, John F. "The *Pietas* of an Ideal Son at Ugarit." *UF* 11 (1979): 353–56.

Herrmann, Virginia Rimmer. "The Architectural Context of the KTMW Stele from Zincirli and the Mediation of Syro-Hittite Mortuary Cult by the Gods." Pages 73–87 in *Contextualising Grave Inventories in the Ancient Near East: Proceedings of a Workshop at the London Seventh ICAANE in April 2010 and an International Symposium in Tubingen in November 2010, Both Organised by the Tubingen Post-graduate School*

"Symbols of the Dead." Edited by Peter Pfälzner, Herbert Niehr, Ernst Pernicka, Sarah Lange, and Tina Koster. Wiesbaden: Harassowitz, 2014.

———. "The Katumuwa Stele in Archaeological Context." Pages 49–56 in *In Remembrance of Me: Feasting with the Dead in the Ancient Middle East.* Edited by Virginia Rimmer Herrmann and J. David Schloen. Chicago: Oriental Institute of the University of Chicago, 2014.

Hiebert, Paula S. "'Whence Shall Help Come to Me?': The Biblical Widow." Pages 125–41 in *Gender and Difference in Ancient Israel.* Edited by Peggy L. Day. Minneapolis: Fortress, 1989.

Hoffner, Harry A. "Hittite Tarpiš and Hebrew Terāphim." *JNES* 27 (1968): 61–68.

Holladay, John S. "Religion in Israel and Judah under the Monarchy: An Explicitly Archaeological Approach." Pages 249–99 in *Ancient Israelite Religion: Essays in Honor of Frank Moore Cross.* Edited by Patrick D. Miller Jr., Paul D. Hanson, and Samuel D. McBride. Philadelphia: Fortress, 1987.

Holladay, William. *Jeremiah 2: A Commentary on the Book of the Prophet Jeremiah 26–52.* Minneapolis: Fortress, 1989.

Huehnergard, John. "Five Tablets from the Vicinity of Emar." *RA* 77 (1983): 11–43.

———. *Ugaritic Vocabulary in Syllabic Transcription.* Winona Lake, IN: Eisenbrauns, 2008.

Hulster, Izaak J. de. *Iconographic Exegesis and Third Isaiah.* Tübingen: Mohr Siebeck, 2009.

Huntington, Richard, and Peter Metcalf, eds. *Celebrations of Death: The Anthropology of Mortuary Ritual.* Cambridge: Cambridge University Press, 1979.

Japheth, Sara. *"jd wšm* [Isa. 56:5]—A Different Proposal." *Maarav* 8 (1992): 69–80.

Jeffers, Ann. *Magic and Divination in Ancient Palestine and Syria.* Leiden: Brill, 1996.

———. "Magic from before the Dawn of Time: Understanding Magic in the Old Testament: A Shift in Paradigm (Deuteronomy 18.9–14 and Beyond)." Pages 123–32 in *A Kind of Magic: Understanding Magic in the New Testament and Its Religious Environment.* Edited by Michael Labahn and Bert Jan Lietaert Peerbolte. New York: T&T Clark, 2007.

Johnston, Philip S. *Shades of Sheol: Death and Afterlife in the Old Testament.* Leicester: Apollos, 2002.

Jonker, Gerdien. *The Topography of Remembrance: The Dead, Tradition, and Collective Memory in Mesopotamia*. New York: Brill, 1995.

Kamlah, Jens. "Grab und Begräbnis in Israel/Juda: Materielle Befunde, Jenseitsvorstellungen und die Frage des Totenkultes." Pages 257–97 in *Tod und Jenseits im alten Israel und in seiner Umwelt*. Edited by Angelika Berlejung and Bernd Janowski. Tübingen: Mohr Siebeck, 2009.

Katz, Dina. "Sumerian Funerary Rituals in Context." Pages 167–88 in *Performing Death: Social Analyses of Funerary Traditions in the Ancient Near East and Mediterranean*. Edited by Nicola Lanieri. Chicago: Oriental Institute of the University of Chicago, 2007.

Katzenstein, Hannah J. "The Royal Steward (*Asher ʿal ha-Bayith*)." *IEJ* 10 (1960): 149–54.

Kaufmann, Yehezkel. *The Religion of Israel: From Its Beginnings to the Babylonian Exile*. Translated and abridged by Moshe Greenberg. New York: Schocken Books, 1972.

Keel, Othmar, and Christoph Uehlinger. *Gods, Goddesses, and Images of God in Ancient Israel*. Translated by Thomas H. Trapp. Minneapolis: Fortress, 1998.

Kelle, Brad E. *Hosea 2: Metaphor and Rhetoric in Historical Perspective*. Atlanta: Society of Biblical Literature, 2005.

Klein, Ralph W. *2 Chronicles: A Commentary*. Minneapolis: Fortress, 2012.

Kletter, Raz. *The Judean Pillar-Figurines and the Archaeology of Asherah*. BARIS 636. Oxford: Tempvs Reparatvm, 1996.

Kloner, Amos, and David Davis. "A Burial Cave of the Late First Temple Period on the Slope of Mount Zion." Pages 107–10 in *Ancient Jerusalem Revealed*. Edited by Hillel Geva. Jerusalem: Israel Exploration Society, 1994.

Klutz, Todd E. "Reinterpreting 'Magic': An Introduction." Pages 1–9 in *Magic in the Biblical World: From the Rod of Aaron to the Ring of Solomon*. Edited by Todd E. Klutz. New York: T&T Clark, 2003.

Knohl, Israel. *Sanctuary of Silence*. Minneapolis: Fortress, 1995.

Knoppers, Gary. *1 Chronicles 1–9*. New York: Doubleday, 2003.

König, Eduard. *Das Buch Jesaja*. Gütersloh: Bertelsmann, 1926.

Kramer, Samuel Noah. *History Begins at Sumer*. Philadelphia: University of Pennsylvania Press, 1981.

Kuemmerlin-McLean, Joanne K. "Magic (OT)." *ABD* 4:468–71.

Lacheman, Ernest R., and David I. Owen. "Texts from Arrapḫa and from Nuzi in the Yale Babylonian Collection." Pages 377–432 in vol. 1 of *Studies on the Civilization and Culture of Nuzi and the Hurrians*.

Edited by Martha A. Morrison and David I. Owen. Winona Lake, IN: Eisenbrauns, 1981.

Lambert, Wilfred G. "An Address of Marduk to the Demons: New Fragments." *AfO* 19 (1959/1960): 114–19.

———. *Babylonian Wisdom Literature*. Oxford: Clarendon, 1960.

———. "Old Akkadian Ilaba = Ugaritic Ilib?" *UF* 13 (1981): 299–301.

Landsberger, Benno. "Die Basaltstele Nabonids von Eski-Harran." Pages 115–51 in *Halil Edhem Hâtira Kitabi*. Ankara: Türk Tarih Kurumu Basimevi, 1947.

Lange, Sarah. "Food Offerings in the Royal Tomb of Qaṭna." Pages 243–57 in *Contextualising Grave Inventories in the Ancient Near East: Proceedings of a Workshop at the London Seventh ICAANE in April 2010 and an International Symposium in Tubingen in November 2010, Both Organised by the Tubingen Post-graduate School "Symbols of the Dead."* Edited by Peter Pfälzner, Herbert Niehr, Ernst Pernicka, Sarah Lange, and Tina Koster. Wiesbaden: Harassowitz, 2014.

Laqueur, Thomas W. *The Work of the Dead: A Cultural History of Mortal Remains*. Princeton: Princeton University Press, 2015.

Layton, Scott C. "The Steward in Ancient Israel: A Study of Hebrew ('ăšer) ʿal-habbayit in Its Near Eastern Setting." *JBL* 109 (1990): 633–49.

Lehmann, Reinhard G. *Die Inschrift(en) des Ahirom-Sarkophags und die Schachtinschrift des Grabes V in Jbeil (Byblos)*. Mainz: Von Zabern, 2005.

Lenzen, Heinrich von. *Vorläufiger Bericht über die von der Deutschen Forschungsgemeinschaft in Uruk-Warka unternommenen Ausgrabungen*. Vol. 15. Berlin: Akademie, 1959.

Leonard, Jeffery M. "Identifying Inner-Biblical Allusions: Psalm 78 as a Test Case." *JBL* 127 (2008): 241–65.

Leuchter, Mark. "Between Politics and Mythology: Josiah's Assault on Bethel in 2 Kings 23:15–20." Pages 67–91 in *Ritual Violence in the Hebrew Bible: New Perspectives*. Edited by Saul M. Olyan. New York: Oxford University Press, 2015.

Levenson, Jon D. *Resurrection and the Restoration of Israel: The Ultimate Victory of the God of Life*. New Haven: Yale University Press, 2006.

Levine, Baruch. "Leviticus: Its Literary History and Location in Biblical Literature." Pages 9–23 in *The Book of Leviticus: Composition and Reception*. Edited by Rolf Rendtorff and Robert A. Kugler. Leiden: Brill, 2003.

Levine, Baruch A., and Jean-Michel Tarragon. "Dead Kings and Rephaim: The Patrons of the Ugaritic Dynasty." *JAOS* 104 (1984): 649–59.

Levtow, Nathaniel B. *Images of Others: Icon Politics in Ancient Israel.* Winona Lake, IN: Eisenbrauns, 2008.

Lewis, Theodore J. *Cults of the Dead in Ancient Israel and Ugarit.* Atlanta: Scholars Press, 1989.

———. "Dead, the Abode of the." *ABD* 3:787–78.

———. "Divine Images and Aniconism in Ancient Israel." *JAOS* 118 (1998): 36–53.

———. "Feasts for the Dead and Ancestor Veneration in Levantine Traditions." Pages 69–74 in In Remembrance of Me: Feasting with the Dead in the Ancient Middle East. Edited by Virginia Rimmer Herrmann and J. David Schloen. Chicago: Oriental Institute of the University of Chicago, 2014.

———. "How Far Can Texts Take Us? Evaluating Textual Sources for Reconstructing Ancient Israelite Beliefs about the Dead." Pages 189–202 in *Sacred Time, Sacred Place.* Edited by Barry M. Gittlen. Winona Lake, IN: Eisenbrauns, 2002.

———. "Teraphim." *DDD* 1588–1601.

L'Heureux, Conrad E. *Rank among the Canaanite Gods: El, Baʿal and the Rephaim.* Missoula, MT: Scholars Press, 1979.

Lincoln, Bruce. "The Tyranny of Taxonomy." Pages 131–41 in *Discourse and the Construction of Society: Comparative Studies of Myth, Ritual, and Classification.* New York: Oxford University Press, 1992.

Lohfink, Norbert. "Recent Discussion on 2 Kings 22–23: The State of the Question." Pages 45–61 in *A Song of Power and the Power of Song: Essays on the Book of Deuteronomy.* Edited by Duane L. Christensen. Winona Lake, IN: Eisenbrauns, 1993.

Long, Burke O. *2 Kings: The Forms of the Old Testament Literature.* Grand Rapids: Eerdmans, 1991.

Longman, Tremper, III. *Fictional Akkadian Autobiography.* Winona Lake, IN: Eisenbrauns, 1991.

Loretz, Oswald. "Die Teraphim als 'Ahnen-Götter-Figur(in)en' im Lichte der Texte aus Nuzi, Emar und Ugarit." *UF* 24 (1992): 134–78.

Lundbom, Jack. *Deuteronomy: A Commentary.* Grand Rapids: Eerdmans, 2013.

———. *Jeremiah 37–52.* New York: Doubleday, 2004.

MacDonald, Nathan. "The Hermeneutics and Genesis of the Red Cow Ritual." *HTR* 105 (2012): 351–71.

Margalit, Baruch. *The Ugaritic Poem of Aqht*. New York: de Gruyter, 1989.

Mayer, Werner. *Untersuchungen zur Formensprache der Babylonischen Gebetsbeschwörungen*. StPohl 5. Rome: Biblical Institute Press, 1976.

Mays, James Luther. *Hosea: A Commentary*. Philadelphia: Westminster, 1969.

Mazar, Amihai. *The Archaeology of the Land of the Bible, 10,000–586 BCE*. New York: Doubleday, 1990.

McCarter, P. Kyle. *I Samuel: A New Translation with Introduction, Notes, and Commentary*. New York: Doubleday, 1980.

McCarter, P. Kyle. *II Samuel: A New Translation with Introduction, Notes, and Commentary*. Garden City: Doubleday, 1984.

———. "The Sarcophagus Inscription of Tabnit, King of Sidon." *COS* 2:56.

McMahon, Gregory. "Comparative Observations on Hittite Rituals." Pages 127–35 in *Recent Developments in Hittite Archaeology and History: Papers in Memory of Hans G. Guterbock*. Edited by K. Aslihan Yener and Harry A. Hoffner Jr. Winona Lake, IN: Eisenbrauns, 2002.

Meier, Gerhard. "Die zweite Tafel der Serie *bīt mēseri*." *AfO* 14 (1941–1944): 139–52.

Mettinger, Tryggve. *No Graven Image? Israelite Aniconism in Its Ancient Near Eastern Context*. Stockholm: Almqvist & Wiksell, 1995.

Meyers, Carol. "The Family in Early Israel." Pages 1–47 in *Families in Ancient Israel*. Edited by Leo G. Perdue, Joseph Blenkinsopp, John J. Collins, and Carol Meyers. Louisville: Westminster John Knox, 1997.

———. *Households and Holiness: The Religious Culture of Israelite Women*. Minneapolis: Fortress, 2005.

Meyers, Jacob M. *II Chronicles*. New York: Doubleday, 1965.

Michalowski, Piotr. "The Death of Šulgi." *Or* 46 (1977): 220–25.

Michel, Céline. "Femmes et ancêtres: Le cas des femmes d'Aššur." Supplement, *Topoi* 10 (2009): 1027–39.

Milgrom, Jacob. "HR in Leviticus and Elsewhere in the Torah." Pages 24–40 in *The Book of Leviticus: Composition and Reception*. Edited by Rolf Rendtorff and Robert A. Kugler. Leiden: Brill, 2003.

———. *Leviticus 1–16: A New Translation with Introduction and Commentary*. New York: Doubleday, 1991.

———. *Leviticus 17–22: A New Translation with Introduction and Commentary*. New York: Doubleday, 2000.

Monroe, Lauren A. S. *Josiah's Reform and the Dynamics of Defilement: Israelite Rites of Violence and the Making of a Biblical Text*. New York: Oxford University Press, 2011.

Moor, Johannes C. de. "Standing Stones and Ancestor Worship." *UF* 27 (1995): 1–20.

Neiman, David. "PGR: A Canaanite Cult Object in the Old Testament." *JBL* 67 (1948): 55–60.

Niditch, Susan. "Legends of Wise Heros and Heroines." Pages 445–63 in *The Hebrew Bible and Its Modern Interpreters*. Edited by Douglas A. Knight and Gene M. Tucker. Chico, CA: Scholars Press, 1985.

Niehr, Herbert. "The Changed Status of the Dead in Yehud." Pages 136–55 in *Yahwism after the Exile: Perspectives on Israelite Religion in the Persian Era*. Edited by Rainer Albertz and Bob Becking. STR 5. Assen: Van Gorcum, 2003.

———. "Two Stelae Mentioning Mortuary Offerings from Ugarit (KTU 6.13 and 6.14)." Pages 149–60 in *(Re-)Constructing Funerary Rituals in the Ancient Near East: Proceedings of the First International Symposium of the Tübingen Post-graduate School "Symbols of the Dead" in May 2009*. Edited by Peter Pfälzner, Herbert Niehr, Ernst Pernicka, and Anne Wissing. QSS 1. Wiesbaden: Harrassowitz, 2012.

Nihan, Christophe. "1 Samuel 28 and the Condemnation of Necromancy in Persian Yehud." Pages 23–54 in *Magic in the Biblical World: From the Rod of Aaron to the Ring of Solomon*. Edited by Todd E. Klutz. London: T&T Clark, 2003.

Nowack, Wilhelm. *Lehrbuch der hebräischen Archäologie*. Leipzig: Mohr, 1894.

Olmo Lete, Gregorio del. *Canaanite Religion according to the Liturgical Texts of Ugarit*. 2nd ed. Translated by Wilfred G. E. Watson. Münster: Ugarit-Verlag, 2014.

———. *Mitos y leyendas de Canaan: Según la tradición de Ugarit*. Monterrey: Institución San Jerónimo, 1981.

Olmo Lete, Gregorio del, and Joaquin Sanmartín, trans. and ed. *Dictionary of the Ugaritic Language in the Alphabetic Tradition*. 2 vols. Leiden: Brill, 2015.

Olyan, Saul M. *Asherah and the Cult of Yahweh in Israel*. Atlanta: Scholars Press, 1988.

———. *Biblical Mourning: Ritual and Social Dimensions*. New York: Oxford University Press, 2004.

———. "Family Religion in Israel and the Wider Levant of the First Millennium BCE." Pages 113–26 in *Household and Family Religion in Antiquity*. Edited by John Bodel and Saul M. Olyan. Oxford: Blackwell, 2008.

------. *Friendship in the Hebrew Bible*. New Haven: Yale University Press, 2017.

------. "Is Isaiah 40–55 Really Monotheistic?" *JANER* 12 (2012): 190–201.

------, ed. *Ritual Violence in the Hebrew Bible: New Perspectives*. New York: Oxford University Press, 2015.

------. "Some Neglected Aspects of Israelite Interment Ideology." *JBL* 124 (2005): 601–16.

------. "The Status of the Covenant during the Exile." Pages 333–44 in *Berührungspunkte: Studien zur Social- und Religionsgeschichte Israels und seiner Umwelt: Festschrift für Rainer Albertz zu seinem 65. Geburtstag*. Edited by Ingo Kottssieper, Rüdiger Schmitt, and Jakob Wöhrle. Münster: Ugarit-Verlag, 2008.

------. "Stigmatizing Associations: The Alien, Things Alien, and Practices Associated with Aliens in Biblical Classification Schemas." Pages 17–28 in *The Foreigner and the Law: Perspectives from the Hebrew Bible and the Ancient Near East*. Edited by Reinhard Achenbach, Rainer Albertz, and Jakob Wökrle. Wiesbaden: Harrassowitz, 2011.

------. "Unnoticed Resonances of Tomb Opening and Transportation of the Remains of the Dead in Ezekiel 37:12–14." *JBL* 128 (2009): 491–501.

------. " 'We Are Utterly Cut Off': Some Nuances of לנו נגזרנו in Ezek 37:11." *CBQ* 65 (2003): 43–51.

------. "What Do We Really Know about Women's Rites in the Israelite Family Context?" *JANER* 10 (2010): 55–67.

Oppenheim, A. Leo. *The Interpretation of Dreams in the Ancient Near East*. Philadelphia: American Philosophical Library, 1956.

Osborne, James. "Secondary Mortuary Practice and the Bench Tomb: Structure and Practice in Iron Age Judah." *JNES* 70 (2011): 35–53.

Pardee, Dennis. "*Marzihu, Kispu*, and the Ugaritic Funerary Cult: A Minimalist View." Pages 273–87 in *Ugarit, Religion, and Culture: Proceedings of the International Colloquium on Ugarit, Religion and Culture, Edinburgh, July 1994*. Edited by John C. L. Gibson, Nick Wyatt, Wilfred G. E. Watson, and Jeffrey B. Lloyd. Münster: Ugarit-Verlag, 1996.

------. "A New Aramaic Inscription from Zincirli." *BASOR* 356 (2009): 51–71.

------. *Ritual and Cult at Ugarit*. WAW 10. Leiden: Brill, 2002.

------. "West Semitic Canonical Compositions." *COS* 1:239–375.

Parker, Simon. *Ugaritic Narrative Poetry*. Atlanta: Scholars Press, 1997.

Pearson, Michael Parker. *The Archaeology of Death and Burial.* College Station: Texas A&M University Press, 1999.

Pedersén, Olof. *Archives and Libraries in the City of Aššur: A Survey of the Material from the German Excavations.* Part 2. Uppsala: Almqvist & Wiksell, 1986.

Perdue, Leo G., Joseph Blenkinsopp, John J. Collins, and Carol Meyers, eds. *Families in Ancient Israel.* Louisville: Westminster John Knox, 1997.

Pfälzner, Peter. "Archaeological Investigations in the Royal Palace of Qatna." Pages 29–64 in *Urban and Natural Landscapes of an Ancient Syrian Capital Settlement and Environment at Tell Mishrifeh/Qatna and in Central-Western Syria: Proceedings of an International Conference Held at Udine 9–11 December 2004.* Edited by Daniele Morandi Bonacossi. SAQPC 1. DAS 12. Udine: Forum, 2007.

———. "How Did They Bury the Kings of Qatna?" Pages 205–21 in *(Re-) Constructing Funerary Rituals in the Ancient Near East: Proceedings of the First International Symposium of the Tübingen Post-graduate School "Symbols of the Dead" in May 2009.* Edited by Peter Pfälzner, Herbert Niehr, Ernst Pernicka, and Anne Wissing. QSS 1. Wiesbaden: Harrassowitz, 2012.

———. "Royal Funerary Practices and Inter-regional Contacts in the Middle Bronze Age Levant: New Evidence from Qatna." Pages 141–56 in *Contextualising Grave Inventories in the Ancient Near East: Proceedings of a Workshop at the London Seventh ICAANE in April 2010 and an International Symposium in Tubingen in November 2010, Both Organised by the Tubingen Post-graduate School "Symbols of the Dead."* Edited by Peter Pfälzner, Herbert Niehr, Ernst Pernicka, Sarah Lange, and Tina Koster. Wiesbaden: Harassowitz, 2014.

Pinker, Aron. "Qohelet 9:3b–7: A Polemic against Necromancy." *JJS* 63 (2012): 218–37.

Pitard, Wayne. "Care of the Dead at Emar." Pages 123–63 in *Emar: The History, Religion, and Culture of a Syrian Town in the Late Bronze Age.* Edited by Mark W. Chavalas. Bethesda, MD: CDL, 1996.

———. "The *Rpum* Texts." Pages 259–69 in *Handbook of Ugaritic Studies.* Edited by Wilfred G. E. Watson and Nick Wyatt. Leiden: Brill, 1999.

———. "Tombs and Offerings: Archaeological Data and Comparative Methodology in the Study of Death in Israel." Pages 145–68 in *Sacred Time, Sacred Place.* Edited by Barry Gittlen. Winona Lake, IN: Eisenbrauns, 2002.

———. "The Ugaritic Funerary Text RS 34.126." *BASOR* 232 (1978): 65–75.

Pope, Marvin H. "The Cult of the Dead at Ugarit." Pages 159–79 in *Ugarit in Retrospect*. Edited by Gordon D. Young. Winona Lake, IN: Eisenbrauns, 1981.

———. "Notes on the Rephaim Texts from Ugarit." Pages 185–224 in *Essays on the Ancient Near East in Memory of Jacob Joel Finkelstein*. Edited by Maria deJong Ellis. Hamden, CT: Archon Books, 1977.

Porada, Edith. "Notes on the Sarcophagus of Ahiram." *JANESCU* 5 (1973): 354–72.

Porter, Barbara Nevling, ed. *What Is a God? Anthropomorphic and Nonanthropomorphic Aspects of Deity in Ancient Mesopotamia*. Winona Lake, IN: Eisenbrauns, 2009.

Prichard, James B., and Daniel E. Fleming. *The Ancient Near East: An Anthology of Texts and Pictures*. Princeton: Princeton University Press, 2010.

Propp, William H. *Exodus 19–40*. New York: Doubleday, 2006.

Rad, Gerhard von. *The Theology of Israel's Historical Traditions*. Vol. 1 of *Old Testament Theology*. Louisville: Westminster John Knox, 2001.

Rahmani, Levi Y. "Ancient Jerusalem's Funerary Customs and Tombs: Part One." *BA* 44 (1981): 171–77.

Rakita, Gordon F. M., and Jane E. Buikstra, eds. *Interacting with the Dead: Perspectives on Mortuary Archaeology for the New Millennium*. Gainesville: University Press of Florida, 2005.

Rendsburg, Gary A. *Israelian Hebrew in the Book of Kings*. Bethesda, MD: CDL, 2002.

Richardson, Seth. "Death and Dismemberment in Mesopotamia: Discorporation between the Body and the Body Politic." Pages 189–208 in *Performing Death: Social Analyses of Funerary Traditions in the Ancient Near East and Mediterranean*. Edited by Nicola Lanieri. Chicago: Oriental Institute of the University of Chicago, 2007.

Ricks, Stephen D. "The Magician as Outsider in the Hebrew Bible and the New Testament." Pages 131–43 in *Ancient Magic and Ritual Power*. Edited by Marvin Meyer and Paul Mirecki. RGRW 129. Leiden: Brill, 1995.

Ritner, Robert. "Necromancy in Ancient Egypt." Pages 89–96 in *Magic and Divination in the Ancient World*. Edited by Leda Ciraolo and Jonathan Seidel. Leiden: Brill, 2002.

Roberts, Jimmy J. M. *The Earliest Semitic Pantheon: A Study of the Semitic Deities Attested in Mesopotamia before Ur III*. Baltimore: Johns Hopkins University Press, 1972.

Robinson, Gnana. "The Meaning of *jd* in Isa 56,5." *ZAW* 88 (1976): 282–84.

Robson, Eleanor. "The Tablet House: A Scribal School in Old Babylonian Nippur." *RA* 95 (2001): 39–66.

Römer, Thomas. *The So-Called Deuteronomistic History: A Sociological, Historical, and Literary Introduction*. London: T&T Clark, 2005.

Sahlins, Marshall. *What Kinship Is—And Is Not*. Chicago: University of Chicago Press, 2013.

Sanders, Seth. "Naming the Dead: Funerary Writing and Historical Change in the Iron Age Levant." *Maarav* 19 (2012): 11–36.

———. "Words, Things, and Death: The Rise of Iron Age Literary Monuments." Pages 327–48 in *Language and Religion*. Edited by Robert Yelle, Courtney Handman, and Christopher Lehrich. Berlin: de Gruyter, 2019.

Schaudig, Hanspeter. *Die Inschriften Nabonids von Babylon und Kyros' des Großen: Samt den in ihrem Umfeld entstandenen Tendenzschriften*. Münster: Ugarit-Verlag, 2001.

Schloen, J. David. *House of the Father as Fact and Symbol: Patrimonialism in Ugarit and the Ancient Near East*. Winona Lake, IN: Eisenbrauns, 2001.

Schloen, J. David, and Amir S. Fink. "New Excavations at Zincirli Höyük in Turkey (Ancient Sam'al) and the Discovery of an Inscribed Mortuary Stele." *BASOR* 356 (2009): 1–13.

Schmid, Konrad. "The Quest for 'God': Monotheistic Arguments in the Priestly Texts of the Hebrew Bible." Pages 271–89 in *Reconsidering the Concept of Revolutionary Monotheism*. Edited by Beate Pongratz-Leisten. Winona Lake, IN: Eisenbrauns, 2011.

Schmidt, Brian. *Israel's Beneficent Dead: Ancestor Cult and Necromancy in Ancient Israelite Religion and Tradition*. Winona Lake, IN: Eisenbrauns, 1994.

———. "The 'Witch' of En-Dor, 1 Samuel 28, and Ancient Near Eastern Necromancy." Pages 111–29 in *Ancient Magic and Ritual Power*. Edited by Marvin Meyer and Paul Mirecki. RGRW 129. Leiden: Brill, 1995.

Schmitt, Rüdiger. *Magie im Alten Testament*. Münster: Ugarit-Verlag, 2004.

———. "The Problem of Magic and Monotheism in the Book of Leviticus." *JHS* 8 (2008): 2–12.

————. "Totenversorgung, Totengedenken und Nekromantie. Biblische und archäologische Perspektiven ritueller Kommunikation mit den Toten." Pages 501–24 in *Tod und Jenseits im alten Israel und in seiner Umwelt*. Edited by Angelika Berlejung and Bernd Janowski. Tübingen: Mohr Siebeck, 2009.

Scurlock, JoAnn. "Ghosts in the Ancient Near East: Weak or Powerful." *HUCA* 68 (1997): 77–96.

————. "Magic: Ancient Near East." *ABD* 4:464–68.

————. "Magical Means of Dealing with Ghosts in Ancient Mesopotamia." PhD diss., University of Chicago, 1988.

————. *Magico-Medical Means of Treating Ghost-Induced Illnesses in Ancient Mesopotamia*. Boston: Brill, 2006.

————. "Ritual 'Rubbing' Recitations from Ancient Mesopotamia (A Review of Barbara Böck, *Das Handbuch Muššuʾu 'Einreibung': Ein Serie sumerischer und akkadischer Beschwörungen aus dem 1.Jt vor Chr.* Biblioteca del Próximo Oriente Antiguo, 3." *Or* 80 (2011): 88.

Segal, Alan F. "Hellenistic Magic: Some Questions of Definition." Pages 349–75 in *Studies in Gnosticism and Hellenistic Religions*. Edited by Roel van den Broek and Maarten J. Vermaseren. EPRO 91. Leiden: Brill, 1981.

Segert, Stanislav. *A Basic Grammar of the Ugaritic Language*. Berkeley: University of California Press, 1984.

Seitz, Gottfried. *Redaktiongeschichtliche Studien zum Deuteronomium*. BWANT 93. Stuttgart: Kohlhammer, 1971.

Seow, Choon-Leong. *Ecclesiastes: A New Translation with Introduction and Commentary*. AYB 18C. New Haven: Yale University Press, 1997.

Shaffer, Aaron. "The Sumerian Sources of Tablet XII of The Epic of Gilgamesh." PhD diss., University of Pennsylvania, 1963.

Smelik, Karen. "The Witch of Endor: 1 Samuel 28 in Rabbinic and Christian Exegesis Till 800 A.D." *VC* 33 (1977): 160–79.

Smith, Jonathan Z. "A Matter of Class: Taxonomies of Religion." Pages 160–78 in *Relating Religion: Essays in the Study of Religion*. Chicago: University of Chicago Press, 2004.

————. "Trading Places." Pages 11–27 in *Relating Religion*. Chicago: University of Chicago Press, 2004.

Smith, Mark S. *The Early History of God: Yahweh and the Other Deities in Ancient Israel*. Grand Rapids: Eerdmans, 2002.

————. *The Origins of Biblical Monotheism: Israel's Polytheistic Background and the Ugaritic Texts*. New York: Oxford University Press, 2001.

Smith, Mark S., and Elizabeth M. Bloch-Smith. "Death and Afterlife in Ugarit and Israel." *JAOS* 108 (1988): 277–84.

Smith, Morton. "A Note on Burning Babies." *JAOS* 95 (1975): 477–79.

Smith, Sidney, with Cyril J. Gadd. "Tablets of Kirkuk." *RA* 23 (1926): 49–161.

Smoak, Jeremy. *The Priestly Blessing in Inscription and Scripture: The Early History of Numbers 6:24–26.* New York: Oxford University Press, 2016.

Soden, Wolfram von. "Aus einem Ersatzopferritual für den assyrischen Hof." *ZA* 45 (1939): 42–61.

Sonia, Kerry. "'In My House and within My Walls': The Shared Space of Yahweh and the Dead in Israelite Religion." In *With the Loyal You Show Yourself Loyal: Essays on Relationships in the Hebrew Bible in Honor of Saul M. Olyan.* Edited by T. M. Lemos, Debra Scoggins Ballentine, Karen B. Stern, and Jordan D. Rosenblum. AIL. Atlanta: SBL Press, forthcoming.

Spronk, Klaas. *Beatific Afterlife in Ancient Israel and the Ancient Near East.* AOAT 219. Neukirchen-Vluyn: Neukirchener Verlag, 1986.

Stavrakopoulou, Francesca. "Exploring the Garden of Uzza: Death, Burial, and Ideologies of Kingship." *Bib* 87 (2006): 1–12.

———. *Land of Our Fathers: The Roles of Ancestor Veneration in Biblical Land Claims.* New York: T&T Clark, 2010.

Stol, Marten, and Sven P. Vleeming, eds. *The Care of the Elderly in the Ancient Near East.* Boston: Brill, 1998.

Stowers, Stanley K. "The Religion of Plant and Animal Offerings versus the Religion of Meanings, Essences and Textual Mysteries." Pages 35–56 in *Ancient Mediterranean Sacrifice.* Edited by Jennifer Wright Knust and Zsuzsa Varhelyi. New York: Oxford University Press, 2011.

Strickert, Fred. *Rachel Weeping: Jews, Christians, and Muslims at the Fortress Tomb.* Collegeville, MN: Liturgical Press, 2007.

Struble, Eudore J., and Virginia Rimmer Herrmann. "An Eternal Feast at Sam'al: The New Iron Age Mortuary Stele from Zincirli in Context." BASOR 356 (2009): 15–49.

Suriano, Matthew J. "Breaking Bread with the Dead: Katumuwa's Stele, Hosea 9:4, and the Early History of the Soul." *JAOS* 134 (2014): 385–405.

———. *A History of Death in the Hebrew Bible.* New York: Oxford University Press, 2018.

———. *The Politics of Dead Kings: Dynastic Ancestors in the Book of Kings and Ancient Israel.* Tübingen: Mohr Siebeck, 2010.

Tadmor, Hayim. "The Inscriptions of Nabunaid: Historical Arrangement." Pages 351–64 in *Studies in Honor of Benno Landsberger*. Edited by Hans G. Güterbock and Thorkild Jacobsen. AS 16. Chicago: University of Chicago Press, 1965.

———. "Was the Biblical *sārîs* a Eunuch?" Pages 317–25 in *Solving Riddles and Untying Knots: Biblical, Epigraphic, and Semitic Studies in Honor of Jonas C. Greenfield*. Edited by Ziony Zevit, Seymour Gitin, and Michael Sokoloff. Winona Lake, IN: Eisenbrauns, 1995.

Tawil, Hayim. "A Note on the Ahiram Inscription." *JANESCU* 3 (1970–1971): 32–36.

Teixidor, Javier. "L'inscription d'Aḥiram à nouveau." *Syria* 64 (1987): 137–40.

Tigay, Jeffrey. *The Evolution of the Gilgamesh Epic*. Philadelphia: University of Pennsylvania Press, 1982.

———. *The JPS Torah Commentary: Deuteronomy*. Philadelphia: Jewish Publication Society of America, 1996.

Tigay, Jeffrey. *You Shall Have No Other Gods: Israelite Religion in the Light of Hebrew Inscriptions*. HSS 31. Atlanta: Scholars Press, 1986.

Toorn, Karel van der. "The Domestic Cult at Emar." *JCS* 47 (1995): 35–49.

———.Echoes of Judean Necromancy in Isaiah 28,7–22." *ZAW* 100 (1988): 199–217.

———. *Family Religion in Babylonia, Ugarit, and Israel: Continuity and Changes in the Forms of Religious Life*. Leiden: Brill, 1996.

———. "Family Religion in Second Millennium West Asia (Mesopotamia, Emar, Nuzi)." Pages 20–36 in *Household and Family Religion in Antiquity*. Edited by John Bodel and Saul M. Olyan. Oxford: Blackwell, 2008.

———. "Gods and Ancestors at Emar and Nuzi." *ZA* 84 (1994): 38–59.

———. "Ilib and the 'God of the Father.'" *UF* 25 (1993): 379–87.

———. "The Nature of the Biblical Teraphim in the Light of the Cuneiform Evidence." *CBQ* 52 (1990): 203–22.

———. "Second Millennium West Asian Family Religion." Pages 20–36 in *Household and Family Religion in Antiquity*. Edited by John Bodel and Saul M. Olyan. Oxford: Blackwell, 2008.

———. *Sin and Sanction in Israel and Mesopotamia*. Assen: Van Gorcum, 1985.

Toorn, Karel van der, and Theodore J. Lewis. "תרפים." *TDOT* 15:777–89.

Tropper, Josef. *Die Inschriften von Zincirli*. Münster: Ugarit-Verlag, 1993.

———. *Nekromantie: Totenbefragung im Alten Orient und im Alten Testament*. Neukirchen-Vluyn: Neukirchener, 1989.

——. *Ugaritische Grammatik*. Münster: Ugarit-Verlag, 2012.

Trotter, James M. *Reading Hosea in Achaemenid Yehud*. London: Sheffield Academic, 2001.

Tsevat, Matitiahu. "Traces of Hittite at the Beginning of the Ugaritic Epic of Aqhat." *UF* 3 (1971): 351–52.

Tsukimoto, Akio. *Untersuchungen zur Totenpflege (kispum) im alten Mesopotamien*. AOAT 216. Neukirchen-Vluyn: Neukirchener Verlag, 1985.

Turner, Bryan S. "The Sociology and Anthropology of the Family." Pages 232–45 in *Classical Sociology*. London: Sage, 1999.

Ucko, Peter J. "Ethnography and Archaeological Interpretation of Funerary Remains." *WA* 1 (1969): 262–80.

Ussishkin, David. "On the Shorter Inscription from the 'Tomb of the Royal Steward.'" *BASOR* 196 (1969): 16–22.

Van Winkle, Dwight W. "The Meaning of *yād wāšēm* in Isaiah LVI 5." *VT* 47 (1997): 378–85.

VanderKam, James C. "Jewish High Priests of the Persian Period: Is the List Complete?" Pages 67–91 in *Priesthood and Cult in Ancient Israel*. Edited by Gary A. Anderson and Saul M. Olyan. Sheffield: Sheffield Academic, 1991.

Vaux, Roland de. *Ancient Israel: Its Life and Institutions*. London: Darton, Longman & Todd, 1961.

Vayntrub, Jacqueline. "Like Father, Like Son: Theorizing Transmission in Biblical Literature." *HBAI* 7 (2018): 500–526.

Wade, George W. *The Book of the Prophet Isaiah*. London: Methuen, 1911.

Watson, James L. "Death Pollution in Cantonese Society." Pages 55–86 in *Death and the Regeneration of Life*. Edited by Maurice Bloch and Jonathan Parry. Cambridge: Cambridge University Press, 1982.

Weiher, Egbert von. *Uruk: spätbabylonische Texte aus dem Planquadrat U 18. Teil IV*. Mainz am Rhein: von Zabern, 1993.

Weinfeld, Moshe. *Deuteronomy 1–11*. New York: Doubleday, 1964.

——. "The Worship of Molech and of the Queen of Heaven and Its Background." *UF* 4 (1972): 133–54.

Westermann, Claus. *Isaiah 40–66*. Philadelphia: Westminster, 1969.

Wilson, Robert R. *Genealogy and History in the Biblical World*. New Haven: Yale University Press, 1977.

Wolff, Hans Walter. *Hosea: A Commentary on the Book of the Prophet Hosea*. Philadelphia: Fortress, 1974.

Wright, G. Ernest. *Deuteronomy, IB*. New York: Abingdon, 1953.

Wright, Jacob L., and Michael J. Chan. "King and Eunuch: Isaiah 56:1–8 in Light of Honorific Royal Burial Practices." *JBL* 131 (2012): 99–119.

Wyatt, Nicholas. *Religious Texts from Ugarit: The Words of Ilimilku and His Colleagues.* Biblical Seminar 53. London: Sheffield Academic Press, 2002.

Younger, K. Lawson. "Two Epigraphic Notes on the New Katumuwa Inscription from Zincirli." Maarav 16 (2011): 159–79.

Zevit, Ziony. *The Religions of Ancient Israel: A Synthesis of Parallactic Approaches.* New York: Continuum, 2001.

Zimmerli, Walther. *Ezekiel.* Vol. 2. Philadelphia: Fortress, 1983.

Ancient Sources Index

Modern Authors Index

Subject Index